Get Real with Storytime

Get Real with Storytime

52 Weeks of Early Literacy Programming with Nonfiction and Poetry

Julie Dietzel-Glair and Marianne Crandall Follis

An Imprint of ABC-CLIO, LLC
Santa Barbara, California • Denver, Colorado

Library of Congress Cataloging-in-Publication Data

Names: Dietzel-Glair, Julie, 1976– author. | Follis, Marianne Crandall, author.
Title: Get real with storytime : 52 weeks of early literacy programming with nonfiction and poetry / Julie Dietzel-Glair and Marianne Crandall Follis.
Description: Santa Barbara, CA : Libraries Unlimited, an imprint of ABC-CLIO, LLC, [2016] | Includes bibliographical references and indexes.
Identifiers: LCCN 2015025224| ISBN 9781440837388 (paperback) | ISBN 9781440837395 (ebook)
Subjects: LCSH: Children's libraries—Activity programs—United States. | Storytelling—United States. | Libraries and preschool children—United States. | Poetry and children. | Children's literature—Bibliography. | BISAC: LANGUAGE ARTS & DISCIPLINES / Library & Information Science / General.
Classification: LCC Z718.3 .D545 2016 | DDC 027.62/51—dc23 LC record available at http://lccn.loc.gov/2015025224

ISBN: 978-1-4408-3738-8
EISBN: 978-1-4408-3739-5

20 19 18 17 16   1 2 3 4 5

This book is also available on the World Wide Web as an eBook.
Visit www.abc-clio.com for details.

Libraries Unlimited
An Imprint of ABC-CLIO, LLC

ABC-CLIO, LLC
130 Cremona Drive, P.O. Box 1911
Santa Barbara, California 93116-1911

This book is printed on acid-free paper ∞

Manufactured in the United States of America

Contents

Introduction

Storytimes are one of the biggest perks of being a children's librarian. You get to connect with children. You get to read fun books. You get to act silly—and get paid to do it.

Planning storytime can be just as much fun as the actual program; as you look through stacks and stacks of well-illustrated picture books that make you chuckle or even tear up. But what about the other side of the children's room? The side where the stacks are typically taller and the books are often thicker? What about the nonfiction books filled with fascinating photographs and interesting facts? What about the rhythm, rhyme, and delicious language of poetry? Do you include those books in your storytime? You should.

Many children (and adults), especially boys, prefer nonfiction to fiction. They like facts and "true stuff." By reading nonfiction in storytime you can connect with more children. Including poetry in storytime opens the doors for a love of words in children. Too many children dislike poetry units in school, but exposing them to poetry at an earlier age may dissuade those negative feelings. Many educational standards (e.g., Common Core) have a focus beyond fiction. Libraries can link their programs to these standards and better prepare children for school. Reading nonfiction and poetry also educates parents and caregivers about the wealth of resources available for young children. Plus, with so many incredible nonfiction and poetry books being published, it would be a shame not to include them in programming.

This book is for librarians, early educators, and anyone who like to read with children. It is their ticket to adding nonfiction and poetry to preschool storytimes. It is a year's worth of programs that include nonfiction, poetry, picture books, rhymes, songs, flannel board, and follow-up activities. Along the way you'll find early literacy tips that provide more information about the benefits of various storytime activities. So buckle up and prepare yourself for storytimes that will have kids begging for more.

Tips for Including Nonfiction Books in Storytime

Look for books with large, clear photographs or illustrations. Preschoolers want a visual treat while you share facts about their favorite animal or vehicle. Just like a picture book, you want illustrations that show well across the room. Photographs are ideal, but there are also many quality life-like looking illustrations in nonfiction books. Books that feature cartoony illustrations will provide a level of familiarity to kids who are accustomed to picture books. Uncertain if the illustrations will work in your storytime space? Open up the book and take a few steps back to see if the illustrations are appealing from a distance. As a general rule, books with a larger trim size are going to be seen better by a crowd.

Look for spare text but don't be afraid of a text-heavy book. Books with minimal text are easy because you can simply read the entire book like a story. However, if a text-heavy book has great illustrations, you may be able to read just the captions in order to share the book with a group. Many nonfiction books provide just the right amount of information in headings to be of interest to a crowd. Mark stimulating sentences with Post-it notes and read just portions of a text. Don't forget to make the book available after storytime for a family to check out. While you may have read only portions of the book, a family may wish to delve into it more.

Remember that a challenging vocabulary is your friend. Kids do not need text watered down for them. They will understand many words in context and will be broadening their own word bank at the same time. It is a good idea to look up the correct pronunciation of words and practice them in advance. While everyone (even many three-year-olds) can say *Tyrannosaurus Rex*, there are many difficult dinosaur names.

Consider the age-appropriateness of a topic. This resource contains 52 topics that preschoolers will enjoy and are suitable for a crowd environment. Kids want to know more about animals and where they go in winter. They are interested in cars and trucks. They love playing in dirt and finding cool rocks. Remember that the mind of a preschooler is like a sponge, and they are capable of understanding more than many people give them credit for. With that in mind, there are certainly topics (an obvious one is death) that three-year-olds may need to learn about; however, storytime is not an appropriate place to introduce that topic. The same consideration goes for your particular community and suitability of topics.

Be aware of outdated facts. You are probably already weeding your nonfiction collection and removing nonfiction books with obsolete information. When choosing a nonfiction book for storytime, double check to be sure that the information is still valid. While the books recommended in this resource are up to date as of publication, it is possible that some of them may become outdated at some point in the future. Who knows, maybe another planet will be knocked off the list.

Avoid didactic or agenda-driven books. This is not a comment on overall collection management as those books often have a place in a library collection. When planning a storytime, message-driven nonfiction and picture books are often poor fits. Children are the ultimate lie detectors; they can tell that there is medicine mixed in with that sugar. Fortunately there are plenty of good nonfiction books out there that are great fits. Hopefully, this book will serve as an introduction to many of them.

Last but not least, only use nonfiction books that you like. This same rule goes for every book, rhyme, and song in a storytime. Use books that you like and your enthusiasm will resonate throughout the room. Children who like nonfiction will pick up on your excitement, and it will further their interest in the topic. Boys especially have a keen interest in facts and real stuff, and this is a great opportunity to connect with them.

Tips on Including Poetry in Storytime

Children are natural poets. They are in the process of acquiring language and enjoy the basic building block of the spoken (or sung) word. They respond to meter, the feel of a word in their mouths. Sadly adults can sometimes have an aversion to poetry. No one is pointing fingers, but the hope is that while exploring this book you may encounter a poem that reignites the love of a well-crafted poem in you. There will not be a quiz at the end of this book, and aside from right now, there will be no mention of iambic pentameter.

When selecting poems to share in storytime, pay attention to this beautiful language and tune in to things like assonance and alliteration. These repetitive sounds are fun to recite and even more fun to hear. Again, remember that young children are naturally attracted to the sound of language. And while poetry can rhyme, it doesn't have to.

You may find that some of the poems here have a higher reading level than others and may contain words that are beyond a child's understanding. Don't shy away from advanced language. Sometimes they will understand the actual meaning of the word, and sometimes they won't. If a poem's complete understanding hinges on one word, then it may not be the best poem to convey a thought or feeling. We also know that children are building their vocabulary and world knowledge every day. Poetry can be a bridge to understanding.

You may come across a poem in this book that was written a long time ago, or originally for an adult reader. Don't fear. There is nothing in this book that is not appropriate. There is, however, poetry from Benjamin Franklin, Langston Hughes, and Robert Frost. Beautiful words strung together to evoke a mood or thought don't know what year it is or how many years the listener has been on the earth.

The poems in this book come from many sources. Some are beautifully illustrated single poem picture books; this format is welcome and familiar to both children and adults. It may not seem like poetry, but because it is tucked away in the nonfiction section of the library, it isn't getting the attention it would if it was in the picture book section of the library.

Some of the poems suggested here are a single poem in an anthology. It can take time to become comfortable sharing this single text–driven message to a crowd accustomed to illustrated works. Don't worry about simply reading aloud, but if you want to give a visual representation of the poem, consider typing out the poem and sharing via PowerPoint, or display the page using an overhead projector or ELMO. You may even want to write out the poem on a piece of poster paper. Remember, children this age are becoming aware of print, and displaying language is an important part of this developmental stage.

While you aren't required to memorize the poetry you share, you will want to practice reading the poem aloud. Sometimes punctuation or a rhyme may trip off your tongue instead of roll. Practicing helps you become familiar with the way the words flow together and fall on your ears.

Lastly, this should not be painful. There will be poems that speak to you and those that don't. There are too many great poems out there for you to struggle with one. Explore the anthologies we have listed here. Flip through; stop and sample one or two (or more). You just may surprise yourself. And your storytime audience.

How to Use This Book

Each chapter is a new topic. You'll find old favorites like dogs, cars, and shapes. You'll also find new ideas from math to being eco-friendly. Every chapter has everything you need to create a fun-filled, informative, and poetic storytime for the preschool crowd.

Each chapter has multiple poetry, nonfiction, picture book, and rhyme/song selections. Programmers can pick and choose the items they like from each chapter to create their personalized storytime. Put things in an order that makes sense for your individual storytime personality. If you prefer to end, rather than start, storytime with a poem, you have the right to move things around. Everything in this resource is a suggestion.

Every recommended book in this resource was published in the year 2000 or later. There are hundreds (if not thousands) of fantastic books on each subject published before 2000. Programmers should certainly include those books in their storytimes as they see fit. Newer books were chosen for this resource in hopes that there is a higher chance that the books can be found in libraries or may still be in print.

The chapters are broken down into the following segments:

Welcome Song: Routine is important in any child's life; it provides cues on what is happening next in a world that can still be confusing to a young brain. The concept of routine is also important in storytime. A familiar welcome song that is used every week lets young patrons know that it is time to settle down and get ready for storytime. Throughout the chapters you will see the headings for welcome, transitional, and closing songs. While there are occasional suggestions for particular songs or rhymes based on a topic, you should feel free to use your favorite tried and true songs during this portion of the program. However, if you are looking to tweak your routine, here are a few suggestions:

- Good Morning to You
- Shake My Sillies Out (from More Singable Songs by Raffi)
- Open Shut Them
- Hi, Hello and How Are You (Tune: London Bridge)
- If You're Ready for a Story (Tune: If You're Happy and You Know It)
- Head, Shoulders, Knees, and Toes
- Two Little Hands
- Teddy Bear, Teddy Bear
- Hokey Pokey
- Happy Trails
- The More We Get Together
- If You're Happy and You Know It
- Skinnamarink

Opening Poem: Poetry can set the mood for the rest of the program. It encompasses delicate language and precise order. An especially appropriate poem is highlighted in this section as a way to set the stage for the storytime subject. Read the recommended poem aloud or choose another based on your preferences. Check out "Tips on Including Poetry in Storytime" for more information on reading poetry.

Action Rhyme: Children are learning to sit still and listen, but their little bodies need to move. Every topic has a rhyme that involves action that you can use to get everyone (adults included) up and moving in between books and/or poems.

Nonfiction for Storytime: Time for facts. The book highlighted here is specifically chosen for its appeal to a crowd of preschoolers. Don't be afraid of nonfiction titles—kids love "real stuff." Be sure to read the "Tips for Including Nonfiction Books in Storytime" for more information.

Transitional Song: See WELCOME SONG.

Flannel Board Activity: Books provide one form of visual cue to a story or rhyme. Flannel boards are another fun way to tell a story, act out a rhyme, sing a song, or explain a concept. Patterns are provided at the end of the chapter for many of the flannel board activities; however, there are many other resources for flannel board patterns. Check your professional resource collection or search online for playful clip art that can be printed and laminated for flannel board use. When a pattern is provided, it is intended as a suggestion; programmers may use any patterns or pre-made pieces that they already have.

Picture Books for Storytime: No storytime would be complete without stories. This section has two picture books that can be shared at any point in your storytime.

Closing Song: See WELCOME SONG.

Follow-Up Activities: This section has extension activities. Things families can do at the library or on their own after storytime. This is where you will find craft activities, science activities, and field trip suggestions. Many librarians like to provide a hands-on activity after a 30-minute storytime. This is the perfect place to look for those more time-intensive ideas.

Other Songs, Rhymes, and Fingerplays: An action rhyme is suggested earlier in each chapter, but many people include a song, rhyme, fingerplay, or other movement activity in between each book of a storytime. You'll find more suggestions here. This section also has fun YouTube videos that can be shown to provide a different format.

Additional Poetry: This underutilized section of the library has a plethora of lovely words and books on each of the topics in this book. Feel free to browse through the titles suggested here and swap out the OPENING POEM with something that suits your fancy.

Additional Nonfiction: One fact book simply isn't enough. This section houses more age-appropriate nonfiction that can be shared in storytime or displayed for families to check out after the program.

Additional Fiction Picture Books: There is no way the authors of this resource could choose only two picture books for each topic. More favorites can be found here.

Early Literacy Tips: These are sprinkled throughout the chapters. They are intended to provide information on the reasons for much of what we do for children and families in a library setting (or other early reading setting).

Airplanes

Look up on any given day and what do you see? Airplanes! Many small children are fascinated by these winged giants. How does something so big glide through the air? While most adults may try to avoid that question, do not avoid airplane storytime!

Sample Storytime

Welcome Song

Routine is important when working with children. Be sure to include welcome, transitional, and closing songs or activities to signify what is coming next. Don't be afraid to use the same ones; children take comfort in knowing what is coming next.

Opening Poem

"Wake Up, Wings!" from Hopkins, Lee Bennett, compiler, and Ponder Goembel, illus. Give Me Wings. New York: Holiday House, 2010.
"Prepare to fly!" This 23-word poem by Rebecca Kai Dotlich will set the tone for a storytime about airplanes and flight.

Action Rhyme

See the Little Airplanes
By M. Follis
(Tune: I'm a Little Teapot)

See the little airplanes in the sky (shade eyes with hands and look up)
Watch and count them as they fly (put hand up)
One, two, three, four, look! there's five (count on fingers)
Way up high, as clouds go by (wave)

Nonfiction for Storytime

Downs, Mike and David Gordon, illus. The Noisy Airplane Ride. Berkeley, CA: Tricycle Press, 2003.
Your first plane ride can be a bit frightening, especially with all those weird sounds. All of the sounds are explained from walking down the jetway to the thrum of the engines. Reading a nonfiction book has never been so noisy and fun.

Transitional Song

See Welcome Song earlier.

Flannel Board Activity

Five Little Airplanes

For this you will need five airplanes. You can either use free clip art found as part of the standard office processing software or search the Internet for free clip art. There is a sample pattern at the end of the chapter as well.

Once you have the patterns cut and colored to your liking, attach a sticky backing as needed.

Count the airplanes as you place them on the board. When all five are in place, recite the following rhyme, removing an airplane from the right as each one departs.

Early Literacy Tip:
When counting and placing items on the flannel board, please remember to do so from left to right. Think of the number line and how we read numbers, like words in English, from left to right.

Five Little Airplanes
Rhyme by M. Follis

Five little airplanes in the sky
Watch them as they fly so high
One goes off to look for more
How many are left?
Just these four.

Four little airplanes happy as you please
Watch them as they catch a breeze
One goes off high above the tree
How many do we have left?
Now there are only three.

Three little airplanes, shiny and new
They are looking for something new to do
One flies off to look for you
How many are left?
Only two!

Two little airplanes, flying in the sun
They are looking for some fun
One decides that he is done
How many left?
Just this one.

One little airplane, feeling alone
She decides it's time to go home.

Picture Books for Storytime

Lyon, George Ella and Mick Wiggins, illus. Planes Fly! New York: Atheneum Books for Young Readers, 2013.
This book is fictional but it still shows many types of planes and the experience of flying on a commercial jet. The rhyming text and full-page illustrations make it a fun storytime read.

Sturges, Philemon and Shari Halpern, illus. I Love Planes! New York: HarperCollins Publishers, 2003.
What starts as a child folding a paper airplane becomes a celebration of many flying machines from planes to hot air balloons to spacecraft. Children will enjoy the uncluttered images and simple text.

Closing Song

See Welcome Song earlier.

Follow-Up Activities

Draw an Airplane

Court, Rob. How to Draw Aircraft. Chanhassen, MN: The Child's World, 2007.
Using only four simple steps, this title shows how to draw a seaplane, helicopter, biplane, blimp, space shuttle, cargo plane, glider, hot air balloon, Harrier jet, passenger jet, commuter plane, ultralight, jet fighter, and Spirit of St. Louis. Draw one of the planes together after storytime or put the book on display for families to try at home.

Make Paper Airplanes

Use either of these two books for ideas on making a variety of different paper airplanes together.

Harbo, Christopher L. The Kids' Guide to Paper Airplanes. Mankato, MN: Capstone Press, 2009.
Recommend this title to children looking for harder paper airplanes to create.

Harbo, Christopher L. Paper Airplanes: Flight-School Level 1. Mankato, MN: Capstone Press, 2011.
Start with the simpler paper airplane models: Dynamic Dart, Spinning Blimp, and Whirly.

Early Literacy Tip:
Making paper airplanes requires strong fine motor skills—skills that they need to develop in order to write. Children develop at different rates. Some may be ready to create an entire airplane on their own. Others will need much more help. Choose paper airplane models with simple directions and consider completing part of the project for the children.

Clouds and Airplanes

Materials:

- Airplane coloring sheet (you may choose to use the pattern at the end of the chapter or look for your own coloring sheet)
- Paper plates
- (Optional) Blue poster paint (diluted)
- Cotton balls
- Liquid glue

Directions:

- Place diluted paint on a paper plate. The thinness of the paint, due to dilution, will allow for quicker drying time.
- Allow children to "paint" the sky of the airplane coloring sheet using cotton balls and blue paint.
- Discard the cotton balls used for painting.

- Pour liquid glue onto clean paper plate.
- Dip clean cotton balls into glue, and adhere them as "clouds" on the coloring sheet.

Airplane Observation

Many airports have observation areas where people can park and watch the planes take off and land. Research your closest airports to see if they offer this option and share the information with caregivers in your storytime. The observation area near the Baltimore-Washington International Airport also has a playground to occupy busy little bodies.

Other Songs, Rhymes, and Fingerplays

The Wings on the Airplane
Adapted by J. Dietzel-Glair
(Tune: The Wheels on the Bus)

The wings on the airplane fly, fly, fly (hold your arms out like you are flying)
Fly, fly, fly,
Fly, fly, fly
The wings on the airplane fly, fly, fly
All through the sky.

Additional verses:
The people on the airplane buckle their seatbelt (hold your hands as if they are holding the ends of a seatbelt and bring them together around your waist)
The bags on the airplane stow away (pretend to lift a bag into the overhead bin)

Pete the Pilot
Adapted by M. Follis
(Tune: Old MacDonald)

Pete the pilot has a plane
Zoom, zoom, zoom, zoom, zoom (hold arms out straight to mimic wings)
And on that plane he has two wings (hold arms out straight to mimic wings)
Zoom, zoom, zoom, zoom, zoom (hold arms out straight to mimic wings)
With a zoom, zoom here (lean wings left)
And a zoom, zoom there (lean wings right)
Here a zoom, there a zoom, everywhere a zoom, zoom.
(quickly alternate between left and right with each zoom)
Pete the pilot has a plane (hold arms out straight to mimic wings)
Zoom, zoom, zoom, zoom, zoom (hold arms out straight to mimic wings)

Additional verses (substitute for underlined phrase):
Many lights—blink (use fingers to suggest blinking by gently closing and opening them)
Many passengers—wave (wave)

Did You Ever See an Airplane?
Adapted by M. Follis
(Tune: Did You Ever See a Lassie)

Did you ever see an airplane, an airplane, an airplane
Did you ever see an airplane, flying way up in the sky?
There are red ones and blue ones
And old ones and new ones
Did you ever see an airplane way up in the sky?

Additional Poetry

Martin Jr., Bill, Michael Sampson, and various illustrators. The Bill Martin Jr. Big Book of Poetry. New York: Simon & Schuster, 2008.
"Clouds" by Christina G. Rossetti (p. 30) is a great tie in for anyone who has ever marveled at flying above the clouds.

Vardell, Sylvia and Janet Wong, ed. The Poetry Friday Anthology for Science: Poems for the School Year Integrating Science, Reading and Language Arts, K-5 Teacher Edition. Princeton, NJ: Pomelo Books, 2014.
In "Clouds" by Kate Coombs (p. 85) the narrator describes some of the things she sees in the shapes of clouds overhead, just imagine flying in an airplane through those shapes. Filled with simile the poem ends with the fact that clouds "should really look wet" as they are a large body of water in the sky. A great way to introduce the differences between appearances and the water cycle through lyrical language.

Additional Nonfiction

Carr, Aaron. Jumbo Jets. New York: AV2 by Weigl, 2014.
Did you know that "some jumbo jets can fly more than 10,000 miles without landing?" This book is full of interesting tidbits about jumbo jets and is appropriate as a storytime read-aloud. Two pages with additional facts can be shared one on one with a caregiver.

Mitton, Tony and Ant Parker, illus. Amazing Airplanes. New York: Kingfisher, 2002.
The animals are going on a plane and readers can learn about air travel while hearing about their trip. The cartoon-like illustrations provide a familiar storybook feel to a topic that can scare many children.

Roberts, Cynthia. Airplanes. Mankato, MN: The Child's World, 2007.
With full-page photographs and minimal text, this title can be used as a read-aloud in storytime.

Additional Fiction Picture Books

Hubbell, Patricia, and Megan Halsey and Sean Addy, illus. Airplanes: Soaring! Turning! Diving! Tarrytown, NY: Marshall Cavendish, 2008.
There is something exciting about a book that you have to turn on its end in order to read the text, and this book has two pages like that. Rhyming text complements the illustrations of a variety of type of airplanes.

Hubbell, Patricia and Nancy Speir, illus. My First Airplane Ride. Las Vegas, NV: Two Lions, 2008.

A great book for sharing some of the parts and routines a first time young flier may see and experience on a flight. In this story, single rhyming sentences per page take us through the wait to "board," the slow movement of "taxiing," and the "shudders" and "shakes" of lift off—all worth the while to reach your final destination.

London, Jonathan and Denis Roche, illus. A Plane Goes Ka-ZOOM! New York: Henry Holt and Company, 2010.

Ideal for a younger storytime crowd, rhyming text introduces children to planes of all shapes and sizes.

Airplane pattern for Flannel Board

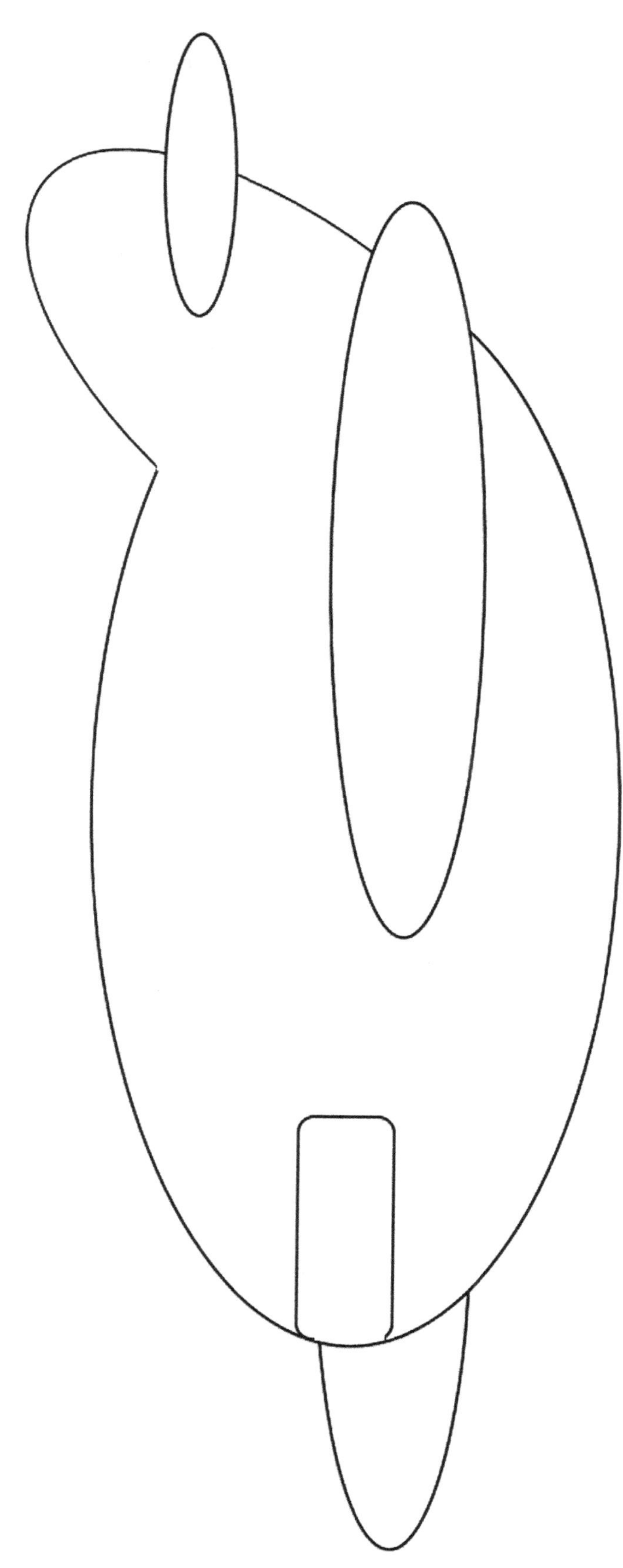

Alphabet

From beginning toys and books as well as singing the ABC song, little ones are introduced to the alphabet in many ways. Pointing out letters during a drive, a walk down the grocery store aisle, and in books is something most adults already do with their young ones. This storytime is a natural extension of this important early literacy practice.

Sample Storytime

Welcome Song

Routine is important when working with children. Be sure to include welcome, transitional, and closing songs or activities to signify what is coming next. Don't be afraid to use the same ones; children take comfort in knowing what is coming next.

Opening Poem

"Parrot" from Belle, Jennifer and David McPhail, illus. Animal Stackers. New York: Hyperion Books for Children, 2005.

In this acrostic poem the reader politely asks a parrot to "stop repeating the alphabet . . . A to Z." The first letter of each of the first words of the six line poem spells out PARROT. This would be a great poem to present to your audience visually so they can see that the meaning of the poem's title has to do with the content of the poem in a funny play on words. Tweet.

Action Rhyme

A is for Alligator
Traditional Rhyme

A is for Alligator
Chomp Chomp Chomp (extend arms out straight in front like a large alligator mouth and bring them together in a big chomp)
B is for Ball
Bounce Bounce Bounce (jump up and down like you are a bouncy ball)
C is for Circle
Spin Round and Round (spin around twice)
D is for where we all sit down (sit down)

Nonfiction for Storytime

Zuckerman, Andrew. Creature ABC. San Francisco: Chronicle Books, 2009.

On the very first page, you see the letter "Aa" and just a glimpse of an alligator. Turn the page to see the entire beast and the word "alligator." Stunning photographs of animals are highlighted against a crisp white background. You may choose to present this book as a guessing game on pages with only a hint of the animal to come. Quick facts about each animal are provided in the back.

Transitional Song

See Welcome Song earlier.

Flannel Board Activity

Chicka Chicka Boom Boom

Using the classic and popular chant from Chicka Chicka Boom Boom, create a flannel board of the infamous coconut tree (pattern at the end of the chapter) and add letters while going through. Be sure to ask the audience to help with the repeating verse!

Martin Jr., Bill, John Archambault, and Lois Ehlert, illus. Chicka Chicka Boom Boom. New York: Beach Lane Books, 2009. (anniversary edition)

Early Literacy Tip: Rhyme, rhythm, and repetition play an important role in the acquisition of language for the very young, and this book has all three!

Picture Books for Storytime

Bingham, Kelly and Paul O. Zelinsky, illus. Z Is for Moose. New York: Greenwillow Books, 2012.

When the zebra referee lines up items and animals for your typical ABC book, Moose can't wait until M. When his letter comes and goes without including him, Moose has a meltdown. Fortunately Zebra is a good friend who finds a solution that makes everyone happy, most of all Moose. Young readers will identify with Moose's full range of over-the-top emotions.

Hills, Tad. How Rocket Learned to Read. New York: Schwartz & Wade Books, 2010.

When Rocket falls in love with a story, he realizes the need to learn to read. Good thing little yellow bird is an excellent teacher. Soon Rocket learns all the ways the letters of the alphabet can combine to form the words that fill stories and the world. Rocket's feelings launch off the page in sweet illustrations of expressive eyes and body language. Your young readers will enjoy sharing Rocket's journey into the world of words.

Early Literacy Tip: Stories that mimic a child's own experiences are an important part of their development. Children will be able to relate to Rocket's struggle, which will validate their own learning process.

Closing Song

See Welcome Song earlier.

Follow-Up Activities

Alphabet Soup

Materials:

- Bowl coloring sheet (pattern at the end of the chapter)
- Liquid glue
- Paint brushes

- Paper plate
- Alphabet-shaped breakfast cereal
- Optional: Crayons or markers

Directions:

- Reproduce the included bowl coloring page
- Optional: Allow children to decorate the bowl as they like
- Pour liquid glue onto a paper plate
- Allow children to use paint brushes and liquid glue to adhere alphabet-shaped cereal to bowl creating alphabet soup!

NOTE: Depending on allergies, and your library's policies, extra cereal can be used as a snack.

Other Songs, Rhymes, and Fingerplays

The Alphabet Song

A-B-C-D-E-F-G-H-I-J-K-L-M-N-O-P-Q-R-S-T-U-V-W-X-Y-and Z
Now I know my ABCs, next time won't you sing with me?

Sesame Street—Sing the Alphabet Song

The zany gang from Sesame Street has a rhyming song sharing words that go with each letter of the alphabet. The song is sung twice on the video so you can join in with verses you know: https://www.youtube.com/watch?v=783EsrHchXA

Sesame Street—C Is for Cookie

As far as the Cookie Monster is concerned, "C" is the only important letter. Sing along with his ode to his favorite tasty treat. The letter "C" is clear throughout the video reinforcing the shape for children learning their letter: https://www.youtube.com/watch?v=BovQyphS8kA

Additional Poetry

Belle, Jennifer and David McPhail, illus. Animal Stackers. New York: Hyperion Books for Children, 2005.
This collection of acrostic poems plays heavily on the identification of letters, as the first letter of each of the first words of the poems spells out the topic of the poem. This would be a great poem to present to your audience visually so they can see that the meaning of the poem's title has to do with the content of the poem in a funny play on words. "The Ostrich" tells how all the creatures on the beach stop and wonder at the big bird with its head in the sand. Be sure to make note of the contents, as many poems can be used other storytimes (animals, fairy tales, etc.) as well.

Nesbitt, Kenn and Ethan Long, illus. My Hippo Has the Hiccups: And Other Poems I Totally Made Up. Naperville, IL: Sourcebooks Jabberwocky, 2009.
"Alphabet Break" (p. 19) goes through all the letters A-P only stopping because the speaker needs to "P." This is a quirky way to say your ABCs. The poem is Track 11 on the included CD so you can share the author reading the poem aloud.

Additional Nonfiction

Ernst, Lisa Campbell. The Turn-Around, Upside-Down Alphabet Book. New York: Simon & Schuster Books for Young Readers, 2004.

What better way to learn the shapes of the letters than by looking at them from every possible direction. Have you ever thought that "B" can look like "half a butterfly?" What about "O" being "a fried egg?" Each letter is clear on the page and in the correct position when the book is held normally so the book can be used as an educational tool. After kids know their letters a little better, play around with them by holding the book upside down.

Prochovnic, Dawn Babb and Stephanie Bauer, illus. A to Z Sign with Me: Sign Language for the Alphabet. Minneapolis, MN: Magic Wagon, 2012.

This is an alphabet book you can really grab hold of with both hands or at least use your hands to learn the basic letter signs. A slight story is told and little ones are asked to join in by signing letters they see and hear. Bright colorful illustrations are joined by clear images of handshapes and movements.

Additional Fiction Picture Book

Baker, Keith. LMNO Peas. New York: Beach Lane Books, 2010.

"We are peas-alphabet peas! We work and play in the ABCs!" And off we go as page by page and letter by letter, the alphabet peas demonstrate the many things they can be. Our P peas are poets and painters and plumbers fixing leaks! Big bold letters juxtaposed by tiny active peas are set against large white pages. Perfect for sharing.

Bottner, Barbara and Michael Emberley, illus. An Annoying ABC. New York: Alfred A. Knopf, 2011.

The morning was going well until "Adelaide annoyed Bailey." Each page continues the tale of annoyances with each action mirroring the annoyers name in an alliterating fashion. Never fear, peace is restored once another "A" word is introduced: apologize.

Fleming, Denise. Shout! Shout It Out! New York: Henry Holt and Company, 2011.

This book isn't just fun for sharing, it is fun for shouting! Children can join in, and loudly, while reciting numbers, letter, colors, animals, and other fun concepts. Illustrated in Fleming's bright bold patterned fashion.

Pearson, Debora. Alphabeep: A Zipping, Zooming ABC. New York: Holiday House, 2003.

An A to Z story that features vehicles of all sorts, from Ambulances to Zambonis and everything in between. Also a fun addition for the "Community Helpers" and "Cars and Trucks" storytime themes.

Pfister, Marcus. Animal ABC. New York: NorthSouth Books, Inc., 2013.

Each page is marked with patterned upper and lowercase letters, with a textured print illustration of an animal, along with a riddle like clue to help young readers guess the animal. "I have scales and a toothy smile. Just don't call me 'crocodile.' " The answer, of course, represents Aa: Alligator! A great way to have young readers interact by guessing the animals, while handily associating the letters with the creature. Some fanciful creatures are thrown in for added fun.

Coconut Tree Pattern

Bowl Pattern for Alphabet Soup

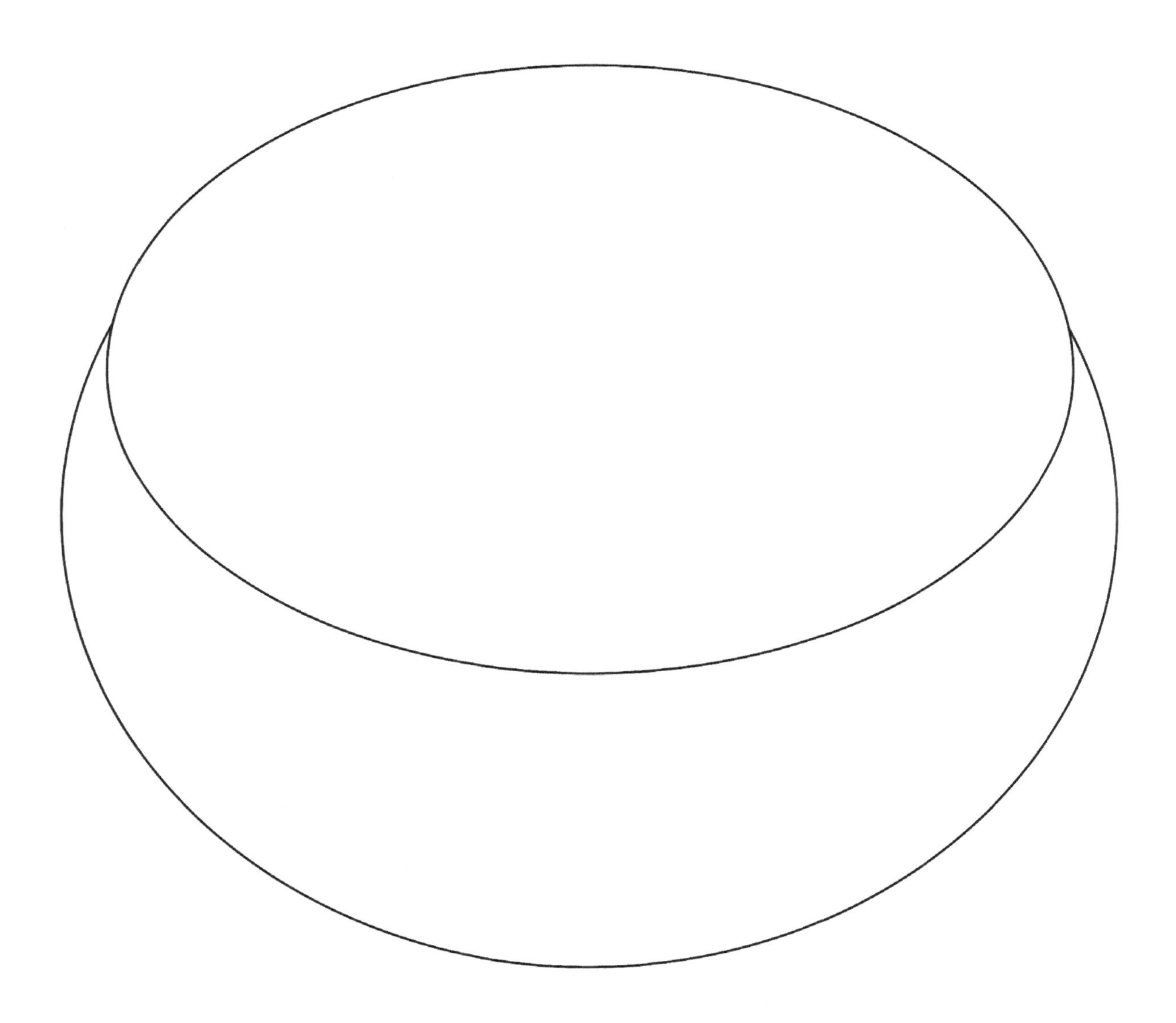

Apples

Red, yellow, green, and pink, juice, sauce, and slice! Apples are bright, colorful, and part of a little one's everyday experience. Celebrate the ordinary in this sweet and crisp storytime.

Sample Storytime

Welcome Song

Routine is important when working with children. Be sure to include welcome, transitional, and closing songs or activities to signify what is coming next. Don't be afraid to use the same ones; children take comfort in knowing what is coming next.

Opening Poem

"Core" from Powell, Consie. Amazing Apples. Morton Grove, IL: Albert Whitman & Company, 2003.
This simple acrostic poem reveals the flower design created by seeds inside an apple. After reading the poem aloud, cut open an apple to show everyone the design.

Action Rhyme

Two Red Apples
Adapted by J. Dietzel-Glair

Two red apples hanging from a branch (hold up two fists)
One named Mac (shake one fist)
The other named Tosh (shake the other fist)
Pull down Mac (pretend to pick an apple from a tree)
Pull down Tosh (pretend to pick the other apple)
Take a bite of Mac (hold a pretend apple and take a bite)
Take a bite of Tosh (hold a pretend apple in the other hand and take a bite)

Nonfiction for Storytime

Koontz, Robin Michal and Nadine Takvorian, illus. Apples, Apples, Everywhere!: Learning about Apple Harvests. Mankato, MN: Picture Window Books, 2011.
While it may seem that way, apples don't just magically appear in the grocery story. Illustrations in browns, reds, oranges, and yellows give a true sense of the autumn apple season.

Transitional Song

See Welcome Song earlier.

Flannel Board Activity

A-P-P-L-E

This flannel board uses simple die-cut letters and an apple shape. If you don't have access to a die cut, see whether a neighboring library will give you access to theirs, or find simple letters online.

Place the letters A-P-P-L-E on the flannel board one at a time and ask the children to help you spell out the word.

Once all are on the board, sing this song:

A-P-P-L-E
Modified by M. Follis
(Tune: BINGO)

I know a fruit that's red and sweet and apple is its name-o
A-P-P-L-E
A-P-P-L-E
A-P-P-L-E
And apple is its name-o

For additional choruses, remove one letter and instead of replacing a letter with a clap, replace it with a pretend bite of apple and a loud CHOMP!

example: "CHOMP-P-P-L-E"

Picture Books for Storytime

Matheson, Christie. Tap the Magic Tree. New York: Greenwillow Books, 2013.
Follow along as a bare brown apple tree grows leaves, flowers, and apples, and then goes bare again before winter. Much like Tullet's *Press Here*, this book encourages interaction to make the story progress.

Murray, Alison. Apple Pie ABC. New York: Disney-Hyperion Books, 2010.
Much more than just an alphabet book, this title is the story of a dog that really wants that freshly baked apple pie. Each letter is displayed clearly on the page making it a good choice for children learning the alphabet.

Early Literacy Tip:
Sing the Alphabet Song after reading an ABC book to reinforce the letters.

Closing Song

See Welcome Song earlier.

Follow-Up Activities

Apple Samples

Materials:

- Fresh apples cut into pieces
- Applesauce served in dixie cups with spoons
- Dried apples

- Apple juice served in small cups
- Any other apple products you wish to share
- Paper towels or napkins

Direction:

- Allow everyone to try the apples in different forms.

Apple Picking

Research local apple farms in the area and provide a sheet with hours, addresses, and other pertinent information for parents. Picking apples is an activity that is fun for the whole family. It encourages a healthy lifestyle by getting people outdoors and eating nutritious apples.

Other Songs, Rhymes, and Fingerplays

10 Little Apples
Adapted by J. Dietzel-Glair
(Tune: 10 Little Indians)

One little, two little, three little apples
Four little, five little, six little apples
Seven little, eight little, nine little apples
Ten little apples in a pie. Yum!

Apples and Bananas

This fun song plays with vowel sounds. A karaoke version can be found here: https://www.youtube.com/watch?v=OKEUAzzn-lg. If you have projection ability, show the video so everyone can sing along.

Early Literacy Tip:
Songs with silly sounds are fun, and they also help children learn letter sounds.

Additional Poetry

Katz, Bobbi, sel. and Deborah Zemke, illus. More Pocket Poems. New York: Dutton Children's Books, 2009.
"Happy Apple" by Anon (p. 16) is a simple rhyming pattern sharing that a happy apple would give joy by falling on "a nice boy like me." After all, apples beg to be eaten.

Powell, Consie. Amazing Apples. Morton Grove, IL: Albert Whitman & Company, 2003.
This collection of acrostic poems follows apples through spring, harvest, baking and canning, and winter. Preschoolers may be too young to create their own acrostic poems, but they can enjoy being introduced to them.

Additional Nonfiction

Esbaum, Jill. Apples for Everyone. Washington, DC: National Geographic Society, 2009.
Explore different types of apples, how they grow, and how they can be enjoyed. Children will enjoy the photographs in this title as a caregiver reads to them.

Smucker, Anna Egan and Kathleen Kemly, illus. Golden Delicious: A Cinderella Apple Story. Morton Grove, IL: Albert Whitman & Company, 2008.
Where did the Golden Delicious apple come from? This longer nonfiction picture book can be shared between a child and caregiver.

Additional Fiction Picture Books

Boldt, Claudia. Odd Dog. New York: NorthSouth, 2012.
Most dogs are very protective of their bones. Peanut is a little different, he is protective of his apples and apple tree. When the juiciest apple hangs over his neighbor's yard, he fears the worst but ends up making a new friend.

Holub, Joan and Jan Smith, illus. Apple Countdown. Morton Grove, IL: Albert Whitman & Company, 2009.
This fun tale of a class field trip to an apple farm offers great opportunities to count backwards from 20.

McClure, Nikki. Apple. New York: Abrams Appleseed, 2012.
A single word on each page enhances the illustrations that tell the tale of an apple from when it falls on the ground to when a new tree grows.

Art and Drawing

Most little ones have, at one time or another, expressed their creativity in less than ideal ways. Channel their self-expression with this artistic storytime and follow up with some controlled mess activities.

Sample Storytime

Welcome Song

Routine is important when working with children. Be sure to include welcome, transitional, and closing songs or activities to signify what is coming next. Don't be afraid to use the same ones; children take comfort in knowing what is coming next.

Opening Poem

"Behind the Museum Door" from Hopkins, Lee Bennett and Stacey Dressen-McQueen, illus. Behind the Museum Door: Poems to Celebrate the Wonders of Museums. New York: Abrams Books for Young Readers, 2007.
Museums house many wonders to behold. An art storytime introduces children to these wonders. Use "Behind the Museum Door" to open the door to wonder.

Action Rhyme

The Artist Paints a Picture
Adapted by J. Dietzel-Glair
(Tune: The Farmer in the Dell)

The artist paints a picture (pretend to hold a paint brush in one hand and paint a picture in front of you)
The artist paints a picture
Heigh-ho the museum is full
The artist paints a picture

The sculptor makes a statue (use both hands and pretend to mold clay in front of you)
The sculptor makes a statue
Heigh-ho the museum is full
The sculptor makes a statue

Nonfiction for Storytime

Niepold, Mil and Jeanyves Verdu. Oooh! Picasso. Berkeley, CA: Tricycle Press, 2009.
Explore five sculptures made by Pablo Picasso. Each sculpture is shown over four double-page spreads that zoom in on specific parts of the sculpture. The text is minimal, yet lyrical, making for an ideal storytime read.

Transitional Song

See Welcome Song earlier.

Flannel Board Activity

Shapes Make Shapes

Bertier, Anne. Wednesday. New York: Enchanted Lion Books, 2014.
In this simple story, two shapes, Big Square and Little Round, meet to play a game of transformation. They each say a word, and then break into pieces to give the word a shape.

- Use a simple small circle shape and a medium-sized square. Print multiple copies of them or create them from colored paper. Laminate and apply velcro or double-sided tape. You can also use felt.
- Taking clues from the book, cut the square and circle as needed to re-create some of the images in the book. (Example: The butterfly shape is made by cutting each shape in half.)
- Some of the images are complex, but many are simple and fun. Pick and choose according to your comfort level.
- Read portions of the story and re-create the image on the flannel board.
- Ask children what other fun things could be made.
- If you have a small enough group, invite children up to participate in their own creations.

Picture Books for Storytime

Beaumont, Karen and David Catrow, illus. I Ain't Gonna Paint No More. Boston: Houghton Mifflin Harcourt, 2005.
When a little boy gets in trouble for painting on the walls, he decides to use his body as a canvas. Seeing red, he paints his head, adding some black onto his back. For some reason his mom doesn't find this any more acceptable than the walls. With colors dripping off the pages, and a fun refrain (best done in an accent if you can manage it) this is a big hit at storytime.

Verde, Susan and Peter H. Reynolds, illus. The Museum. New York: Abrams Books for Young Readers, 2013.
On a visit to the museum, a young girl finds inspiration and emotion in the works of art she sees. Filled with action words, the rhyming text is a fun introduction to a museum.

Closing Song

You may wish to close storytime with the poem "Museum Farewell." This short poem closes the doors and turns out the lights after a visit to the museum. The poem by Rebecca Kai Dotlich can be found in:

Hopkins, Lee Bennett and Stacey Dressen-McQueen, illus. Behind the Museum Door: Poems to Celebrate the Wonders of Museums. New York: Abrams Books for Young Readers, 2007.

Follow-Up Activities

Lines All Around

Whitman, Candace and Steve Wilson, illus. Lines That Wiggle. Maplewood, NJ: Blue Apple Books, 2009.
How can you go wrong with glittery lines in a book? Lines can do so many things from wiggling to curling to criss-crossing. Sprout creativity and build observation

Early Literacy Tip:
Look for ways to encourage skills that children will build upon later in their education. *Lines That Wiggle* encourages the use of observation skills which is a key part of the scientific process.

skills by reading this book then following the instructions on the last page to "find some lines not in this book" in your library.

Museum Visits

Many museums have family-friendly events and/or child-focused exhibits. Call the museums in your area (or research them on the Internet) and put together a handout for families of upcoming events and exhibits. The museums will love the free publicity.

Other Songs, Rhymes, and Fingerplays

I Use Colors
Adapted by M. Follis and J. Dietzel-Glair
(Tune: Old MacDonald)

I use colors when I paint
P-A-I-N-T
Blue and yellow create green
P-A-I-N-T
With a blue swish here
And a yellow swish there
Here a blue, there a yellow
Now the green is everywhere
I use colors when I paint
P-A-I-N-T

Use the other color mixtures for more verses:
Red and yellow create orange. . . .
Red and blue create purple . . .
And if you want to have a little more fun:
Red and white create pink . . .

Early Literacy Tip:
Breaking down words into their corresponding letters helps build phonemic awareness.

I'm an Artist
By M. Follis and J. Dietzel-Glair
(Tune: London Bridge)

Dip the brush into the paint,
Into the paint
Into the paint
Dip the brush into the paint
Now I'm painting!

Additional verses:
Place the pencil on the paper—now I'm drawing
Run the crayons over the page—now I'm coloring
Squeeze the clay into a shape—now I'm sculpting

Additional Poetry

Heard, Georgia, ed. Falling Down the Page. New York: Roaring Brook Press, 2009.
"Creativity" by Eileen Spinelli tells that an artist takes both traditional and household materials and "turns it happily to art" displaying that even our youngest can engage their creativity each day and be an artist as well.

Hopkins, Lee Bennett, ed. and Sachiko Yoshikawa, illus. Hamsters, Shells and Spelling Bees: School Poems. New York: HarperCollins, 2008.
"Art Class" by Leslie Danford Perkins lists the many reasons why art class is a "feast for my eyes and my hands."

Additional Nonfiction

MacLachlan, Patricia and Hadley Hooper, illus. The Iridescence of Birds: A Book about Henri Matisse. New York: Roaring Book Press, 2014.
In this simplest of biographies, the reader learns why Henri Matisse became a great painter and how his upbringing inspired him. A majority of each double-page spread is absorbed by engaging illustrations. The poetic text gives life to his artistic mind and flows like a fictional picture book.

Micklethwait, Lucy. I Spy Shapes in Art. New York: Greenwillow Books, 2004.
On each page, readers are directed to find a particular shape in a famous work of art. This book is great for a detail-oriented child who loves to sit and study illustrations.

Niepold, Mil and Jeanyves Verdu. Oooh! Matisse. Berkeley, CA: Tricycle Press, 2007.
Explore five collages made by Henri Matisse. In small parts, the pieces of the collages look like something new which is described with minimal text. This title is a fun storytime read-aloud.

Additional Fiction Picture Books

Light, Kelly. Louise Loves Art. New York: HarperCollins, 2014.
Louise has created a masterpiece and is ready to hang it on "The Gallery du Fridge." Unfortunately, her little brother gets hold of her drawing first and creates his own masterpiece from the same piece of paper. Luckily, Louise loves her little brother even more than she loves her art. Lots of white space and minimal use of color let readers focus on the action of the story.

The Metropolitan Museum of Art. Museum ABC. Boston: Little, Brown and Company, 2002.
This title is an alphabet book and introduction to art. For example, four examples of apples in art face the page that reads "A is for APPLE." If used in storytime, share just a couple of pages with the audience.

Reynolds, Peter H. The Dot. Somerville, MA: Candlewick Press, 2003.
When a young girl encounters the pressure of a blank page and doubts about her own ability to create art, her teacher finds a unique way to encourage her creativity. Our young artists then learns to pass the gift of encouragement along. A great discussion starter and prompt for creative expression.

Tullet, Herve. Mix It Up. San Francisco: Chronicle Books, 2014.

Using an interactive format, Tullet asks readers to touch the pages and mix it up combining colors and creating patterns replicated in the textual illustrations. When getting your hands dirty with paint isn't an option, this is the next best thing.

Wiesner, David. Art & Max. Boston: Clarion Books, 2010.

Max's enthusiasm about painting makes up for his lack of skills, well almost. His artistic friend, Arthur, becomes the unwilling recipient of unexpected consequences. Be prepared for the strangest art you've ever seen.

Zalben, Jane Breskin. Mousterpiece: A Mouse-Sized Guide to Modern Art. New York: Roaring Brook Press, 2012.

Janson the Mouse lives in a museum and starts creating works of art like the ones she sees in the modern wing. This is a child-friendly introduction to some famous works of art.

Baby Animals

Nothing is cuter than a baby animal—even a baby crocodile or a baby skunk. Kids and adults alike can never get enough of baby animal pictures and videos. Create a storytime to go along with that fascination.

Sample Storytime

Welcome Song

Routine is important when working with children. Be sure to include welcome, transitional, and closing songs or activities to signify what is coming next. Don't be afraid to use the same ones; children take comfort in knowing what is coming next.

Opening Poem

"How a Puppy Grows" from Chorao, Kay. The Baby's Book of Baby Animals. New York: Dutton Children's Books, 2004.

Add movements to this poem by Leroy F. Jackson. Wiggle your bottom when the poem mentions the puppy's "wiggle-tail." Then touch your nose, tummy, and ears when they are mentioned.

Action Rhyme

Two Little Tadpoles
Adapted by M. Follis and J. Dietzel-Glair

Two little tadpoles
Sitting in a bog (hold up one finger on each hand)
One named Polly (wiggle one finger)
The other named Wog (wiggle the other finger)
Swim away Polly (move one hand behind your back)
Swim away Wog (move the other hand behind your back)
Come back Polly (bring back the first hand)
Come back Wog (bring back the other hand)

Nonfiction for Storytime

Stockdale, Susan. Carry Me!: Animal Babies on the Move. Atlanta, GA: Peachtree Publishers, 2005.

Animals around the world use various techniques for carrying their babies: from propping them on their shoulders to gathering them in their mouths. Most of the double-page spreads feature only one animal with their young. Friendly illustrations and minimal text make this appropriate as a storytime read-aloud. More information about each animal and where they are found in the world is located in the back.

Transitional Song

See Welcome Song earlier.

Flannel Board Activity

What Baby Animal Is in This Egg?

Materials:

- A large oval shape as an egg
- Photographs of animals that hatch from an egg (cute animal photographs seem to make up a majority of the Internet; find ones that suit your fancy). Make sure your felt egg is large enough to hide the image. Ideas for animals include turtle, chicken, duck, and tadpole. If you want to have fun with the activity, include a dinosaur.

Directions:

- Hide one animal picture behind the egg.
- Give clues about the animal until the kids are able to correctly guess the animal.
- Examples include: I have a shell. My shell is my home. I am a reptile. I can swim and crawl. I am a turtle.
- Once the kids guess the animal, pull off the egg to reveal the animal.
- Then hide another animal and do it again.

Picture Books for Storytime

Blackstone, Stella and Clare Beaton. Who Are You, Baby Kangaroo? Cambridge, MA: Barefoot Books, 2004.
A puppy asks many animals what the baby kangaroo is called. This title has repetitive phrasing and the chance to learn the names of a variety of baby animals.

Na, Il Sung. A Book of Babies. New York: Alfred A. Knopf, 2013.
Different animal babies act in a variety of ways on the day they are born. Each animal is described in only one sentence making this a quick storytime read.

Closing Song

See Welcome Song earlier.

Follow-Up Activities

Matching Game

Use a basic Internet search to find images of mother animals and corresponding images of baby animals. Be sure to seek out images where the baby animal is named something different.

Examples:

Cow and calf
Horse and foal
Elephant and calf

Goat and kid
Kangaroo and joey
Pig and piglet
Porcupine and porcupette
Duck and duckling
Frog and tadpole

Allow children to the come to the flannel board and match a set of animals. Be sure to give the correct name for the baby animal.

Early Literacy Tip: Introducing new and often complex words like porcupette in a familiar environment and in context is a great way for children to grow vocabulary.

Other Songs, Rhymes, and Fingerplays

Mommy Has a Baby
Adapted by M. Follis and J. Dietzel-Glair
(Tune: Old MacDonald)

Mommy swan has a cygnet
Honk honk honk honk honk
Mommy swan has a cygnet
Honk honk honk honk honk
With a honk honk here
And a honk here there
Here a honk, there a honk
Everywhere a honk honk
Mommy swan has a cygnet
Honk honk honk honk honk

Other verses:
Mommy duck has a duckling—quack quack quack quack quack
Mommy cow has a calf—moo moo moo moo moo
Mommy cat has a kitten—mew mew mew mew mew
Mommy kangaroo has a joey—hop hop hop hop hop
Mommy porcupine has a porcupette—ouch ouch ouch ouch ouch

Early Literacy Tip: It is fun and simple to expand vocabulary through songs.

Mary Had a Little Lamb
English Nursery Rhyme

Mary had a little lamb, little lamb, little lamb
Mary had a little lamb
It's fleece was white as snow.
And everywhere that Mary went, Mary went, Mary went
Everywhere that Mary went
The lamb was sure to go.

He followed her to school one day, school one day, school one day
He followed her to school one day
Which was against the rule,
It made the children laugh and play, laugh and play, laugh and play
It made the children laugh and play
To see a lamb at school.

And so the teacher turned it out, turned it out, turned it out
And so the teacher turned it out
But still it lingered near,
And waited patiently about, patiently about, patiently about
It waited patiently about
Till Mary did appear.

"Why does the lamb love Mary so? Mary so? Mary so?"
"Why does the lamb love Mary so?"
The eager children cry.
"Why, Mary loves the lamb, you know. Lamb, you know, Lamb you know."
"Why, Mary loves the lamb, you know."
The teacher did reply.

Note: Many rhymes have expanded versions. Sing just the popular first verse or the whole thing depending on your comfort level.

Wright, Danielle, collected by, and Mique Moriuchi, illus. My Village: Rhymes from around the World. London: Frances Lincoln Children's Books, 2010.
"Little Donkey" is a traditional Irish rhyme that reads like a poem. Poor little one-day-old donkey, he wants to play but his young body just needs to rest.

Additional Poetry

Chorao, Kay. The Baby's Book of Baby Animals. New York: Dutton Children's Books, 2004.
Adorable illustrations of ducklings, kittens, puppies, and piglets adorn these pages of nursery rhymes, poems, and lullabies.

Martin Jr., Bill, Michael Sampson, and various illustrators. The Bill Martin Jr. Big Book of Poetry. New York: Simon & Schuster, 2008.
"Baby Chick" (p. 21) by Aileen L. Fisher ponders the question how baby chicks know how to escape their eggshell home and be born into the great big world. Turn the page to read "A Kitten" by Eleanor Farjeon (p. 22) who had "a giant purr . . . and a midget mew."

Sidman, Joyce. Dark Emperor and Other Poems of the Night. New York: Houghton Mifflin Harcourt, 2010.
"I am a Baby Porcupette." Despite the vulnerability of the baby porcupette, he can fend off the enemy! "I raise my quills and pirouette." The simple four line stanzas are lyrical and filled with information and the double-page spread of this poem also includes a more fact-based paragraph for elaboration of the life of a baby porcupette.

Worth, Valerie and Steve Jenkins, illus. Animal Poems. New York: Farrar Straus Giroux, 2007.
"Kangaroos" shows just how lucky joeys are; they get to hop back into that comfy pouch whenever they want. No other animals get this privilege after they are born. The joey in the illustration looks so tiny compared to the mama kangaroo that is taller than the page, it's easy to see how he fits into her pouch.

Additional Nonfiction

Evans, Lynette and Guy Troughton, illus. Whose Egg? San Rafael, CA: Insight Kids, 2013.
Read the clues then lift the flaps to reveal the animal that hatches from a particular egg. Readers will be delighted to find birds, alligators, platypuses, snakes, turtles, and butterflies (the last animal hatching from a loose definition of an "egg").

Jenkins, Steve and Robin Page. My First Day. Boston: Houghton Mifflin Books for Children, 2013.
From kiwis to Siberian tigers, and giraffes to emperor penguins, baby animals have very different first days of life. Classic Steve Jenkins illustrations enhance the text of this interesting topic. If the text is too long for a particular group, choose favorite pages to share with a storytime crowd.

Posada, Mia. Guess What Is Growing Inside This Egg. Minneapolis, MN: Millbrook Press, 2007.
Rhyming verses and watercolor illustrations give hints about the animals that hatch from each of the eggs in this book. More information about each animal is provided on the reveal pages. Read just the verses and animal names for a storytime read-aloud.

Additional Fiction Picture Books

Butler, John. Bedtime in the Jungle. Atlanta, GA: Peachtree Publishers, 2009.
Count along as jungle mamas put one rhino, two monkeys, three leopards, and so on, to bed for the night. With satisfying rhyming text, storytime attendees will be excited to yell out the next number.

Butler, John. Whose Nose and Toes? New York: Penguin Publishing, 2004.
Take a peek at a nose or toes and guess the baby animal. This book acts as a turn-the-page guessing game that can be played during storytime.

Esbaum, Jill and Jen Corace, illus. I Hatched! New York: Dial Books for Young Readers, 2014.
Told from the point of view of a new hatched Killdeer chick, this rhyming story captures the enthusiasm of a baby wanting to learn everything. Readers will find themselves wanting to read quickly to mimic the mood of the book.

Freymann, Saxton. Baby Food. New York: Arthur A. Levine Books, 2003.
What could be cuter than a garlic kitten or a radish mouse? Be prepared for lots of oohs and aahs as you share baby animals fashioned out of fruits and vegetables. To make this book interactive ask your storytime attendees to identify the food used on each page.

Bathtime

Everyone's favorite time of day! Adults are happy because it means that their little ones are clean and it's almost bedtime. Little ones see it as a time to splash and play with their favorite bath toys. And let's not forget about the bubbles!

Sample Storytime

Welcome Song

Routine is important when working with children. Be sure to include welcome, transitional, and closing songs or activities to signify what is coming next. Don't be afraid to use the same ones; children take comfort in knowing what is coming next.

Opening Poem

Katz, Alan and David Catrow, illus. Take Me Out of the Bathtub: And Other Silly Dilly Songs. New York: Margaret K. McElderry Books, 2001.
In the titular poem/song, sung to the tune of "Take Me Out to the Ballgame" a young child begs to be taken out of the tub as he is wrinkle-y and clean, but a little stuck!

Action Rhyme

This is a fun little song that can only lead to good clean fun. If you have prop scarves handy, pass them out and let little ones practice their scrubbing skills!

Scrub, Scrub, Scrub, Scrub
By M. Follis and J. Dietzel-Glair
(Tune: Row, Row, Row Your Boat)

Soap, toys, tub and towel
And hot water please!
Scrub, scrub, scrub, scrub,
Wash your dirty knees

Soap, toys, tub and towel
Bubbles on my nose
Scrub, scrub, scrub, scrub,
Wash your dirty toes

Soap, toys, tub and towel
Everything's all wet
Scrub, scrub, scrub, scrub
Wash your dirty neck

Soap, toys, tub and towel
Bubbles everywhere
Scrub, scrub, scrub, scrub
Wash your dirty hair

Soap, toys, tub and towel
My toy boats make a fleet
Scrub, scrub, scrub, scrub
Wash your dirty feet

Nonfiction for Storytime

Barner, Bob. Animal Baths. San Francisco: Chronicle Books, 2011.
Vibrant illustrations accompany this brief introduction to the bathing habits of animals. The last page suggests acting like the animals in the book while taking a bath; add pretend movements to your storytime for nonfiction fun.

Transitional Song

See Welcome Song earlier.

Flannel Board Activity

Five Little Ducks

Create five felt ducks using the pattern at the end of the chapter. You may also wish to enlarge the bathtub pattern to put all the ducks in the bath. Put the ducks (and tub) on the flannel board and share this rhyme.

Five Little Ducks in the Tub
By M. Follis

Five little ducks, splishing and splashing
Cleaning behind their ears, soapy and laughing
One jumps out, sliding across the floor
How many are left?
Just these four

Four little ducks, splishing and splashing
Cleaning behind their ears, soapy and laughing
One jumps out, shaking the bubbles free
How many are left
Just these three!

Three little ducks, splishing and splashing
Cleaning behind their ears, soapy and laughing
One jumps out saying "My lips are turning blue!"
How many are left?
Just these two.

Two little ducks, splishing and splashing
Cleaning behind their ears, soapy and laughing
One jumps out saying "I'm DONE!"
How many are left?
Just this one.

One little duck, splishing and splashing
Cleaning behind his ears, soapy and laughing
He jumps out saying "Alone is no fun!"
How many are left?
Now there are none

Early Literacy Tip:
Talking about ideas like the concept of "none" helps build a young child's general world knowledge.

Picture Books for Storytime

Krosoczka, Jarrett J. Bubble Bath Pirates. New York: Penguin Books, 2003.
Bathtime is taken up a notch when you add soap, water, and pirates!

Peck, Jan and Valeria Petrone, illus. Way Down Deep in the Deep Blue Sea. New York: Simon & Schuster, 2004.
A little boy goes searching for pirate treasure way down deep in the deep blue bathtub!

Closing Song

See Welcome Song earlier.

Follow-Up Activities

Soap Bubbles

Materials:

- Liquid dishwashing soap
- Water
- A variety of bubble wands

Directions:

- Add a small amount of dishwashing soap to the water.
- Dip your wand in the soapy solution.
- Take the wand back out and gently blow on the hole to create a bubble.

Other Songs, Rhymes, and Fingerplays

Dirty Fingernails
By J. Dietzel-Glair
(Tune: Twinkle Twinkle Little Star)

Dirty, dirty fingernails
All because of mud in pails
I like to play in dirt all day
Shovel, shovel mud away
Dirty, dirty fingernails
All because of mud in pails

I'm Singing in the Tub
Adapted by J. Dietzel-Glair
(Tune: I'm Singing in the Rain)

I'm singing in the tub
Just singing in the tub
I know I sound so lovely
Just singing in the tub

Early Literacy Tip:
Don't worry about how you sound. Singing is an important bonding activity between a parent and a child.

Sesame Street—Ernie and His Rubber Ducky

No bathtime storytime would be complete without Ernie's ode to his favorite bath toy. Share the classic Sesame Street clip from YouTube: https://www.youtube.com/watch?v=Mh85R-S-dh8.

Additional Poetry

Katz, Alan and David Catrow, illus. Take Me Out of the Bathtub and Other Silly Dilly Songs. New York: Margaret K. McElderry Books, 2001.
"I'm Filthy, I'm Dirty" to the tune of "It's Raining, It's Pouring" brings up one of the chief reasons for taking a bath, being disgusting!

McNaughton, Colin. Wish You Were Here (And I Wasn't): A Book of Poems and Pictures for Globe Trotters. Cambridge, MA: Candlewick Press, 2000.
"Row, Row, Row Your Bath" (p. 21) is a humorous adaptation of the well-known song.

Philip, Neil, sel. and Claire Henley, illus. The Fish Is Me: Bathtime Rhymes. New York: Clarion Books, 2002.
Humor abounds when water, soap, and fun collide. Share poems about the joys of a bath (and getting dirty again), misbehaving soap, and the best ways to get clean. All of the poems in this book are suitable for the preschool crowd. Share the illustrations while reading your favorite selections from this title.

Additional Nonfiction

Bradley, Kimberly Brubaker and Margaret Miller, photo. Pop! A Book about Bubbles. New York: HarperCollins Publishers, 2001.
Photographs and clear text explain the science behind soap bubbles in child-friendly language. Put this book on display for families to check out after a bathtime storytime.

Jenkins, Steve and Robin Page. Time for a Bath. Boston: Houghton Mifflin Books for Children, 2011.
Some animals take baths in the dirt, while others let ants do the dirty work. Kids and adults will be fascinated by the odd bathtime rituals of animals from tigers to pangolins to tomato groupers. Share one-on-one or choose a couple favorite pages to share with a group.

Schuh, Mari C. Brushing Teeth. Mankato, MN: Capstone Press, 2008.
Don't forget to "bathe" your teeth. Through large pictures and only a couple sentences per page, you can follow along with Luke's brushing routine. This is an important topic as preschoolers start brushing their own teeth.

Additional Fiction Picture Books

Ficocelli, Elizabeth and Glin Dibley, illus. Kid Tea. Tarrytown, NY: Cavendish Children's, 2007.

After a week full of messy fun, a brother and sister are dunked in the tub each night to create an interesting "kid tea." For example: "Monday is fun day, mud-pies-in-the-sun day . . . Dunk me in the tub please for some brown kid tea." In addition to being a fun bathtime rhyme, other concepts such as days of the week and colors are brightly presented.

O'Garden, Irene and Cynthia Jabar, illus. The Scrubbly-Bubbly Car Wash. New York: HarperCollins Publishers, 2003.

Even cars need a bathtime and this car wash is "lathery-blathery" and "scrubbly-bubbly." The illustrations make this car wash feel like a carnival ride.

Willems, Mo. The Pigeon Needs a Bath! New York: Hyperion Books for Children, 2014.

Oh, Pigeon, will you ever learn? Pigeon stinks and does *not* want to take a bath. He even goes so far as to point out that in some cultures it is "impolite to bathe." As in all of the pigeon books, the audience is part of the story.

Duck Pattern

Bathtub Pattern

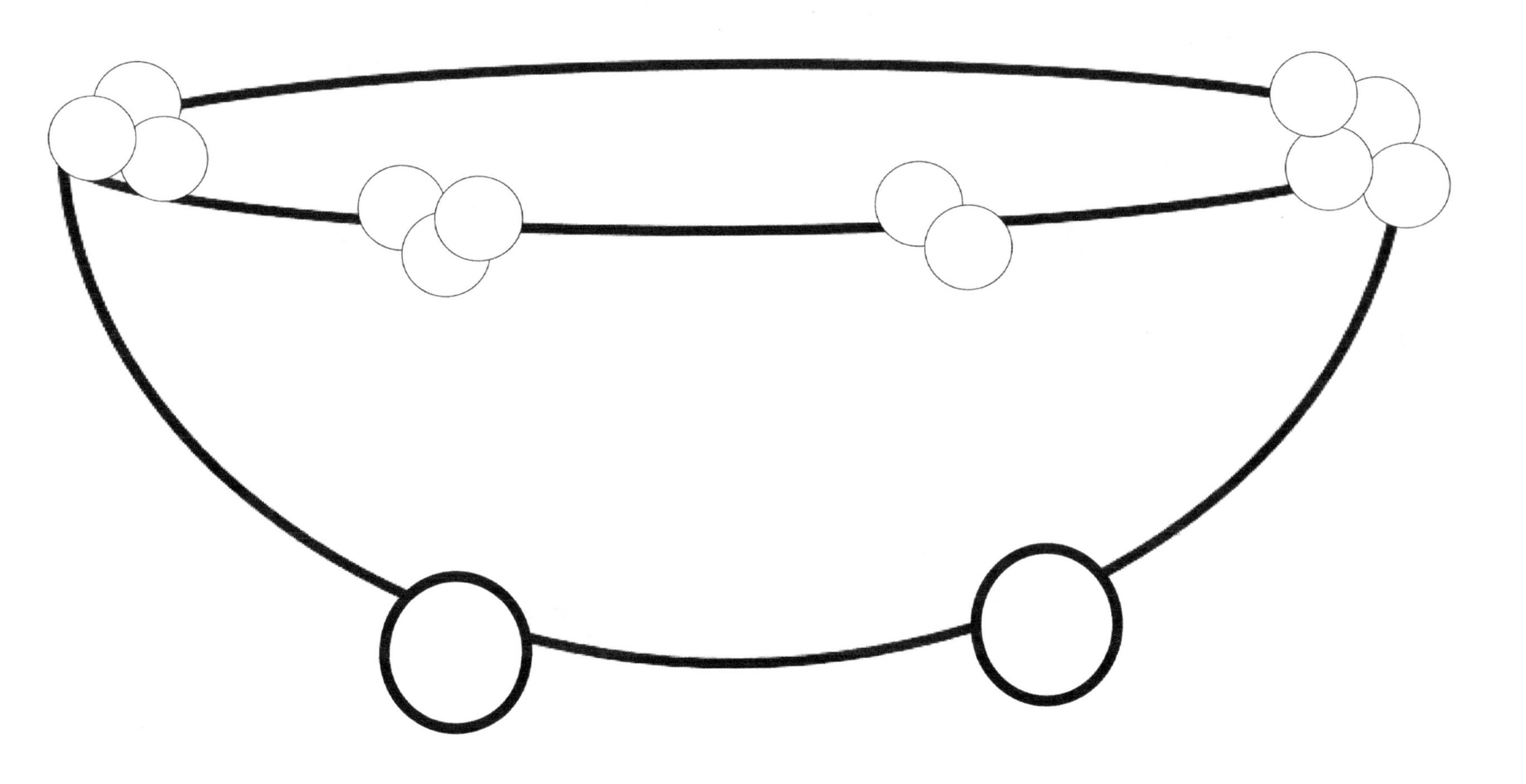

Beach

Sand between your toes and breezy, salty air. Bring a piece of a favorite family vacation spot to storytime.

Sample Storytime

Welcome Song

Routine is important when working with children. Be sure to include welcome, transitional, and closing songs or activities to signify what is coming next. Don't be afraid to use the same ones; children take comfort in knowing what is coming next.

Opening Poem

"Look" from Ode, Eric and Erik Brooks, illus. Sea Star Wishes: Poems from the Coast. Seattle, WA: Sasquatch Books, 2013.
This poem ends with the words "look, watch, wonder" making it an ideal start to a storytime. Display the accompanying illustration of two children exploring the beach while reading this poem.

Action Rhyme

The Waves at the Beach
Adapted by M. Follis
(Tune: The Wheels on the Bus)

The waves at the beach go up and down, (use hands to make a wave-like motion)
Up and down, up and down,
The waves at the beach go up and down,
In the summertime!

Additional verses:
Clams go open and shut (cup hands together to form clamshell shape then open and close)
Crabs go back and forth (wiggle fingers in a left and right motion as if playing a piano)
Jellyfish go wiggle, wiggle, wiggle (hold hands with fingers facing downwards to imitate tentacles, and wiggle fingers)
Lobsters go pinch, pinch, pinch (use thumb and index finger and make pinching motion)
End by repeating first verse

Nonfiction for Storytime

Serafina, Frank. Looking Closely Along the Shore. Tonawanda, NY: Kids Can Press, 2008.
Close-up photographs of common seaside animals and plants create a guessing game for young beach dwellers. Once revealed through a full page photograph, there is more information for the curious family. Read just the text on the guessing page and the name of the plant or animal for storytime.

Transitional Song

See Welcome Song earlier.

Flannel Board Activity

Beach Supplies

"I Must Go Down to the Beach Again" from Shapiro, Karen Jo and Judy Love, illus. I Must Go Down to the Beach Again and Other Poems. Watertown, MA: Charlesbridge, 2007.

Lots of supplies are needed for a fun day at the beach. Make this poem a visual experience by printing pictures for the flannel board of all the items this child brings with him. Put them on the board as they are mentioned in the poem. You'll need pictures of a red toy boat, bathtub duck, yellow truck, plastic squirt-toy, blow-up raft, pail and shovel, towel, hat, kite, green glasses, water shoes, sandwich, plum, lemonade, pudding, and a spoon.

Picture Books for Storytime

Docherty, Thomas. To the Beach. Somerville, MA: Templar Books, 2007.

A beach book about a boy that uses extraordinary methods of transportation for his beach excursion. When he is done swimming and building sand castles, he uses more unique forms of transportation.

Konagaya, Kiyomi and Masamitsu Saito, illus. Beach Feet. New York: Enchanted Lion Books, 2012.

A child experiences the sights, smells, sounds, and physical sensations of a day at the beach through text and illustrations that are full of action.

Closing Song

See Welcome Song earlier.

Follow-Up Activities

Kinetic Sand

Kinetic Sand offers a fun, clean way for children to recreate a day of playing in the sand at the beach. Purchasing enough sand for everyone to play may be too costly, but you can use the following link to access an easy and inexpensive recipe for a homemade version.

http://www.duchessnduke.com/diy-kinetic-sand/

Depending on what objects you may have on hand, bring additional supplies, like toy cars to drive through sand, and buttons and other appropriate objects to bury.

Early Literacy Note: Giving children a tactile experience related to a storytime's theme offers them a fun follow-up activity that engages multiple senses including motor skills.

Other Songs, Rhymes, and Fingerplays

Seashell Seashell
By J. Dietzel-Glair
(Tune: Bicycle Built for Two)

Seashell seashell
I like to look for you
On the beaches
Where my family goes each June
You might be a lovely clam shell
Or perhaps a broken piece
But I add each one
To my collection
To remember you all year through

My Bonnie Lies Over the Ocean
Traditional Scottish Folk Song

My Bonnie lies over the ocean
My Bonnie lies over the sea
My Bonnie lies over the ocean
Oh, bring back my Bonnie to me.

Bring back, bring back
Oh, bring back my Bonnie to me, to me
Bring back, bring back
Oh, bring back my Bonnie to me.

Early Literacy Note: Work on distinguishing letter sounds by alternating between standing up and sitting down every time you sing a word that begins with "B" when singing "My Bonnie Lies Over the Ocean."

Additional Poetry

Michelson, Richard and Doris Ettlinger, illus. S Is for Sea Glass: A Beach Alphabet. Ann Arbor, MI: Sleeping Bear Press, 2014.
A variety of poetic forms are used to vividly describe different aspects of the beach from A to Z. Common beach themes such as gulls and kites are juxtaposed with less common ideas such as the ice in winter. Designed like a picture book, hold open the book while reading your favorite selection. To use as an alphabet book, read just the titles of each poem "A Is for Angel," "B Is for Boardwalk," and so on, in storytime.

Ode, Eric and Erik Brooks, illus. Sea Star Wishes: Poems from the Coast. Seattle, WA: Sasquatch Books, 2013.
The beach is more than just sand and waves. It is tidal pools and stunt kites and geoducks. Charming illustrations complement each of the child-friendly poems in this title.

Wolfe, Frances. Where I Live. Plattsburgh, NY: Tundra Books, 2001.
A young narrator shares a poem about the seaside where she lives. Each two-line verse is spread over two double-page spreads with a large illustration. Read the entire book aloud in a storytime.

Additional Nonfiction

Himmelman, John. Who's at the Seashore? Lanham, MD: NorthWord Books for Young Readers, 2008.

One line per page describes the animals found on the seashore. Kids will be interested to learn more about the unique animals included such as turnstones, moon snails, and killifish. A short paragraph about each of the nine animals is included in the back.

Kudlinski, Kathleen V. and Lindy Burnett, illus. The Seaside Switch. Minnetonka, MN: NorthWord, 2007.

Each page reads like a mini-vignette as the tides change and seaside plants and animals are stranded in tidal pools or whisked back out to sea.

Mannis, Celeste Davidson. Snapshots: The Wonders of Monterey Bay. New York: Viking, 2006.

Take a trip to the coast of California through vivid photographs. Further information is provided on each page but the rhyming text that accompanies the featured photographs can be read aloud to a group.

Additional Fiction Picture Books

Ashman, Linda and Nadine Bernard Westcott, illus. To the Beach! Orlando, FL: Harcourt, Inc., 2005.

This family has to turn around so many times for beach accessories that it seems they will never make it. Humor and a surprise ending add to the fun.

Elya, Susan Middleton and Steven Salerno, illus. Bebé Goes to the Beach. Orlando, FL: Harcourt, Inc., 2008.

Spanish words are sprinkled through this rhyming text about a toddler's trip to the beach with his mother. A glossary with definitions and pronunciation guides makes this book accessible to those without Spanish-language skills.

Williams, Karen Lynn and Floyd Cooper, illus. A Beach Tail. Honesdale, PA: Boyds Mills Press, 2010.

When Gregory gets lost at the beach, he follows the lion tale he drew until he makes it back to dad. Cooper's gentle illustrations add a softness to this beach adventure.

Bears

Teddy Bears have been around since 1902 and named for President Teddy Roosevelt. Since then these stuffed animals have been a household item for many children around the world. Featured in children's fairy tales, songs, and books, bears are a great hook for storytimes and follow-up activities.

Sample Storytime

Welcome Song

Routine is important when working with children. Be sure to include welcome, transitional, and closing songs or activities to signify what is coming next. Don't be afraid to use the same ones; children take comfort in knowing what is coming next.

Opening Poem

Brown, Margaret Wise and Susan Jeffers, illus. Love Songs of the Little Bear. New York: Hyperion Books for Children, 2001.
This title contains four illustrated poems. Each poem is broken up over multiple pages creating a mini picture book. Choose the one that speaks to you to read aloud in storytime.

Action Rhyme

Teddy Bear, Teddy Bear
Traditional Rhyme
(Act out the movements as they are mentioned in the song)

Teddy bear, teddy bear turn around
Teddy bear, teddy bear touch the ground
Teddy bear, teddy bear show your shoe
Teddy bear, teddy bear that will do

Teddy bear, teddy bear go upstairs
Teddy bear, teddy bear say your prayers
Teddy bear, teddy bear turn out the light
Teddy bear, teddy bear say goodnight.

Nonfiction for Storytime

Markle, Sandra. How Many Baby Pandas? New York: Walker & Company, 2009.
Through photographs taken at the Wolong Giant Panda Breeding Center, readers learn about baby pandas from birth through two years old. Read just the red text on each page for a fun storytime read-aloud. Be sure to count along with the book by pointing at the designated number of pandas on each page.

Transitional Song

See Welcome Song earlier.

Flannel Board Activity

Square Bear

Campbell, Kathy Kuhtz and Emily Muschinske, illus. Let's Draw a Bear with Squares. New York: The Rosen Publishing Group's PowerStart Press & Editorial Buenas Letras, 2004.
This book gives simple page-by-page instructions on how to draw a bear using colored squares. Instead of drawing the bear, cut the squares out of felt and create the bear on the flannel board as you read (or tell) the book.

Picture Books for Storytime

Ruzzier, Sergio. Bear and Bee. New York: Disney-Hyperion Books, 2013.
Bear wakes up from winter hibernation and goes in search of honey. He is scared of meeting a big scary bee until he befriends one. A humorous tale of friendship and misunderstandings.

Seeger, Laura Vaccaro. Dog and Bear: Two Friends, Three Stories. New York: Neal Porter Book, 2007.
Three short stories about the friendship between a Dachshund and a toy teddy bear showing that there's fun to be had no matter how different you are. The short chapters make this fun for reading as a whole, or picking and choosing from among the "chapters." Colorful acrylic paints and plenty of white space make this a great book for sharing with a group. Check out the three other installments of this friendship including **Two's Company** (2008), **Three to Get Ready** (2009), and **Tricks and Treats** (2014).

Closing Song

See Welcome Song earlier.

Follow-Up Activities

Build a Bear

Using the pattern attached you can both build a bear to go with this storytime theme and discuss shapes and colors.

Materials:

- Construction paper in:
  - brown
  - light brown
  - pink
  - black
- Glue or glue sticks

Directions:

- Cut out the pattern pieces ahead of time from the appropriate color construction paper.
- Cut the brown ear and pink inner ear (heart shape) in half.
- Glue the inner pink ear to the brown outer ear, then attach on the outer edges of brown bear face.

- Adhere small black circles onto brown circle bear face in the appropriate places for eyes, as shown in pattern.
- Glue light brown circle bear "snout" onto face, and build a smile and nose by attaching an inverted pink heart, and small black dot as shown in the pattern.
- Attach head to body.
- Glue on light brown oval to represent the bear's belly.
- Adhere the bear's upper and lower paws by attaching light brown circles and ovals as shown in pattern.
- Now give a rumbly growl!

Early Literacy Tip:
Use easily recognizable shapes and expand vocabulary and concept skills by differentiating between circles and ovals, and light and dark brown.

Other Songs, Rhymes, and Fingerplays

We're Going on a Bear Hunt
Traditional Folk Song

We're going on a bear hunt, (slap hands on thighs to mimic sound of walking)
We're gonna catch a big one,
What a beautiful day,
We're not scared.
Oh oh!
Grass,
Long, wavy, grass.
We can't go over it,
We can't go under it,
We've gotta go through it!
Swishy swashy, swishy swashy. (rub hands together in a back and forth motion)
We're going on a bear hunt,
We're gonna catch a big one,
What a beautiful day,
We're not scared.
Oh oh!
Mud,
Thick, oozy mud.
We can't go over it,
We can't go under it,
We've gotta go through it!
Squelch squelch, squelch squelch (lift feet slowly as if feet are stuck in mud)
We're going on a bear hunt,
We're gonna catch a big one,
What a beautiful day,
We're not scared.
Oh oh!
A river,
A deep, cold river.
We can't go over it,
We can't go under it,
We've gotta go through it!
Splish splosh, splish splosh. (pretend to swim through the water)
We're going on a bear hunt,

We're gonna catch a big one,
What a beautiful day,
We're not scared.
Oh oh!
A cave,
A scary, dark cave.
We can't go over it,
We can't go under it,
We've gotta go through it!
Tiptoe, tiptoe. (crouch low and tiptoe)
(Say the following verse all together and quickly.)
OH NO IT'S A BEAR!!!
Quick! (do all actions quickly in reverse)
Through the cave, tiptoe, tiptoe,
Through the river, splish splosh, splish spolosh,
Through the mud, squelch squelch, squelch squelch,
Through the grass, swishy swashy, swishy swashy.
Run to the house, run up the stairs, (pretend to run with arms racing at sides)
Oh oh forgot to shut the door!
Run back downstairs, shut the door, (run and mime shutting door)
Run back up, to the bedroom, (run)
Jump into bed, pull up the covers, (mime pulling covers over head)
WE ARE NEVER GOING ON A BEAR HUNT AGAIN!!

Trapani, Iza. The Bear Went Over the Mountain. New York: Sky Pony Press, 2012.
In addition to the well-known song, this bear goes over the mountain to see what he can see, hear, smell, touch, and taste. A musical score is included in the back so you can sing the entire book.

Early Literacy Tip:
Kids learn about the five senses early in school. Help them learn this information at the end of each verse. Touch your eyes, ears, nose, fingertips, and tongue.

Additional Poetry

Lewis, J. Patrick, ed. National Geographic Book of Animal Poetry: 200 Poems with Photographs That Squeak, Soar, and Roar! Washington, DC: National Geographic, 2012.
"Grandpa Bear's Lullaby" by Jane Yolen is a soothing ode to hibernation and the sweet dreams of the bear's long sleep.

Schertle, Alice and Linda Hill Griffith, illus. Teddy Bear, Teddy Bear. New York: HarperCollins Publishers, 2003.
Snuggly teddy bears, misbehaving teddy bears, and overly loved teddy bears, you'll find them all in this collection of odes to everyone's favorite stuffed animal. The paintings add color and warmth to the poetry, and perhaps a bit of nostalgia for adults in the room.

Worth, Valerie and Steve Jenkins, illus. Animal Poems. New York: Farrar Straus Giroux, 2007.
The "Bear" may look soft and cuddly, but his fierce eyes show something else. The bear on the facing page stares you down as you read.

Additional Nonfiction

Baines, Rebecca. A Den Is a Bed for a Bear: A Book about Hibernation. Washington, DC: National Geographic, 2008.

Just the right amount of information about hibernation is told in rhyming text. Other fun facts are included along the way, such as bears eating calories equal to 65 cheeseburgers in one day. Share just the main text or include your favorite facts in a storytime read.

Barner, Bob. Bears! Bears! Bears! San Francisco: Chronicle Books, 2010.

With only one line per page, children can be introduced to the eight types of bears in the world. A page in the back gives quick facts about baby bears that will interest young listeners. Barner's collage-style art is attractive and will show well across a room.

Brett, Jeannie. Wild about Bears. Watertown, MA: Charlesbridge, 2014.

Each of the eight species of bears has things in common with each other and traits that make them unique. Each species receives each own double-page spread. The watercolor illustrations and measured amount of information on each page makes this a book that can be shared one-on-one with a child. Programmers may wish to show each bear and read one trait for use in storytime.

Additional Fiction Picture Books

Foley, Greg. Thank You Bear. New York: Viking, 2007.

The other animals think Bear's box is boring and unuseful. But Bear knows that his friend Mouse will love the empty box. This tale of friendship will delight storytime attendees.

Morris, Jackie. Something about a Bear. London: Frances Lincoln Children's Books, 2014.

Breathtaking watercolor paintings fill the pages of this story book filled with factual information about each of the eight types of bears. Lyrical prose describes each bear. A toy teddy bear, the very best bear, makes a quick appearance at the beginning and the end.

Pinkwater, Daniel and Will Hillenbrand, illus. Bear in Love. Somerville, MA: Candlewick Press, 2012.

Bear and a mysterious friend exchange gifts on a rock until they finally meet. Hillenbrand's soft illustrations are just right for this quiet story.

Yoon, Salina. Found. New York: Walker Books for Young Readers, 2014.

When Bear finds a lost stuffed bunny, he strives to find its home. Children will understand the concept of losing a beloved toy. Adults will like the subtle humor found on the end pages.

Completed Bear Pattern

Bear Pattern

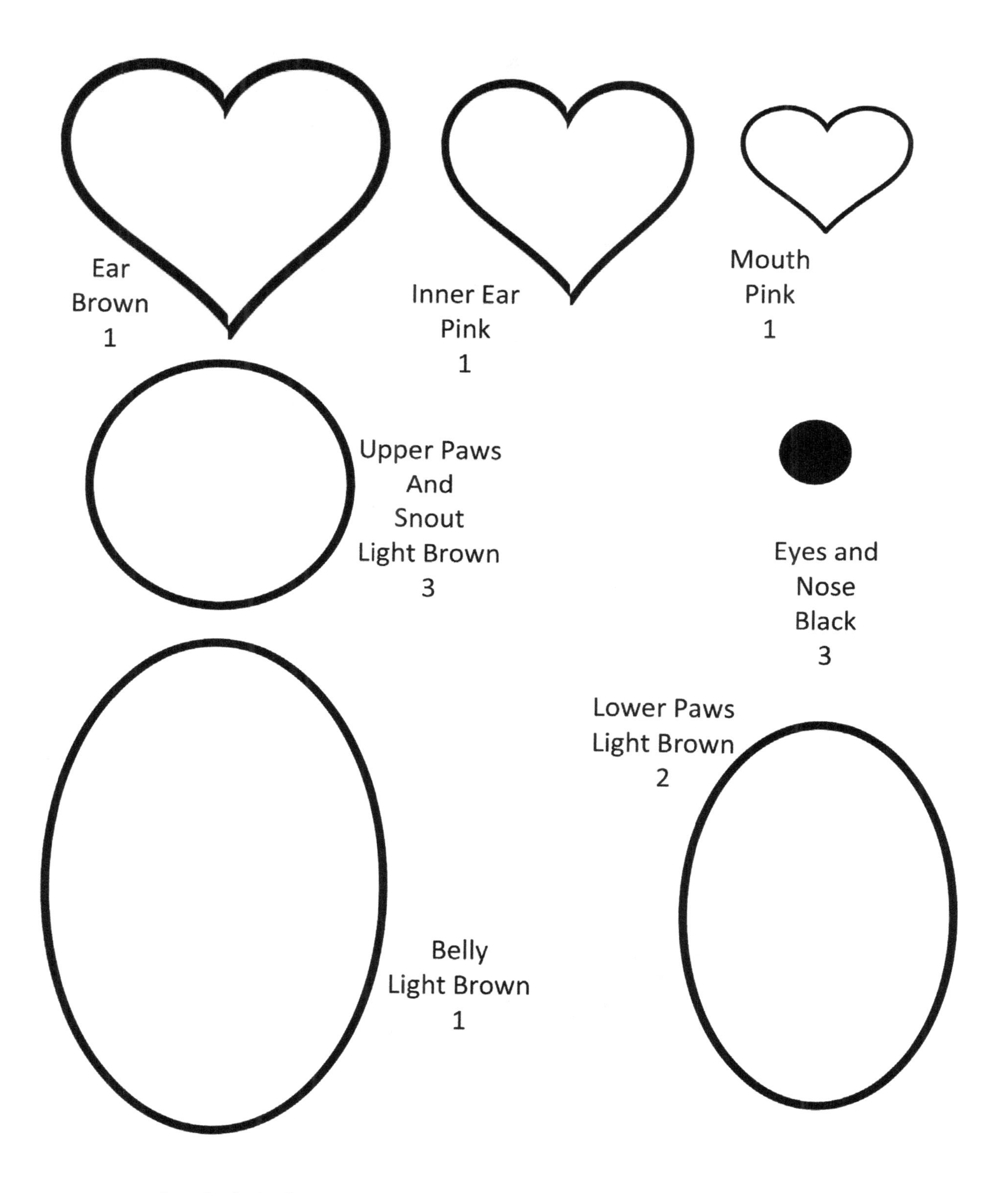

Bear Pattern

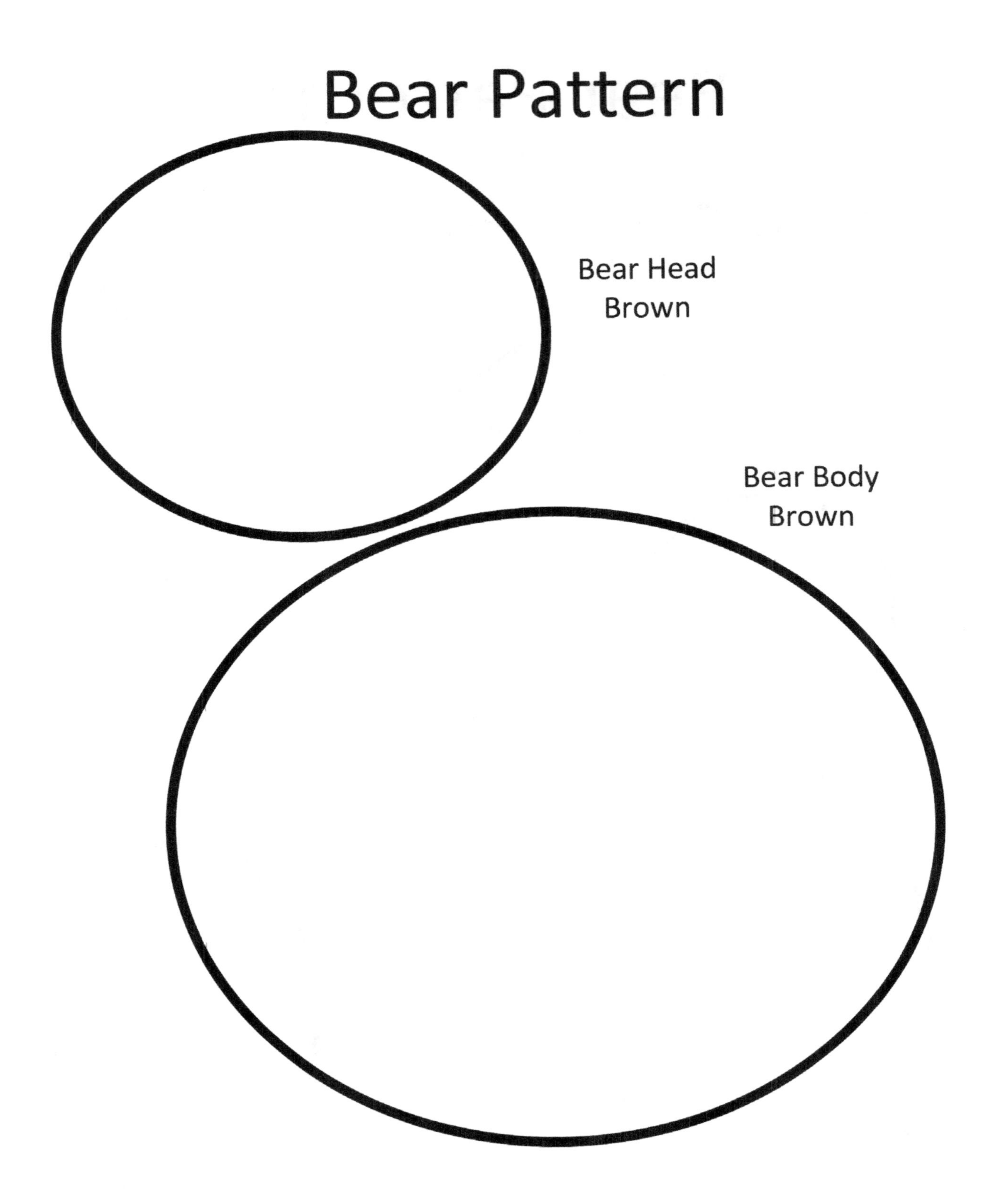

Bedtime/Nighttime

While most children will tell you that this is their least favorite time of day, it is a daily event that everyone can relate to. If your storytime is scheduled for the evening, this might be a great chance to schedule a pajama storytime. Have your little friends come to the event dressed appropriately, with a snack and pillows brought from home.

Sample Storytime

Welcome Song

Routine is important when working with children. Be sure to include welcome, transitional, and closing songs or activities to signify what is coming next. Don't be afraid to use the same ones; children take comfort in knowing what is coming next.

Opening Poem

"Set, Sun" from Hopkins, Lee Bennett, compiler, and Mariusz Stawarski, illus. Sky Magic. New York: Dutton Children's Books, 2009.
Set the tone for storytime through this poem that literally tells the sun it is time for day to end. Use it to create an evening feel to a daytime program or as an apt descriptor for the darkening sky during an evening storytime. "Moon Lullaby" is also a scene setter for a program about sleepy time.

Action Rhyme

Ready for Bedtime
Written by M. Follis
(Tune: London Bridge)

Every night we take a bath, take a bath, take a bath (mime washing)
Every night we take a bath
Ready for bedtime!

Additional verses:
Put on jammies (mime putting on clothes)
Brush our teeth (mime brushing teeth)
Read a book (mime reading a book and turning page)
Say goodnight (mime kissing parent)

Nonfiction for Storytime

Lunde, Darrin and Patricia J Wynne, illus. Hello, Bumblebee Bat. Watertown, MA: Charlesbridge, 2007.
Not all animals sleep at night. Told like a question and answer book, the responses are given from the point of view of this tiny bat. Further information about the species is shared in the back; it is short enough to read to a storytime crowd that wants to know more.

Transitional Song

See Welcome Song earlier.

Flannel Board Activity

Five in the Bed

Pretend your flannel board is a bed. Put five felt animals in bed. (Note: You don't need to reinvent the wheel by creating new flannel pieces for this rhyme. Use any five animals you have created for other rhymes.) Remove one and let it fall on the floor each time an animal falls out. When the little one is lonely, put everyone back in bed together.

Five in the Bed
British Playground Song

There were five in the bed
And the little one said
"Roll over! Roll over!"
So they all rolled over
And one fell out.

There were four in the bed . . .
There were three in the bed . . .
There were two in the bed . . .

There was one in the bed
And the little one said
"I'm lonely!"

Picture Books for Storytime

Horáček, Petr. When the Moon Smiled. Cambridge, MA: Candlewick Press, 2003.
All is not well on the farm. The day animals are awake and the night animals are asleep. Count along with the moon as he lights stars one by one as a signal to the animals. The star cutouts on each page will be a big hit with any child.

Howatt, Sandra J. and Joyce Wan, illus. Sleepyheads. New York: Beach Lane Books, 2014.
The dark palette matches the sleepytime feel as all the animals snuggle in for the night. Ending with a child asleep in mama's arms, parents will enjoy being introduced to this delightful bedtime read.

Closing Song

See Welcome Song earlier.

Follow-Up Activities

Stuffed Animal Sleepover

Directions:

- Ask everyone to bring a stuffed animal to storytime. (Note: Suggest to parents that the child *not* bring their most favorite animal that may be sorely missed at bedtime.)

- Before they leave storytime, have everyone add a name tag to a ribbon tied around their stuffed animal.
- Everyone leaves his or her stuffed animal after storytime so that the stuffed animal can have a sleepover at the library.
- After all the children have left, the librarian arranges the animals in fun activities (i.e., listening to a bedtime story, eating milk and cookies, climbing on the bookshelves) and takes pictures of the fun.
- In the morning everyone picks up his or her stuffed animals and can see the pictures of all the fun.

Other Songs, Rhymes, and Fingerplays

Rock-a-Bye, Baby
Traditional Lullaby

Rock-a-bye, baby
In the tree tops
When the wind blows
The cradle will rock.
When the bough breaks,
The cradle will fall,
And down will come baby,
Cradle and all.

Twinkle Twinkle Little Star
Traditional Rhyme

Twinkle, twinkle little star (open and close hands in front of you like stars)
How I wonder what you are
Up above the world so high (raise hands above your head)
Like a diamond in the sky
Twinkle, twinkle little star
How I wonder what you are

Check your collection for a CD of lullabies. You can play the CD as people are coming into storytime or as they are leaving to set the tone.

Early Literacy Tip:
Singing together is one of the five basic practices that helps lay groundwork for literacy. Sing new songs and old favorites in storytime and encourage parents to sing at home.

Additional Poetry

Pearson, Susan, selector, and Peter Malone, illus. The Drowsy Hours: Poems for Bedtime. New York: HarperCollins Publishers, 2002.
Pearson has selected poems from greats such as Robert Louis Stevenson and Walter de la Mare. "The Starlighter" by Arthur Guiterman and "Manhattan Lullaby" by Norma Farber are especially good choices for the end of storytime as they signal the beginning of night and sleep.

Sidman, Joyce and Rick Allen, illus. Dark Emperor & Other Poems of the Night. New York: Houghton Mifflin Books for Children, 2010.
The opening poem in this collection, "Welcome to the Night" celebrates those who wake at the end of the day and make the night come alive with sound and movement. A beautiful lyrical way to begin or end a nighttime storytime.

Worth, Valerie, and Steve Jenkins, illus. Animal Poems. New York: Farrar Straus Giroux, 2007.
Read "Bat" or "Owl" to match night animal nonfiction books. Both poems are set on dark colored pages alongside detailed illustrations.

Yolen, Jane and Andrew Fusek Peters, collectors, and G. Brian Karas, illus. Switching on the Moon: A Very First Book of Bedtime Poems. Somerville, MA: Candlewick Press, 2010.
Sixty poems are collected in three sections: Going to Bed, Sweet Dreams, and In the Night. The large trim size and attractive illustrations make this an ideal book to hold up and share while reading a few favorite selections.

Additional Nonfiction

Early Literacy Tip: Expand a child's mind by broadening a bedtime storytime with the related topic of nighttime animals.

Gibbons, Gail. Owls. New York: Holiday House, 2005.
This book is on the longer side for a storytime audience but it is filled with interesting owl facts. Leave the illustration captions for a one-on-one session. Many kids will be fascinated by the depictions of an owl capturing prey; the fact that the illustrations are drawn lightens the "violence" for sensitive children.

Johnson, J. Angelique. Bats. North Mankato: MN: Capstone Press, 2011.
Bats are fascinating animals, especially since many kids are already in bed before they come out for the night. A book with short sentences and large photographs can introduce kids to this elusive animal.

Olson, Gillia M. Phases of the Moon. Mankato, MN: Capstone Press, 2007.
Large photographs and minimal text introduce young people to the changing moon. The book doesn't shy away from terms like crescent, quarter, and gibbous phases yet is simple enough for a storytime crowd.

Ward, Jennifer and Jamichael Henterly, illus. Forest Bright, Forest Night. Nevada City, CA: Dawn Publications, 2005.
Who's awake at night? Rhythmic text and darker hues show owls, porcupines, opossums, and more. Flip the book over for bright colors and daytime animals.

Additional Fiction Picture Books

Edwards, Pamela Duncan. While the World Is Sleeping. New York: Orchard Books, 2010.
A young child takes a ride on an owl to see all the animals that are awake while everyone else is sleeping.

Ismail, Yasmeen. Time for Bed, Fred! New York: Walker Books for Young Readers, 2013.
Fred the dog will do anything to avoid going to bed, until he does so much he wears himself out. The entire text is told as if the narrator is speaking to the dog and kids will recognize the tone of voice.

McFarland, Clive. A Bed for Bear. New York: Harper, 2014.
Poor Bear. He is getting ready to hibernate but wasn't looking forward to sharing a big cave with other noisy bears, so he sets off to find the perfect bed. In true Goldilocks fashion he gives many other choices a try until he finds the one that is just right. Watercolors and paper collage with plenty of white space make page details pop.

Ohora, Zachariah. Stop Snoring Bernard. New York: Henry Holt and Company, 2011.
Bernard loves his life at the zoo. Sadly, not everyone loves Bernard's loud snores. When nap time comes to the otter pond, Bernard's snores keep everyone awake. When he is told to find somewhere else to sleep, Bernard seeks out another bed. His snores and the complaints follow until he finally finds his way back home.

Willems, Mo. Don't Let the Pigeon Stay Up Late. New York: Hyperion, 2006.
As usual, Pigeon is being difficult and creative in coming up with excuses for not going to bed. Have children help you convince Pigeon that everyone needs to sleep.

Yolen, Jane and Mark Teague, illus. How Do Dinosaurs Say Good Night? New York: The Blue Sky Press, 2000.
When it is time for bed you would think that a dinosaur would act up. Not these dinosaurs. They peacefully climb into bed and give mom and dad a hug and kiss. This bedtime story is filled with humor. Look closely on each page to find the name of each illustrated dinosaur.

Birds

Whether up in the air, in the tree, or swimming in a pond, our feathered friends are all around. There's no reason for them to not be in storytime, too! Their wide array of colors and sounds make them perfect for an interactive storytime.

Sample Storytime

Welcome Song

Routine is important when working with children. Be sure to include welcome, transitional, and closing songs or activities to signify what is coming next. Don't be afraid to use the same ones; children take comfort in knowing what is coming next.

Opening Poem

"Chickadee-dee" from Yolen, Jane and Jason Stemple, photography. Birds of a Feather. Honesdale, PA: Wordsong, 2011.
"With your black cap on" is repeated three times in the eight-line "Chickadee-dee" (p. 9). Act out the poem by pretending to put on a hat and encouraging storytime attendees to do the same. You can also put on and take off a real black hat each time that line is read.

Action Rhyme

Two Little Blackbirds
English Nursery Rhyme

Two little blackbirds (hold out both hands with fingers folded, thumbs up)
Sitting on a wall
One named Peter (indicate left thumb)
The other named Paul (indicate right thumb)
Fly away Peter (put left hand behind back)
Fly away Paul (put right hand behind back)
Come back Peter (return left hand to front)
Come back Paul (return right hand to front)

Other verses:
One named Short, the other named Tall
One named Big, the other named Small
One named Soft, the other named Loud (When using this verse, the birds can be sitting on a "cloud" so everything still rhymes.)

Nonfiction for Storytime

Stockdale, Susan. Bring On the Birds. Atlanta, GA: Peachtree Publishers, 2011.
Rhythmic text introduces young readers to both exotic and familiar birds. The illustrations are large enough for a storytime crowd. Each bird is identified in the back along with a couple additional facts.

Transitional Song

See Welcome Song earlier.

Flannel Board Activity

Five Little Birdies

Materials:

- Clip art of five different birds in the following colors: blue, yellow, red, brown, and green or use the pattern at the end of this chapter
- Glue and felt (or velcro) to be attached to all of the clip art pieces so they will "stick" to the flannel board

Early Literacy Tip:
Including adjectives, and in this case basic concepts such as color, expands vocabulary and memory.

Directions:

- Place the birds on the flannel board.
- Count the birds with the children.
- Point to each bird individually and ask the children to call out their color.
- Recite the following, removing birds as indicated:

Five Little Birds
By M. Follis

Five little birdies, flying by our door
The blue one flew away and then there were (have children shout number)
FOUR (count the remaining birds)
Four little birdies flying over the tree
The yellow one flew away and then there were (have children shout number)
THREE (count the remaining birds)
Three little birdies didn't know what to do
The red one flew away (make him say "I'm bored") and then there were (have children shout number)
TWO (count the remaining birds)
Two little birdies sitting in the sun
The brown one flew away and then there was (have children shout number)
ONE
The little green birdie felt so all alone
With no one left to play with he decided to go (see if kids can guess the rhyming word)
HOME.
And no how many birdies are left, now that we are done (see if kids can guess the word)
NONE.

While we are suggesting a flannel board activity, feel free to use a digital device if available. You can create a PowerPoint presentation with five birds (in the appropriate colors) on the first slide. On the next slide, there will be four birds as the blue one has flown away. Continue creating slides for each of the verses of the rhyme.

Picture Books for Storytime

Horacek, Petr. Puffin Peter. Somerville, MA: Candlewick Press, 2011.
Peter gets swept out to sea and needs the help of a whale to find his friend Paul. Along the way they meet parrots, penguins, and toucans.

Yuly, Toni. Early Bird. New York: Feiwel and Friends, 2014.
The early bird goes across, through, under, up, around, and over until she reaches her friend the early worm and they share breakfast. The bright illustrations will show well across a storytime crowd.

Closing Song

See Welcome Song earlier.

Follow-Up Activities

Colorful Birds

Materials:

- White paper plates
- Nontoxic poster paint and applicators
- Feathers
- Assorted color construction paper, cut in strips to use as tail feathers
- Orange or yellow construction paper cut in diamond pattern to use as beak
- Googley eyes (Warning: choking hazard. Use with adult supervision.)
- Glue or glue sticks

Directions:

- Fold the white paper plate in half, creating a heavy seam.
- Paint the exposed side of the plate.
- When dry, glue on feathers as desired.
- Fold orange diamond shape construction paper and glue on plate as beak.
- Glue googley eyes on above beak.
- Glue strips of colorful construction paper to the inside of the plate, sticking out to serve as tail feathers.

An example of the completed project can be found at the end of the chapter.

Bird Songs

Franco, Betsy and Steve Jenkins, illus. Bird Songs. New York: Margaret K. McElderry Books, 2007.
This book introduces children to the variety of sounds made by birds. Use the Cornell Lab of Ornithology website (http://www.allaboutbirds.org/guide/search) to search for the birds in the book and hear a recording of their song.

Other Songs, Rhymes, and Fingerplays

What Does the Bird Say?
Adapted by M. Follis
(Tune: Wheels on the Bus)
This song can also be converted to a singing flannel board activity.
You can create birds for each verse to display as you sing.

The birds in the tree say tweet, tweet, tweet,
Tweet, tweet, tweet; tweet, tweet, tweet
The birds in the tree say tweet, tweet, tweet
All day long

The chicks at the farm say peep, peep, peep
Peep, peep, peep; peep, peep, peep
The chicks at the farms say peep, peep, peep
All day long

The crows in the field say caw, caw, caw
Caw, caw, caw; caw, caw, caw
The crows in the field say caw, caw, caw
All day long

The seagulls at the beach say mine, mine, mine
Mine, mine, mine; mine, mine, mine
The seagulls at the beach say mine, mine, mine
All day long

(sing this verse softly)
The owls in the night say who, who, who
Who, who, who; who, who, who
The owls in the night say who, who, who
All night long

Have You Ever seen. . . .
Adapted by M. Follis
(Tune: Have you ever seen a lassie?)

Have you ever seen a blue bird, a blue bird, a blue bird
Have you ever seen a blue bird, fly across the sky
His wings flap this way and that way and this way and that way (imitate flapping motion with arms)
Have you ever seen a blue bird, fly across the sky?

Have you ever seen a chicken, a chicken, a chicken
Have you ever seen a chicken, peck at its corn?
It pecks this way and that way and this way and that way (imitate pecking motion)
Have you ever seen a chicken peck at its corn

Have you ever seen a pelican, a pelican, a pelican
Have you ever seen a pelican, fishing for food
Its mouth opens this way and that way, and this way and that way (open mouth wide and scoop)
Have you ever seen a pelican fishing for food?

Have you ever seen a flamingo, flamingo, flamingo
Have you ever seen a flamingo, standing on one leg?
It stands this way and that way and this way and that way (stand on one leg then switch)
Have you ever seen a flamingo standing on one leg.

Additional Poetry

Ruddell, Deborah and Joan Rankin, illus. Today at the Blue-Bird Café: A Branchful of Birds. New York: Margaret K. McElderry Books, 2007.
Explore the personalities of 22 different birds through poetry. Consider the ultimate redness of "The Cardinal." See the majesty that is "The Eagle." And laugh at meal of "The Woodpecker."

Worth, Valerie and Steve Jenkins, illus. Animal Poems. New York: Farrar Straus Giroux, 2007.
The poem titled "Owl" is short and easy for young children to understand. The illustration on the facing page is intriguing enough to hold up for children to see while the poem is being read.

Yolen, Jane and Jason Stemple, photography. Birds of a Feather. Honesdale, PA: Wordsong, 2011.
Fourteen double-page spreads feature photographs of each bird, a corresponding poem, and a short paragraph with factual information about the bird.

Yolen, Jane and Jason Stemple, photography. Fine Feathered Friends: Poems for Young People. Honesdale, PA: Wordsong, 2004.
Just like *Birds of a Feather* (the previous book) this book features dazzling photographs, poetry, and information about 14 different birds. In the author's note, Yolen encourages young readers to write their own poetry. While this task will be too difficult for preschoolers, you can show them the photographs and ask them for adjectives to describe the birds.

Early Literacy Tip:
Encourage story-building skills by asking open-ended questions about the illustrations/photographs in books. Examples for Jane Yolen's poetry books include: What is this bird thinking? Where is this bird?

Additional Nonfiction

Hurley, Jorey. Nest. New York: Simon & Schuster Books for Young Readers, 2014.
This simple book follows the life cycle of a robin using only one word per page.

Sayre, April Pulley and Steve Jenkins, illus. Vulture View. New York: Henry Holt and Company, 2007.
Share in the day of a vulture through simple text and the engaging illustrations of Steve Jenkins. Kids who like gross things will especially like the page where the vultures eat the stinky dead deer.

Stewart, Melissa and Sarah S. Brannen, illus. Feathers: Not Just for Flying. Watertown, MA: Charlesbridge, 2014.

Designed like a field notebook, each page of this book gives another quality of a bird's feathers. Read just the large text in a storytime setting. There is a sentence or two of further explanation on each page for those who want more.

Ward, Jennifer and Steven Jenkins, illus. Mama Built a Little Nest. New York: Beach Lane Books, 2014.

Each page features a four-line rhyming verse about a different type of bird nest. Large illustrations present each bird and the nest. Read just the rhyming verse in storytime and leave the additional information for parents to share with a child one-on-one.

Additional Fiction Picture Books

DePalma, Mary Newell. Two Little Birds. Grand Rapids, MI: Eerdmans Books for Young Readers, 2014.

A soft color palette conveys the first migration of a young pair of birds. Onomatopoeic words and repetition will make this a storytime favorite.

Esbaum, Jill and Jen Corace, illus. I Hatched! New York: Dial Books for Young Readers. 2014.

This whirlwind adventure is told from the point of view of a newly hatched killdeer that can't wait to explore everything in his new world. When he finally gets back to the nest, he is ready to share all he knows with another new hatchling.

Horacek, Petr. Silly Suzy Goose. Cambridge, MA: Candlewick Press, 2006.

Suzy Goose wants to squawk like a toucan, stretch like a giraffe, and jump like a kangaroo until she needs the help of her goose friends to protect her from a lion. Add movement to the story by pretending to act like the different animals Suzy admires.

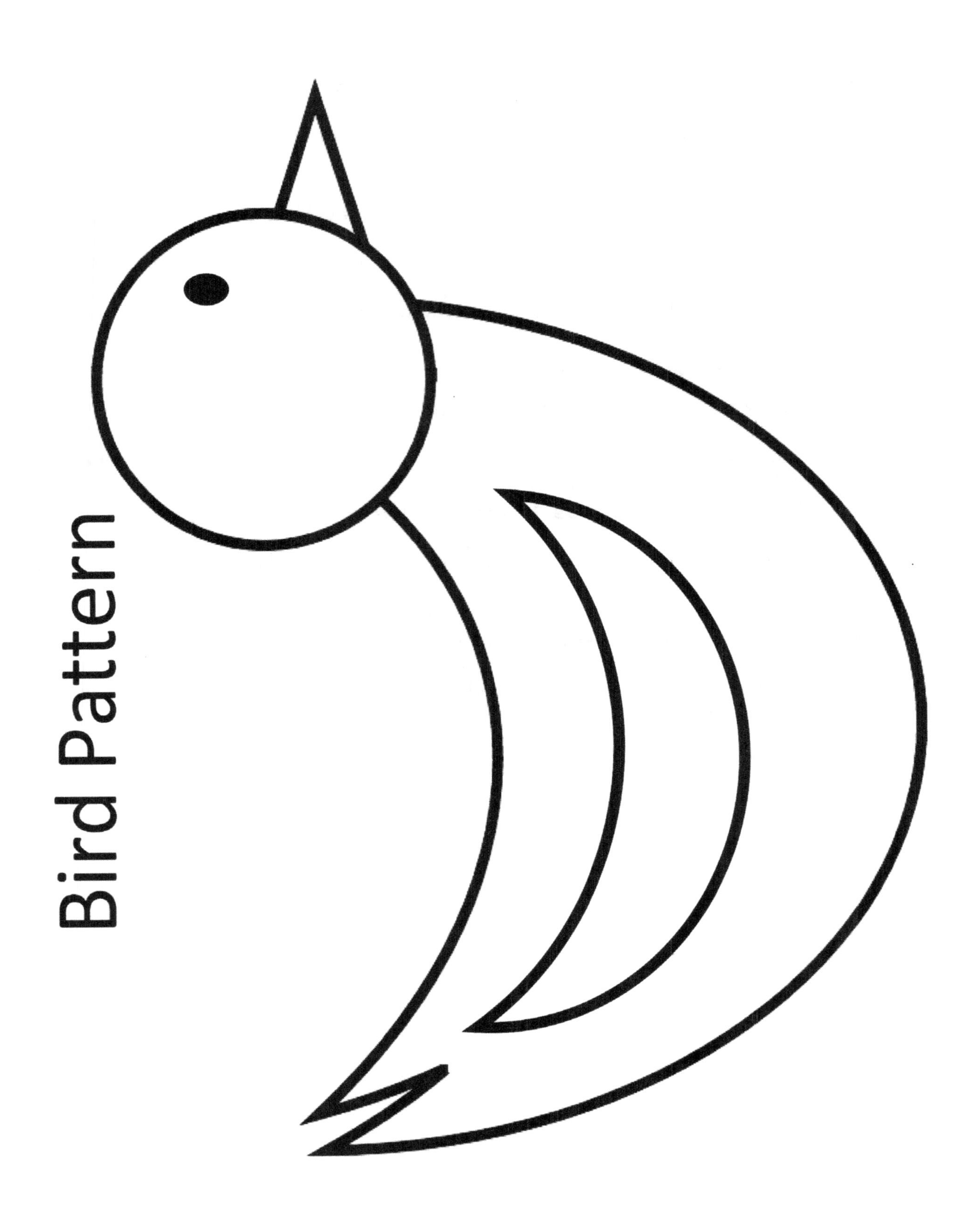
Bird Pattern

Pattern for Colorful Birds

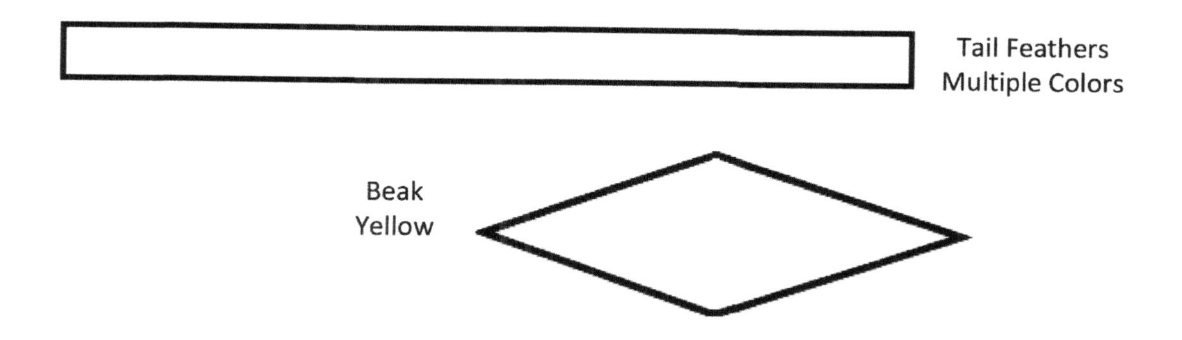

Completed Colorful Birds

Boats

Oh the places you can go on a boat and the things you can see! Whether at sea, on a river or lake, and even in the tub, float this storytime past your young readers and then follow up with a floating experiment.

Sample Storytime

Welcome Song

Routine is important when working with children. Be sure to include welcome, transitional, and closing songs or activities to signify what is coming next. Don't be afraid to use the same ones; children take comfort in knowing what is coming next.

Opening Poem

"The Beginning of Boat" from Sturges, Philemon and Giles Laroche, illus. Down to the Sea in Ships. New York: G.P. Putnam's Sons, 2005.

This poem is fun because you can act it out while reading it. Fill a bucket with water then put in a rock. Watch as the rock sinks. Then put in a toy boat and watch it float.

Action Rhyme

Row, Row, Row Your Boat
English Nursery Rhyme

(move your arms and torso back and forth as if you are rowing a boat)
Row, row, row your boat
Gently down the stream
Merrily, merrily, merrily, merrily
Life is but a dream

Early Literacy Tip:
Children enjoy repeating familiar rhymes again and again. It helps them build confidence in their knowledge.

Nonfiction for Storytime

Garland, Michael. Tugboat. New York: Holiday House, 2014.

From morning to night, a little tugboat stays busy tugging heavy barges and pushing ocean liners. This nonfiction title looks and reads like a storybook.

Transitional Song

See Welcome Song earlier.

Flannel Board Activity

Docking Fun

Materials:

- Brown felt cut to look like boat docks. (Make the docks different widths and length. An example is at the end of the chapter. Note that the example is not to scale. Create a large dock shape that will fit many size boats.)
- Felt boats of various sizes (They don't need to be elaborate, just a simple boat shape. A simple wooden boat pattern is included at the end of the chapter.)

Directions:

- Try sliding each boat into the different boat slips.
- Ask "Does this boat fit here?" "Is it too long?" "Is it too wide?" "Is it just right?"
- Keep adding boats until everyone has a perfect boat slip.

You may wish to finish the activity with this rhyme.

This Is a Tugboat
By M. Follis

This is a tugboat, pull pull pull
This is a speedboat, zoom zoom zoom
This is a sailboat, catch the wind
This is the marina where they all go in

Picture Books for Storytime

Bunting, Eve and Nancy Carpenter, illus. Big Bear's Big Boat. Boston: Clarion Books, 2013.
After following the suggestions of other animals, Big Bear's perfect new boat becomes ugly so he follows his heart and puts it back to the way he wants it. The text in this book is a little longer making it a smart choice for the first book in storytime.

Hubbell, Patricia, and Megan Halsey and Sean Addy, illus. Boats: Speeding! Sailing! Cruising! Tarrytown, NY: Marshall Cavendish Children, 2009.
While fictional, this rhyming book still introduces children to many types of boats from little dinghies to mighty aircraft carriers. Many of the boats seem to move across the page drawing the reader to the next page.

Closing Song

See Welcome Song earlier.

Follow-Up Activities

Boat Fun

Put a couple inches of water in a clear Tupperware container. (Look for a short one that would fit under a bed.) Add toy boats and let the children play.

Notes: This activity is best done outside. Make sure there is ample adult supervision. Test the toy boats to be sure they float before doing the activity.

Early Literacy Tip:
Tactile experiences help children learn. (Even if they are a little messy.)

Other Songs, Rhymes, and Fingerplays

The Boats Out in the Sea
Adapted by M. Follis
(Tune: The Farmer in the Dell)

The boats out in the sea
The boats out in the sea
Float up and down and all around
The boats out in the sea

Have You Ever Seen?
Adapted by M. Follis
(Tune: Have You Ever Seen a Lassie)

Have you ever seen a sailboat a sailboat a sailboat
Have you ever seen a sailboat, gliding along?
It glides this way and that way and this way and that way,
Have you ever seen a sailboat gliding along?

Additional verses:
Row boat, rowing along
Motor boat, speeding along
Tug boat, chugging along
Fishing boat, trawling along

Here Is the Sea
Traditional Rhyme

Here is the sea, the wavy sea.
Here is a boat, and here is me.
And all the fishes down below,
Wriggle their tails and away they go.

A Sailor Went to Sea
Traditional Rhyme
(Make this rhyme interactive by clapping or jumping every time you say "sea" or "see.")

A sailor went to
Sea, sea, sea,
To see what he could
See, see, see.
But all that he could
See, see, see,
Was the bottom of the deep blue
Sea, sea, sea.

Additional Poetry

Collins, Billy and Karen Romagna, illus. Voyage. Piermont, NH: Bunker Hill Publishing, Inc., 2014.
An illustrated poem of a boy, his boat, and the places his imagination brings him. While out to sea his boat becomes a book and readers are drawn into the pages as they ride the waves and fight a pirate. Read the book as a story or focus on the words as the text is featured in poetic form on the last page.

Coombs, Kate and Meilo So, illus. Water Sings Blue: Ocean Poems. San Francisco: Chronicle Books, 2012.
Push off from the docks and "fly" away from land in "Song of the Boat." A hint of the city sits in the corner of the illustration but the boat is all alone on the blue sea.

Sturges, Philemon and Giles Laroche, illus. Down to the Sea in Ships. New York: G.P. Putnam's Sons, 2005.
"The Beginning of Boat" (see Opening Poem above) and "Tugboat" are especially appropriate for the early literacy crowd. "Tugboat" has many onomatopoeic words making it a fun read.

Vardell, Sylvia and Janet Wong, ed. The Poetry Friday Anthology for Celebrations. Princeton, NJ: Pomelo Books, 2015.
Celebrate "what sails and floats" with Sara Holbrook's poem "Boats" (p. 195). The rolling rhythm of the poem will make you think of the gentle waves of the water.

Additional Nonfiction

Floca, Brian. Lightship. New York: Atheneum Books for Young Readers, 2007.
Lightships once stood where lighthouses could not be built. They aided in the safe passage of other vessels. Floca has illustrated the layout and the work of one such ship. Detailed-oriented readers will delight in searching for the cat that is included on many of the pages. This title is suitable for a storytime crowd that is ready for a longer read.

Additional Fiction Picture Books

Biggs, Brian. Everything Goes by Sea. New York: Balzer+Bray, 2013.
This oversized picture book is jammed full of information and detailed illustrations of water travel of all sorts, including the parts of a variety of boats. Share this by highlighting a few key points in each page to peak interest. Ideal for one-on-one sharing.

Dunbar, Polly. Arthur's Dream Boat. Somerville, MA: Candlewick Press, 2012.
Arthur dreams about an amazing boat but no one in his family wants to hear about it until his imagination takes him away. This book is filled with onomatopoeic words that will be fun to sound out in storytime.

Lund, Deb and Howard Fine, illus. Dinosailors. Orlando: Harcourt, Inc., 2003.
The dinosaurs crave adventure and set off on a boat. This seaworthy romp includes nautical terms to boost vocabulary. Prepare for lots of laughter and ewws when the dinos lose their lunch after a squall.

Steggall, Susan. Busy Boats. London: Frances Lincoln Children's Books, 2010.
Come to the busy harbor in the morning to see all the boats as they set out for their day. The illustrations bring a lot of life to the spare text.

Waddell, Martin and Susan Varley, illus. Captain Small Pig. Atlanta, GA: Peachtree, 2009.
A unique trio of an Old Goat, Turkey, and Small Pig go out for a boat ride. Small Pig may be too little but he still wants to do everything himself. This is a gentle and reassuring tale of family.

Dock and Boat Patterns

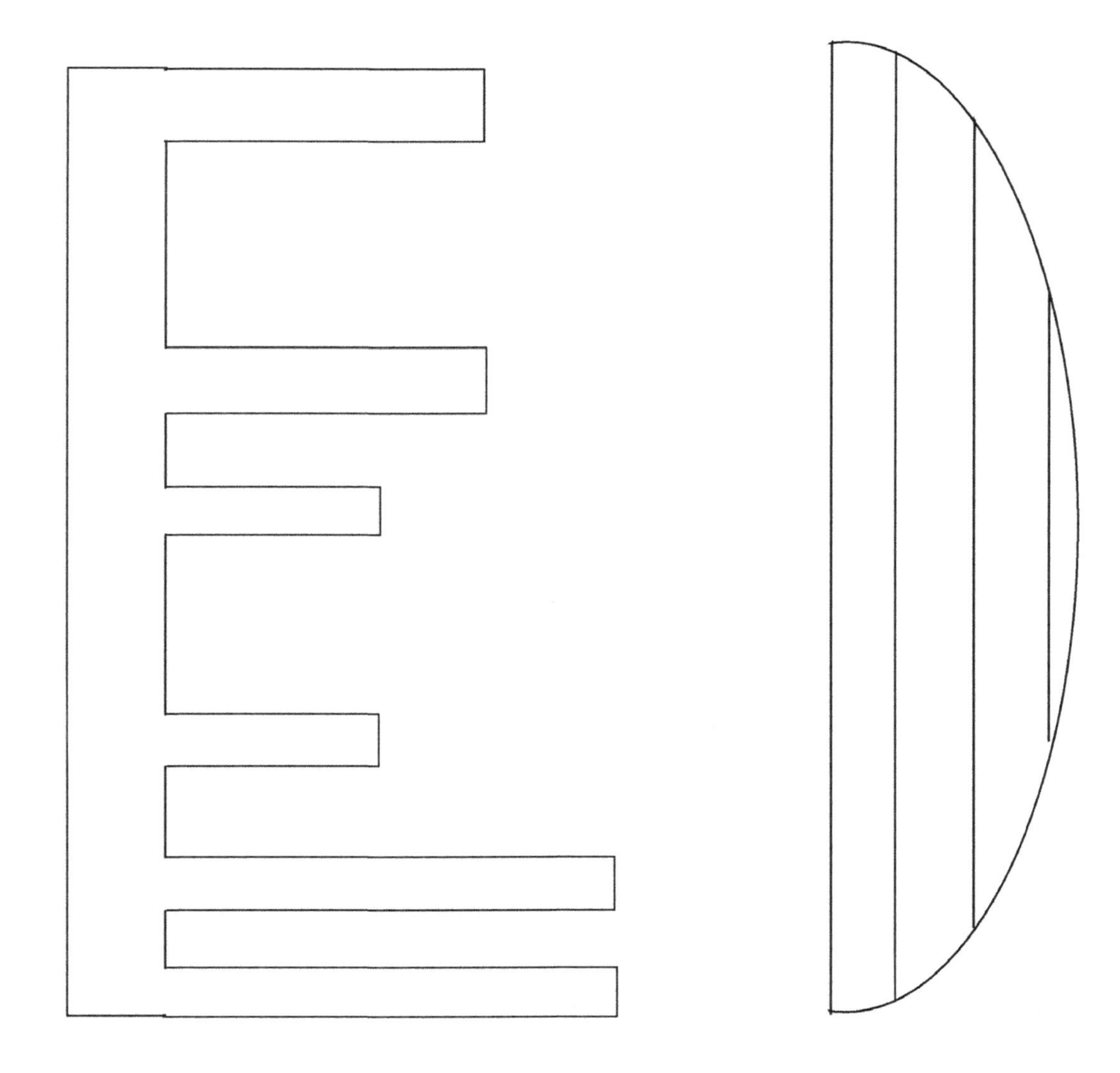

Butterflies and Caterpillars

It's hard to imagine that a small, green creeping caterpillar can turn into a light bright butterfly, but this is the perfect subject for so many discussions and a process children can observe. If you are hesitant to involve actual live insects, be sure to have large colorful photos for up close observation.

Sample Storytime

Welcome Song

Routine is important when working with children. Be sure to include welcome, transitional, and closing songs or activities to signify what is coming next. Don't be afraid to use the same ones; children take comfort in knowing what is coming next.

Opening Poem

"Always Hungry" from Gerber, Carole and Eugene Yelchin, illus. Seeds, Bees, Butterflies, and More! Poems for Two Voices. New York: Henry Holt and Company, 2013.
Best told in two voices yet suitable for only one, "Always Hungry" tells the tale of a Monarch caterpillar that wants milkweed. The poem is short, and the illustrations are lovely; hold the book up for all to see while reading this poem.

Action Rhyme

Yoo, Taeeun. You Are a Lion and Other Yoga Poses. New York: Nancy Paulsen Books, 2012.
Turn to the second yoga pose, found on pages 7–10. Recite the lines, follow the directions, and flex your wings! Children will enjoy seeing the animal in the yoga poses, and may enjoy getting to do something a bit more athletic in storytime.

Early Literacy Tip:
Print motivation is encouraged and engaged when little ones (adults, too) interact with books. While reading aloud is one way to do this, acting out scenes, or yoga poses, also helps build the bond between words and actions. The end result is the same: building the love of books.

Nonfiction for Storytime

Aston, Dianna and Sylvia Long, illus. A Butterfly Is Patient. San Francisco: Chronicle Books, 2011.
The traits and lives of a variety of butterflies is illustrated in this elegant book. Read just the large script text in a storytime then make the book available for families that want to read more.

Transitional Song

See Welcome Song earlier.

Flannel Board Activity

Match the Butterflies

Using the pattern at the end of the chapter, create multiple pairs of matching butterflies. If you have an Ellison butterfly shape, you can easily create two felt butterflies each in matching colors.

Put the butterflies on the flannel board in random order.

Hold up one butterfly and ask a child to come up and find the matching butterfly.

Set those two butterflies aside and continue until all butterflies have been matched.

Early Literacy Tip:
Playing matching games (alike and different) helps to build letter recognition skills.

Picture Books for Storytime

Foley, Greg. Don't Worry Bear. New York: Viking, 2008.
Caterpillar makes a cocoon and bear comes to check on him at night, in the wind, in the rain, and in the snow. At last, caterpillar turns into a silk moth. Uncluttered illustrations and clear text will make this a storytime favorite.

Martin, Jr. Bill and Lois Ehlert, illus. Ten Little Caterpillars. New York: Beach Lane Books, 2011.
Ten caterpillars venture out into the world. Some climb flowers. One becomes part of a show and tell activity. Finally, the 10th caterpillar becomes a butterfly. Each of the 10 unique caterpillars is identified in the back along with an illustration of their butterfly/moth. With simple text and a white background, this is classic Martin and Ehlert.

Closing Song

See Welcome Song earlier.

Follow-Up Activities

Metamorphosis

The metamorphosis from caterpillar to butterfly can be a difficult idea to grasp for small children. Depending on your setting, you may want to acquire caterpillars and watch the change unfold over the course of weeks. Again, this is very time intensive but fun.

Another suggestion would be to re-create the one of the more popular stories, *The Very Hungry Caterpillar* (Eric Carle) using this fun puppet from Folkmanis: http://www.folkmanis.com/prod-67-1-283-1/caterpillar-butterfly.htm.

Further re-create the story by displaying foods on the flannel board, to demonstrate all that our hungry friend has eaten.

Early Literacy Tip:
Retelling stories with puppets builds narrative skills.

Other Songs, Rhymes, and Fingerplays

The Caterpillars Go Marching
Adapted by J. Dietzel-Glair
(Tune: The Ants Go Marching)

The caterpillars go marching up the milkweed, the milkweed
The caterpillars go marching up the milkweed, the milkweed
The little one stops to spin a cocoon
He says "I'll see you guys real soon"
And he slowly turns into a Monarch Butterfly
But-ter-fly

The Itsy Bitsy Caterpillar
Adapted by M. Follis and J. Dietzel-Glair
(Tune: Itsy Bitsy Spider)

The itsy bitsy caterpillar
Climbed up the leafy plant
He created a cocoon
And took a long nap
Many days went by
And he metamorphosized
And turned into a butterfly
That flew off in the sky

Additional Poetry

Early Literacy Tip:
Don't shy away from using advanced vocabulary words in your made-up rhymes. Kids will start to understand them through context.

Gerber, Carole and Eugene Yelchin, illus. Seeds, Bees, Butterflies and More!: Poems for Two Voices. New York: Henry Holt and Company, 2013.
In addition to this chapter's opening poem "Always Hungry" there are two other poems that discuss the life cycle of the butterfly including "Now We're Sleepy" covering the chrysalis stage and "New Baby" telling of the birth of a butterfly. There are many other poems in the collection that cover insects, pollination, butterflies, and other garden residents.

Katz, Bobbi, sel., and Deborah Zemke, illus. More Pocket Poems. New York: Dutton Children's Books, 2009.
"Butterfly" by Benjamin Franklin (p. 14). What is a butterfly? Read and find out in this short two-line poem. "Caterpillars" by Aileen Fisher (p. 15) asks the important questions like what caterpillars do and know and responds with how they chew and grow. A fun way to learn more about what caterpillars do and know and you do not!

Lewis, J. Patrick, ed. National Geographic Book of Animal Poetry: 200 Poems with Photographs That Squeak, Soar, and Roar! Washington, DC: National Geographic, 2012.
A photograph of a monarch caterpillar curves around "The Tickle Rhyme" by Ian Serraillier and "What's a Caterpillar?" by Graham Denton; each poem (p. 10) is a super short ode to these wriggly creatures. More easy-to-understand poems on caterpillars and butterflies, with a photograph of a tiger swallowtail butterfly, can be found on pages 46–47.

Sidman, Joyce and Beth Krommes, illus. Butterfly Eyes and Other Secrets of the Meadow. Boston: Houghton Mifflin Company, 2006.
What do butterflies see when they are looking at flowers? They see all the colors of the world and the secret ultraviolet ones that are hidden to humans. Beauty and science intermingle in Sidman's "Ultraviolet" poem. Flip the page for more on the science to share after reading the poem aloud.

Additional Nonfiction

Barner, Bob. Dinosaurs Roar, Butterflies Soar! San Francisco: Chronicle Books, 2009.
Barner's classic colorful style educates us all on how delicate butterflies outlasted the dinosaurs. Read just the main text or include the extra facts (in smaller font) while reading this book to a crowd. It is sure to appeal to butterfly and dinosaur lovers alike.

Bishop, Nic. Nic Bishop Butterflies and Moths. New York: Scholastic, 2009.
Detailed, vivid, and up close photos bring these fleeting, flitting creature right to your fingertips. The book is designed so that you can flit from page to page and read the bold text as a small factoids, which are the perfect bite-sized bits for storytime. If these don't get your little listeners involved, be sure to show them the photo of a caterpillar fighting off its attacker with its stinky osmeterium (even though it looks like he is sticking his tongue out at them!).

Bredeson, Carmen and Lindsey Cousins. Can You Find These Butterflies? Berkeley Heights, NJ: Enslow Publishers, Inc., 2012.
This is a guided reading book so the text is quite simple; however, it gives nice basic information about nine different butterflies from a Monarch to a Gray Hairstreak. Children who want to know about specific butterflies will enjoy seeing this book.

Ehlert, Lois. Waiting for Wings. San Diego: Harcourt, Inc., 2001.
Uniquely cut pages and jewel-tone illustrations add to the beauty of this information book. The sparse rhyming text lends itself to being read aloud in storytime. An illustrated identification guide is provided in the back for curious readers who wish to name the butterflies, caterpillars, chrysalises, and flowers featured in the book.

Frost, Helen and Leonid Gore, illus. Monarch and Milkweed. New York: Atheneum Books for Young Readers, 2008.
The life cycles of a monarch butterfly and the milkweed plant are juxtaposed through spare, poetic text. Share this lovely book with a smaller storytime group.

Additional Fiction Picture Books

Jarrett, Clare. Arabella Miller's Tiny Caterpillar. Cambridge, MA: Candlewick Press, 2008.
Arabella Miller finds a caterpillar which she cares for until it turns into a butterfly. Rhyming text and the large trim size of the book make this good for storytime.

Kleven, Elisa. Glasswings: A Butterfly's Story. New York: Dial Books for Young Readers, 2013.
Claire's clear wings allow her to look like whatever is around her. When she gets swept away to a city she needs the help of new friends to find the flowers that she loves.

Butterfly Pattern

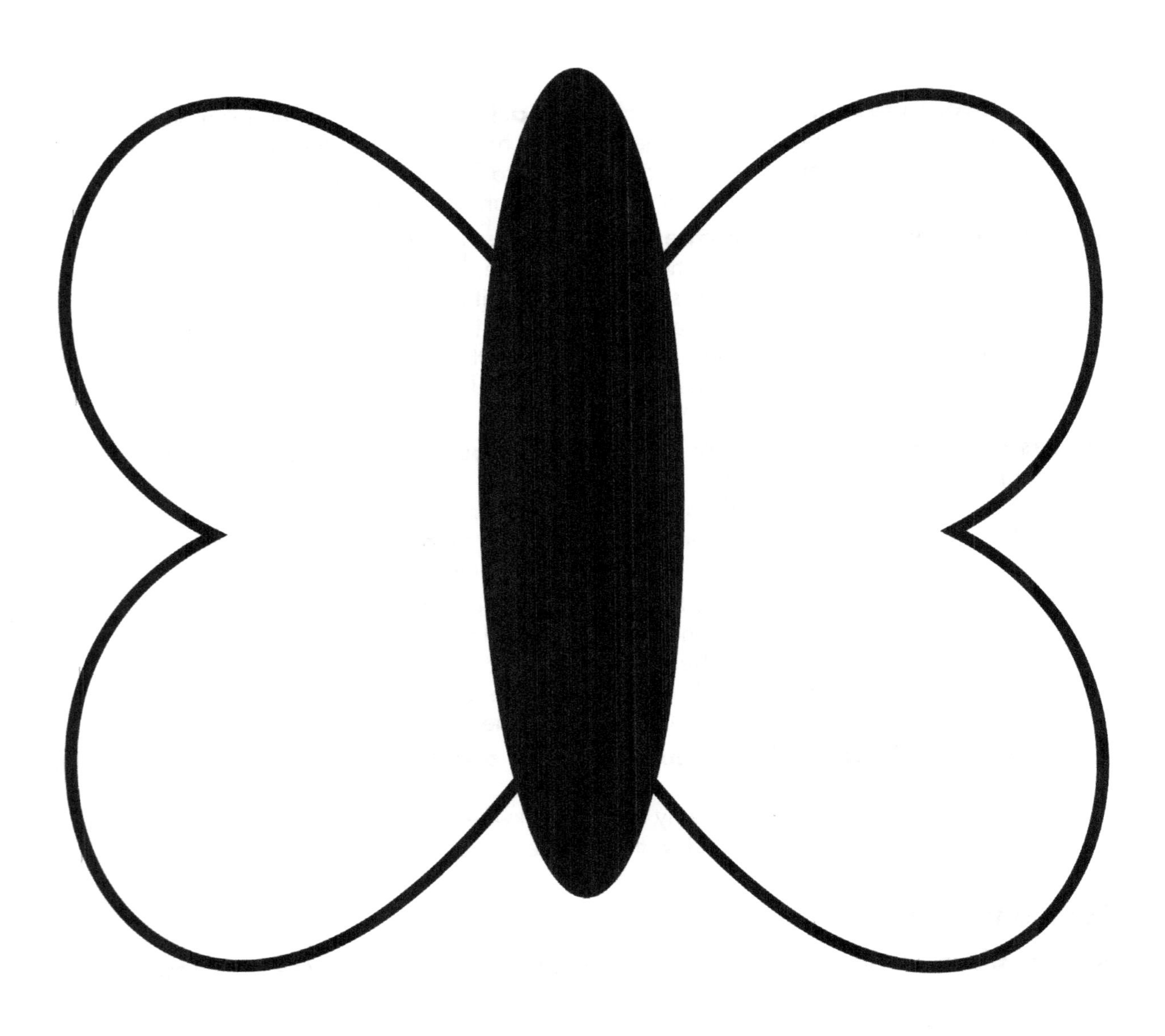

Cars and Trucks

Coming in all shapes, sizes, and colors, cars are a prominent figure in the lives of most children. Look! A yellow one! Can you find one that's blue? We are sure this storytime on cars and trucks will keep them coming and the storytime energy going.

Sample Storytime

Welcome Song

Routine is important when working with children. Be sure to include welcome, transitional, and closing songs or activities to signify what is coming next. Don't be afraid to use the same ones; children take comfort in knowing what is coming next.

Opening Poem

"Ice Cream Truck" by Lillegard, Dee and Valeri Gorbachev, illus. Go! Poetry in Motion. New York: Alfred Knopf. 2006.
A short three lines say all that you need to know about the ice cream truck and its "welcome tune."

Action Rhyme

Wheels on the Bus
American Folksong

The wheels on the bus go round and round
Round and round
Round and round
The wheels on the bus go round and round
All through the town

Additional verses:
Horn goes beep, beep, beep (pretend to press a horn while saying beep)
Wipers goes swish, swish, swish (sway arms in a parallel fashion, mimicking windshield wipers)
Doors go open and shut (extend arms and then bring hands together)
People go up and down (stand up straight then stoop)
Babies go wah, wah, wah (put fists to eyes and rub while saying wah)
Mommies go shhh, shhhh, shhhh. (put fingers to mouth and shush)

Nonfiction for Storytime

Coppendale, Jean and Ian Graham. The Great Big Book of Mighty Machines. Buffalo, NY: Firefly Books, 2009.
Nine double-page spreads of this book focus on cars from convertibles to off-road vehicles. Read the large text on each page to appeal to the car aficionados in your storytime. The

large photographs and trim size and makes this book especially good for storytime. Note: This book also has a chapter on motorcycles/bicycles, trains, tractors, fire trucks, dump trucks, and monster trucks.

Transitional Song

See Welcome Song earlier.

Flannel Board Activity

Vehicle Patterns

Steggall, Susan. Red Car, Red Bus. London: Frances Lincoln Children's Books, 2012.
This cumulative story adds vehicles onto the page in a pattern according to color and vehicle type, for example: blue van, blue truck, orange truck, orange van, yellow van, yellow car, red car, red bus.

Read the story in advance and if you choose to follow along with the book, create flannels to match the set pattern. You can use the patterns found at the end of this chapter.

Even if you don't use the book during the flannel board, find clip art that can be used in the same manner. Sort them by color, sort them by vehicle type, or have children create a logical pattern of their own.

Early Literacy Tip:
Playing matching games and recognizing patterns helps to build letter recognition skills even when not using letters!

Picture Books for Storytime

Bee, William. And the Cars Go . . . Somerville, MA: Candlewick, 2013.
A policeman on patrol encounters a long line of traffic. Wanting to clear the road he makes his way up the street passing onomatopoetic vehicles along the way from a station wagon that goes "brrrmm brrrmm brrrmm" to a Rolls Royce with an understated "whisper whisper whisper." These fun sounds make for an interactive storytime, especially when the reason for the traffic is revealed! (baaaaa!) The illustrations are colorful and fun and contain loads of details for individual sharing, while still big and clear enough for a large group. Look out for the pesky seagulls who make themselves at home among the vehicles. For added fun there are 15 snails hidden in the pages. Can you find them all?

Savage, Stephen. Supertruck. New York: Roaring Brook Press, 2015.
While all of the trucks in the city have jobs, there is one truck that is called upon during special times of need. When the city is covered in snow and all of the other trucks are stuck, the lowly, mild mannered garbage truck ducks into his garage lair and returns as SUPERTRUCK!, able to move snow and return things to normal. High-contrast illustrations with strong geometric elements make this visually appealing and easy to share with a large group who will happily cheer for this unlikely hero.

Early Literacy Tip:
Taking the time to study an image (e.g., looking for the hidden snails in *And the Cars Go . . .*) helps children learn to look for small details, which aids in building narrative skills.

Closing Song

See Welcome Song earlier.

Follow-Up Activities

Car and Truck Play

Materials:

- Toy cars and trucks
- Masking tape
- Mini traffic cones (optional)

Directions:

- Use the masking tape to create roads on your floor.
- Add optional traffic cone obstacles (slalom areas).
- Open up the course for open driving time.

Draw Cars and Trucks

Court, Rob. How to Draw Cars and Trucks. Clanhassen, MN: The Child's World, 2007. Using four simple steps each, learn how to draw a sports car, small car, tow truck, limousine, dump truck, cement truck, police car, fire truck, delivery truck, race car, ambulance, school bus, monster truck, and drag racer. Put crayons and paper out for families to try drawing the cars and trucks together.

Other Songs, Rhymes, and Fingerplays

I'm a Little Race Car
Adapted by J. Dietzel-Glair
(Tune: I'm a Little Teapot)

I'm a little race car
I have four wheels
When I go fast
It makes people squeal
When I rev my engine
At the start of the race
I vroom vroom vroom
At a supersonic pace.

Safety First
By M. Follis
(Tune: Twinkle, Twinkle, Little Star)

When I'm driving near or far
Always buckle up in the car
Car seats for little ones who ride
In the backseat, side by side
When I'm driving near or far
Safety first inside the car

"Obsessed by Trucks" by Justin Roberts. From Jungle Gym (2010).
Kids (especially little boys) get so excited when they see big trucks. This rocking song mentions dump trucks, fire trucks, and more. You can also find a fun YouTube video with a young girl lip-syncing the song here: https://www.youtube.com/watch?v=jTpHAbuEQac.

Additional Poetry

Lewis, J. Patrick, Douglas Florian and Jeremy Holmes, illus. Poem-Mobiles. New York: Schwartz & Wade Books, 2014.
A collection of funny, zany, and reimagined automobiles live on the pages of this book. One example is the "Mini-Mini-Car" using a whole, heaping, bunch of synonyms for language expansion. Also check out 23rd-Century Motors and its prediction about the cars of tomorrow! Bold yet detailed illustrations work for both storytime sharing and up close exploration.

Lillegard, Dee and Valeri Gorbachev, illus. Go! Poetry in Motion. New York: Alfred Knopf. 2006.
This collection of poetry that moves includes all sorts of vehicles such as ice cream trucks, mail trucks, school buses, garbage trucks and pickup trucks. Climb on up and let them take you for a ride!

Nesbitt, Kenn and Ethan Long, illus. My Hippo Has the Hiccups: And Other Poems I Totally Made Up. Naperville, IL: Sourcebooks Jabberwocky, 2009.
"My Car Is Constructed of Pickles" (p. 142) is an automobile that feeds the hungry but doesn't get them very far, at least once they've eaten the wheels. Laugh at the absurdity of this crazy car then listen to the author read it aloud on the included CD.

Additional Nonfiction

Rex, Michael. My Race Car. New York: Henry Holt and Company, 2000.
Learn about race cars and pit crews as one driver tries to win the race. The facts are blended into the illustrated story making it a storytime read-aloud.

Tuchman, Gail. Race Day. Washington, DC: National Geographic, 2010.
Preschoolers who are beginning to read will enjoy this action-packed "Pre-Reader" level book about car racing.

Additional Fiction Picture Books

Bell, Babs and Rob Hefferan, illus. The Bridge Is Up. New York: HarperCollins, 2004.
When the bridge is up, everyone has to wait. And during the course of this cumulative story, traffic builds to include a nice assortment of vehicles. Invite children to join with you in the refrain "Now everyone has to wait!"

Knudsen, Michelle and Scott Magoon, illus. Big Mean Mike. Somerville, MA: Candlewick, 2012.
Big Mean Mike is a big mean guy. He wears combat boots and drives a big mean car that roars through the streets. Then one day Big Mean Mike is surprised to find a small, white, fluffy bunny hiding in his car. Worried about what people might think, Mike shoos the bunny away only to find two bunnies the next day, and three the next, until Mike finds he has to make a decision about his big mean image and confess that maybe he isn't so mean after all. Big bold illustrations fill many double-page spreads, with an occasional oases of white fluff. The big mean dialog makes this a fun read-aloud.

Lewis, Kevin and Daniel Kirk, illus. My Truck Is Stuck. New York: Hyperion Books for Children, 2002.

When a dump truck carrying a great big load gets stuck, its two drivers ask for help from passing by vehicles. Even with the help of several kindly drivers, the poor truck remains stuck. Heavy on rhyme, refrain, counting, and a hidden story featuring some mischievous prairie dogs this is a sure to be a hit at storytime.

Pearson, Debora. Alphabeep: A Zipping, Zooming ABC. New York: Holiday House, 2003.

An A to Z story that features vehicles of all sorts, from Ambulances to Zambonis and everything in between.

Rockwell, Anne. Truck Stop. New York: Viking, 2013.

A young boy details the tasks he and his family do to welcome drivers of all types of trucks to their family truck stop. They ready themselves by squeezing orange juice and brewing coffee and wait for their parking lot to fill with produce trucks, moving vans, and flatbeds carrying construction equipment. For truck lovers, this stop is heavenly!

Rylant, Cynthia and Brian Biggs, illus. Brownie & Pearl Go for a Spin. New York: Beach Lane Books, 2012.

This short and simple story features a little girl and her cat that decide to run some errands in their toy car. When the day is done, Pearl decides she isn't ready to leave the car. Thankfully Brownie is a good problem solver. With sweet, short sentences, this is a perfect little story for your younger audiences.

Scieszka, Jon and Dani Jones, illus. Race from A to Z. New York: Simon & Schuster, 2014.

"A is for Axle, Bumper starts with B. Jack shouts out to Trucktown, 'Let's all race to Z!' " And so the race begins over the next 30 pages and 26 letters. With great vocabulary building words, onomatopoeic sounds and kid friendly illustrations, this is a great choice for car and truck storytimes, as well as those focusing on the alphabet.

Steen, Sandra, Susan Steen, and G. Brian Karas, illus. Car Wash. New York: G.P. Putnam's Sons, 2001.

Did you know that octopuses and a coral reef can be found in a car wash? Take a trip to the deep with two imaginative children. Everyone will love making the fun sounds in this book: "whish," "thomp," and "whirr!"

Vehicle Patterns

Cats

There is something mysterious about cats. Even if a child doesn't have one of his or her own at home, they can be seen on walks through the neighborhood, peering out windows, watching from behind trees. Cats seem to know more than they are letting on, and this is part of their appeal. Children want to be close to this creature, but we all know, unless the cat is willing, that's not going to happen. This cat-themed storytime is the next best thing!

Sample Storytime

Welcome Song

Routine is important when working with children. Be sure to include welcome, transitional, and closing songs or activities to signify what is coming next. Don't be afraid to use the same ones; children take comfort in knowing what is coming next.

Early Literacy Tip:
To encourage print motivation it is a good idea to engage children and adults in acting out parts of a story (or in this case a poem). A bonus is inspiring an enjoyment of poetry that will last through their education years and beyond.

Opening Poem

"Her Tail" from Kuskin, Karla and Lisze Bechtold, illus. Toots the Cat. New York: Henry Holt and Company, 2005.
A cat's tail is silky and billowing. Read this six line poem then give everyone a scarf so they can wave their tail around.

Action Rhyme

Kittens
By M. Follis and J. Dietzel-Glair
(Tune: Farmer in the Dell)

The kittens lap the milk (pretend to lick milk from a bowl)
The kittens lap the milk
Meow, meow, meow, meow, meow, meow
The kittens lap the milk

Additional verses:
Bat the ball (pretend to pass a ball from hand to hand)
Arch their back (arch back)
Flick their tail (wiggle behind)
Clean their face (wipe hand over face)

Nonfiction for Storytime

Piven, Hanoch. What Cats Are Made Of. New York: Atheneum Book, 2009.
Not your typical cat book, *What Cats Are Made Of* uses adjectives, collage art, and a brief description to capture cat characteristics. "Cats are made of Origami" with an origami cat describes the Scottish Fold cat, with the forward-bending ears from a genetic mutation. Did you know that these kittens are born with normal ears and when they are a month old they will either fold or not.

Transitional Song

See Welcome Song earlier.

Flannel Board Activity

Pete the Cat and His Four Groovy Buttons

The beauty of Pete the cat is that he is simple to draw or trace. Using felt or a variety of colored construction paper, create an yellow-shirted Pete the Cat. Using four different colors of felt or paper, create four buttons. Once you have all the pieces, sing the story of Pete the Cat and his Four Groovy Button, stopping to count along the way. If you are creating a paper Pete, it's a good idea to laminate it for better durability.

Don't know the song? You can find it at the following YouTube address: http://youtu.be/V7YMN2ia8z4. Don't worry, I sang it wrong the first time too.

Litwin, Eric. Pete the Cat and His Four Groovy Buttons. New York: Harper, 2012.

Picture Books for Storytime

Schwarz, Viviane. There Are Cats in This Book. Cambridge, MA: Candlewick Press, 2008.
This interactive book invites storytellers and young participants to turn the page, look under flaps, and blow dry a group of curious cats, ending with "Did you like the cats? I think they liked you too!"

Wardlaw, Lee and Eugene Yelchin, illus. Won-Ton: A Cat Tale Told in Haiku. New York: Henry Holt and Company, 2011.
The tale of a cat's journey from shelter to home told through a series of cat-centric haikus. Accompanied by playful illustrations, the book ends with the revelation of the cat's secret name.

Closing Song

See Welcome Song earlier.

Follow-Up Activities

Three Little Kittens Laundry Line

Materials:

- Paper (or real) mittens attached in pairs by string
- A laundry line (you can just use masking tape to attach a string to opposite walls in your storytime space)

Directions:

- Sing the song of the "Three Little Kittens" (words later in this chapter)
- When you get to the part when the kittens hang up their mittens to dry, have all the kids hang a pair of mittens over the laundry line.

The Three Little Kittens
English Nursery Rhyme

Three little kittens they lost their mittens,
And they began to cry,
Oh, mother dear, we sadly fear
Our mittens we have lost.
What! lost your mittens, you naughty kittens!
Then you shall have no pie.
Mee-ow, mee-ow, mee-ow.
No, you shall have no pie.

The three little kittens they found their mittens,
And they began to cry,
Oh, mother dear, see here, see here,
Our mittens we have found!
Put on your mittens, you silly kittens,
And you shall have some pie.
Purr-r, purr-r, purr-r,
Oh, let us have some pie.

The three little kittens put on their mittens,
And soon ate up the pie;
Oh, mother dear, we greatly fear
Our mittens we have soiled.
What! soiled your mittens, you naughty kittens!
Then they began to sigh,
Mee-ow, mee-ow, mee-ow.
Then they began to sigh.

The three little kittens they washed their mittens,
And hung them out to dry;
Oh! mother dear, do you not hear,
Our mittens we have washed!
What! washed your mittens, then you're good kittens,
But I smell a rat close by.
Mee-ow, mee-ow, mee-ow.
We smell a rat close by

Early Literacy Tip:
Help build narration skills by doing a rhyme twice. Sing the "Three Little Kittens" song once all the way through. On the second singing, stop to hang up the mittens then ask who remembers how the rhyme ends.

Other Songs, Rhymes, and Fingerplays

What Are Cats Made Of?
Adapted by J. Dietzel-Glair and M. Follis

What are nice cats made of?
Whiskers and fur

And lots of purrs
That's what nice cats are made of

What are naughty cats made of?
Scratches and hisses
And near claw misses
That's what naughty cats are made of.

Don't forget about some famous cat songs from Disney-animated movies:

"Everybody Wants to Be a Cat" from *Aristocats*
"The Siamese Cat Song" from *Lady and the Tramp*

Additional Poetry

Florian, Douglas. Bow Wow Meow Meow: It's Rhyming Cats and Dogs. San Diego, CA: Harcourt, Inc., 2003.
This title has four fun poems about house cats. Hold up the page showing the accompanying illustration while reading the poem aloud.

Franco, Betsy and Michael Wertz, illus. A Curious Collection of Cats. Berkeley, CA: Tricycle Press, 2009.
This collection of 34 concrete poems is best shown. If possible project on an overhead projector while reading the poem.

Kuskin, Karla and Lisze Bechtold, illus. Toots the Cat. New York: Henry Holt and Company, 2005.
A collection of poems about the author's cat, Toots. Show the playful illustrations while reading a selection of favorite poems to a group.

Additional Nonfiction

Graubart, Norman D. My Cat. New York: PowerKiDS Press, 2014.
This introduction to pet cats has a small trim size making it easy for little hands to manipulate. The large photographs will show well in a storytime room. The pictures are sure to get a lot of "awwws" as you turn the pages.

Hibbert, Clara. If You Were a Cat. Mankato, MN: Smart Apple Media, 2013.
Cats hunting, cats stretching, cats hissing, cats balancing, so many photographs of cats fill this book. The clean layout of each two-page spread makes it easy to choose one section of text for each page flip. Read quick facts, questions, or the "If you were a cat . . ." section. Read through the book ahead of time and mark your chosen sections with a Post-it note.

Walker, Sarah. Big Cats. New York: DK Publishing, Inc., 2002.
Linger on the large photographs in this book while asking open-ended questions. For example, on page 19 there is a tiger splashing in the water. Ask "Do you think this tiger likes the water?" This particular question is fun since most house cats despise water. The caption on the same page notes that tigers actually enjoy lounging in water on hot days. The book is text heavy for the preschool age group, but programmers can choose particular facts to read aloud or just share the pictures.

Additional Fiction Picture Books

Henkes, Kevin. Kitten's First Full Moon. New York: Greenwillow Books, 2004.
When a young kitten sees her first full moon, she mistakes it for a very large bowl of milk. Her quest for the milk leads her to mishaps and frustration, but in the end all is well. This Caldecott Medal recipient is both beautiful and fun for a wide range of audience ages.

Lloyd, Sam. Mr. Pusskins. New York: Atheneum Books for Young Readers, 2007.
Grumpy Cat, Mr. Pusskins learns to appreciate his life after spending a night out "on the town."

Watt, Melanie. Chester. Toronto: Kids Can Press, 2007.
Never one to take the backseat, Chester decides that what the story about a mouse needs is a new lead character. Maybe even a cat named Chester.

Yolen, Jane and Mark Teague, illus. How Do Dinosaurs Love Their Cats? New York: Blue Sky Press, 2010.
As in the other books in this picture book series, correct cat ownership behaviors are exemplified by dinosaurs. What is not to love in a book with both dinosaurs and cats?

Clothing

One of the biggest, and often hardest and challenging decisions of the day: What to wear? Clothing is a constant conversation in the lives of many young people. There are favorite shirts, pants whose tags irritate, and shoes. Does anyone like to wear shoes? And don't forget what to wear under it all!

This storytime is sure to a-DRESS issues shared by kids and their adults who fight the good fight each and every day.

Sample Storytime

Welcome Song

Routine is important when working with children. Be sure to include welcome, transitional, and closing songs or activities to signify what is coming next. Don't be afraid to use the same ones; children take comfort in knowing what is coming next.

Opening Poem

"Emily's Undies" from Schertle, Alice and Petra Mathers, illus. Button Up! New York: Harcourt Children's Books, 2009.

No clothing storytime would be complete without a reference to underwear. In only 16 lines, this poem has humor and a subtle encouragement of potty training (so you can show your cool underwear everywhere you go).

Action Rhyme

Socks, Pants, Shirt and Shoes
Adapted by M. Follis
(Tune: Head, Shoulders, Knees and Toes)

Socks, pants, shirt and shoes (as singing pat ankles, legs, chest, feet)
Shirt and shoes
Socks, pants, shirt and shoes
Shirt and shoes
Getting dressed is easy
When you're only wearing blue
Socks, pants, shirt and shoes
Shirt and shoes

Shoes, pants, socks and shirt (changing order to: feet, legs, ankles, chest)
Socks and shirt
Shoes, pants, socks and shirt
Socks and shirt
When you're out to play
Be sure to avoid dirt
Shoes, pants, socks and shirt
Socks and shirt

Socks, shirt, shoes and pants (changing order to: ankles, chest, feet, legs)
Shoes and pants
Socks, shirt, shoes and pants
Shoes and pants
Be careful where you sit or
You may end up in ants
Socks, shirt, shoes and pants
Shoes and pants.

Note to programmers: Don't be afraid to use a cheat sheet when presenting a new rhyme in storytime.

Early Literacy Tip:
Good listening skills are a building block for reading skills. By switching the clothing order for each verse you are encouraging active listening.

Nonfiction for Storytime

Ajmera, Maya, Elise Hofer Derstine, and Cynthia Pon. What We Wear: Dressing Up around the World. Watertown, MA: Charlesbridge, 2012.

Some kids dress just like you and me. Some wear special and unique outfits. Revel in the photographs of children from around the world celebrating, going to school, and playing sports.

Transitional Song

See Welcome Song earlier.

Flannel Board Activity

Getting Dressed

Oud, Pauline. Getting Dressed with Lily and Milo. New York: Clavis, 2007.

Before little bunny Lily can go outside to play with her friend Milo, she needs to get dressed. For each item, she needs to make a decision on what to choose. For example, she needs to choose her striped underpants.

Using the pattern at the end of this chapter, create articles of clothing in different colors or simple patterns.

Read the story and have young storytime goers help you select the proper article.

Picture Books for Storytime

Long, Ethan. Chamelia. New York: Little Brown and Company, 2011.

While most chameleons work hard to blend in, Chamelia was born to stand out. But sometimes her fashion choices rub people the wrong way and Chamelia learns to find ways to make her mark without clashing. Digital collage illustrations featuring fabric prints make this a fetching read.

Schories, Pat. Pants for Chuck. New York: Holiday House, 2014.

Chuck the woodchuck is determined to wear a pair of pants that he found, even if they are way too small. Perhaps his friends are right and he should take them off before they rip. This "I Like to Read" title has expressive illustrations and a fun storyline.

Early Literacy Tip:
Many beginning reader titles are now made to look like picture books. Be sure to check those shelves for fun storytime reads that can also encourage emerging readers.

Closing Song

See Welcome Song earlier.

Follow-Up Activities

Dress-Up Time

Materials:

- Costumes and/or random dress-up clothes (hint: you can go to your local goodwill for deals on fun dress-up clothes)
- A full-length mirror
- Camera (optional)

Directions:

- Allow free time for kids to dress up how they choose.
- Make sure everyone can see their crazy outfits in the mirror.
- If you choose, take pictures of their outfits and e-mail the photos to parents.

Other Songs, Rhymes, and Fingerplays

This Little Piggy
Adapted by J. Dietzel-Glair

This little piggy wore sandals
And this little piggy wore sneaks
This little piggy wore snow boots
And this little piggy wore cleats
And this little piggy went barefoot—Ouch! Ouch! Ouch!
All the way home.

I Can Dress Myself
By M. Follis

I want to go outside and play
I want to dress myself
I am growing every day
I can reach my shelf
I chose some shorts
And my favorite tee
Put some sandals on my feet
But when my mother saw
She screamed:
"There is snow covering the street!"

Where Is My T-Shirt?
Adapted by J. Dietzel-Glair
(Tune: Where Has My Little Dog Gone?)

Oh where, oh where is my favorite t-shirt?
Oh where, or where can it be?

I've looked in my dresser
And looked on the floor
Oh Mommy, please help me.

Oh! Look! I'm already wearing it!

Additional Poetry

Kennedy, X.J. and Philippe Béha, illus. City Kids: Street & Skyscraper Rhymes. Vancouver: Tradewind Books, 2010.
No matter what you do, your clothes are going to get dirty and that means a trip to the "Laundromat" (p. 70) where "socks leapfrog over other socks."

Schertle, Alice and Petra Mathers, illus. Button Up! New York: Harcourt Children's Books, 2009.
This collection covers all types of clothing from shoelaces to jammies to hand-me-down sweatshirts. The accompanying illustrations show animals wearing the clothing; there is a snoozing alligator in pajamas and an ostrich in an itchy wool sweater. What type of clothing is appropriate for the current weather outside? Pick that poem to read.

Singer, Marilyn and Hiroe Nakata, illus. Shoe Bop! New York: Dutton Children's Books, 2008.
These shoes are made for walking. And dancing. And fishing. And dressing up. When a young girl's purple sneakers fall apart, she visits the shoe store with mom. Her shoe shopping trip is captured through catchy poetry. If possible, bring in a few styles to display while reading about those types of shoes.

Vardell, Sylvia and Janet Wong, ed. The Poetry Friday Anthology for Celebrations. Princeton, NJ: Pomelo Books, 2015.
Clothing helps us express our personality, especially a hat! How do you wear yours? Tilted? Backward? Be sure to don your chapeau while reading Joan Bransfield Graham's "Hats Off to Hat Day" (p. 37).

Additional Nonfiction

Heling, Kathryn, Deborah Hembrook, and Andy Robert Davies, illus. Clothesline Clues to Jobs People Do. Watertown, MA: Charlesbridge, 2012.
See that uniform hanging on a clothesline? Who could it belong to? What job do they do? Kids will readily recognize the uniform for a mail carrier, farmer, chef, artist, carpenter, firefighter, and astronaut.

Swinburne, Stephen R. Whose Shoes?: A Shoe for Every Job. Honesdale, PA: Boyds Mills Press, 2010.
Play the guessing game in the middle of the book. See the shoes then flip the page to see who wears them for their occupations. Jobs range from a ballerina to a postal worker.

Additional Fiction Picture Books

Barnett, Mac and Jon Klassen, illus. Extra Yarn. New York: Balzar + Bray, 2012.
Annabelle finds a magic box of yarn and is able to knit a sweater for everyone and everything in her town, even those that claim they don't want anything. The illustrations are subdued yet humorous, especially when she knits sweaters for trees and houses.

Hines, Anna Grossnickle and LeUyen Pham, illus. Whose Shoes? San Diego: Harcourt, Inc., 2001.
Lift the flaps to solve the riddle of whose shoes this little mouse is wearing.

Ji, Zhaohua and Cui Xu. No! That's Wrong! La Jolla, CA: Kane Miller Books, 2008.
When the wind blows an errant pair of red underwear off a clothesline, a little rabbit finds it and decides it is a hat. An off-page narrator (and your young readers) all chime in saying "No, that's wrong. It's not a hat" while the rabbit and his wide assortment of animal friends try on the hat. Finally a donkey points out the obvious, but after trying to wear the underwear properly, rabbit decides that his initial assessment suits him best. The silliness of rabbit's fashion choices, combined with the general amusement of underwear, makes this a story sure to elicit giggles and audience participation.

Kushkin, Karla and Fumi Kosaka. Under My Hood I Have a Hat. New York: HarperCollins, 2004.
"Under my hood I have a hat. Under that . . . my hair is flat." A little girl undressing and dressing for the cold reveals layer after layer of winter clothing. While all of the layers keep her warm, she warns against falling down. Simple sweet illustrations and rhyming text make this a fun share that will warm up any storytime.

McDonald, Megan and Katherine Tillotson, illus. Shoe Dog. New York: Atheneum Books for Young Readers, 2014.
Shoe Dog is so excited to have a place to call home. There is only one problem. He loves to chew on shoes. If he can't control his impulses, he may never get to jump on the Big Bed in the Land of Upstairs. The energy of this little pup is perfectly illustrated through quirky and squiggly lines.

Melling. David. Don't Worry, Douglas! Wilton, CT: Tiger Tales, 2011.
Douglas's brand-new hat becomes unraveled while he is playing. The other animals try to help but he eventually has to tell his dad what really happened. Kids who are starting to learn about responsibility will appreciate this tale of forgiveness.

Reidy, Hannah and Emma Dodd, illus. All Sorts of Clothes. Minneapolis, MN: Picture Window Books, 2005.
A variety of children describe what they love to wear. Bold illustrations against solid colors make this a good choice for large group sharing. The last page of the book asks "What do you like to wear?" ending the story with a natural conversation starter.

Sendelback, Brian. The Underpants Zoo. New York: Scholastic, 2011.
Come visit the absolutely silly new zoo in town. All of the animals wear underpants just like our young readers. In hilarious pairs of rhyming lines, lists of particular needs and favorites are given. "Hippo's have hearts, because she's such a romantic. Elephant's size is Extra-Jumbo Gigantic!" Comical bug-eyed creatures wearing everything from tighty whiteys to wild boxers are sure to elicit giggles galore!

Bunny Pattern

Clothing Patterns

Colors

One of the first adjectives we use in the world of children is color. Colors are the topic of songs, rhymes, and conversations. Explore this primary concept further in this colorful storytime.

Sample Storytime

Welcome Song

Routine is important when working with children. Be sure to include welcome, transitional, and closing songs or activities to signify what is coming next. Don't be afraid to use the same ones; children take comfort in knowing what is coming next.

Opening Poem

"Green Frog" from Larios, Julie and Julie Paschkis, illus. Yellow Elephant: A Bright Bestiary. Orlando, FL: Harcourt, Inc., 2006.
"Green Frog" (p. 4) uses the colors green and blue as the predominant adjectives in a short, quick ode to the familiar amphibian. A full-page illustration complements the poem making it suitable for display in storytime.

Action Rhyme

I See Color
Adapted by J. Dietzel-Glair
(Tune: London Bridge)

I see red in this room
In this room
In this room
I see red in this room
Can you see it too?
(ask children to point to red objects in the room)
Additional verses: Have children identify other colors.

Nonfiction for Storytime

Brocket, Jane. Ruby, Violet, Lime: Looking for Color. Minneapolis, MN: Millbrook Press, 2012.
Striking photographs accompany text about the colors. The book also discusses the concepts of primary and secondary colors but the text is not overwhelming.

Early Literacy Tip:
Not every book needs to be read straight through. When reading a book like *Ruby, Violet, Lime,* you can stop and point out the colors around you after each page to echo the concept.

Transitional Song

See Welcome Song earlier.

Flannel Board Activity

Color Time

"Crayons: A Rainbow Poem" from Yolen, Jane and Jason Stemple, photography. Color Me a Rhyme: Nature Poems for Young People. Honesdale, PA: Wordsong, 2000.

Create a felt crayon (pattern at the end of the chapter) for all of the colors mentioned in this poem: blue, green, yellow, orange, red, lime, brown, black, pink, chocolate, burnt sienna, and ivory. Read "Crayons: A Rainbow Poem" aloud and put each felt crayon on the flannel board as it is mentioned in the poem.

Picture Books for Storytime

Foley, Greg. Purple Little Bird. New York: Balzer + Bray, 2011.

Purple Bird lives in a purple world but goes in search of a more perfect place. Purple Bird discovers animals and worlds of different colors and decides to bring more color into his home.

Wilson, Karma and Jane Chapman, illus. Bear Sees Colors. New York: Margaret K. McElderry Books, 2014.

Reinforce the colors blue, red, yellow, green, and brown with Bear and friends. White backgrounds give way to pages full of the focus color. When you finish a color page, can you find more of that color in your storytime space?

Closing Song

See Welcome Song earlier.

Follow-Up Activities

Mix the Colors

Materials:

- Red, yellow, and blue fingerpaints
- Paper plates
- Plastic bags (optional)

Directions:

- Put a small blob of red, yellow, and blue fingerpaint on each plate.
- With adult supervision, everyone can mix red and yellow together to make orange, yellow and blue together to make green, and blue and red together to make purple.
- If you are concerned about the mess, put a small amount of two colors in a plastic Ziploc bag and instruct the kids to mix the paints without opening the bag.

Other Songs, Rhymes, and Fingerplays

The Colors
Adapted by J. Dietzel-Glair
(Tune: Farmer in the Dell)

Red and blue make purple
Red and blue make purple

The colors mix so beautifully
Red and blue make purple

Additional verses:
Yellow and red make orange
Blue and yellow make green

I Use Colors
Adapted by M. Follis and J. Dietzel-Glair
(Tune: Old MacDonald)

I use colors when I paint
P-A-I-N-T
Blue and yellow create green
P-A-I-N-T
With a blue swish here
And a yellow swish there
Here a blue, there a yellow
Now the green is everywhere
I use colors when I paint
P-A-I-N-T

Use the other color mixtures for more verses:
Red and yellow create orange. . . .
Red and blue create purple . . .
And if you want to have a little more fun:
Red and white create pink . . .

Baa, Baa, Black Sheep
Traditional English Nursery Rhyme

Baa, baa, black sheep
Have you any wool?
Yes sir, yes sir
Three bags full
One for my master
And one for my dame
And one for the little boy
Who lives down the lane.

Continue with other colored sheep: baa, baa, red sheep . . . baa, baa, purple sheep. Add to the fun by creating a felt sheep in each color to put on the flannel board as you sing along. (There is a sheep pattern in Chapter 24, Family Animals.)

Color Hokey Pokey
Adapted by M. Follis and J. Dietzel-Glair
(Tune: Hokey Pokey)

Note: Give children two tongue depressors at the beginning of the song. One tongue depressor has a red dot and the other has a green dot.

You put your red stick in
You put your red stick out

You put your red stick it
And you shake it all about
You do the color pokey
And you turn yourself around
That's what it's all about

You put your green stick it
You put your green stick out
You put your green stick in
And you shake it all about
You do the color pokey
And you turn yourself around
That's what it's all about

You can also do this rhyme with stickers on their feet.

Early Literacy Tip: Use lime green or lavender on the left foot and red on the right foot. This will help them to learn left and right, which is related to literacy because we read left to right.

Additional Poetry

Larios, Julie and Julie Paschkis, illus. Yellow Elephant: A Bright Bestiary. Orlando, FL: Harcourt, Inc., 2006.

The colors green, red, white, orange, yellow, purple, pink, black, gold, brown, silver, turquoise, blue, and gray are the focus of 14 poems about animals. Each poem also has an illustration of the colorful animal on the facing page. Some animals are realistic, such as the Gold Finch; others are more playful, like the Purple Puppy.

Martin Jr., Bill, Michael Sampson, and various illustrators. The Bill Martin Jr. Big Book of Poetry. New York: Simon & Schuster, 2008.

"What Is Pink?" (p. 36), by Christina G. Rossetti, asks the question of a variety of colors, and poetically answers them. Except for orange which is "just an orange!"

Yolen, Jane and Jason Stemple, photography. Color Me a Rhyme: Nature Poems for Young People. Honesdale, PA: Wordsong, 2000.

These poems are based on photographs that feature specific colors in nature. Yolen also provides additional descriptors for the colors that can be read aloud before or after the poem.

Additional Nonfiction

Doran, Ella, David Goodman, and Zoe Miller. Color. London: Tate Publishing, 2006.

The first nine pages of this book have amazing full-page spreads illustrating primary and secondary colors through photographs. Use this book to introduce each color in storytime. Then open a discussion of other things that are red, blue, yellow, orange, green, purple, and brown.

Gonyea, Mark. A Book about Color: A Clear and Simple Guide for Young Artists. New York: Henry Holt and Company, 2010.

Seven chapters break down color concepts such as primary and secondary colors, the meanings associated with colors, color saturation, and the color wheel. With minimal text and bright illustrations, the first two chapters lend themselves to being read aloud to a storytime group.

Micklethwait, Lucy. I Spy Colors in Art. New York: Greenwillow Books, 2007.
Fourteen paintings are explored with an "I spy" that makes the reader study the work of art. For example, the "I spy" for Pablo Picasso's *Maya with a Doll* is "I spy with my little eye two blue eyes." Children can then search the full-page reproduction of the painting for the two blue eyes on the doll. This book is great for a small group where everyone can play along.

Additional Fiction Picture Books

Daywalt, Drew and Oliver Jeffers, illus. The Day the Crayons Quit. New York: Philomel Books, 2014.
Tired of being used and abused in the same boring fashion, a young child's crayons have decided they have had enough and have quit! Blue is worn out from all of the ocean pictures, and black wants to be used as a color, not just an outline! When each color makes its complaints known, their clever owner finds a way to make everyone happy.

Dodd, Emma. Dog's Colorful Day: A Messy Story about Colors and Counting. New York: Dutton Children's Books, 2000.
When our hero Dog starts his day, he is all white with one black spot on his ear. After encountering orange juice, paint, jelly, markers, mud, ice cream, chocolate, grass, and a bee, dog is covered with 10 colorful spots. This book offers young reader opportunities to count and identify colors as they read.

Ficocelli, Elizabeth and Glin Dibley, illus. Kid Tea. Tarrytown, NY: Marshall Cavendish Children's, 2007.
Follow a brother and sister through the week, colorful messes and the grime of the day ends up coloring the water of their nightly bath creating "kid tea."

Seeger, Laura Vaccaro. Green. New York: Roaring Brook Press, 2012.
Green is so much more than just green. It is a place. It is a food. It is a speed. Small cut-outs on the pages add to the homage to this lively color.

Wolff, Ashley. Baby Bear Sees Blue. New York: Beach Lane Books, 2012.
After Baby Bear wakes, he explores the world outside his cave and sees colors everywhere. He is even treated to a rainbow before settling back down for the night. Many of the illustrations provide a unique visual perspective to Baby Bear's world.

Crayon Pattern

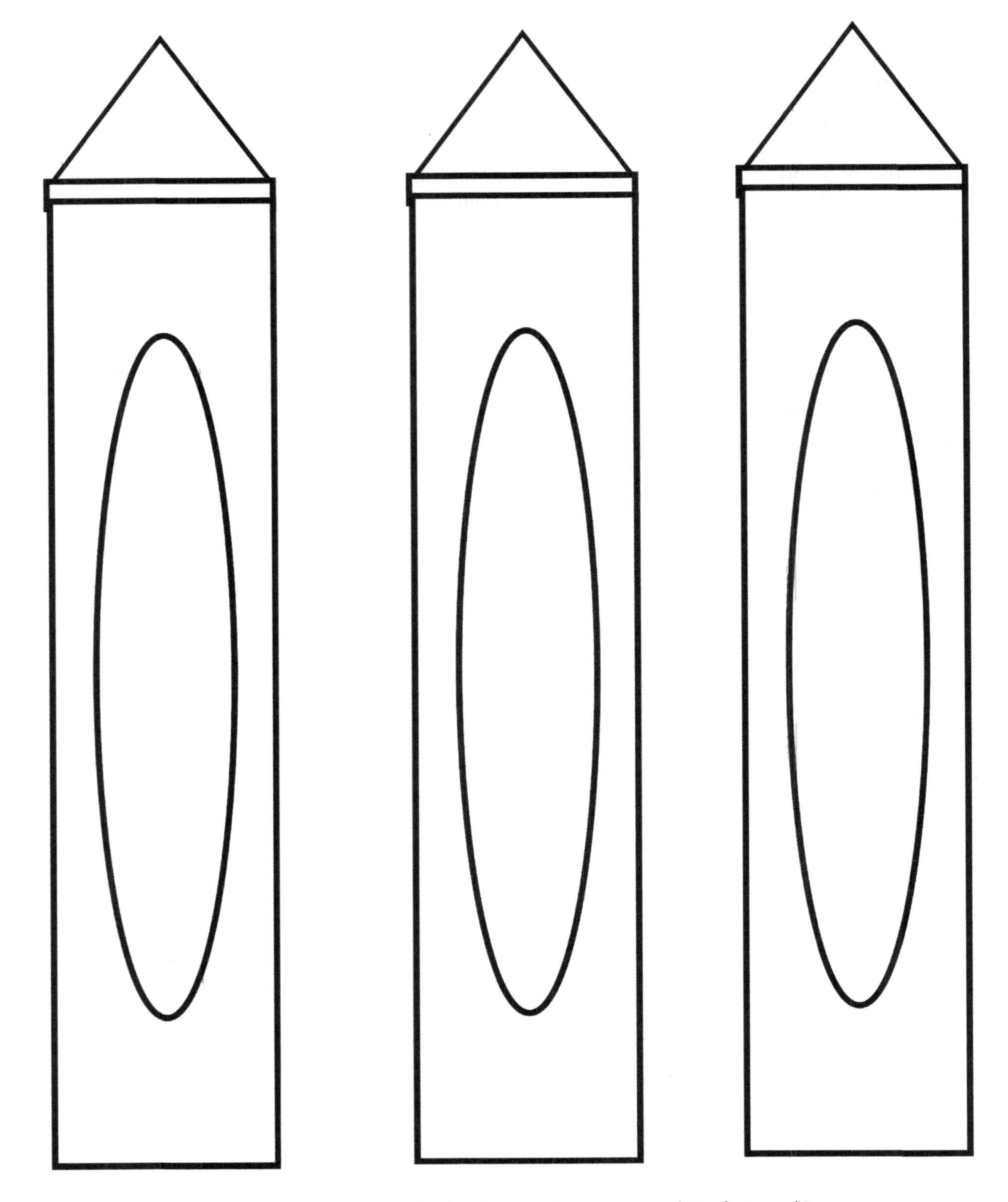

Community Helpers

Children are fascinated by firemen and policemen. They want to visit the firehouse and see the cool trucks. They want to grow up to save the world from "bad guys." Don't forget some of the other heroes who keep the streets clean and deliver important messages. Satisfy their curiosity with an entire storytime devoted to these brave men and women.

Sample Storytime

Welcome Song

Routine is important when working with children. Be sure to include welcome, transitional, and closing songs or activities to signify what is coming next. Don't be afraid to use the same ones; children take comfort in knowing what is coming next.

Opening Poem

"Gabby the Garbage Collector" from Nesbitt, Kenn and Ethan Long, illus. My Hippo Has the Hiccups. Naperville, IL: Sourcebooks, Inc., 2009.
Gabby loves her job and is thrilled that you save your trash for her. She goes on to list some of the many things she finds and treasures and is willing to view her "awesome assemblage," on display at the local dump! A fun and jaunty ode to the unsung hero: the garbage collector! This title comes with a CD featuring some of the poems read by the author. For a change of pace (and voice), pop in the CD to hear Nesbitt's version of this poem.

Action Rhyme

I'm a Firefighter
Adapted by M. Follis
(Tune: Here We Go Round the Mulberry Bush)

This is the way I pull on my boots (pretend to pull on boots)
Pull on my boots, pull on boots
This is the way I pull on my boots
I'm a firefighter

This is the way I drive my truck (hold pretend steering wheel in front of you)
Drive my truck, drive my truck
This is the way I drive the truck,
I'm a firefighter

Additional verses:
Slide down the pole (hold two hands together like you are holding a pole and slide down)
Spray the fire (hold a pretend hose in front of you and spray it back and forth)
Climb the ladder (use both your arms and legs to climb a pretend ladder)

Nonfiction for Storytime

Carr, Aaron. The Police Station. New York: AV2 by Weigl, 2014.
Photographs and short text show the police interacting with people in a neighborhood. Kids looking at this book will get positive vibes about the police force and will know who to go to if they ever need help.

Transitional Song

See Welcome Song earlier.

Flannel Board Activity

Who Am I?

Find images using an Internet search or any clip art you may own. Create flannel board pieces for the following community helpers: police officer, firefighter, garbage man, and postman.

Recite the following poem and have children guess who the community helper is.

Who Am I?
By M. Follis

I visit your house every day
Bringing messages from far away
When you see me walking by
Please be sure to wave and say hi!
Can you guess who I am?

I spend my days walking a beat
Or in my squad car's drivers seat
I often dress in a uniform of blue
My job is to keep things safe for you!
Can you guess who I am?

I clean up messes from your house
No one has ever said, "You're as quiet as a mouse!"
Put bags outside, close to the street
I keep our cities and towns nice and neat!
Can you guess who I am?

I wear a uniform and helmet on my head
I drive a big truck that's all red
I use a ladder and a long hose
I protect you from fire,
Everyone knows . . .
Can you guess who I am?

Early Literacy Tip:
Guessing games encourage children to listen closely. As they are listening, they are processing what they are hearing and trying to think ahead. This helps to build comprehension skills.

Picture Books for Storytime

Elya, Susan Middleton and Dan Santat, illus. Fire! ¡Fuego! Brave Bomberos. New York: Bloomsbury, 2012.
Follow along with this crew of brave bomberos as they answer a call to put out a fire and save a poor gatito. Loads of Spanish words are sprinkled throughout and placed in context so meaning is clear, but just in case, there is a glossary, too. Wonderfully detailed

illustrations by Dan Santat including a diverse fire crew, and some dejected dalmatians.

McMullan, Kate and Jim. I'm Brave. New York: Balzer + Bray, 2014.
What do you call a big red truck with lights, sirens, and a hose? Brave! (and good looking!) This fun read-aloud is filled with sounds and actions that can be replicated by little ones during storytime, while giving young fire truck enthusiasts loads of details about all that a fire truck carries and can do.

Early Literacy Tip:
Exposure to a foreign language at an early age helps connect synapses in the brain that will make it easier for a child to learn that language.

Closing Song

See Welcome Song earlier.

Follow-Up Activities

Red Light Green Light with Steering Wheels

Materials:

- White paper plates with fluted sides
- Scissors, crayons, markers, and so on
- Premade signs
    - RED LIGHT with STOP in the middle
    - GREEN LIGHT with GO in the middle
    - YELLOW LIGHT with SLOW in the middle

Give out simple paper plates and have children use crayons and scissors, where warranted, to create a more realistic and decorative steering wheel.

While children are working, give them the directions for the game.

What do we do when we see a red light? STOP!
And the green light tells us it is safe to do what? GO!
What does the yellow light mean? GO SLOW!
So when I say RED LIGHT! you are all going to? STOP!
And when I say green light you are all going to? GO!
And when I say YELLOW light you are all going to . . .? GO SLOW!

Once everyone has their wheel completed, have the children form a circle.

Ask the little ones to start their engines and say that you want to hear their motors. Model car like noises for the children to imitate, such and vroom, rumble, etc. Add a horn or two by saying beep beep.

Flash the signs in alternating order and have the kids drive, stop, and go slow according to the signal signs.

Vehicle Visits

Contact your local fire department, police department, or post office to see if they do vehicle visits. If you have a parking lot, rope off part of the lot for safety. Let everyone explore the vehicles and ask questions of the community helpers.

Other Songs, Rhymes, and Fingerplays

The Wheels on the Fire Engine
Adapted by M. Follis
(Tune: The Wheels on the Bus)

The wheels on the fire engine
Go round and round
Round and round
Round and round
The wheels on the Fire Engine
Go round and round
All through the town

Additional verses:
Siren goes wah, wah, wah
Bell goes clang, clang, clang
Ladder goes up and down, up and down, up and down
Hose goes spray, spray spray

I'm a Little Fireman
Adapted by M. Follis
(Tune: I'm a Little Teapot)

I'm a little fireman, dressed in red
With my fire helmet on my head
I can drive a fire truck, hose fires down
I am a helper in your town

Policemen Are Your Friend
By M. Follis
(Tune: Farmer in the Dell)

The policemen are your friends, policemen are your friends
When you're in trouble
They're there on the double
Policemen are your friends

They always keep you safe, they always keep you safe
When you're in trouble
They're there on the double
They always keep you safe

The People in Your Neighborhood

This is a classic Sesame Street song with verses about the postman and the fireman. You can find the video at YouTube at: https://www.youtube.com/watch?v=W5cRukvx850.

Hurry, Hurry Drive the Firetruck

YouTube offers opportunities to let the storytime crowd hear other people singing songs and rhymes. Two librarians perform this fun song here: https://www.youtube.com/watch?v=n9Dhlp9VQ-w. Be sure to mime the actions along with the words so the kids can follow along.

Additional Poetry

Kennedy, X.J. and Philippe Béha, illus. City Kids: Street & Skyscraper Rhymes. Vancouver: Tradewind Books, 2010.

"Hydrants" (p. 60) are an important tool "waiting for hire" by a fireman. But on hot days they sometimes become a playful fountain.

Lillegard, Dee and Valeri Gorbachev, illus. Go! Poetry in Motion. New York: Alfred Knopf. 2006.

This collection of poetry that moves includes all sorts of vehicles such as mail and garbage trucks.

Martin Jr., Bill, Michael Sampson, and various illustrators. The Bill Martin Jr. Big Book of Poetry. New York: Simon & Schuster, 2008.

Margaret Wise Brown's "Postman's Song" (p. 76) sings the praises of these dedicated community helpers and ponders what they are carrying in their mail sacks and from where the letters have traveled.

Additional Nonfiction

Owen, Ann and Eric Thomas, illus. Delivering Your Mail: A Book about Mail Carriers. Minneapolis, MN: Picture Window Books, 2004.

Everyone likes getting mail and packages and this book tells you how they get to you. Friendly mail carriers walk or drive in the city and the country, in the snow and the rain, to deliver your mail to you.

Roberts, Cynthia. Fire Trucks. Mankato, MN: The Child's World, 2007.

This title uses a question-and-answer format to provide information about fire trucks. Read a few pages or display the book for checkout by a family. Also look for **Police Cars** (2007) by the same author.

Additional Fiction Picture Books

Beaty, Andrea and Pascal Lemaitre. Firefighter Ted. New York: McElderry Books, 2009.

Ted is a bear who knows how to use his imagination. When he smells smoke, he quickly transforms into Firefighter Ted, using household items to fashion a fire extinguisher and quickly puts out the burnt toast. The fun continues as he keeps his firefighter persona through the school day.

Hamilton, Kersten and R.W. Alley, illus. Police Officers on Patrol. New York: Viking, 2009.

Who is always ready to "rock and roll" and save the day? Office Mike on traffic patrol, Office Jan on mounted patrol, and Officer Carl on crime patrol. Along with rhyming text and fun details in the illustrations, children learn to trust and call the police when they need help.

Hubbell, Patricia and Viviana Garofoli, illus. Firefighters: Speeding! Spraying! Saving! Tarrytown, NY: Marshall Cavendish Corporation, 2007.

This short, simple rhyming text filled with action and sound is the perfect read-aloud for toddlers and preschoolers.

Luthardt, Kevin. Larabee. Atlanta: Peachtree, 2004.

Larabee loves helping Mr. Bowman deliver the mail; he just wishes someone would send him something. Unfortunately, dogs don't get mail. Still, Larabee makes his rounds saying hello to everyone and yips with delight when he finds an envelope addressed to him.

Mortensen, Denise Dowling and Cece Bell, illus. Bug Patrol. New York: Clarion Books, 2013.
Captain Bob of Bug Patrol keeps the peace on the mean streets. In this light-hearted tale, Captain Bob keeps ants in line, speeding spiders sedate, and helps a baby flea find its way home.

Steffensmeier, Alexander. Millie Waits for the Mail. New York: Walker & Company, 2007.
Most mail carriers have to worry about dogs along their route. This one has to worry about Millie, the cow that loves nothing more than frightening the mail carrier. In the end, the mail carrier and Millie come to a unique arrangement. Take time to study the illustrations; there is much humor to be found from a skateboarding ant to a flock of curious chickens.

Teague, Mark. Firehouse. New York: Orchard Books, 2010.
When a little pup goes on a field trip to the firehouse, he gets to ride along on a call with the rest of the firefighters. Cooperation and teamwork save the day in this kid friendly read aloud with an (almost) all canine cast.

Whiting, Sue and Donna Rawlins. The Firefighters. Cambridge, MA: Candlewick Press, 2008.
After a fun morning of imaginative play, the children in Ms. Mia's class are visited by real firefighters and learn about fire safety.

Construction Equipment and Work Trucks

It seems that no matter where you live, or where you drive, there is construction. While this may cause headaches for the adults of storytime, it can provide little ones with lots of excitement. Have fun bringing that excitement into your storytimes.

Sample Storytime

Welcome Song

Routine is important when working with children. Be sure to include welcome, transitional, and closing songs or activities to signify what is coming next. Don't be afraid to use the same ones; children take comfort in knowing what is coming next.

Opening Poem

"Skyscraper" from Janeczko, Paul B., ed. and Robert Rayevsky, illus. Hey You!: Poems to Skyscrapers, Mosquitoes, and Other Fun Things. New York: HarperCollins, 2007.

Why are these tall buildings called skyscrapers? Because they "scrape the sky" and "tickle the stars" a quick poem by Dennis Lee celebrating what construction workers create.

Action Rhyme

Johnny Works with One Hammer

The song starts off easy with only one hammer, which only requires one hand. Everyone will be laughing; you slowly add hammers and try to use five.

Watch three cartoon kids do a version of this song on YouTube at: https://www.youtube.com/watch?v=NYk8Gmwt_Cc.

For even more fun, watch this video of real kids singing the song. Coordination issues are solved by having the kids lay on the floor: https://www.youtube.com/watch?v=QVf3DJD9TaM.

Nonfiction for Storytime

Murrell, Deborah and Christiane Gunzi. Mega Trucks: The Biggest, Toughest Trucks in the World! New York: Scholastic, 2005.

The large trim size of this book makes these massive trucks look larger than life. Programmers have many options in presenting this book. (1) Choose just the pages with construction equipment and read everything on the page. (2) Read just the introductory sentences for each truck.

Early Literacy Tip:
Help children with vocabulary by asking them to point out a specific item or two on each page. *Mega Trucks* helps with this fun task by including "Can you point to . . ." boxes on many pages of the book.

Transitional Song

See Welcome Song earlier.

Flannel Board Activity

Construction Song

Create or find images online for the following pieces of equipment, or if you want to change up your flannel board routine you can share pictures from a big bold nonfiction book featuring some of these pieces of equipment, such as:

Perritano, John. Construction Machines. New York: Gareth Stevens Publishing, 2014.

Construction Friends
By M. Follis
(Tune: Ten Little Indians)

Grumble, grumble goes the excavator
Grumble, grumble goes the excavator
Grumble, grumble goes the excavator
Scooping up the dirt

Round and round goes the mixer
Round and round goes the mixer
Round and round goes the mixer
Mixing up the cement

Grrr, grrr, grrr goes the paver
Grrr, grrr, grrr goes the paver
Grrr, grrr, grrr goes the paver
Smoothing out the road

Bumpity, bumpity goes the dump truck
Bumpity, bumpity goes the dump truck
Bumpity, bumpity goes the dump truck
Dumping out its load

Reaching, reaching goes the tall crane
Reaching, reaching goes the tall crane
Reaching, reaching goes the tall crane
Stretching way up high

Picture Books for Storytime

Harper, Charise Mericle. Go! Go! Go! Stop! New York: Alfred A. Knopf, 2014.
A bulldozer, dump truck, tow truck, crane, mixer, and backhoe build a bridge with a little help from Little Green. But when things get too crazy, Little Red knows how to make everyone stop. Storytime attendees will love this funny book.

Holub, Joan and James Dean, illus. Mighty Dads. New York: Scholastic Press, 2014.
Grown excavators, bulldozers, and cranes help their children learn how to build in this rhyming book with lots of action words and sounds.

Closing Song

See Welcome Song earlier.

Follow-Up Activities

What Can You Build

Materials:

- Toy building supplies.
    - These may be Legos, blocks, lincoln logs, or another building toy

Directions:

- Allow for free building time.
- Be sure to encourage the adults in the room to participate fully with their children.
- As children are working on their creations, walk around and ask what they are working on.

Other Songs, Rhymes, and Fingerplays

Cranes
By M. Follis

(have children extend arms together)
Cranes reach up (reach up)
Crane reach down (bend down low)
Cranes reach out (reach over to one side)
And all around (turn around)

London Bridge
Traditional English Nursery Rhyme

London Bridge is falling down
Falling down, falling down
London Bridge is falling down
My fair lady

Ashburn, Boni and Sergio De Giorgi, illus. Builder Goose: It's Construction Rhyme Time! New York: Sterling Children's Books, 2012.
If Mother Goose ran a construction site her rhymes would look a lot like this. Have fun with "The Itsy-Bitsy Skid Steer," "Crumbling Bridge Is Falling Down," "Twinkle, Twinkle, Wrecking Ball," and many more.

Early Literacy Tip:
Nursery rhymes are very familiar to preschoolers. Rhymes that use the well-known format and melody are a fun treat.

Scieszka, Jon, David Gordon, Loren Long, and David Shannon, illus. Truckery Rhymes. New York: Simon & Schuster Books for Young Readers, 2009.
Scieszka has taken well-known nursery rhymes and changed the words to a truck theme. Look for these fun construction equipment-related rhymes: "Rock-a-Bye Mixer," "This Is the Way," "Patty Cake Patty Cake," "Swing around with Rosie," and "Wrecker Rosie Sat on a Wall."

"Obsessed by Trucks" by Justin Roberts. From Jungle Gym (2010)
Kids (especially little boys) get so excited when they see big trucks. This rocking song mentions dump trucks, fire trucks, and more. You can also find a fun YouTube video with a young girl lip-syncing the song here: https://www.youtube.com/watch?v=jTpHAbuEQac.

Additional Poetry

Vestergaard, Hope and David Slonim, illus. Digger, Dozer, Dumper. Somerville, MA: Candlewick Press, 2013.
Big trucks from backhoes to cement mixers are personified through poetry. With fun illustrations, you can share multiple selections from this title in a storytime.

Additional Nonfiction

Low, William. Machines Go to Work. New York: Henry Holt and Company, 2009.
What could be better than a flap book? Why a flap book with big trucks, of course! Hear the machine's sound then see what work it is accomplishing when you lift the flap. Also look for ***Machines Go to Work in the City*** (2012) by the same author.

Maass, Robert. Little Trucks with Big Jobs. New York: Henry Holt and Company, 2007.
One or two sentences give a short description of trucks from street sweeper to zambonis and ending with everyone's favorite—the ice cream truck. Kids will enjoy seeing photographs of less common trucks like a glass truck and a plane tug.

Pallotta, Jerry and Rob Bolster, illus. The Construction Alphabet Book. Watertown, MA: Charlesbridge, 2006.
"A is for Aerial Lift . . . B is for Bulldozer . . . C is for Cement Mixer." Follow along as a piece of construction equipment is illustrated and described in a short paragraph for each letter of the alphabet. Read just the first sentence of each page as a storytime read aloud.

Roberts, Cynthia. Dump Trucks. Mankato, MN: The Child's World, 2007.
Children ask lots of questions and this book answers the types of questions they ask: "How are dump trucks used?" "How does a dump truck move?" "How does a dump truck dump?" This book is a little longer than some other recommended titles so programmers may wish to read only a couple pages in a storytime.

Early Literacy Tip:
One of the first letters that children learn is the first letter of their first name. They are oftentimes very proud of this knowledge. During or after reading an alphabet book, ask children to raise their hands if their name starts with "A." Continue through each letter.

Additional Fiction Picture Books

Clement, Nathan. Job Site. Honesdale, PA: Boyds Mills Press, 2011.
Every piece of heavy machinery has a very special job to do and they keep going it until the job is done. The computer-rendered illustrations are crisp and clean in the messy job site. Kids always want to see construction equipment in action, and this book fills that dream.

Mandel, Peter and Peter Catrow, illus. Jackhammer Sam. New York: Roaring Brook Press, 2011.
Sam is the man! The jackhammer man. He jackhammers all day long causing more and more destruction as he goes. Yet he sings such a cheerful little tune that it doesn't matter

when he causes doom. Kids will be singing the playful words and nonsense sounds long after the book is done.

Early Literacy Tip:
Preschool kids love nonsense words. They help kids learn sounds and how they can fit together.

Rinker, Sherri Duskey and Tom Lichtenheld, illus. Goodnight, Goodnight, Construction Site. San Francisco: Chronicle Books, 2011.
After a long, hard day, the work trucks are ready to rest. The rhyming text makes the book feel like a rough and tumble lullaby. The illustrations add personality to the trucks by giving a teddy bear to the crane and a blanket to the cement mixer. The sturdy and glossy pages will show well across a storytime room.

Dinosaurs

Dinosaurs are the perfect obsession for little ones. Large and in charge, but no longer with us. There is a safety in learning about something so ferocious, yet being reassured that you are completely out of its reach. Enjoy these extinct beasts!

Sample Storytime

Welcome Song

Routine is important when working with children. Be sure to include welcome, transitional, and closing songs or activities to signify what is coming next. Don't be afraid to use the same ones; children take comfort in knowing what is coming next.

Opening Poem

"Barosaurus" from Florian, Douglas. Dinothesaurus. New York: Atheneum Books for Young Readers, 2009.
"Barosaurus" (p. 23) compares the ancient lizard to the height of five elephants and length of a whale. Children will be able to picture this huge dinosaur and laugh when they are offered a ride in the last line.

Action Rhyme

If You're a Dinosaur and You Know It
Adapted by M. Follis
(Tune: If You're Happy and You Know It)

Each dinosaur has unique features so please make sure to include them as you introduce each verse.

Sadly, we can't ask the T-Rex to clap his hands, but we can ask him to give a roar.

If you're and T-Rex and you know it, give a roar!
Roar, Roar
If you're a T-Rex and you know it give a roar!
Roar, Roar
If you're a T-Rex and you know it, then your roar will really show it
If you're a T-Rex and you know it, give a roar!
Roar, Roar.

The Apatosaurus had a long graceful neck it used to bow its head to reach its food—plants!
Apatosaurus—take a bow

The most famous of the flying dinosaurs with large wings!
Pterodactyl—flap your wings

This dinosaur has three spiked scales on its head; perfect for protecting itself.
Triceratops—bump your head

Nonfiction for Storytime

Munro, Roxie. Inside-Outside Dinosaurs. Tarrytown, NY: Marshall Cavendish Children, 2009.

See a dinosaur skeleton then turn the page to see an illustration of the same dinosaur as they may have lived so many years ago. Children will love seeing the inside and the outside of these eight dinosaurs. Dinosaurs are so popular and exciting for children that the simple text of the dinosaur name and name definition will be interesting enough. Programmers who want more can use the back matter to add interesting facts to each page.

Transitional Song

See Welcome Song earlier.

Flannel Board Activity

Dinosaur Time

Place a found or purchased flannel piece of each dinosaur on the board while singing its verse.

You may also have dinosaur die cuts available at your library or another local public library. There are also sets that you can purchase from an educational resource center or online.

Millions of Years Ago
Adapted by M. Follis
(Tune: Wheels on the Bus)

The pterodactyl's wings went
Flap, flap, flap!,
Flap, flap, flap!
Flap, flap, flap!
Millions of years ago!

Additional verses:
Triceratops's horn went bump, bump, bump!
The Apatosaurus's teeth went chomp, chomp, chomp!
T-Rex's growl went roar, roar roar!

Early Literacy Tip:
Using visual cues (flannel board pieces) with a rhyme engages the senses of sight and hearing which will reach more types of learners.

Picture Books for Storytime

O'Connor, George. If I Had a Raptor. Somerville, MA: Candlewick Press, 2014.

This title, about a young girl fantasizing about having a pet velociraptor, will be especially funny to children with pet cats. Laugh along as the raptor snuggles on clean laundry, scratches the furniture, and stalks birds through a window.

Early Literacy Tip:
Encourage caregivers to talk with children about the silliness of a book while they are reading. For *If I Had a Raptor*, they can ask who else snuggles on clean laundry? Would a raptor really do that?

Shea, Bob. Dinosaur vs. Bedtime. New York: Hyperion Books for Children, 2008.

Little Dinosaur is pretty tough. He tackles and defeats anything that stands in his way; just ask that has been pile of leaves or the big slide. But bedtime is Dinosaur's biggest challenge and fight as he might, he may have met an opponent he just can't defeat. But then again, there are such things as a win-win situation. Shea's multimedia collage illustrations are perfect, and the overly dramatic comic book–style text explosions add drama to this little guy's strong will. Be sure to check out the other books in the Dinosaur Vs. collection.

Closing Song

See Welcome Song above.

Follow-Up Activities

Draw Dinosaurs

Court, Rob. How to Draw Dinosaurs. Chanhassen, MN: The Child's World, 2007.
Using only four simple steps each, this title illustrates how to draw an ammonite, ichthyosaur, ankylosaurus, plesiosaurus, iguanodon, pterodactyl, spinosaurus, diplodocus, dimorphodon, stegosaurus, velociraptor, triceratops, tyrannosaurus, and a fossil skeleton. Using a white board, chalk board, or piece of paper taped to a flannel board, draw one of the dinosaurs and have everyone follow along on their own sheet of paper. This activity is great for building fine motor skills in older preschoolers.

Dinosaur Footprint Craft

Either trace your young storytime goers feet on green construction paper or use the pattern provided at the end of the chapter.

Materials:

- Green construction paper
- Light brown sand paper
- Glue or glue sticks

Directions:

- Cut out the pattern pieces ahead of time from the appropriate color construction paper.
- Cut out dinosaur footprint from green construction paper according to pattern.
- Cut out the dinosaur nails or "claws" from brown sandpaper according to pattern.
- Have children adhere "claws" to the footprint.

Other Songs, Rhymes, and Fingerplays

I'm a Dinosaur
By J. Dietzel-Glair
(Tune: I'm a Little Teapot)

I'm a great big dinosaur
From long ago
I used to rule
Now I'm just bones
Everyone is still
Fascinated by me
But if I was here now
You'd want to flee! ROAR! (pretend to run quickly in place)

This Dinosaur
Adapted by J. Dietzel-Glair
(Rhyme: This Little Piggy)

This great big T-Rex eats meat.
This long apatosaurus eats plants.
This flying pterodactyl rules the skies.
And this speedy raptor isn't shy.
And this dinosaur egg holds a reptilian surprise. CRACK!

Additional Poetry

Florian, Douglas. Dinothesaurus. New York: Atheneum Books for Young Readers, 2009.
Florian devotes a two-page spread to each poem and his corresponding illustrations. A "Glossarysaurus" in the back offers a paragraph with more information about each dinosaur.

Hopkins, Lee Bennett and Barry Gott, illus. Dizzy Dinosaurs: Silly Dino Poems. New York: Harper, 2011.
Part of the "I Can Read!" series, the poems in this title are clever and fun. Topics include a messy triceratops, dinosaurs riding the bus to school, and bathtime. A helpful guide to dinosaur name pronunciation is given in the front of the book.

Lewis, J. Patrick and Frank Remkiewicz, illus. Scientrickery: Riddles in Science. New York: Harcourt, Inc., 2004.
Even though they have long since stopped roaming the planet, they still exist in the "corners of your mind." "T-Bones" is a riddle poem that will be quickly solved by dinosaur enthusiasts.

Weinstock, Robert. Can You Dig It? New York: Disney Hyperion, 2010.
With poems on fossils, stegosauruses, as well as other types of dinosaurs, this lends some light-hearted fun to these long-gone creatures. There's plenty of silliness as well, and it may be fun to point out some of the fiction here, like dinosaurs counting and eating sheep, and cave people living alongside the great lizards.

Additional Nonfiction

Ashby, Ruth and John Sibbick, illus. My Favorite Dinosaurs. New York: Milk and Cookies Press, 2005.
The illustrations in this volume are exquisite which is no surprise since they were done by a famed dinosaur artist. Pull the featured dinosaur type out of the text to share while everyone admires the art. Kids will look at this book for hours.

Jenkins, Steve. Prehistoric Actual Size. Boston: Houghton Mifflin, 2005.
Lots of animals lived during prehistoric times, not just dinosaurs. Explore life-size illustrations of the itty-bitty spiny shark, the giant millipede, and just the claw (it's all that will fit on the page) of the baryonyx. One fact or two on each animal is provided within the main text. Further information can be found at the back.

Judge, Lita. How Big Were Dinosaurs? New York: Roaring Brook Press, 2013.
Did you know the fearsome velociraptor was only the size of a dog? Unless you go to a museum, it is difficult to picture the true size of the mighty dinosaurs. Through illustrations and text, this title compares dinosaur sizes to familiar animals and objects. Read the entire text or just show the pictures and talk about the comparisons.

Additional Fiction Picture Books

Beaumont, Karen and Daniel Roode, illus. Dini Dinosaur. New York: Greenwillow Books, 2012.

Dini dinosaur has had a long day of playing in the mud. When it comes time for a bath, there seems to be some confusion on what you should wear to the tub. Each time he goes to wash a body part, he discovers it is still clothed. With a fun refrain of "scrub-a- dub-dub" and "Back you go! So . . ." young readers are given plenty of opportunity to participate. A prehistorically good time.

Clanton, Ben. Rex Wrecks It! Somerville, MA: Candlewick Press, 2014.

Where else can a robot, unicorn bunny, monster, and T-Rex be friends but in this alliterative and funny tale of friendship. By the end, Rex learns to play *with* his friends rather than destroying their creations and everyone is happier.

Duddle, Jonny. Gigantosaurus. Somerville, MA: Templar Books, 2014.

The boy who cried wolf, or in this case cried gigantosaurus, is back. Bonehead's friends run and hide every time he cries out a warning, until the time he really means it. Luckily, everyone survives and Bonehead apologizes for his trickery. The digital cartoon illustrations will appeal to kids who are accustomed to Pixar and Disney movies.

Dinosaur Foot Print Activity

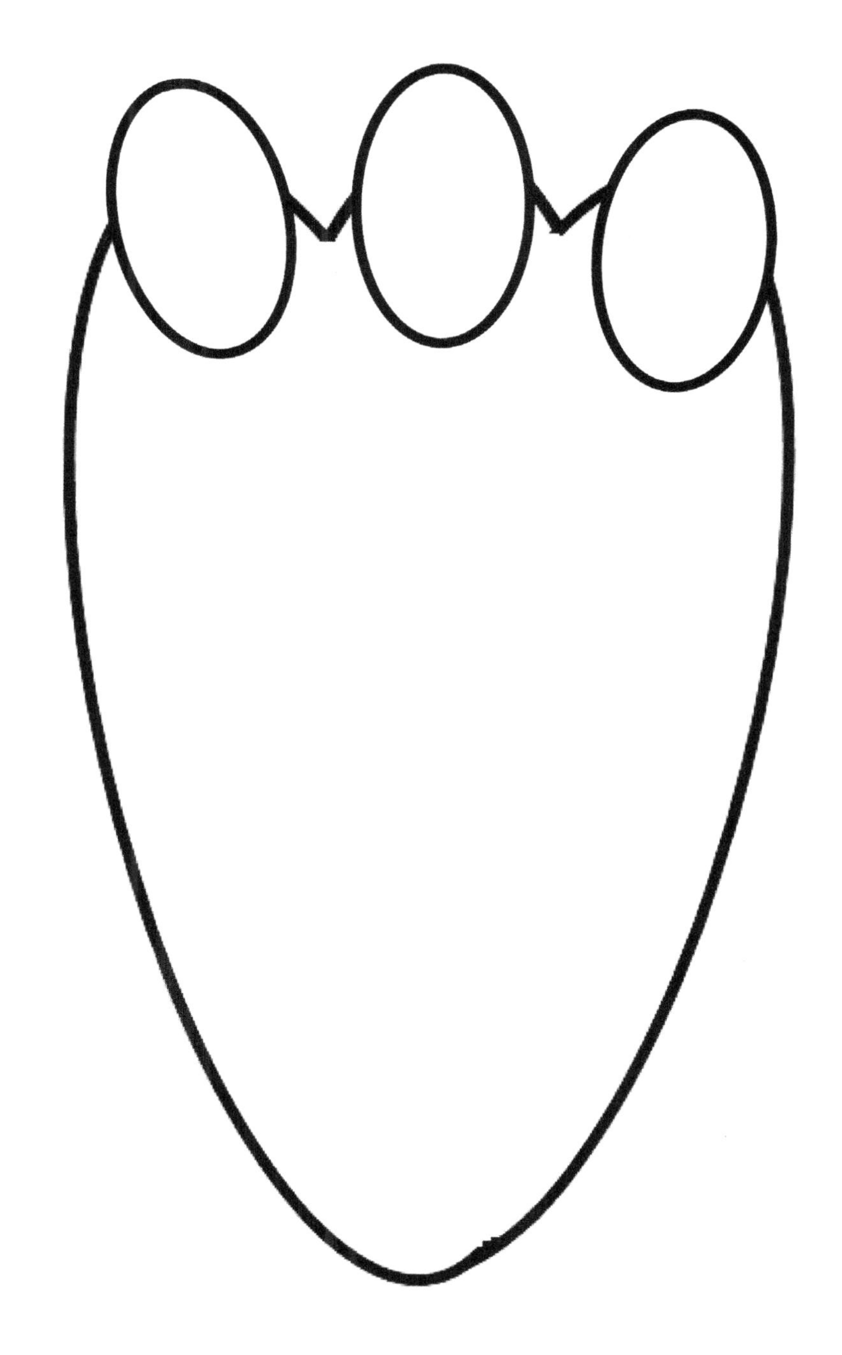

Dinosaur Footprint Pattern

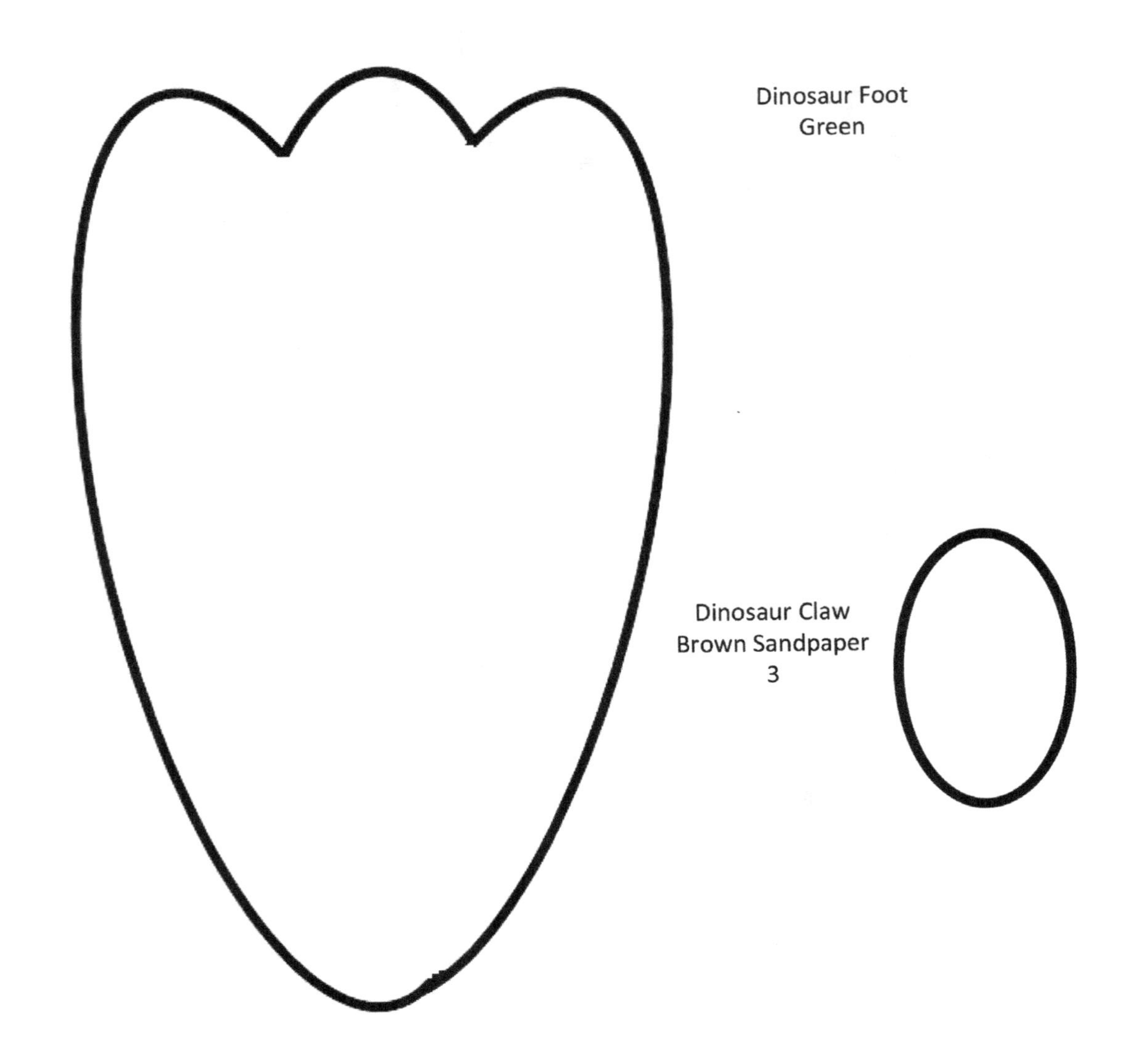

Dogs

With tails a wagging and tongues a drooling, dogs are not subtle creatures. Let them out to play with your little ones at storytime!

Sample Storytime

Welcome Song

Routine is important when working with children. Be sure to include welcome, transitional, and closing songs or activities to signify what is coming next. Don't be afraid to use the same ones; children take comfort in knowing what is coming next.

Opening Poem

"Oh Yes, Oh Yes!" from Gottfried, Maya and Robert Rahway Zakanitch, illus. Good Dog. New York: Alfred A. Knopf, 2005.
Read this poem in an excited tone like a dog that just has too much to say. Be sure to slow down your voice at the end when he finally lays down to rest.

Action Rhyme

Bingo
English Folk Song

There was a man who had a dog
And Bingo was his name-o
B-I-N-G-O
B-I-N-G-O
B-I-N-G-O
And Bingo was his name-o

There was a man who had a dog
And Bingo was his name-o
(clap)-I-N-G-O
(clap)-I-N-G-O
(clap)-I-N-G-O
And Bingo was his name-o

There was a man who had a dog
And Bingo was his name-o
(clap)-(clap)-N-G-O
(clap)-(clap)-N-G-O
(clap)-(clap)-N-G-O
And Bingo was his name-o

Keep replacing letters with claps until you are completely clapping the letters of the dog's name.

Nonfiction for Storytime

Montalván, Luis Carlos, Bret Witter, and Dan Dion, photography. Tuesday Tucks Me In: The Loyal Bond between a Soldier and His Service Dog. New York: Roaring Brook Press, 2014.
Tuesday is a service dog. He lives with Luis and helps him every day. This book is a gentle and sometimes funny introduction to service dogs. There are a couple of pages about Luis going to war; those uncomfortable sharing that topic with young children can skip those pages without losing the beauty of the rest of the book.

Transitional Song

See Welcome Song earlier.

Flannel Board Activity

Dog's Colorful Day

Create a flannel dog pattern using the pattern attached. Cut "spots" of color that correspond with the story and add as you read along. You'll need spots in the following colors: black, red, blue, green, brown, yellow, pink, gray, orange, and purple.

Dodd, Emma. Dog's Colorful Day: A Messy Story about Colors and Counting. New York: Dutton Children's Books, 2000.
When the day starts out, Dog has only one black spot on his ear. Throughout the day he gets into all sorts of messes and ends up with 10 colorful spots before a bath.

Be sure to have children recount the story with you, repeating the color names of all the spots and then recap by counting them.

Picture Books for Storytime

Seeger, Laura Vaccaro. Dog and Bear: Two Friends, Three Stories. New York: Neal Porter Book, 2007.
Three short stories about the friendship between a Dachshund and a toy teddy bear showing that there's fun to be had no matter how different you are. The short chapters make this fun for reading as a whole, or picking and choosing from among the "chapters." Colorful acrylic paints and plenty of white space make this a great book for sharing with a group. Check out the three other installments of this friendship including **Two's Company** (2008), **Three to Get Ready** (2009), and **Tricks and Treats** (2014).

Stein, David Ezra. I'm My Own Dog. Somerville, MA: Candlewick Press, 2014.
Told from the dog's point of view, this pup thinks he runs his own life. Eventually he gets a human that he trains to play fetch and that he cleans up after when the human spills food. This is a unique play on a pet story.

Closing Song

See Welcome Song earlier.

Follow-Up Activities

Dog Puppet

Using a brown paper bag and some simple cutout shapes, create a paper bag puppet. Patterns and a sample finished product are at the end of the chapter.

Materials:

- Construction paper in:
  - brown
  - pink
  - white
  - black
- Glue or glue sticks
- Brown paper lunch bags

Directions:

- Cut out the pattern pieces ahead of time from the appropriate color construction paper.
- Have children assemble the dog puppet by placing the following pieces on the puppy according to pattern.
  - ears
  - eyes
  - nose
  - tummy
- Sing "How Much Is That Doggie in the Window" and have puppets chime in with "Ruff, Ruff!"

Service Dogs

Invite service dogs into the library to visit and have the dog's handler explain what the dogs do and why they do it. Try contacting one of the following organizations to find service/therapy dogs in your area:

Karma Dogs: http://www.karmadogs.org/
National Association of Service Dogs: http://www.naservicedogs.org/
Patriot Paws: http://www.patriotpaws.org/
Pets on Wheels: http://petsonwheels.org/
Therapy Dogs International: http://www.tdi-dog.org/
Your local SPCA.

Other Songs, Rhymes, and Fingerplays

Church, Caroline Jayne. Do Your Ears Hang Low? New York: Scholastic, 2002.
Two floppy-eared puppies play along with this children's song. Pages in the back have suggested movements to make the song more interactive.

Early Literacy Tip:
Illustrated books of familiar songs give children the opportunity to "read" a book to you. This boosts narrative and print awareness skills.

Puppies
Adapted by J. Dietzel-Glair
(Tune: Ten Little Indians)

One little, two little, three little puppies
Four little, five little, six little puppies
Seven little, eight little, nine little puppies
Ten little puppies—WOOF WOOF WOOF!

Additional Poetry

Florian, Douglas. Bow Wow Meow Meow: It's Rhyming Cats and Dogs. San Diego, CA: Harcourt, Inc., 2003.
The first half of this title features poems about specific dog breeds. Each double-page spread contains one poem and an accompanying illustration. Hold up the book while reading the poem.

Gottfried, Maya and Robert Ralway Zakanitch, illus. Good Dog. New York: Alfred A. Knopf, 2005.
The varying personalities of dogs shines in this collection of poems. Each page also has an illustration of a different breed of dog making it accessible for sharing in storytime.

Rosen, Michael J. and Mary Azarian, illus. The Hound Dog's Haiku: And Other Poems for Dog Lovers. Somerville, MA: Candlewick Press, 2011.
Twenty breeds of dog are portrayed through haiku and woodcut illustrations. The book has the appearance of a storytime picture book. Choose a group of your favorites to read aloud.

Sklansky, Amy E. and Karla Firehammer, Karen Dismukes, Sandy Koeser, and Cathy McQuitty, illus. From the Doghouse: Poems to Chew On. New York: Henry Holt and Company, 2002.
This book of poetry is an ode to big dogs, little dogs, city dogs, and country dogs. The unique illustrations were created with beads.

Additional Nonfiction

Ajmera, Maya and Alex Fisher. A Kid's Best Friend. Watertown, MA: Charlesbridge, 2002.
No matter where you are in the world a dog can be your best friend. Minimal text speaks of the love between a child and his dog. The real stars of the book are photographs of children and their dogs from New Zealand to Argentina to Poland.

Neuman, Susan B. Jump, Pup! Washington, DC: National Geographic, 2014.
This puppy has a lot of energy to share through photographs and minimal text (some pages have only one word). Share the whole book with a storytime crowd. No one will be able to resist the adorable puppy.

Early Literacy Tip:
There are so many ways to effectively interact with a book: read the text, read parts of the text, look at the illustrations and talk about them without reading the text, let kids make up a story based on the illustrations. Be sure to model many different ways to "read" a book.

Simon, Seymour. Dogs. New York: HarperCollins Publishers, 2004.
Dogs come in so many shapes and sizes, as is evident from the variety shown in the full-page photographs. Use the pictures to introduce kids to the different types of dogs, simply show the picture, and tell them what kind of dog it is. You can also have fun with this book by asking the audience to give names to the dogs in each picture. The text in this book is simple yet lengthy; leave a copy available for a family to check out and share if they wish.

Additional Fiction Picture Books

Gal, Susan. Please Take Me for a Walk. New York: Alfred A. Knopf, 2010.
A perky black and white puppy gives a list of reasons why his owner should take him for a walk. He has things to do like chase the neighbor's cat, say hello to neighbors; he wants to see and be seen with his best friend (the walker!).

Haughton, Chris. Oh No, George! Somerville, MA: Candlewick Press, 2012.
When his owner leaves for the day, he asks his long-eared, sweet-eyed dog George if he will be good. Of course he will! Right? But temptation gets the better of George when he see the cat (who surely wants to play) and the cake (what good is an uneaten cake?). Of course his owner forgives his misdeeds, and takes George out for a walk where he shows remarkable restraint. Or does he? This book allows the readers to respond to George, and the bright art bursts off the page making this a great book for storytime sharing.

Kirk, Katie. Eli, No! New York: Abrams Books for Young Readers, 2011.
"Eli is a good dog, but sometimes bad . . . What do we say when we get mad? Eli, no!" And Eli is often bad over the next few pages, getting into all sorts of mischief. Invite young storytime goers to join you in the refrain "Eli, no!" But of course, no matter how poorly our puppy (or little storytime goers) misbehaves, the answer at the end of the day is always "yes" to the question, "Do they still love me?" Retro graphics in bright bold colors make this a fun book to peruse with loads of clean, clear details, and mischief.

Pritchett, Andy. STICK! Somerville, MA: Candlewick Press, 2013.
After finding a new stick, a little dog tries to get other animals to join in his fun and excitement with no luck. The pig is more excited about mud, and the cow grass. But soon the little pup meets another dog just as happy about the stick as he is. After the rest of the animals hijack the fun stick, the two dogs are left with something even better, a friend. Simple graphic designs, and one word per double page spread make this a short fun and very visually impactful book for sharing with young storytime goers.

Dog Flannel Board Pattern

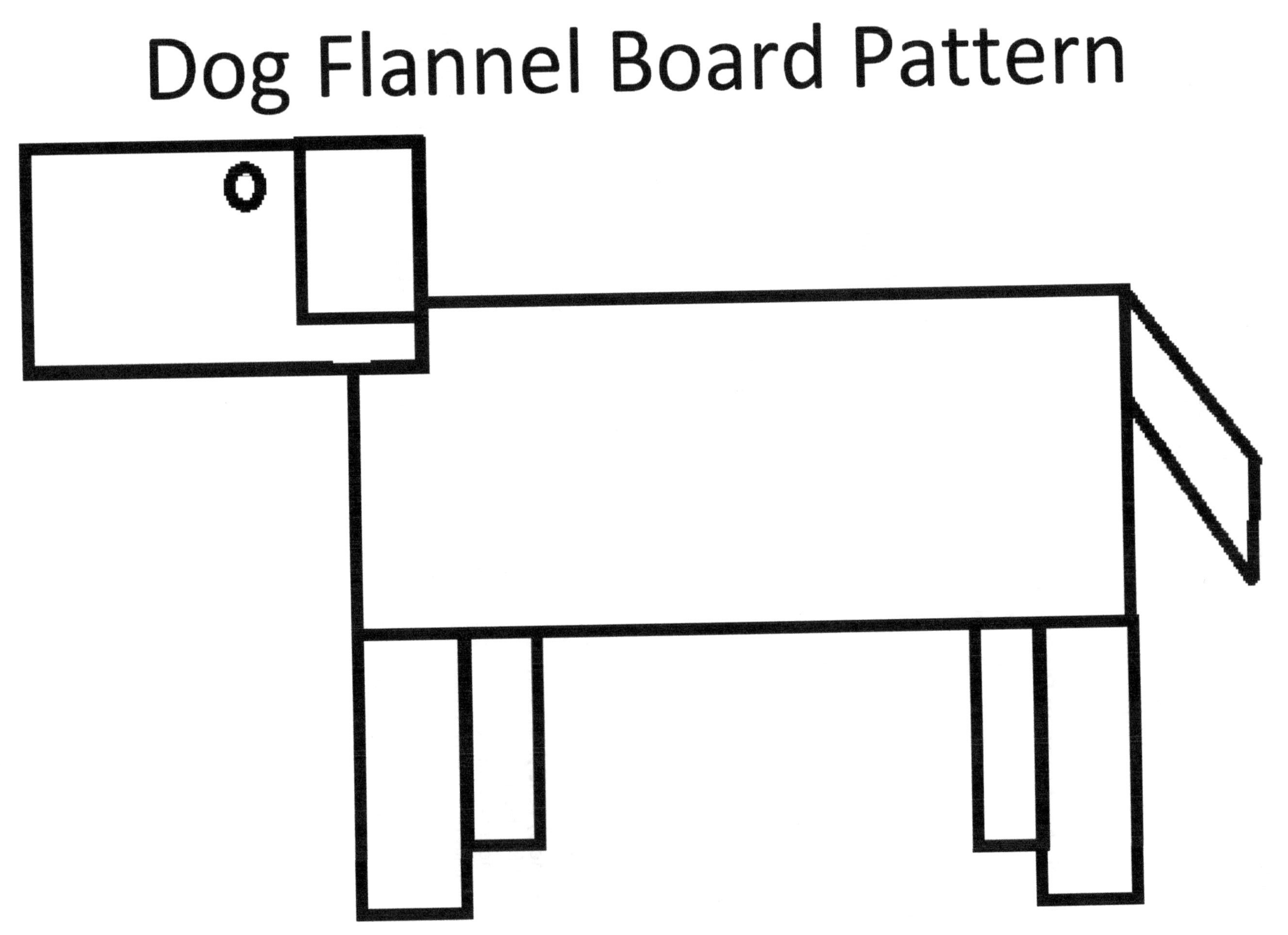

Finished Dog Puppet Pattern

Dog Puppet Pattern

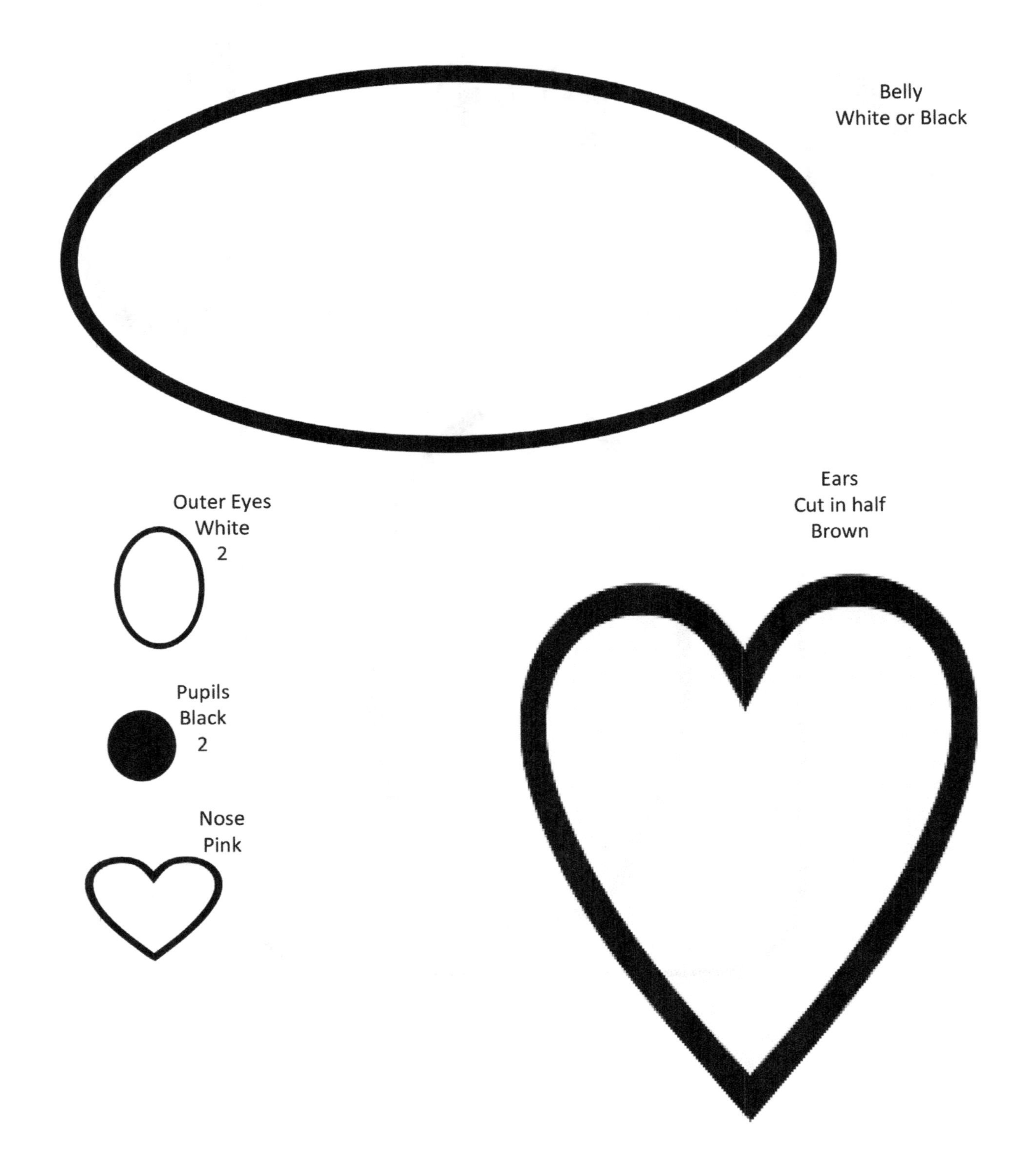

Ducks

More than any other bird, ducks have garnered the attention of young and old alike. Perhaps it is because they seem to share their fluffy little ones with the world. Have a quacking good time in this duck storytime.

Sample Storytime

Welcome Song

Routine is important when working with children. Be sure to include welcome, transitional, and closing songs or activities to signify what is coming next. Don't be afraid to use the same ones; children take comfort in knowing what is coming next.

Opening Poem

"A Solitary Wood Duck" from Yolen, Jane and Jason Stemple, photography. Birds of a Feather. Honesdale, PA: Wordsong, 2011.
Oh, wood duck, all alone on the pond, "we surrender to your beauty." Show the accompanying photograph and share a bit from the informational paragraph on the page. Did you know that wood ducks make their nests in tree holes?

Action Rhyme

Mr. Duck
Traditional Rhyme

Mr. Duck went out to walk, (hold one hand up forming a beak,
fingers together as the top, thumb as the bottom)
One day in pleasant weather.
He met Mr. Turkey on the way (hold up other hand as a beak)
And there they walked together.
"Gobble, gobble, gobble." (make one hand "talk")
"Quack, quack, quack." (make the other hand "talk")
"Goodbye, goodbye." (make both hands "talk")
And then they both walked back. (put hands behind your back)

Nonfiction for Storytime

Davies, Nicola and Salvatore Rubbino, illus. Just Ducks! Somerville, MA: Candlewick Press, 2012.
Learn about mallard ducks as a young girl shares her experience with the ducks in her city. The colorful mixed media illustrations make it an appealing storytime read. Additional facts are included on each page in a smaller font.

Transitional Song

See Welcome Song earlier.

Flannel Board Activity

Five Little Ducks

Use the pattern at the end of this chapter to create five little duck flannels. Start with all five on the board, and remove as indicated in the song.

Five Little Ducks
Traditional Rhyme

Five little ducks went out one day
Over the hill and far away,
Til the Momma Duck went "quack, quack, quack"
And four little ducks came waddling back

Continue the story, counting backwards as the ducks fail to return.

For a child friendly finish, you can always add these lines and actions:

Ask the crowd: "How do you think the Momma Duck feels? Is she happy? No. She may be a little . . . mad?"

Continue . . .
So Momma Duck went:
Quack, quack, quack, quack quack, quack (huffily with hands on hip)
Quack, quack, quack, quack quack, quack (wagging finger)
Quack, quack, quack, quack quack, quack
(pointing right index finger to left palm indicating
RIGHT HERE, RIGHT NOW!)
And who do you think came back

COUNT
1, 2, 3, 4, 5 (as you place ducks back on the flannel board)
And they went to bed without dinner
Because you should always listen to your Momma!

Picture Books for Storytime

Cronin, Doreen and Betsy Lewis, illus. Giggle, Giggle, Quack. New York: Simon & Schuster, 2002.
When Farmer Brown goes on vacation, he leaves his brother Bob in charge warning him to "keep an eye on Duck. He's trouble." And trouble he is. When Duck finds a pencil on the ground, he makes some small changes to Farmer Brown's instructions that lead to hilarious results. Be sure to have the children pay close attention to Duck too, and follow the unspoken story of our funny feathered friend.

Lurie, Susan and Murrary Head, photography. Swim, Duck, Swim! New York: Feiwel and Friends, 2014.
The expressive full-page photographs are the highlight in this story about trying something new. Preschoolers are also learning to swim so this book will echo many of their lives.

Closing Song

See Welcome Song earlier.

Follow-Up Activities

Five Little Ducks

This quick craft for children will allow them to re-create five little ducks song at home.

Materials:

- Photocopies of the pattern included at the end of this chapter
  - If possible, photocopy onto yellow copy paper
  - You will need five ducks per child
- Glue or glue sticks
- Craft sticks
- Optional: A typed copy of the song "Five Little Ducks"

Directions:

- Photocopy the duck pattern
- Depending on the motor skills of the child, you may want to cut out the ducks. It may be easiest to cut them into stamp-sized squares with the ducks centered.
- Have children adhere ducks onto craft sticks.
- Sing "Five Little Ducks" together.

Early Literacy Tip: Giving children props like puppets and letting them re-create the story or rhyme boosts narrative skills.

Other Songs, Rhymes, and Fingerplays

Silly Lil' Duck Goes . . .
Adapted by M. Follis
(Tune: Here We Go Round the Mulberry Bush)

Silly lil' duck goes waddle, waddle
Waddle, waddle
Waddle, waddle
Silly lil' duck goes waddle, waddle
So early in the morning!

Silly lil' duck goes quack, quack, quack, quack
Quack, quack, quack, quack
Quack, quack, quack, quack
Silly lil; duck goes quack, quack, quack, quack
Early in the morning!

Six Little Ducks

Watch adults and children play with puppets to this song on this YouTube video: https://www.youtube.com/watch?v=oq8qMjm6_8E. Along with modeling positive play, the video shows the words to the song as they are being sung.

Early Literacy Tip: Help parents and caregivers learn the words to rhymes and songs by posting the words on your flannel board during storytime. You can also locate YouTube videos that include the words.

Weines, Teri, illus. Five Little Ducks. Mankato, MN: The Child's World, 2011.
An illustrated version of a favorite duck song. Page 14 includes fun movements to go with each line of the song. The five ducklings in the illustrations have such personality, especially the leader.

Additional Poetry

Lewis, J. Patrick, ed. National Geographic Book of Animal Poetry: 200 Poems with Photographs That Squeak, Soar, and Roar! Washington, DC: National Geographic, 2012.
"Four Ducks on a Pond" by William Allingham (p. 149) are a memory "to remember for years." Adding to the joy of the seven-line poem is a photograph of four ducklings that seem to be swimming toward the rabbit on the facing page.

Ruddell, Deborah and Joan Rankin, illus. Today at the Blue-Bird Café: A Branchful of Birds. New York: Margaret K. McElderry Books, 2007.
Ducks get all the attention but there are lots of different aquatic birds. Expand the storytime topic by including "The Loon's Laugh" or "The Swan."

Early Literacy Tip:
Including loons and swans in storytime is a great way to introduce these birds to children who want to call every swimming bird a duck.

Additional Nonfiction

Hall, Margaret. Ducks and Their Ducklings. Mankato, MN: Capstone Press, 2004.
The short sentences contain duck vocabulary such as drake, egg tooth, and down. Large photographs give everyone lots to look at while you read the minimal text. Of specific interest is a double-page spread that shows four pictures of a duck from right after it hatches to four-five months of age.

Rustad, Martha E.H. A Baby Duck Story. Mankato, MN: Capstone Press, 2012.
The two snuggly ducklings on the cover of this book just beg to be read about. Full-page photographs show the progression of a duckling from egg to flying time. The text is simple and easy to understand.

Steinkraus, Kyla. Ducks on the Farm. Vero Beach, FL: Rourke Publishing, 2011.
Simple information about ducks is presented beside full-page photographs. Read the book or use some of the photographs to introduce a duck storytime. The up close photograph on the title page looks like the duck is staring you down and telling you to "Read this book."

Zobel, Derek. Ducks. Minneapolis, MN: Bellweather Media, 2012.
Part of the Blastoff! Readers series, this book has easy-to-read basic facts about ducks. The book focuses on Mallards but has pictures of a couple other types of duck. Those learning to read will be excited to attempt a book that was shared in storytime.

Additional Fiction Picture Books

Beaumont, Karen and Jose Aruego and Ariane Dewey, illus. Duck, Duck, Goose! (A Coyote's On the Loose!). New York: HarperCollins Publishers, 2004.
When word spreads that a coyote is on the loose the entire barnyard begins to panic, including the initial duck and goose who spread the tale in this fun rhyming cumulative romp. As the story nears its climax, those attentive to the illustration will be clued in to what is really going on at the farm!

Krilanovich, Nadia. Chicken, Chicken, Duck! Berkeley, CA: Tricycle Press, 2011.
A patterned choral of animal sounds make this a fun storytime read-aloud allowing for prediction and participation.

McCully, Emily Arnold. Little Ducks Go. New York: Holiday House, 2014.
When six little ducks fall down a storm drain, mama duck frantically runs along until they stop under a manhole cover and she is able to get help from a kind man. With only 39 unique words, this "I Like to Read" title can also be shared with new readers.

Moore, Eva and Nancy Carpenter, illus. Lucky Ducklings. New York: Orchard Books, 2013.
Based on a true story, when Mamma Duck and her five little duckling babies head out for a walk to town, they are stopped when the five ducklings fall into a storm grate. That might be the end of the story, but it's not! Learn about the rescue of the baby ducks by the citizens and community helpers of the town.

Nedwidek, John and Lee White, illus. Ducks Don't Wear Socks. New York: Penguin Books for Young Readers, 2008.
One day a very serious young girl named Emily encountered a duck wearing socks. "Ducks don't wear socks!" she said. "Cold feet" replied the duck." And for the next several days Emily continues to encounter this very silly duck until she finally breaks down and becomes a little silly herself. A laugh-out loud storytime book for those silly at heart.

Sloat, Teri. I'm a Duck! New York: Puffin Books, 2006.
The life and life cycle of a duck is told in this sweet picture book that combines a vintage feel and natural facts with a duck that fully celebrates his duckness: his quack, his wings, his flight, and soon his role as dad to some new ducklings.

Willems, Mo. The Duckling Gets a Cookie? New York: Hyperion Books for Young Children, 2012.
Of course Pigeon is not happy with the title! How did the Duckling get a cookie when Pigeon wants one too? No one ever hands *him* a cookie! What is the big deal about the Duckling? Pigeon asks for things all the time and is always told no! A slightly skewed lesson on manners in typical Mo Willems fashion.

Yamamura, Anji. Hannah Duck. La Jolle, CA: Kane/Miller Book Publishers, 2005.
A sweet quiet tale about a young duck's fear of the going out alone and the comfort and confidence friends can lend.

Early Literacy Tip:
Many pictures books are involving the reader as a "character" in the story. The Pigeon books by Mo Willems offer a lot of opportunities for audience participation. This adds another level of involvement and enjoyment to the book.

Duck Pattern

Eco-Friendly

All of us play a role in keeping our planet clean and safe and it's never too early to share this message with our children. The following books will help you convey this often weighty and controversial message in a fun and age-appropriate manner.

Sample Storytime

Welcome Song

Routine is important when working with children. Be sure to include welcome, transitional, and closing songs or activities to signify what is coming next. Don't be afraid to use the same ones; children take comfort in knowing what is coming next.

Opening Poem

"Where Are the Bees?" from Florian, Douglas. UnBEElievables. New York: Beach Lane Books, 2012.
Every living thing, from the biggest to the smallest, is affected by pollution, viruses, and pesticides. In a child-friendly way, this poem starts the conversation about bees and how they have been disappearing. Use this poem to start small and then build upon the concept.

Action Rhyme

Plant a Tree
By J. Dietzel-Glair and M. Follis
(Tune: Are You Sleeping)

Plant a tree, plant a tree (wave hands above your head like tree branches)
Dig a hole, dig a hole (pretend to dig a hole with a shovel)
Make sure it gets water, make sure it gets water (pretend to use a watering can)
It will grow, it will grow. (squat down, slowly stand up
like you are growing, and raise your hands in the air)

Nonfiction for Storytime

Root, Phyllis and Betsy Bowen, illus. Plant a Pocket of Prairie. Minneapolis, MN: University of Minnesota Press, 2014.
Plant foxglove beardtongue to attract hummingbirds or asters to entice silvery checkerspot butterflies. Follow along as a pocket of prairie grows and grows. The back matter is for older readers, but the illustrated beginning can be shared with a storytime crowd.

Early Literacy Tip:
Nonfiction books introduce vocabulary words through animal names. In *Plant a Pocket of Prairie* there aren't just butterflies; there are great spangled fritillaries and dakota skippers.

Transitional Song

See Welcome Song earlier.

Flannel Board Activity

E-A-R-T-H

Using die cuts of the letters E-A-R-T-H. Place the letters on the flannel board and ask kids to identify them as they go up.

Then sing this song:
(Tune: Bingo)

There's a big blue planet that I love
And EARTH is its name-0
E-A-R-T-H, E-A-R-T-H,
E-A-R-T-H,
And EARTH is its name-o!

Remove letters one by one and replace with a clap.
(ex. CLAP-A-R-T-H, CLAP-A-R-T-H, CLAP-A-R-T-H and Earth is its name-o!)

Picture Books for Storytime

Muldrow, Diane and Bob Staake, illus. We Planted a Tree. New York: A Golden Book, 2010.
Families from around the world, from New York to Kenya, plant a tree to make their world a better place. The tree provides a sanctuary for animals, fruit for the dinner plate, and clean air. A nod to the fact that saving the earth is a worldwide issue.

Schaefer, Carole Lexa and Pierr Morgan, illus. Cool Time Song. New York: Viking, 2005.
It's so very hot in the desert, but the animals come together at dusk to cool off and celebrate together. They beckon for people to join in their song of conservation and joy. Illustrations full of color and imagination will engage a storytime crowd.

Closing Song

See Welcome Song earlier.

Follow-Up Activities

Earth Craft

Materials:

- Coffee filters
- Washable blue and green markers
- Spray bottles filled with water
- White paper plates

Directions:

- Have children color coffee filters using blue and green markers. The pattern or design doesn't matter, as a matter of fact it makes it more interesting to have such a wide variety of results.
- When filters are colored, place filters on white paper plate.
- Have children "help" staff and/or parents spray the filters gently with water.

  Note: The wetter the filter the longer the drying time and the blurrier the colors. Three pumps should do it but experiment beforehand with your specific bottle.

- Let filter dry.

  Note: Because most follow-up activities are done at the end of storytime, the paper plate will help get the project home in one piece, even if we are creating a bit more trash. Ask parents to recycle the plate when the earth is dry.

Other Songs, Rhymes, and Fingerplays

I Love the Mountains

Popular with Girl Scout troops, this song celebrates the beauty of nature. A nice version with rolling photographs of natural scenes can be found on YouTube: https://www.youtube.com/watch?v=5ExQGwF0Z3g. Share the video or sing the song yourself.

I Love Trash

Oscar the Grouch loves trash most of all. Share this classic Sesame Street song with your storytime. Remember, if they put trash where it belongs they make Oscar happy: https://www.youtube.com/watch?v=rxgWHzMvXOY.

Trash that is put where it belongs helps to keep streets and streams clean. Encourage children to clean up after themselves by starting with their toys. After playtime, make clean up a game by singing a little song. Create your own rhythm for this short song. Keep singing until everything is back in its place. You can also use this tune in storytime as you put away scarves, shakers, or other instruments.

Toys Away

Toys away, toys away
Time to put the toys away.

Pick It Up!
M. Follis
(Tune: I've Been Working on the Railroad)

I put litter in a trash can
Not just on Earth Day
Bottles, cans are recycled
Each and every day
We take care of our planet
Keep it neat and tidy too
Together we can make a difference
I will! How 'bout you?

Additional Poetry

Coombs, Kate and Meilo So, illus. Water Sings Blue: Ocean Poems. San Francisco: Chronicle Books, 2012.

Look for poems that speak to the beauty and interconnectedness of the earth such as "Song of the Boat," "Sand's Story," "What the Waves Say," "Coral," and "Tideline." The watercolor illustrations capture the coolness of the water and the colors of the sea.

Heard, Georgia, ed. Falling Down the Page. New York: Roaring Brook Press, 2009.

"What Is Earth?" by J. Patrick Lewis asks some of the planet's inhabitants the same question . . . "What Is Earth?" Some answers are silly, but others poignant and important like that of the whale "A sea where I sing." Ask your little listeners what Earth is to them.

Martin Jr., Bill, Michael Sampson, and various illustrators. The Bill Martin Jr. Big Book of Poetry. New York: Simon & Schuster, 2008.

"Hurt No Living Thing" by Christina G. Rossetti (p. 49) reminds us all to be kind to the world we live in and its fellow inhabitants. A short sweet and gentle reminder to be kind.

Additional Nonfiction

Brenner, Barbara and Tom Leonard, illus. One Small Place in a Tree. New York: HarperCollins Publishers, 2004.

After a hole forms in a tree, it serves as a home for timber beetles, a flying squirrel, bluebirds, white-footed mice, and a redback salamander. Use this book with older preschoolers to show how a "dead" tree can be full of life.

Lyon, George Ella and Katherine Tillotson, illus. All the Water in the World. New York: Atheneum Books for Young Readers, 2011.

Lyrical verse brings the water cycle to life for young listeners. The celebration of keeping the Earth green is matched by textured and playful illustrations. This book begs to be read aloud.

Martin Jr., Bill, Michael Sampson, and Dan Lipow, illus. I Love Our Earth. Watertown, MA: Charlesbridge, 2006.

Travel across the planet with these photographs accompanied by short, lyrical text. Share the book with a storytime crowd to instill a love of the beauty that can be found.

Sayre, April Pulley and Kate Endle, illus. Trout Are Made of Trees. Watertown, MA: Charlesbridge, 2008.

We are all connected and this book illustrates that in the simplest manner. Collage illustrations demonstrate the food web and will give storytime attendees lots to look at.

Toft, Kim Michelle. The World That We Want. Watertown, MA: Charlesbridge, 2005.

Vibrant illustrations practically jump off the page while the interconnectedness of the planet is told through a sequential story. The back matter identifies each of the animals in the book.

Early Literacy Tip:

Encourage everyone to "read along" with sequential storylines. After reading a few pages, people may start to say the last line along with you. You can also pause before the last line to encourage people to say it with you.

Additional Fiction Picture Books

Base, Graeme. The Water Hole. New York: Harry N. Abrams, Inc., 2001.

Graeme's intricate illustrations show animals from around the world gathering at a watering hole that is slowly disappearing. When the rains finally come, it brings the animals back to harmony. The book started as a focus on the changing African seasons but can be used to explore water conservation.

Ghigna, Charles and Ag Jalkowska, illus. Pick Up the Park. North Mankato, MN: Picture Window Books, 2012.

Young children first list all of the things they enjoy doing while playing in the park and then list some of the ways they can help keep the park a clean and enjoyable place.

Gliori, Debi. The Trouble with Dragons. New York: Walker & Company, 2008.

Dragons are trouble. Not just for humans but for the whole world. They build too many roads. They cut down too many trees. Can they learn how to be better before it's too late? The onus of saving the planet is put on a fictitious animal but the real importance of conservation and protection is evident.

Wright, Maureen and Violet Kim, illus. Earth Day, Birthday. Tarrytown, NY: Marshall Cavendish Children, 2012.

While little monkey is busy counting down the days until his birthday, everyone else is preparing for Earth Day in a variety of ways. He tells everyone he meets, "It's not Earth Day! It's my birthday!" to which everyone responds "It's Earth Day, not your birthday!" The actions of the jungle friends are a great way to share with young readers the simple changes we can all take to celebrate earth day throughout the year. Fun jungle animals and a bright palette make this a good choice for storytime sharing.

Family

Families come in many shapes, colors, and configurations; the only common denominator is love. While children may understand the concept of family, they don't always understand the actual relationships between the members of their families. They don't always realize that grandpa is daddy's dad. A family storytime can help make those connections alongside the celebration of the love, learning, and fun that comes with family.

Sample Storytime

Welcome Song

Routine is important when working with children. Be sure to include welcome, transitional, and closing songs or activities to signify what is coming next. Don't be afraid to use the same ones; children take comfort in knowing what is coming next.

Opening Poem

"Who Is This Girl?" from Greenfield, Eloise and Jan Spivey Gilchrist, illus. Brothers & Sisters: Family Poems. New York: Amistad, 2009.

Told from the point of view of a new baby, this poem tells of the love between sisters. With only six lines, the poem is short and the accompanying illustration will help young children understand it.

Action Rhyme

Me and My Family
By M. Follis

Me and my family, we like to cook (pantomime stirring)
Me and my family, we like to play (bounce or jump)
Me and my family, we read books (mime reading books)
I love them more each and every day. (hug yourself)

Nonfiction for Storytime

Ajmera, Maya, Sheila Kinkade, and Cynthia Pon. Our Grandparents: A Global Album. Watertown, MA: Charlesbridge, 2010.

Photographs of children and their grandparents from around the world accompany brief text about their special bond. Read this book straight through in storytime to celebrate grandparents.

Transitional Song

See Welcome Song earlier.

Flannel Board Activity

My Family, My Heart

Materials:

- One large, red felt heart (large enough to fit all four of the family member felt pieces comfortably)
- A felt mother, father, sister, and brother. Use clip art or pieces you have from other rhymes you have done. You may also choose to use photographs from magazines of a mother, father, sister, and brother. Be sure to be sensitive to the ethnicities of your community.

Directions:

- Put the heart on the flannel board.
- As you sing the rhyme that follows, add each family member on top of the heart.

I Love My Family
By J. Dietzel-Glair
(Tune: Are You Sleeping?)

I love mommy, I love mommy
Yes I do, yes I do
She takes good care of me, she takes good care of me
How 'bout you? How 'bout you?

Additional verses:
I love daddy . . .
I love sister . . .
I love brother . . .

Picture Books for Storytime

Ryder, Joanne and Margie Moore, illus. Bear of My Heart. New York: Simon & Schuster Books for Young Readers, 2007.
A mother's love is like nothing else. It makes exploring better. It makes nighttime cozy. This story is a Mama Bear and her child, but the sentiment relates to all caring families.

Saltzberg, Barney. Tea with Grandpa. New York: Roaring Brook Press, 2014.
A young girl has tea with her grandpa every day. At the end of the story, readers are introduced to a modern twist as the girl and her grandpa are "meeting" through the computer. Many family members are far away yet this title, with minimal text, shows how they can still be close.

Early Literacy Tip:
The American Academy of Pediatrics recommends minimal screen time for young children. However, there are productive and educational ways for adults to use technology with children.

Closing Song

See Welcome Song earlier.

Follow-Up Activities

Draw Your Family

Materials:

- White construction paper
- Crayons

Directions:

- At the end of storytime have everyone draw a picture of their family. They may choose to include extended family members and pets.

Family Tree

Materials:

- Copies of the tree pattern found in the Trees chapter (one for each child)
- Copies of the leaf pattern found in the Tree chapter (multiple for each child)
- Crayons
- Glue sticks

Directions:

- Let every child color their tree coloring sheet.
- With help from the caregiver with them, write the names of their immediate family members on leaves. (One person per leaf.)
- Glue the leaves onto the tree.

Early Literacy Tip:
Don't shy away from concepts that children may not fully understand. The concept of a family tree is complex (especially with blended families) but it is still a fun activity that introduces the topic.

Other Songs, Rhymes, and Fingerplays

My Family Loves Me
Adapted by J. Dietzel-Glair
(Tune: You Are My Sunshine)

My family loves me
They really love me
They make me happy
When skies are grey
We play games and
We read together
My family rocks
In every single way

One Big Family
Adapted by J. Dietzel-Glair
(Tune: Ten Little Indians)

One little, two little, three little brothers
Four little, five, little, six little sisters
Seven little, eight little, nine little cousins
1 big family reunion

Wright, Danielle, collected by, and Mique Moriuchi, illus. My Village: Rhymes from around the World. London: Frances Lincoln Children's Books, 2010.
We have much to learn from our grandparents and the traditional Australian rhyme titled "Grandfather" is a child asking his grandfather to teach him.

Additional Poetry

Greenfield, Eloise and Jan Spivey Gilchrist, illus. Brothers & Sisters: Family Poems. New York: Amistad, 2009.
Broken into sections for Brothers, Sisters, and then the combination of both, each poem has a watercolor illustration to support the text.

Martin Jr., Bill, Michael Sampson, and various illustrators. The Bill Martin Jr. Big Book of Poetry. New York: Simon & Schuster, 2008.
There is a wide variety of family-themed poems on pages 122–128, including "My Little Sister" (William Wise, p. 127), "In My Daddy's Arms" (Folami Abiade, p. 124) and "Grandpa's Stories" (Langston Hughes, p. 122) to name a few.

Vardell, Sylvia and Janet Wong, ed. The Poetry Friday Anthology for Celebrations. Princeton, NJ: Pomelo Books, 2015.
An older sibling compares what they can do and what their little baby brother or sister can do in "I'm Bigger" by Kristy Dempsey (p. 111). And even though they can do so much more, they "still love you best of all!"

It's hard living far away from family, especially your grandparents, abuelo and abuela. But they can still "send . . . besitos across the long miles." Celebrate the love of family with "Far Away on Grandparents Day" by Julie Larios (p. 235).

And no two families look the same, as explained in "Our Blended Family" (p. 245) by Doraine Bennett. We are a colorful lot "stitched together with threads of love."

Vardell, Sylvia and Janet Wong, ed. The Poetry Friday Anthology for Science: Poems for the School Year Integrating Science, Reading and Language Arts, K-5 Teacher Edition. Princeton, NJ: Pomelo Books, 2014.
In "Hand Me Downs" by George Ella Lyon (p. 72), a child ponders the similarities in family appearances. When the child's mother explains that he will learn all about genes when he grows up, but the child looks down at his pants and thinks he can't wait "to learn what jeans can do."

Additional Nonfiction

Adamson, Heather. Families in Many Cultures. Mankato, MN: Capstone Press, 2008.
Simple text and full-page photographs show that families around the world have much in common. While a preschooler may not understand the concept of a family in another country, this book may help them realize that the family next door acts just like their family even though they look different.

Kerley, Barbara. You and Me Together: Moms, Dads, and Kids around the World. Washington, DC: National Geographic Society, 2005.
Large photographs, many of them covering double-page spreads, show children and parents sharing their lives. The idea of doing things "together, me and you" is repeated numerous times in the text.

Additional Fiction Picture Books

Lang, Suzanne & Max. Families, Families, Families! New York: Random House, 2015.
A fun and funny grouping of animals demonstrates all the many combinations that can create a family, but in the end "if you love each other, then you are a family!" Large-eyed cartoon animals pop off photographed backgrounds, in cool framed visuals.

Levine, Arthur A and Julian Hector, illus. Monday Is One Day. New York: Scholastic, 2011.
Several families deal with the challenges of a workweek through snuggles, raspberries on the nose, and counting down the days until the fun day of Sunday.

Yolen, Jane and Laurel Molk, illus. Off We Go! New York: Little, Brown and Company, 2000.
The baby animals are off to visit Grandma. With phrases like "tip-toe, tippety toe," "slither-slee, slithery slee," and "scritch-scratch, scritchity scratch" repeated throughout, this book is as much fun to read as it is to look at.

Farm Animals

Ever since that farmer, what's his name? MacDonald! That's the one! Ever since the MacDonald guy started listing off his farm animals, we have all been able to moo on command. Here's your chance to learn fun facts, quack like a duck, snort like a pig, and basically raise the barn roof during storytime.

Sample Storytime

Welcome Song

Routine is important when working with children. Be sure to include welcome, transitional, and closing songs or activities to signify what is coming next. Don't be afraid to use the same ones; children take comfort in knowing what is coming next.

Opening Poem

Lewis, J. Patrick, ed. National Geographic Book of Animal Poetry: 200 Poems with Photographs That Squeak, Soar, and Roar! Washington, DC: National Geographic, 2012.
The photography in this book is as poetic as the actual words. Pages 20–21 house four cow poems, each suitable and fun for a preschool crowd. Choose the one that you like best and be sure to share the picture of the cow staring you down and daring you to read his lyrical words.

Action Rhyme

Here Is the Barn
By J. Dietzel-Glair

Here is the barn (put your finger tips together to form a triangular barn roof)
Here is the sty (create a box with your fingers)
See all the pigs (oink oink oink)
They can't fly (shake your head while flapping your arms like you are flying)

Here is the barn (put your fingers together to form a triangular barn roof)
Here is the field (hold your arms out wide)
See all the horses (neigh neigh)
Galloping full speed (run quickly in place)

Nonfiction for Storytime

Kalman, Bobbie. Farm Animals. New York: Crabtree Publishing Company, 2011.
A very basic book that is easily accessible for a young audience. It covers the animals that you can typically find on a farm, along with interesting facts about them. Bright bold color photographs and clear simple sentences against a white background make this also a good book for those learning to read. Front matter includes words to know, and helpful back matter help adults build upon the reading content.

Transitional Song

See Welcome Song earlier.

Flannel Board Activity

Baa, Baa Black Sheep

Using the pattern at the end of the chapter (or a die-cut machine), create sheep in a variety of colors. See the familiar song that follows changing the color for each sheep.

Baa, Baa, Black Sheep
Traditional English Nursery Rhyme

Baa, baa, black sheep
Have you any wool?
Yes sir, yes sir
Three bags full
One for my master
And one for my dame
And one for the little boy
Who lives down the lane.

Continue with other colored sheep: baa, baa, red sheep . . . baa, baa, purple sheep.

Picture Books for Storytime

Bunting, Eve and Jeff Mack, illus. Hurry! Hurry! Orlando, FL: Harcourt, Inc., 2007.
The new chick is about to be born and you're going to miss it if you don't hurry. The intensity of the moment is strengthened through the use of only two repetitive words per page.

Gibbs, Edward. I Spy on the Farm. Somerville, MA: Templar Books, 2012.
Part guessing game, part introduction to colors, kids will want to share this book with everyone in their family. A small circular cutout reveals part of the next animal along with their color and the sound they make. Kids will be screaming out the answers before you can flip the page.

Closing Song

See Welcome Song earlier.

Follow-Up Activities

Farm Visits

Many farms allow visitors to come pet animals or just observe farm activities. Check with local farms near you to see if they allow families to visit. If so, create a sheet with addresses and visiting hours to share with storytime families.

Milk a Cow

Materials:

- Rubber gloves
- Milk or water

- Safety pin
- A plastic cup or bucket

Directions:

- Fill the glove with milk or water.
- Tie the open end of the glove so that the milk or water is sealed inside.
- Use the pin to prick a hole in one of the fingers of the glove. (Depending on the strength of the glove, you may need to enlarge the hole by moving the pin in a circular motion. Experiment ahead of time.)
- Hold the glove over the plastic cup and let kids try to "milk the cow."

Other Songs, Rhymes, and Fingerplays

Little Bo Peep
English Nursery Rhyme

Little Bo-Peep has lost her sheep
And doesn't know where to find them
Leave them alone, and they'll come home
Wagging their tails behind them

Little Boy Blue
English Nursery Rhyme

Little Boy Blue,
Come blow your horn,
The sheep's in the meadow,
The cow's in the corn;
Where is that boy
Who looks after the sheep?
Under the haystack
Fast asleep.

Old MacDonald
Traditional Children's Song

Old MacDonald had a farm
E-I-E-I-O
And on that farm he had a cow
E-I-E-I-O
With a moo-moo here
And a moo-moo there
Here a moo, there a moo
Everywhere a moo-moo
Old MacDonald had a farm
E-I-E-I-O

Additional Verses:
Had a horse . . . neigh-neigh
Had a sheep . . . baa-baa
Had a goat . . . maa-maa
Had a pig . . . oink-oink

Horsey, Horsey
Traditional Nursery Rhyme

Horsey, horsey, don't you stop. (gallop to the beat)
Just let your feet go clippety clop,
Your tail goes swish, your feet go round.
Giddyup, we're homeward bound.

Early Literacy Tip:
Don't feel like you have to change things up for every storytime. Familiar songs and rhymes build confidence in children.

Wright, Danielle, collected by, and Mique Moriuchi, illus. My Village: Rhymes from around the World. London: Frances Lincoln Children's Books, 2010.
"Tingalay-o!" is a traditional Jamaican rhyme. It's fun to say with a Jamaican lilt and has a lot of opportunity for fun movements from leaping to kicking to eating to hee-hawing.

Additional Poetry

Elliott, David and Holly Meade, illus. On the Farm. Cambridge, MA: Candlewick Press, 2008.
All the usual suspects are here, plus a few new friends including snake, bees, and turtle. Make this poetry book interactive by having everyone make the animal's sound after reading its poem. By the end of the book, kids will be making the sound as soon as the page is turned.

Gottfried, Maya and Robert Rahway Zakanitch, illus. Our Farm. New York: Alfred A. Knopf, 2010.
Stories of the animals of Farm Sanctuary told in poems and painterly style illustrations.

Lewis, J. Patrick, ed. National Geographic Book of Animal Poetry: 200 Poems with Photographs That Squeak, Soar, and Roar! Washington, DC: National Geographic, 2012.
This title is filled with so many elegant poems, so it is difficult to choose favorites. Aileen Fisher's "Horses" (p. 35) is a practical ode to the usefulness of a horse's tail. Delight in the happiness of a pig that has all he needs in Myra Cohn Livingston's "Summertime" (p. 133).

Shannon, George, Lynn Brunelle, and Scott Menchin, illus. Chicken Scratches: Poultry Poetry and Rooster Rhymes. San Francisco: Chronicle Books, 2010.
This humorous collection of 16 poems borders on irreverent. A rooster is given chicken soup to make him feel better. A chicken lays a cantaloupe after eating a pack of seeds.

Additional Nonfiction

Gibbons, Gail. Chicks & Chickens. New York: Holiday House, 2003.
With diagrams of the different parts of the chicken and child-friendly narrative, this book is a wonderful introduction to nonfiction for preschoolers. With information on the history of chickens, the different way that chickens "sing," and the different varieties of birds, this book can be read up and down the age levels.

Kalman, Bobbie. Baby Pigs. New York: Crabtree Publishing, 2010.
Part of the "It's Fun to Learn about Baby Animals" series, this book covers some great vocabulary words like that baby pigs are called piglets, and that there are many types of

pigs, some domestic and some wild. Big color photographs make the series appropriate for sharing with a group while reading select text.

Marsh, Laura. Ponies. Washington, DC: National Geographic Society, 2011.
Older preschoolers may be able to read parts of this National Geographic Reader that is filled with photographs of ponies. Share the photograph on pages 4–5 to entice a family to bring this book home.

Merritt, Robin. The Life Cycle of a Chicken. Mankato, MN: The Child's World, 2012.
This book is filled with information about chickens; however, each double-page spread has a full-page photograph of a chicken or egg. By reading just the captions, this book can be enjoyed by a young child.

Additional Fiction Picture Books

Beaumont, Karen, Jose Aruego, and Ariane Dewey, illus. Duck, Duck, Goose! (A Coyote's on the Loose!). New York: HarperCollins Publishers, 2004.
When word spreads that a coyote is on the loose, the entire barnyard begins to panic, including the initial duck and goose who spread the tale in this fun-rhyming cumulative romp. As the story nears its climax, those attentive to the illustration will be clued in to what is really going on at the farm!

Fox, Mem and Judy Horacek, illus. Where Is the Green Sheep? Orlando, FL: Harcourt, Inc., 2004.
There's a blue sheep, a thin sheep, even a clown sheep, but the green sheep is missing. Don't worry, he hasn't gone far, he's just sleeping by the green bush. You'll find lots of great descriptor words like braved, scared, near, and far in this woolly book.

Early Literacy Tips:
Many books present opportunities for creativity in storytime attendees. At the end of *Where Is the Green Sheep?* ask children what other kind of sheep they would like to see.

Weeks, Sarah and Holly Berry, illus. I'm a Pig. New York: HarperCollins Publishers, 2005.
There's is nothing better in this world than being a pig, at least according to the narrator and star of this book. Pay attention to the illustrations as they add special humor to the book.

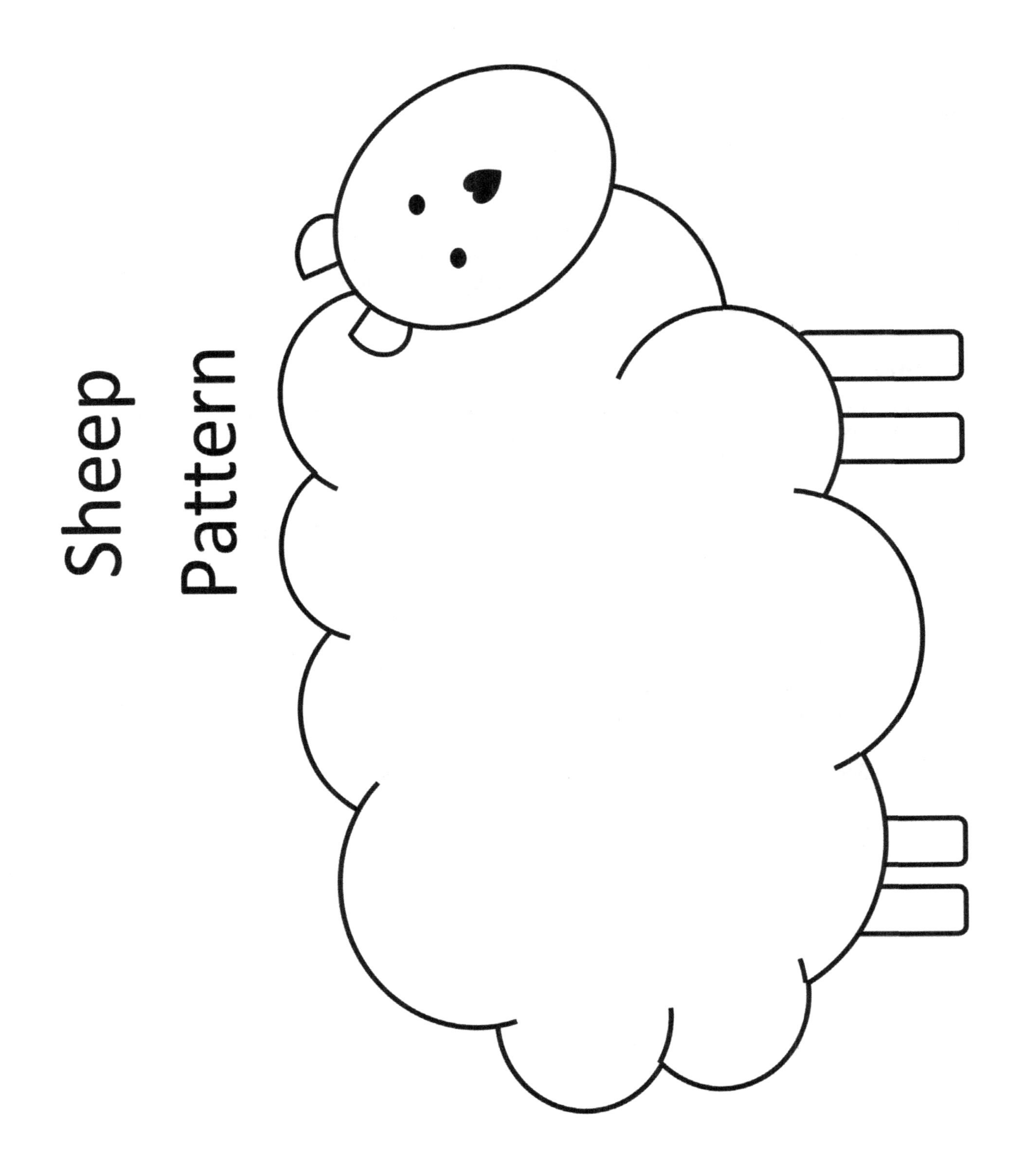
Sheep
Pattern

Feelings

It's tough being a child. From the moment you are born you have feelings you need to express and from that same moment, you try to find ways to convey these feelings to the big people around you. Sadly, these feelings get more and more complicated during the preschool years. Giving children the vocabulary to express themselves and their feelings is an important part of teaching them how to identify these feelings and communicate them. We hope the following storytime makes you happy!

Sample Storytime

Welcome Song

Routine is important when working with children. Be sure to include welcome, transitional, and closing songs or activities to signify what is coming next. Don't be afraid to use the same ones; children take comfort in knowing what is coming next.

Opening Poem

"Happy" from Cain, Janan. The Way I Feel. Seattle, WA: Parenting Press, Inc., 2000.
How can you tell if someone is happy? Could it be the "smile you see on my face?" or the soaring high mood?

Action Rhyme

If You're Happy and You Know It
Created and copyrighted by Joe Raposo

This popular song can include as many verses as you like:
Clap your hands
Stomp your feet
Shout "Hooray"
Do all three

And more verses of your creation.

Nonfiction for Storytime

Miller, Connie Colwell. Happy Is . . . Mankato, MN: Capstone Press, 2012.
From the very first photo of five children smiling down at you, the essence of happiness shines through. The large photographs are then accompanied by rhyming text describing happiness as a tingly tummy, a full heart, and sloppy dog kisses. Preschoolers understand the feeling of happiness, and this book gives them words to go along with that feeling.

Put out other titles in the Know Your Emotions series for families to check out after storytime:

Miller, Connie Colwell. Angry Is . . . Mankato, MN: Capstone Press, 2011.
Nichols, Cheyenne. Scared Is . . . Mankato, MN: Capstone Press, 2012.
Salas, Laura Purdie. Sad Is . . . Mankato, MN: Capstone Press, 2011.

Transitional Song

See Welcome Song earlier.

Flannel Board Activity

There are many posters of emotions available online or in teacher supply stores. The posters show faces for happy, sad, angry, embarrassed, and so on. Purchase one that is on sale and cut it up to make flannel pieces for this story. Each emotion/face should be its own piece. If the poster isn't already a durable material, laminate the pieces before gluing a piece of felt to the back.

Put the appropriate pieces on the flannel board and share this story:

It's Monday morning and Sam just woke up. He gets out of bed and heads to the bathroom to brush his teeth.

Ouch! Sam has bumped his knee on the edge of his toy box.

Which face do you think Sam is wearing right now?

Sam goes downstairs and sees that his grandmother has made him pancakes! His favorite!

Which face do you think Sam is wearing now?

Sam walks to school and remembers he left his lunch at home. Oh no, he is so mad at himself for forgetting!

Which face do you think Sam is wearing now?

When he gets to school, a girl named Maya jumps out of the bushes and yells "Boo!" Sam is so scared he jumps!

Which face do you think Sam is wearing now?

Then he sees that it is just Maya. They are best friends and do everything together . . . including trying to trick each other. Sam laughs!

Which face do you think Sam is wearing now?

When he gets to his classroom he sees his father there, holding his lunch. "Thank you!" Sam says and gives his dad a hug.

Which face do you think Sam is wearing now?

So many faces and so many feelings! And it is only 8 o'clock!

Early Literacy Tip:
Published books aren't the only way to tell stories. Encourage parents to make up simple stories with their child as the lead character.

Picture Books for Storytime

Macdonald, Maryann and Jana Christy, illus. How to Hug. Tarrytown, NY: Marshall Cavendish, 2011.

Hugs can make you feel wonderful, and this is a humorous instruction book on how to do it right. For example, it's okay to say no to a stinky hug from a skunk. Whereas bear hugs can be super special. A cast of animal and human character join this joyous "training" experience.

Seeger, Laura Vaccaro. Bully. New York: Roaring Brook Press, 2013.

No one likes being left out or being made fun of. Bully finds this out the hard way when he discovers that he is being a big bully. With only 22 words, so much of this story is told through the illustrations. The concept of bullying is presented simply yet effectively for the age group.

Closing Song

See Welcome Song earlier.

Follow-Up Activities

Mirror Play

As children are learning about emotions, they are also learning to recognize those emotions in others. One way to help them is to have them practice making different faces in a mirror. Small mirrors can be relatively cheap to purchase at dollar stores.

Directions:

- Give every child and caregiver pair a mirror.
- Ask the caregiver to model a happy face.
- Then ask the kids to try to make a similar face while looking in the mirror.
- Do the same with a sad face, mad face, scared face, and surprised face.

Other Songs, Rhymes, and Fingerplays

What I'm Feeling
By J. Dietzel-Glair
(Tune: Are You Sleeping?)

When I'm happy, when I'm happy
I smile wide, I smile wide (point to your cheeks and smile big)
I giggle and I laugh, I giggle and laugh (hold your stomach like you are laughing hard)
Everyone smiles, everyone smiles

When I'm mad, when I'm mad
I stomp my feet, stomp my feet (stomp your feet)
But I turn it into a song, but I turn it into a song
With a happy beat, with a happy beat (dance happy)

When I'm sad, when I'm sad
Then I cry, then I cry (pretend to rub your eyes like you are crying)
But things will get better, but things will get better
Give it time, give it time (smile)

Early Literacy Tip:
Feelings are difficult. Songs and books can help children understand their feelings and express them appropriately.

"Happy" by Pharrell Williams.
The beat for this song is so infectious that it's not hard to believe it was so popular on the radio. The official music video shows people from all walks of life dancing along. Show the video or just play the song for a happy dance party. (https://www.youtube.com/watch?v=y6Sxv-sUYtM)

Additional Poetry

Brown, Calef. We Go Together: A Curious Collection of Affectionate Verse. New York: Houghton Mifflin Books for Children, 2013.
This title may be small in trim, but it is full of affection, especially the happiness and joy felt when with friends. In "Mirth Makers," friends "laugh and sing and jump and shout"

comparing their day to a birthday cake. In "Laughers" the two separate laughs of friends are combined to create something new.

Greenfield, Eloise and Jan Spivey Gilchrist, illus. Honey I Love. New York: HarperCollins Publishers, 2003.

A young joy-filled girl tells the reader all of the things in her life that she loves and that make her happy. From simple things like the way her cousin talks, her friends laugh, and the feeling of her mother's arms. With the repeating refrain of "Honey, let me tell you that I love . . ." the reader is surrounded by the love this little girl finds in life. Except bedtime. She doesn't love that.

Hopkins, Lee Bennett, ed. and Sachiko Yoshikawa, illus. Hamsters, Shells and Spelling Bees: School Poems. New York: HarperCollins, 2008.

"Not Fair" by David L. Harrison shares a feeling most people experience every now and then, of having to do something when you would rather being doing something else.

Micklos, Jr. John, ed. and Lori McElrath-Eslick, illus. Mommy Poems. Honesdale, PA: Boyds Mills Press, 2001.

When young children misbehave, they go through the emotions of feeling "Bad, Mad, Sad and Glad," after talking over their feelings with mom. A quick rhyme with repetition, this poem by John Micklos, Jr., is easily shared with young ones, who have experienced the same range of emotions.

Additional Nonfiction

Argassi, Martine, PhD. Hands Are Not for Hitting. Minneapolis, MN: Free Spirit Publishing, 2000.

This book asks children if they have ever let their hands be influenced by their feelings and then offers other alternatives to hitting. A great entry point for discussions on feelings and how they influence actions and steps we all can take to redirect these feelings.

Kaiser, Ruth. The Smiley Book of Colors. New York: Golden Books, 2012.

Smiles are all around if you just know where to look. Sometimes there is a smiley face in your bowl of yellow macaroni. Sometimes it's in the way a pink hat is laying on a shelf. Photographs of artistic smiles are accompanied by inspirational text that encourages the reader to smile and choose a good life.

Additional Fiction Picture Books

Diesen, Deborah and Dan Hanna, illus. The Pout-Pout Fish. New York: Farrar Straus Giroux, 2008.

Many animals try to cheer up the pout-pout fish, but he feels he is destined to always spread sadness. As a testament to never giving up, one last fish tries to change his mood. Apparently, all he needed was a kiss. Kids will enjoy the repetition of the pout-pout fish's grief mantra.

Mack, Jeff. Good News Bad News. San Francisco, CA: Chronicle Books, 2012.

With just two words of text and some expressive characters, a series of good and bad events tell the tale of an unfortunate picnic and the range of emotions that go with it.

OHora, Zachariah. No Fits Nilson. New York: Dial Books for Young Readers, 2013.

Amelia and her gorilla friend Nilson do everything together. But sometimes Nilson gets upset and they both have to take a "time-out." When Amelia's mom promises them ice cream in exchange for good behavior during errands, Amelia tries her hardest to keep

Nilson under control with some unexpected results. Many children, and parents too, will be able to relate to Nilson and his outbursts.

Van Hout, Mies. Happy. New York: Lemniscaat, USA, 2012.
Each two-page spread is devoted to one emotion and a fish expressing that feeling. Set against a black background each fish in this book seems to radiate from the page. Even the hand-drawn words are expressive. This book is ideal for asking open-ended questions such as "What tells you that this fish is sad?"

Witek, Jo, and Christine Roussey, illus. In My Heart. New York: Abrams Appleseed, 2013.
When you are sad, your heart can feel "heavy as an elephant." But when it's silly, it is "full of giggles and wiggles." Cutout pages of hearts add whimsy to this simple explanation of emotions.

Yolen, Jane and Mark Teague, illus. How Do Dinosaurs Say I Love You? New York: The Blue Sky Press, 2009.
It can be difficult to love a dinosaur when it fusses with its food or kicks the back of a car seat, but just like any family, its moms and dads always love it. This is a humorous reminder that we are loved even when we make mistakes.

Fish

Swimmy, scaly, silly fish. They are slippery to the touch and fun to watch. Many kids have been to an aquarium or seen a fish tank so this is a familiar animal to them.

Sample Storytime

Welcome Song

Routine is important when working with children. Be sure to include welcome, transitional, and closing songs or activities to signify what is coming next. Don't be afraid to use the same ones; children take comfort in knowing what is coming next.

Opening Poem

"Haiku" from Lewis, J. Patrick, ed. National Geographic Book of Animal Poetry: 200 Poems with Photographs That Squeak, Soar, and Roar! Washington, DC: National Geographic, 2012.

Fish dance in Joan Bransfield Graham's stage-setting haiku (p. 13). The photograph is teeming with fish just ready to jump off the page and into your storytime.

Action Rhyme

Once I Caught a Fish
Traditional Rhyme

One, two, three, four, five (count to five on your fingers)
Once I caught a fish alive (pretend to reel in a fish)
Six, seven, eight, nine, ten (count to ten using the fingers on your other hand)
Then I let him go again (mime throwing the fish back)
Why did you let him go? (hold up both hands as if asking why)
Because he bit my finger so.
Which finger did he bite?
This little finger on the right. (hold up your right pinky finger)

Early Literacy Tip:
When demonstrating right and left (as in the end of "Once I Caught a Fish"), you may wish to hold up your *left* hand. Children will mirror your actions and this will help them learn left from right which is important when they start to read.

Nonfiction for Storytime

Stockdale, Susan. Fabulous Fishes. Atlanta, GA: Peachtree Publishers, 2008.

The waters are full of fishes of all shapes and sizes. Minimal rhyming text describes fish that leap, fish with spots, and fish on land. Read the whole book as a storytime read-aloud. For those who want to know more, each fish is identified on the last two pages.

Transitional Song

See Welcome Song earlier.

Flannel Board Activity

Swim, Swim Blue Fish

Use the pattern at the end of the chapter to create felt fish in a variety of colors. Sing this rhyme changing the color for each fish you add to the flannel board.

Swim Swim Blue Fish
By J. Dietzel-Glair
(Tune: Baa Baa Black Sheep)

Swim swim blue fish
In the deep blue sea
Swim in the rivers
And swim by me
Swim in the lake
And swim in the pond
Swim with your little friends
All day long
Swim swim blue fish
In the deep blue sea
Swim in the rivers
And swim by me

Picture Books for Storytime

Cousins, Lucy. Hooray for Fish! Somerville, MA: Candlewick Press, 2005.
Full of adjectives describing red, happy, and even ele-fish, this eye-catching book has to be large to contain so many scaly friends. What kind of fish can you create in your imagination?

Hendra, Sue. Barry the Fish with Fingers. New York: Alfred A. Knopf, 2010.
Sea Slug thought he had seen it all until he met Barry, the fish with fingers! And oh, the things he could do with fingers! Things like tickle, point, and use finger puppets. Pretty soon all of the fish decide they want fish fingers. Good thing Barry can help! A funny fish tale that will leave kids chuckling at the closing pun.

Closing Song

See Welcome Song earlier.

Follow-Up Activities

Fishing for Shapes and Colors

Materials:

- Construction paper in a variety of colors
- Black marker
- Contact paper to laminate (optional)
- Paper clips
- Stick or dowel

- String
- Magnet
- Kiddie pool or other large "fish pond"

Directions:

- Use the pattern at the end of the chapter to make multiple construction paper fish in a variety of colors.
- Use a marker to draw a shape on the blank side (the one without the fin) of the fish.
- Laminate the fish to make them last longer.
- Attach a paper clip to the front of the fish.
- Put the fish in the "pond."
- Make a fishing pole by tying one end of the sting to the end of the stick. Tie the other end to the magnet.
- Let kids "fish" for fish. When they catch one, ask them to identify the color of the fish and the shape on its back.

Other Songs, Rhymes, and Fingerplays

This Little Fishy
Adapted by J. Dietzel-Glair

This little fishy swims fast
And this little fishy swims slow
This little fishy swims high
And this little fishy swims low
And this little fishy nibbled on my toe! Ouch! Ouch! Ouch! (hop up and down on one foot)

Fish Swim
By J. Dietzel-Glair
(Tune: Ten Little Indians)

Looking, looking in the water (hold hand up to your forehead like you are searching for something)
Looking, looking in the water
Looking, looking in the water
For my fishy friends. (hold palms together and make your hands swim like a fish)

FOUND THEM!

Swimming, swimming in the water (mime swimming)
Swimming, swimming in the water
Swimming, swimming in the water
With my fishy friends. (hold palms together and make your hands swim like a fish)

Additional Poetry

Coombs, Kate and Meilo So, illus. Water Sings Blue: Ocean Poems. San Francisco, CA: Chronicle Books, 2012.

"Prayer of the Little Fish" is like a bedtime wish for safety, food, and life. It also teaches the reader that this particular fish eats plankton and cannot breath out of water. The image features a ruthless shark and a large pool of fish hoping to get away.

Gibson, Amy and Daniel Salmeri, illus. Around the World on Eighty Legs. New York: Scholastic Press, 2011.
The "Piranha" can incite more fear in people than a shark, but this 11-word poem adds a humorous side by mocking his table manners.

Lewis, J. Patrick, ed. National Geographic Book of Animal Poetry: 200 Poems with Photographs That Squeak, Soar, and Roar! Washington, DC: National Geographic, 2012.
Along with the Opening Poem mentioned earlier, this title has a joyful little ode by D. H. Lawrence titled "Little Fish" (p. 45). Be sure to show the photograph of fish swimming through a coral reef.

Worth, Valerie and Steve Jenkins, illus. Animal Poems. New York: Farrar Straus Giroux, 2007.
"Minnows" swim together looking like a "solid silver fish." The two-line stanzas are short and small like a minnow in the water.

Additional Nonfiction

Owens, L. L., The Life Cycle of a Clown Fish. Mankato, MN: The Child's World, 2012.
With the popularity of *Finding Nemo*, kids will love the full-page photographs of clown fish in this book. Each double-page spread features a page of text and a photograph; read just the captions to share this book with a storytime crowd.

Early Literacy Note:
By reading only the captions, you are modeling for parents/caregivers that it is okay to read only parts of a book.

Rake, Jody Sullivan. Puffer Fish. Mankato, MN: Capstone Press, 2007.
Puffer fish are funny looking and fun to imitate. This book has simple, basic facts about puffer fish, but you can use the book to play a game while reading it. Suggest that everyone puff out their cheeks every time you say "puffer fish."

Additional Fiction Picture Books

DiPucchio, Kelly and Bob Shea, illus. Gilbert Goldfish Wants a Pet. New York: Dial Books for Young Readers, 2011.
Poor Gilbert, all he wants is a pet, but the dog was just visiting, the mouse ran away when she discovered Gilbert wasn't cheese, and the fly got swatted right before his eyes. But what about this whiskered fellow? Could he be a good pet for Gilbert? Yes, Fluffy the catfish is just right.

Yaccarino, Dan. The Birthday Fish. New York: Henry Holt and Company, 2005.
Cynthia loves ponies and on each and every birthday wishes for one. But each year she gets something else. This year the something else is a goldfish who convinces Cynthia that she has wish-granting abilities. After spending the day with her new pet, Cynthia still wants a pony, but enjoys her new pet.

Fish Pattern

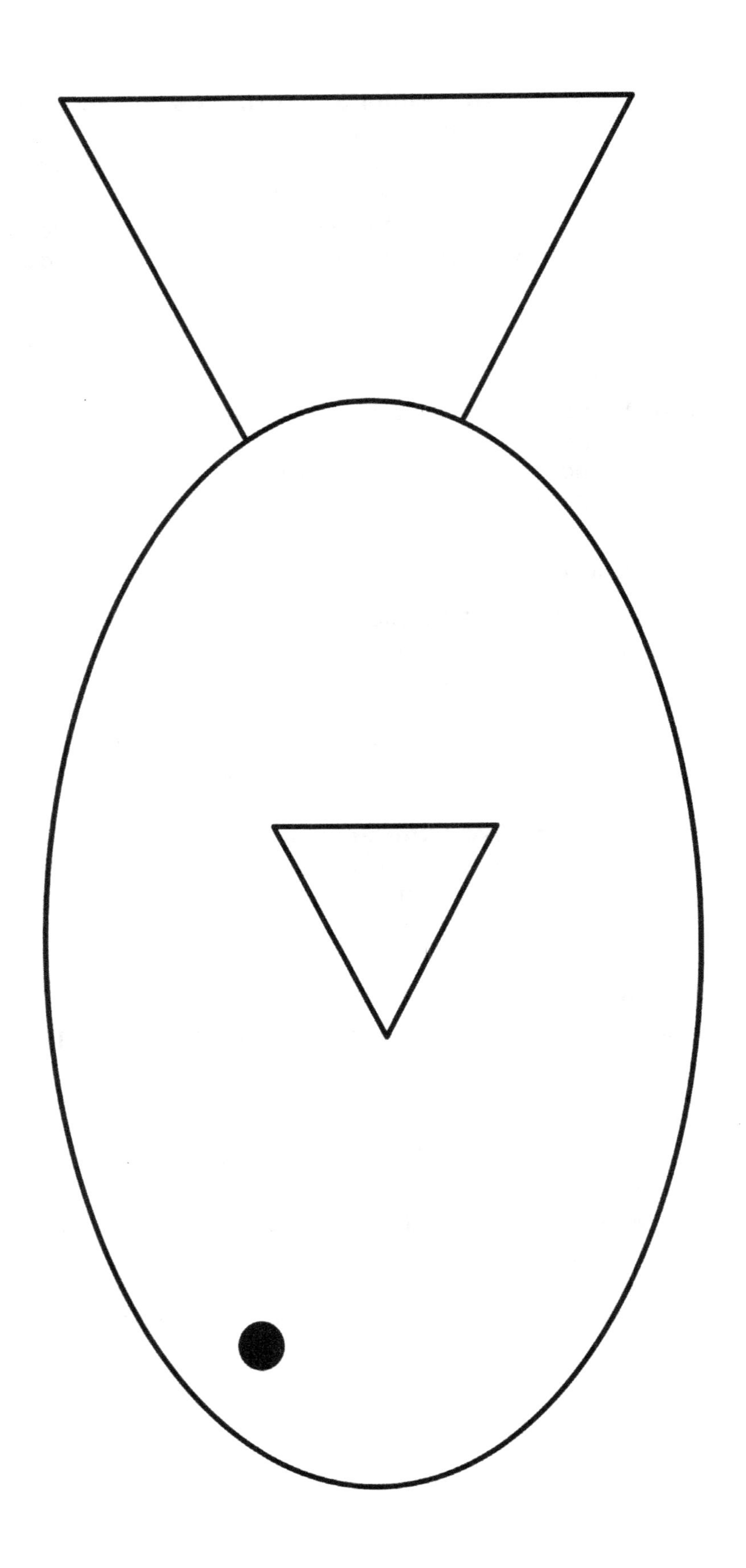

Flowers

Bright, sweet, and colorful, flowers are one of those everyday objects that impact multiple senses and make us smile. Be sure to engage these senses during storytime. If possible have a rose or two of different colors on hand. Have a conversation about the different colors, parts, textures, and smells. Our eyes can see the different colors, but the leaves feel much different from the petals, and if you crush them they smell differently, too. By engaging multiple senses, you can increase young storytime goers' awareness of surroundings and offer them a wider vocabulary for description.

Sample Storytime

Welcome Song

Routine is important when working with children. Be sure to include welcome, transitional, and closing songs or activities to signify what is coming next. Don't be afraid to use the same ones; children take comfort in knowing what is coming next.

Opening Poem

"Pick a Petal" from Shannon, George and Sam Williams, illus. Busy in the Garden. New York: Greenwillow Books, 2006.
He loves me. He loves me not. He loves me; all you end up with is a "bald bouquet." "Pick a Petal" (p. 21) can be read as a flannel board activity. Remove petals as you read until all you are left with is the middle circle.

Early Literacy Tip:
Poetry can be abstract but adding a visual element helps children understand it.

Action Rhyme

From Seed to Flower
Adapted by M. Follis
(Tune: The Farmer in the Dell)

The gardener plants the seeds, the gardener plants the seeds (act out planting a seed)
Heigh Ho it's growing time, the gardener plants the seeds

Additional verses:
The rain begins to fall (act out rain by making sprinkling motions with your fingers)
The sun begins to shine (act out the sun shining by making a circle with both hand, held high)
The plants begin to grow (have one pinched hand "climb out" of a hole made with the other hand)
There are flowers all around (gesture to a field of pretend flowers with open arms)

Nonfiction for Storytime

Gerber, Carole and Leslie Evans, illus. Spring Blossoms. Watertown, MA: Charlesbridge, 2013.
People always think of flowers growing up from the ground in a garden. Introduce everyone to the variety of flowers that grow on trees from white dogwood to magnolia to red maple. The illustrations by Evans capture the beauty of each individual flower.

Transitional Song

See Welcome Song earlier.

Flannel Board Activity

POP! I'm a Flower!

Needed for this flannel board, clip art or simple flannel shapes to represent the following: seed, mound of dirt, sun, a rain cloud complete with rain drops, a stem, leaves, and a flower head. Patterns are included at the end of the chapter.

Pop! I'm a Flower!
Adapted by M. Follis
(Tune: Pop Goes the Weasel)

I'm a seed that grows in the ground (place seed flannel, then cover with dirt flannel)
I need sunshine (place sun flannel in upper corner of the flannel board)
And water (place rain cloud and drops on the board)
I grow a stem (place stem to appear as if growing from dirt)
Some leaves (add leaves to stem)
And then
POP I'm a flower (place flower head flannel on top of stem)

Once all of the parts are on the board, repeat the song, gesturing to the parts previously placed.

Picture Books for Storytime

McQuinn, Anna and Rosaline Beardshaw, illus. Lola Plants a Garden. Watertown, MA: Charlesbridge, 2014.
Lola loves "Mary, Mary Quite Contrary" and she wants to plant a garden of her own. Follow along as she creates her own version of Mary's garden with silver bells, shells, and flowers. The last page features a new version of "Mary, Mary" that focuses on Lola's story.

Swanson, Susan Marie and Margaret Chodos-Irvine, illus. To Be Like the Sun. Orlando: Harcourt, Inc., 2008.
A young girl plants a sunflower seed then watches as it grows strong "to be like the sun." While the sunflower never "speaks," this feels like a conversation between the girl and flower.

Closing Song

See Welcome Song earlier.

Follow-Up Activities

Paper Plate Flowers

Materials:

- White paper plates
- Crayons

Directions:

- The paper plate represents the flower.
- Let children decorate/color their flower however they wish.
- Optional: If you have space available, decorate a part of your children's space as a flower garden. Put chart paper up on a wall (or around the children's desk). Predraw flower stems. As the children finish their paper plate, it can be added to the top of a stem for a community garden.

Early Literacy Tip:
Remember that follow-up activities don't need to be complicated. A paper plate and crayons may seem simple to you but the idea is new to children and will help them remember the flower stories they heard.

Draw Flowers

Court, Rob. How to Draw Flowers and Trees. Chanhassen, MN: The Child's World, 2007. With only four simple steps, children can draw a dandelion, tulip, daisy, violets, rose, and sunflower. Instructions are also given on how to draw various trees. Draw a flower together at the end of the program and put the book on display for families that wish to try to draw more together.

Other Songs, Rhymes, and Fingerplays

Mary, Mary, Quite Contrary
English Nursery Rhyme

Mary, Mary, quite contrary
How does your garden grow?
With silver bells and cockleshells
And pretty maids all in a row

Planting Flowers
Adapted by M. Follis
(Tune: Are You Sleeping)

Planting flowers, planting flowers
In the ground, in the ground
Water them and they grow
Water them and they grow
All around, all around

Ring around the Rosy
Traditional Song

Ring around the rosy (have everyone hold hands as you walk in a circle)
A pocket full of posies
Ashes, ashes
We all fall down. (fall to the ground)

Additional Poetry

Shannon, George and Sam Williams, illus. Busy in the Garden. New York: Greenwillow Books, 2006.
"Pick a Petal" (Opening Poem mentioned earlier) and "Dig In" (p. 10) are child-friendly poems about sharing flowers with someone.

Additional Nonfiction

Blackaby, Susan and Charlene DeLage, illus. Buds and Blossoms: A Book About Flowers. Minneapolis, MN: Picture Window Books, 2003.
The life cycle of a flower from bud, to pollination, to growing seed is explained in very simple language. Bright, colorful illustrations of a variety of flowers put the reader right in the middle of a garden.

Wade, Mary Dodson. Flowers Bloom! Berkeley Heights, NJ: Enslow Publishers, Inc., 2009.
Did you know the biggest flower can grow as large as a bathtub? Told in question-and-answer format, put this title on display for caregivers to share with a child one-on-one.

Additional Fiction Picture Books

Pfister, Marcus. Ava's Poppy. London: NorthSouth, 2012.
When a young girl discovers a lone flower on a hill, she cares for it in drought and wind. But, when the flower's bloom is done, she cares for it still in hopes of seeing it again in the following spring. Vividly illustrated, this book is very easily shared in a large group setting.

Schaefer, Lola M. and Donald Crews, illus. This Is the Sunflower. New York: Greenwillow Books, 2000.
Just like "The House That Jack Built" this cumulative tale starts with one sunflower and then adds more and more to the story until there is a garden full of sunflowers. Encourage everyone to join you in telling the story as they remember the repetitive phrases.

Wellington, Monica. Zinnia's Flower Garden. New York: Dutton Children's Books, 2005.
Zinnia toils gleefully in her garden growing flowers that she can sell on a roadside stand. The true star of this book is the vibrant illustration style that includes photographs of real flowers intermingled with the gouache paintings.

Flower Pattern 1

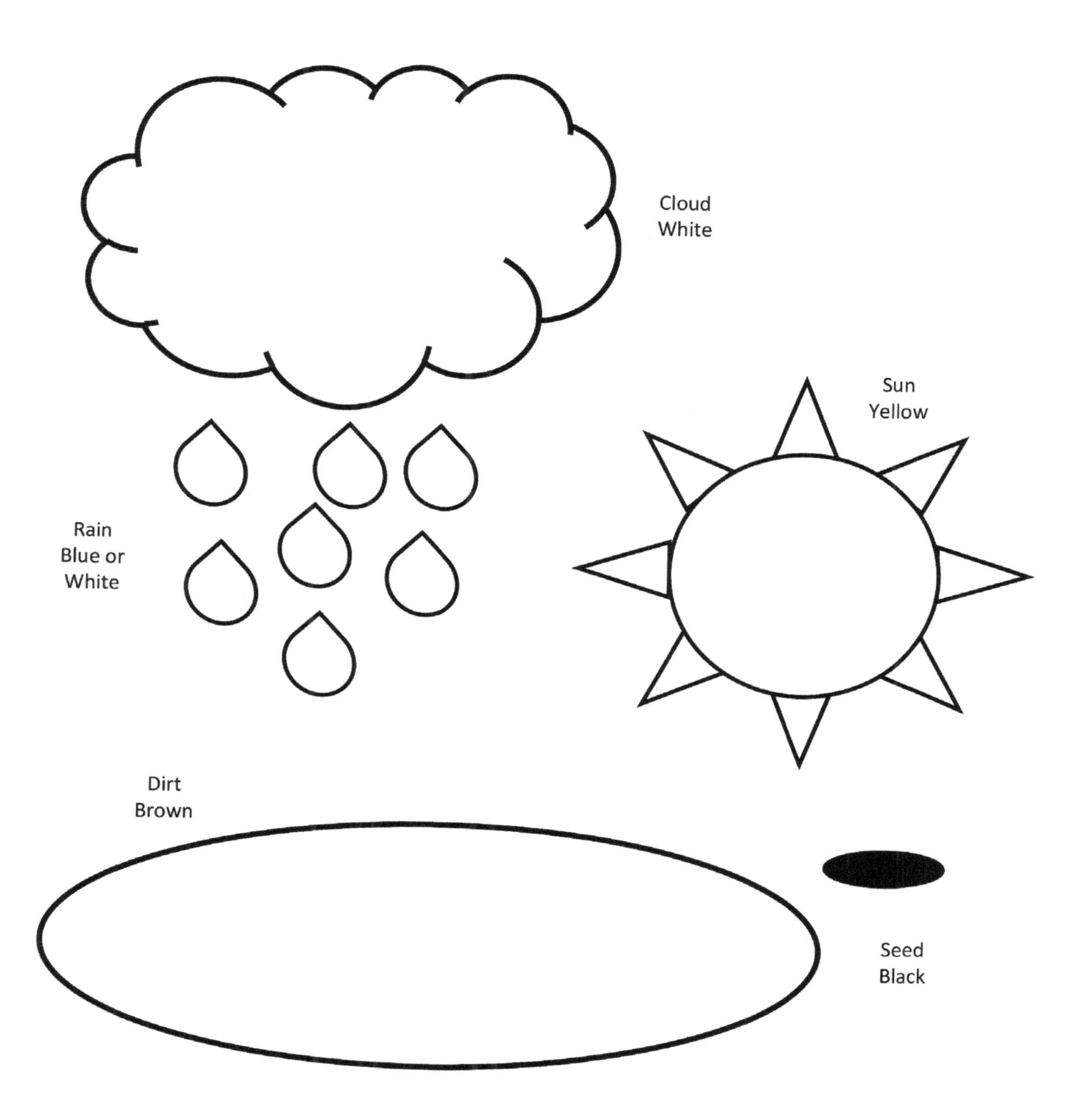

Flower Pattern 2

From *Get Real with Storytime: 52 Weeks of Early Literacy Programming with Nonfiction and Poetry* by Julie Dietzel-Glair and Marianne Crandall Follis. Santa Barbara, CA: Libraries Unlimited.

Food and Cooking

Everyone eats, so in everyone's home, someone cooks. Frying, baking, boiling, broiling, and tossing, there are so many ways to prepare food. And so many flavors to enjoy; because while we all need to eat, not everyone eats the same thing, or the same way. Celebrate these similarities and differences through culinary tales.

Sample Storytime

Welcome Song

Routine is important when working with children. Be sure to include welcome, transitional, and closing songs or activities to signify what is coming next. Don't be afraid to use the same ones; children take comfort in knowing what is coming next.

Opening Poem

Mora, Pat and Rafael López, illus. Yum! MmMm! Qué Rico! New York: Lee & Low Books Inc., 2007.
Haiku and vibrant illustrations pay homage to foods that are native to the Americas. Each page also has information about the origin of the food. The poetry is engaging enough to read the entire book straight through during storytime.

Action Rhyme

Pat-A-Cake
English Nursery Rhyme

Pat-a-cake, Pat-a-cake, baker's man (clap to beat)
Bake me a cake as fast as you can (continue to clap)
Roll it (roll hands)
And pat it (pat)
And mark it with a B (outline B on child's palm or in the air)
Now put it in the oven for baby and me.

Early Literacy Tip:
Having the children outline the letter "B' helps with letter knowledge.

Nonfiction for Storytime

Sayre, April Pulley. Go, Go, Grapes! A Fruit Chant. New York: Beach Lane Books, 2012.
From common (apples, bananas, oranges) to unusual (kiwano, mangosteen, dragon fruit), fruit is celebrated through rhyming text and photographs. If possible, have some fruit available to sample after reading this in storytime. Also look for ***Let's Go Nuts!: Seeds We Eat*** (2013) and ***Rah, Rah, Radishes!: A Vegetable Chant*** (2011) by the same author.

Transitional Song

See Welcome Song earlier.

Flannel Board Activity

Five Little Apples

Use the attached patterns to create the following flannel board. Place the pot on the board and add apples as you read.

Five Little Apples
By M. Follis and J. Dietzel-Glair

The first little apple
Was a nice shiney red
The second apple said
I love our nice warm bed
The third apple said
Oh my, we're getting cozy
The fourth apple said
I'm nice and warm and dozy
The fifth apple said
Our bed is getting hot
Oh no! They cried!
(place handle and lid flannel board piece on pot)
We're applesauce in a pot!

Picture Books for Storytime

Johnson, Paul Brett. On Top of Spaghetti. New York: Scholastic Press, 2006.
Yodeler the dog opens the Spaghetti Emporium and hilarity ensues when someone sneezes. This extension of the favorite children's song will have everyone laughing and singing in storytime.

Martin, David and Valeri Gorbachev, illus. All for Pie, Pie for All. Cambridge, MA: Candlewick Press, 2006.
After the cat family is finished with their apple pie, the leftovers are enjoyed by the mice family, who in turn share the remaining crumbs with the ant family. When all of the pie is done, what's left but to make some more? A fun book about food and sharing.

Closing Song

See Welcome Song earlier.

Follow-Up Activities

All Types of Veggies

Gibbons, Gail. The Vegetables We Eat. New York: Holiday House, 2007.
The middle pages of this book have information and examples about the eight types of vegetables: leaf, bulb, flower bud, root, tuber, stem, fruit, and seed. Show these pages

and real examples of each type. If allowed in your location, sample some of the vegetables as a group.

Other Songs, Rhymes, and Fingerplays

Make the Cake
By J. Dietzel-Glair
(Tune: Are You Sleeping)

Stir the batter, stir the batter
Mix it up, mix it up
Put it in a cake pan, put it in a cake pan
Bake until it's done, yum yum yum!

Humpty Dumpty
English Nursery Rhyme
(While this rhyme never mentions an egg,
popular culture has assigned that identity to Humpty.)

Humpty Dumpty sat on a wall
Humpty Dumpty had a great fall
All the king's horses
And all the king's men
Couldn't put Humpty together again.

Little Jack Horner
English Nursery Rhyme
(The original poem states that it is
a Christmas pie, but we have altered
it here for a wider audience)

Little Jack Horner
Sat in a corner
Eating his holiday pie
He stuck in his thumb
And pulled out a plum
And said
What a good boy am I!

Two Little Eyes
Traditional Rhyme

Two little eyes to look around (point to your eyes)
Two little ears to hear each sound (point to your ears)
One little nose to smell what's sweet (point to your nose)
One little mouth that likes to eat. (point to your mouth or rub your stomach)

Fitzgerald, Joanne. Yum! Yum!! Brighton, MA: Fitzhenry & Whiteside, 2008.
Find 13 nursery rhymes related to food in this book.

Apples and Bananas

This fun song plays with vowel sounds. A karaoke version can be found here: https://www.youtube.com/watch?v=OKEUAzzn-lg. If you have projection ability, show the video so everyone can sing along.

Additional Poetry

Cleary, Brian P. and Andy Rowland, illus. Ode to a Commode: Concrete Poems. Minneapolis, MN: Millbrook Press, 2015.

You may be hungry after sharing these poems about favorite foods: "A Twisted Tale" (pretzels), "I Chews You" (bubble gum), and "Cool, Sweet . . . But Enough about Me" (ice cream cones).

Hopkins, Lee Bennett, sel. and Renée Flower, illus. Yummy!: Eating through a Day. New York: Simon & Schuster Books for Young Readers, 2000.

From the moment you wake up to the scent of breakfast, to the last ice-cream sundae before bed, every day is filled with yumminess. These poems cover childhood favorites like macaroni and cheese, pizza, and Jello. The abstract illustrations are eye-catching and colorful.

Philip, Neil, compiler, and Claire Henley, illus. Hot Potato: Mealtime Rhymes. New York: Clarion Books, 2004.

This collection of fun poems is inspired by food. The poem "Yellow Butter" by Mary Ann Hoberman is especially fun because it encourages saying "Yellow butter purple jelly red jam black bread" as a tongue twister.

Early Literacy Tip:
Tongue twisters are fun and encourage children to practice pronunciation of particular sounds. Children enjoy hearing them even if they are too difficult for them to say.

Vardell, Sylvia and Janet Wong, ed. The Poetry Friday Anthology for Celebrations. Princeton, NJ: Pomelo Books, 2015.

Matt Forrest Esenwine's "Picky Eater" (p. 83) lists some of the narrator's favorite foods; all cereals and all round because it seems our picky eater is very specific in his likes and as he or she says "only eat . . . what's round."

More breakfast food is featured in the syrupy sweet "Waffles, Waffles, Waffles!" by Allan Wold (p. 229). You may never be able to eat waffles again without chanting "Give us waffles, waffles, waffles!"

And stir up some hopping, popping excitement over one of the world's favorite snacks in "Popcorn Party" (p. 43) by Mary Quattlebaum.

In the mood for something sweet? How about some "Cookies" by Cynthia Cotten (p. 315). Please pass the milk because we all know "cookies always do the trick!"

After that we can freeze our brains and tongue with "I Scream!" by Lee Wardlaw. So cold, so creamy, and so delicious "id bade by tung go nub!" But it was worth every lick!

Additional Nonfiction

Nolan, Janet and Julia Patton, illus. PB&J Hooray!: Your Sandwich's Amazing Journey from Farm to Table. Chicago: Albert Whitman & Company, 2014.

What starts as a peanut butter and jelly sandwich then works backward to the grocery store, the delivery trucks, the bakeries and factories, the farmer's fields, and the seeds.

The book builds upon itself as wide-eyed children keep asking questions that delve further and further into the origins of their favorite sandwich.

Stewart, Melissa, Allen Young, and Nicole Wong, illus. No Monkeys, No Chocolate. Watertown, MA: Charlesbridge, 2013.
Without midges, maggots, lizards, fungi, and monkeys there would be no chocolate chip cookies. Double-page illustrations make this title look like a storybook. Read just the large text on each page to a storytime crowd. Those who are interested in more information can read the additional text on each page with a parent.

Additional Fiction Picture Books

Freymann, Saxton. Fast Food. New York: Arthur A. Levine Books, 2006.
Fruits and vegetables are the best form of transportation, at least when they have been made into a train, boat, or even hot-air balloon art. Bright, colorful, and eye-catching, the illustrations in this book are all made out of food. The rhyming text is a quick read but everyone will want to linger on the photographs.

Harper, Charise Mericle. Cupcake. New York: Disney*Hyperion Books, 2010.
Poor vanilla cupcake. He is feeling very blue after all of his brothers and sisters are chosen and he is left alone. Luckily, a plain yet creative candle comes along to brighten the day. A recipe for vanilla cupcakes with buttercream frosting is included in the back.

Wright, Michael. Jake Goes Peanuts. New York: Feiwel and Friends, 2010.
Jake only eats peanut butter sandwiches. He eats them for breakfast, lunch, and dinner. That is, until his parents decide that one week will be peanut butter week. There will be peanut butter pot roast, peanut butter pancakes, even peanut butter soda. The bright cartoon illustrations add more humor to the story.

Applesauce Apple Pattern

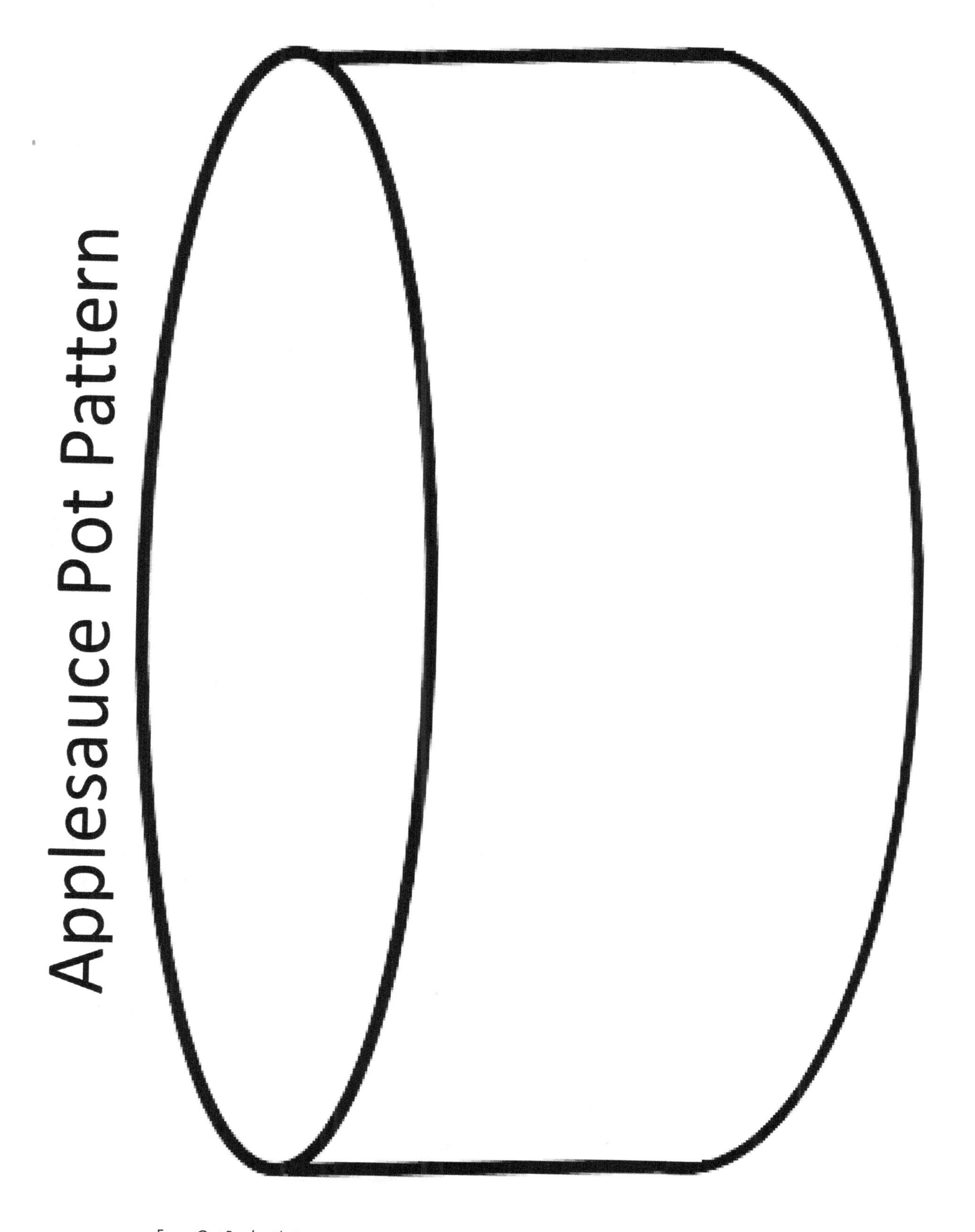
Applesauce Pot Pattern

Applesauce Pot Lid Pattern

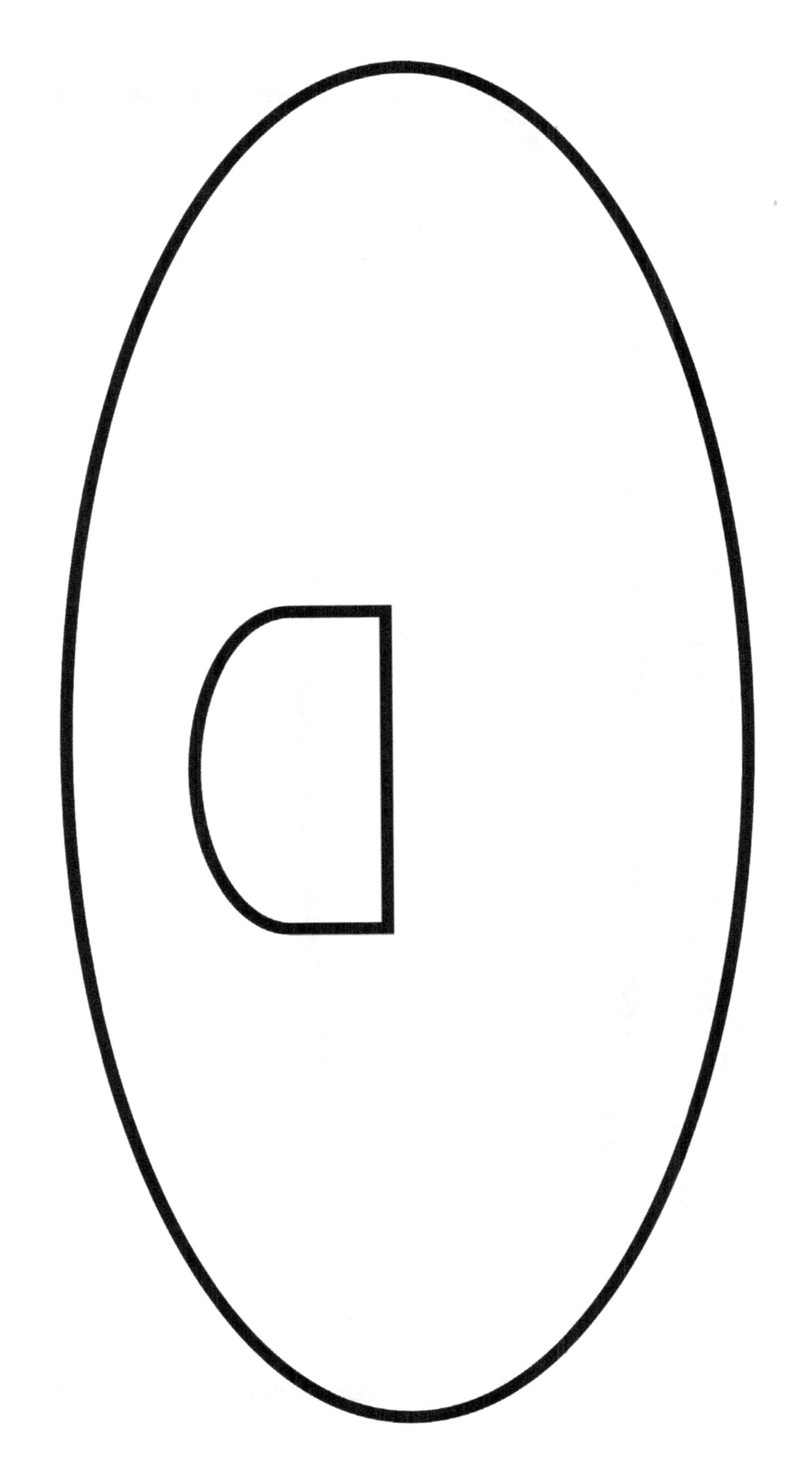

Friends

Friendship comes in many ways. Sometimes your family members are among your earliest friends. Sometimes you will make a friend, who will last a lifetime; and sometimes just a short time. Some friends look like you and enjoy doing the things you do. Sometimes they don't. No matter what kind of friendships you share, you are lucky. Celebrate friendships of all kinds with this storytime.

Sample Storytime

Welcome Song

Routine is important when working with children. Be sure to include welcome, transitional, and closing songs or activities to signify what is coming next. Don't be afraid to use the same ones; children take comfort in knowing what is coming next.

Opening Poem

"Ways to Greet a Friend" from Heard, Georgia. Falling Down the Page. New York: Roaring Brook Press, 2009.
In this welcoming poem by Avis Harley, greetings are given in a wide variety of languages, from Hebrew to Greek, and many in-between. What better way to start a storytime on friends, than with "konichiwa?"

Action Rhyme

Where Is Thumbkin?
Traditional Rhyme adapted by J. Dietzel-Glair

Where is Thumbkin?
Where is Thumbkin?
Here I am. (hold up one thumb)
Here I am. (hold up other thumb)
How are you today Sir? (have one thumb "talk" by wiggling)
Very well, I thank you. (have other thumb "talk")
Run and play. (match up thumbs and have them move away together)
Run and play.

Early Literacy Tip:
You can often change just a word or two in a rhyme to make it fit your theme. Children will also change words around as they learn to play with language.

Nonfiction for Storytime

Thimmesh, Catherine. Friends: True Stories of Extraordinary Animal Friendships. Boston: Houghton Mifflin, 2011.
Sometimes two animals come together in ways that no one can explain. Heartwarming photographs of snuggling animals are set alongside lyrical words about the nature of friendship. Choose a couple of the pages and share the short paragraphs about the character of their relationship.

Transitional Song

See Welcome Song earlier.

Flannel Board Activity

Find child-friendly clip art of five children. Add them to the flannel board as the poem progresses, then remove them as each child departs.

Five Friends Went Walking
By M. Follis

How went out for a walk
And along the way
He met Anna
And turned to her to say
"Want to walk with me on this sunny day?"

How and Anna went walking
Just these two
And they bumped into
Anna's best friend Sue
"Do you want to go walking too?"

How, Anna and Sue
Went walking by the lake
When they happened to meet
A friend from school named Blake
"Come walking with us on this pretty day."

Now the friends four
Went walking merrily by the shore
And who stopped by to say hi?
Their friend from town named Clive
But . . . as they walked together
Someone kicked a BEE HIVE!

Bye said Clive!
"I'm jumping into the lake," said Blake
"Me too," said Sue!
"Hasta mañana," said Anna
"Oh no! OW!" said How.

Picture Books for Storytime

Foreman, Michael. Friends. Minneapolis, MN: Andersen Press USA, 2012.
Cat is sad that his best friend, Bubble the goldfish, isn't free to roam the world. When Cat finds a way to let Bubble be free, Bubble chooses to stay with his best friend. The soft illustrations add to the sentimental feeling of this book.

Springett, Martin and Isobel Springett, photography. Kate & Pippin: An Unlikely Love Story. New York: Henry Holt and Company, 2012.
Based on a true story of an abandoned fawn and the Great Dane that helped to raise her, this unusual friendship is documented through photography. Everyone loves a happy ending, and this one will make your heart melt.

Closing Song

See Welcome Song earlier.

Follow-Up Activities

Make a Chain of Friends

Materials:

- Paper doll chains. The first part of this YouTube video shows you how to make an easy chain of four attached people. https://www.youtube.com/watch?v=AWi9o4AoVal. (This is a great activity for teen volunteers to make in advance.)
- Crayons

Directions:

- Give every child their own paper doll chain to decorate as a set of friends.

Other Songs, Rhymes, and Fingerplays

Make New Friends
Traditional Girl Scout Song

Make new friends
But keep the old
One is silver
And the other gold

The More We Get Together
Traditional British Song

The more we get together
Together, together
The more we get together
The happier we'll be
Cause your friends are my friends
And my friends are your friends
The more we get together
The happier we'll be

Wright, Danielle, collected by, and Mique Moriuchi, illus. My Village: Rhymes from around the World. London: Frances Lincoln Children's Books, 2010.
"Little Friends, Hand in Hand" is a traditional Chinese rhyme that has been translated into English. While the rhyme is about Monkey, Piglet, and Puppy, it encourages everyone to hold hands and walk together.

Additional Poetry

Brown, Calef. We Go Together: A Curious Collection of Affectionate Verse. New York: Houghton Mifflin Books for Children, 2013.
This title may be small in trim, but it is full of affection, especially the happiness and joy felt when with friends. In "We Go Together" the best friends describe all the ways they go together, concluding with "We won the buddy lottery."

Hoberman, Mary Ann, ed. and Michael Emberley, illus. Forget-Me-Nots: Poems to Learn by Heart. New York: Megan Tingley Books, 2012.
In "You Oughta Meet Danitra Brown" by Nikki Grimes (p. 24) a young girl tells you all the reasons you should get to know her friend. She takes dares and takes on challenges and is one of a kind; and the kind of friend we all want to have.

Vardell, Sylvia and Janet Wong, ed. The Poetry Friday Anthology for Celebrations. Princeton, NJ: Pomelo Books, 2015.
In "Sincerely" by Robyn Hood Black (p. 79), one friend writes a sincere letter to another to let them know they notice and are thankful for their kind friend. Something worth mentioning!

Additional Nonfiction

Katz, Jon. Lenore Finds a Friend: A True Story from the Bedlam Farm. New York: Henry Holt and Company, 2012.
Told in simple texts and full-color photographs, this is the true story of Lenore, one of the dogs from the adult book *Meet the Dogs of Bedlam Farm*. When a new puppy arrives on the farm, the other animals aren't interested in becoming friends, especially hardworking Rose, who herds the sheep. When Lenore learns how to befriend a grumpy old ram, she learns how to make friends.

Williams, Marcia. The Elephant's Friend and Other Tales from India. Somerville, MA: Candlewick Press, 2014.
This book contains eight classic folktales updated in language and format. Told in a paneled comic book format, the titular story tells of a lonely elephant who finally makes a friend. When the friend is sold, the elephant misses him so much that the king requests that the friend be returned. The moral: you can't put a price on friendship.

Additional Fiction Picture Books

Bloom, Suzanne. Oh! What a Surprise! Honesdale, PA: Boyds Mills Press, 2012.
Fox loves surprises. When he sees Bear and Goose making gifts she hopes they are for her. Like true friends, Bear and Goose make sure Fox also gets a surprise when they give gifts to each other. There are many other books by Suzanne Bloom featuring this same group of friends including ***Alone Together*** (2014), ***What about Bear?*** (2012), ***A Splendid Friend, Indeed*** (2009), and ***Treasure*** (2007).

Early Literacy Tip:
When there are a series of books about the same characters, put the other books in the series on display after storytime. Children who liked one story will be drawn to others and want to check them out.

Clark, Leslie Ann. Peepsqueak Wants a Friend! New York: Harper, 2013.
All the baby chicks have a partner to play with, except for Peepsqueak. So he hops, skips, jumps, and skitters into the forest to find a friend, despite the warning of many animals along the way. He eventually follows footprints into a dark cave and everyone fears he has met his demise. Instead he finds a friendly bear to be his playmate. The repetition and suspense build as Peepsqueak ventures further and further into the forest.

Ryan, Candace and Mike Lowery, illus. Ribbit Rabbit. New York: Walker & Company, 2011.
Frog and Bunny are best friends but sometimes they fight. This is a gentle reminder that even if friends fight they are still there for each other. The tongue-twisting wording keeps the text from being moralistic.

Santat, Dan. The Adventures of Beekle: The Unimaginary Friend. New York: Little, Brown Books, 2014.

When all of the other imaginary friends get assigned friends, and Beekle is left alone, he decides to go search for one on his own. Leaving the imaginary world and entering the real one on his quest, Beekle meets many obstacles, but in the end learns the true meaning of friendship.

Sauer, Tammi and Michael Slack, illus. Nugget & Fang: Friends Forever—or Snack Time? Boston: Harcourt Children's Books, 2013.

Nugget and Fang are best friends until Nugget goes to Mini Minnows school and discovers that minnows and sharks cannot be friends. It seems their friendship is doomed until disaster strikes and Fang saves the day. There are lots of opportunities for using funny voices in this tale of unlikely friends.

Frogs

Ready! Set! JUMP! What is it about frogs that is so fascinating? Perhaps it is their amazing transformation from tadpole to frog. Perhaps it is their multitude of colors. Perhaps it is just because they are tiny bits of hopping fun.

Sample Storytime

Welcome Song

Routine is important when working with children. Be sure to include welcome, transitional, and closing songs or activities to signify what is coming next. Don't be afraid to use the same ones; children take comfort in knowing what is coming next.

Opening Poem

"Tadpole's Surprise" from Ryder, Joanne and Maggie Kneen, illus. Toad by the Road: A Year in the Life of These Amazing Amphibians. New York: Henry Holt and Company, 2007.
Imagine a tadpole's astonishment as his body slowly changes. Told from his point of view, follow along as he swims, grows legs, loses his tail, and hops away. His whole young life is told in 17 short lines.

Action Rhyme

Two Little Tadpoles
Adapted by M. Follis and J. Dietzel-Glair
(Tune: Two Little Blackbirds)

Two little tadpoles
Sitting in a bog (hold up one finger on each hand)
One named Polly (wiggle one finger)
The other named Wog (wiggle the other finger)
Swim away Polly (move one hand behind your back)
Swim away Wog (move the other hand behind your back)
Come back Polly (bring back the first hand)
Come back Wog (bring back the other hand)

Nonfiction for Storytime

Stewart, Melissa. Frog or Toad?: How Do You Know? Berkeley Heights, NJ: Enslow Publishers, Inc., 2011.
Is it a toad? Is it a frog? It's quite easy to tell if you just follow the rules in this book. Does it have wet, slimy skin? It's a frog. Is the skin dry and bumpy? It's a toad. Each two-page spread has a full-page picture of a frog on one side and a toad on the other along with a method for distinguishing between them. This quick read will have everyone wanting to go outside to find a frog or toad to identify.

Transitional Song

See Welcome Song earlier.

Flannel Board Activity

Use the pattern provided at the end of the chapter and create five green frogs and a log.
Start with all five frogs on the log, and as you proceed through the rhyme, remove one. Be sure to stop and count at intervals.

Five Green and Speckled Frogs
Traditional Rhyme

Five green and speckled frogs
Sitting on a freckled log
Eating some most delicious bugs
YUM! YUM! (rub belly)
One jumped into the pool
Where it is nice and cool
Now there are four green speckled frogs

Continue removing frogs until there are none.

Picture Books for Storytime

Mack, Jeff. Frog and Fly: Six Slurpy Stories. New York: Philomel Books, 2012.
Poor Fly. It seems like Frog always has the upper hand and tricks Fly into being eaten. Six super short stories in one, this looks like a beginners graphic novel but only has three panes per two-page spread and will show well across a room.

Thompson, Lauren and Matthew Cordell, illus. Leap Back Home to Me. New York: Margaret K. McElderry Books, 2011.
Sweet and sentimental yet full of action, a little frog leaps all over the place (even to space) but always returns to find his mother waiting for him. Make this title interactive by jumping along with the little frog.

Closing Song

See Welcome Song earlier.

Follow-Up Activities

Frog Sounds

In the United States, we tend to say that frogs make a "ribbit ribbit" or "croak" sound. Did you know that frogs in China say "guo guo" and the ones in Sweden say "kvack?" Explore sounds of frogs around the world together. http://allaboutfrogs.org/weird/general/songs.html has a list of frog sounds in different languages. It also features real snippets of specific frog and toad calls to listen to.

Other Songs, Rhymes, and Fingerplays

Jumping Frog
By J. Dietzel-Glair

I'm a frog
I like to hop (jump throughout the rhyme)
I jump so much
It's hard to stop
When it's time
For me to sit still
My legs just jump
Against my will

I'm a Little Frog
Adapted by J. Dietzel-Glair
(Tune: I'm a Little Teapot)

I'm a little frog
Sitting on a lily pad
I swim and I hop
Which makes me glad
When I see a fly
Up in the sky
I stick out my tongue
And SLURP! he's mine!
Yum. Yum. (rub your stomach)

Additional Poetry

Florian, Douglas. Lizards, Frogs, and Polliwogs. San Diego: Harcourt, Inc., 2001.
Much more than a typical collection of frog and toad poems, this group includes information about particular species within the rhymes. Learn about a glass frog or poison-dart frogs while having a slimy fun time.

Gibson, Amy and Daniel Salmeri, illus. Around the World on Eighty Legs. New York: Scholastic Press, 2011.
With a nod to the tale of The Frog Prince, kids will enjoy the humorous poem titled "Poison Dart Frog."

Lobel, Arnold. The Frogs and Toads All Sang. New York: HarperCollins Publishers, 2009.
Part poetry, part story, all silly. This collection of rhyming stories was discovered by Lobel's daughter. She added color to his pencil drawings making the poems a lovely addition to any frog storytime.

Ryder, Joanne and Maggie Kneen, illus. Toad by the Road: A Year in the Life of These Amazing Amphibians. New York: Henry Holt and Company, 2007.
Some poems are lyrical, some of funny, all are complemented by illustrations with a natural look. Start in spring and come full circle a year later. Quick facts related to the poem are included at the bottom of each page.

Early Literacy Tip:
Poetic stories are a great way to introduce children to this beautiful art form.

Additional Nonfiction

Bishop, Nic. Nic Bishop Frogs. New York: Scholastic, 2008.
Great facts, often with bite size chunks highlighted, accompany big beautiful photographs taken by Mr. Bishop. Be sure to check out the double-paged spread of the leaping frogs, and the extreme close up of the transparent frog on page 10.

Delano, Marfé Ferguson. Frogs. Washington, DC: National Geographic Kids, 2014.
Frogs come in many colors and sizes, and this book has photographs highlighting the variety. The text focuses on general frog facts, but kids will be more interested in the pictures. Each frog type is identified on the last page so you can name them as you go along.

Guiberson, Brenda Z. and Gennady Spirin, illus. Frog Song. New York: Henry Holt and Company, 2013.
Not all frogs say "ribbit ribbit." Explore the sounds of frogs and toads of the world. Readers are also treated to interesting facts about how the eggs of each species are cared for.

Markovics, Joyce L. My Eyes Are Big and Red. New York: Bearport Publishing, 2014.
Part puzzle, part informational book, each page is a photograph with a few puzzle pieces missing. Different parts of the red-eyed tree frog are revealed alongside a fact on each page. The whole frog is finally shown on the last page. The photos are intriguing even with pieces missing.

Murray, Peter. Frogs. Chanhassen, MN: The Children's World, 2007.
Kids will be amazed by the photos in this book, especially the African bullfrog that has just caught a rat for dinner. Share these photographs while reading the captions to introduce this book to a group.

Early Literacy Tip:
Don't let text-heavy books intimidate you and young listeners. Share the pieces that are appropriate for a group then let interested families read the rest one-on-one.

Additional Fiction Picture Books

Asher, Sandy and Keith Graves, illus. Too Many Frogs! New York: Philomel Books, 2005.
Rabbit has a quiet neat life that he enjoys very much. Every evening he sits down and reads a story. But one stormy night there is a knock at the door. It's Froggy who invites himself in, making a noise and creating a fuss. As days pass and Froggy returns, Rabbit has a decision to make.

Bonning, Tony and Rosalind Beardshaw, illus. Snog the Frog. Hauppauge, NY: Barron's, 2004.
When Frog wakes up on his birthday he decides that he wants to feel like a prince. And since he is a frog, he assumes that he needs a kiss. He visits animal after animal to see if they will give him a kiss. They of course, say no in the most comical of ways. When he finally meets a willing princess, he finally gets his kiss even if she doesn't get her prince.

Kimura, Ken and Yashunari Murakami, illus. 999 Frogs Wake Up. New York: North South Books, 2009.
When spring arrives, mother frog wakes her babies up. The last little sleepy head to wake takes it upon himself to wake the other sleeping creatures like turtles, snakes, and bugs. While many are happy to welcome the first days of spring, not all creatures should be woken by a baby frog. Fun illustrations in bright colors make the frogs hop off the pages.

Frogs Flannel Board Pattern

Gardens

Gardens are full of nutritious food and beautiful flowers. They nourish our bodies and our senses. Storytime is also nourishing; it feeds minds with stories and songs and helps to build social skills.

Sample Storytime

Welcome Song

Routine is important when working with children. Be sure to include welcome, transitional, and closing songs or activities to signify what is coming next. Don't be afraid to use the same ones; children take comfort in knowing what is coming next.

Opening Poem

"Instructions" from Havill, Juanita and Christine Davenier, illus. I Heard It from Alice Zucchini: Poems about the Garden. San Francisco, CA: Chronicle Books, 2006.

"Instructions" (p. 8) is a wonderful start to storytime because it is a poem about planting seeds and the miracle of their growth. The accompanying illustration shows a frog, mouse, and young fairy silently watching a plant grow.

Action Rhyme

Ring around the Rosie
Traditional Song

Ring around the rosie (Start holding hands in a circle.
Walk in a circle while singing.)
A pocket full of posies
Ashes, ashes
We all fall down. (Fall down to the floor.)

Early Literacy Tip:
If you study their history, some nursery rhymes (such as Ring around the Rosie) have a dark past. For preschoolers, the rhymes are just fun games. When they are older and learn the truth, it will give them a connection to that history. Many things that we learn we are little are building blocks for later in life.

Nonfiction for Storytime

Lottridge, Celia Barker. One Watermelon Seed. Brighton, MA: Fitzhenry & Whiteside, 2008.

Count along as seeds are planted and a huge harvest results. The book can be shared in storytime; however, a seek-and-find activity at the back can be shared with a small group.

Transitional Song

See Welcome Song earlier.

Flannel Board Activity

Scarecrow "Monster"

"The Monster" from Havill, Juanita and Christine Davenier, illus. I Heard It from Alice Zucchini: Poems about the Garden. San Francisco, CA: Chronicle Books, 2006.

Build a scarecrow on the flannel board while reading "The Monster" (p. 10). Add parts as they are mentioned in the poem. You will need ragged jeans, a yellow flannel shirt, a straw hat, boots full of holes, and two sparrows. There are patterns at the end of the chapter.

Picture Books for Storytime

Henkes, Kevin. My Garden. New York: Greenwillow Books, 2010.

What would your garden look like if it could grow anything you wanted? Take a look into the imaginative garden of a young girl where the flowers change colors, the rabbits are chocolate, and she can harvest jelly beans from a bush. The vibrant pastel illustrations will show well in a storytime crowd.

Hood, Susan and Matthew Cordell, illus. Rooting for You. New York: Disney*Hyperion Books, 2014.

Poor seed; he is scared to sprout and meet the world. With the help of some creepy crawly friends, he finally makes his way to the surface. The pages grow along with the seed as they fold out. Readers will find lots of fun words like "bonk" and nice language like "snickering snouts" and "keep whirling, unfurling."

Closing Song

See Welcome Song earlier.

Follow-Up Activities

The Curious Garden

Show the DVD of the Carnegie Medal for Excellence in Children's Video winner, *The Curious Garden*, produced by Weston Woods, 2010. Put out copies of the book for families who wish to explore the story again at home:

Brown, Peter. The Curious Garden. New York: Little, Brown and Company, 2009.

Early Literacy Tip: The Andrew Carnegie Medal is awarded by the Association for Library Service to Children and honors the most outstanding video productions for children. Look for more quality book to video adaptations on the award list: http://www.ala.org/alsc/awardsgrants/bookmedia/carnegiemedal and share these with families as another way to enjoy a story after reading the book.

Plant a Seed

Materials:

- An assortment of flower seeds
- Small pots
- Potting soil
- Water

Directions:

- Fill the pots with potting soil.
- Show everyone how to plant a seed in the soil.
- Give it a little water.
- Send the pots home so the flowers can grow. (Optional: Label the pots with the names of the children and put them on a windowsill in the library.)

Other Songs, Rhymes, and Fingerplays

Grow Garden Grow
By J. Dietzel-Glair

Grow garden grow (lift your hands to the sky and grow)
I will tend your soil
Grow garden grow (lift your hands to the sky and grow)
Your seeds will sprout in a little while
Grow garden grow (lift your hands to the sky and grow)
I will water you every day
Grow garden grow (lift your hands to the sky and grow)
Your vegetables are ready to be picked today
Grow garden grow (lift your hands to the sky and grow)
Thank you for this tasty food
Grow garden grow (lift your hands to the sky and grow)
You put me in a happy mood

Mary, Mary, Quite Contrary
English Nursery Rhyme

Mary, Mary, quite contrary
How does your garden grow?
With silver bells, and cockle shells
And pretty maids all in a row.

I Am a Seed
By M. Follis

I am a seed
Small as a bead
Waiting for the sun
Life has begun

Additional Poetry

Gerber, Carole and Eugene Yelchin, illus. Seeds, Bees, Butterflies and More!: Poems for Two Voices. New York: Henry Holt and Company, 2013.
"Seedlings" for two voices starts with "Let's get out of these coats" and continues with great vocabulary like germinate and unfurl. Beautiful language to discuss the ways that gardens start to grow. There are many other poems in the collection that cover insects, pollination, butterflies, and other garden residents.

Havill, Juanita and Christine Davenier, illus. I Heard It from Alice Zucchini: Poems about the Garden. San Francisco, CA: Chronicle Books, 2006.
Twenty poems celebrate a vegetable garden from the spring planting, through a summer storm, into a vegetable stew, and finding a final potato buried in winter.

Shannon, George and Sam Williams, illus. Busy in the Garden. New York: Greenwillow Books, 2006.
Dance with the peppers, cook up some stew, and pull the petals off some flowers. Watercolor paint illustrations accompany 24 poems that are perfectly ripe for storytime.

Vardell, Sylvia and Janet Wong, ed. The Poetry Friday Anthology for Science: Poems for the School Year Integrating Science, Reading and Language Arts, K-5 Teacher Edition. Princeton, NJ: Pomelo Books, 2014.
Planting seeds and charting their progress is a great way for children to learn about seeds and their growth into plants. It is also the subject of Amy Ludwig VanDerwater's "My Bean Plant" (p. 35).
How good are you "at growing beans?" Margarita Engle tells of her time in the garden with her grandfather in "Young and Old Together" (p. 51) as "green towers" of radish seeds quickly spring from the earth.

Additional Nonfiction

Goodman, Emily and Phyllis Limbacher Tildes, illus. Plant Secrets. Watertown, MA: Charlesbridge, 2009.
Follow along as a seed becomes a plant that grows flowers that become fruits that have seeds. Simple descriptions will give kids a true sense of the variety in the plant world. A tiny bit of suspense is added as each stage of the process has a secret to share.

Lendroth, Susan and Kate Endle, illus. Old Manhattan Has Some Farms. Watertown, MA: Charlesbridge, 2014.
The familiar tune of Old MacDonald has been transformed into an informative song about urban gardening. This book traverses the United States through herbs, to beehives, and compost bins. Quick instructions on including your town name are included in the back.

Additional Fiction Picture Books

Ayres, Katherine and Nadine Bernard Westcott, illus. Up, Down, and Around. Somerville, MA: Candlewick Press, 2007.
This garden is full of movement as vegetables grow up toward the sky, down into the ground, and around stakes. Watch them grow then harvest them for a tasty lunch. This fictional tale also provides an introduction to many different vegetables.

Christensen, Bonnie. Plant a Little Seed. New York: Roaring Brook Press, 2012.
Planting a garden takes a lot of watering, working, and waiting. With persistence and patience, these two friends have a bountiful harvest in the fall. Readers will feel like they are gardening along with the boy and girl thanks to the descriptive language.

Fleming, Candace and G. Brian Karas, illus. Muncha! Muncha! Muncha! New York: An Anne Schwartz Book, 2002.
Mr. McGreely is angry when he finds out that rabbits are sneaking into his garden at night and snacking on his plants. Each day he creates another obstacle and each night, the rabbits manage to get through. This cumulative tale is full of onomatopoeia and actions, sure

to get your little listeners involved. And the twist at the end will be sure to have everyone reaching for a fresh crunchy carrot.

Jensen-Elliott, Cindy and Carolyn Fisher, illus. Weeds Find a Way. New York: Beach Lane Books, 2014.

Weeds sure have a bad reputation but they are hardy, persistent, and sometimes beautiful. Filled with lovely language and words like "confetti," "tattered," and "billow" this colorful book may just make you see weeds in a different light. The illustrated weeds are identified in the back of the book.

Salas, Laura Purdie. A Leaf Can Be. Minneapolis, MN: Millbrook Press, 2012.

Poetic lines about all of the things a leaf can be aside from its importance as part of a plant. It can be a "soft cradle . . . (or a) water ladle/a tree topper . . . (or a) rain stopper." Interesting back matter continues the discussion on how different leaves work to be all of these things. For example, animals don't drink water out of a bowl, but they can lap it from leaves, hence its role as a ladle.

Scarecrow Flannel Board Patterns

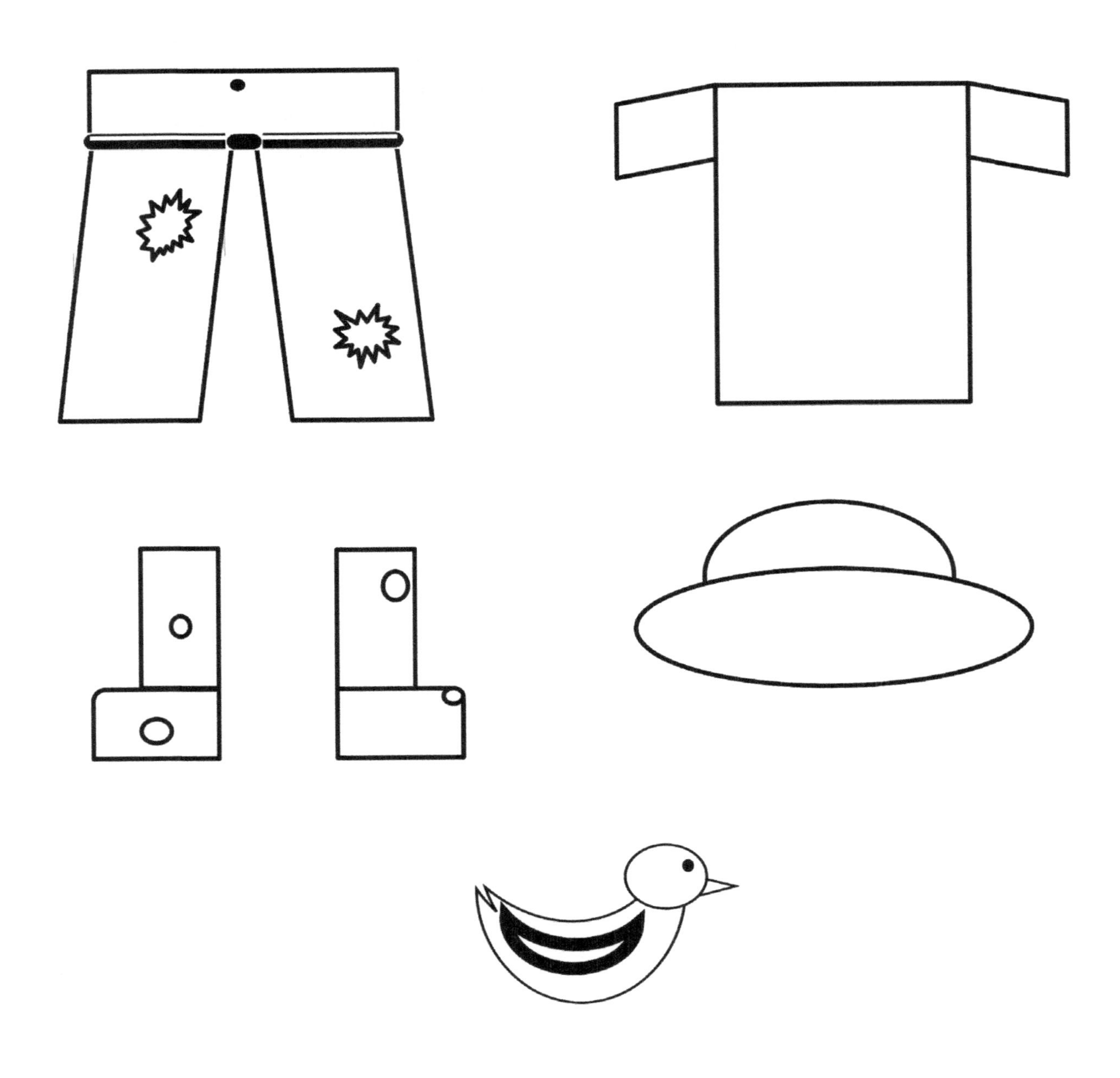

Holidays

Every day has a reason for celebration. Create a montage of holidays for a single storytime or choose elements to celebrate the next holiday on the calendar. In storytime, every holiday can be the most wonderful time of the year.

Sample Storytime

Welcome Song

Routine is important when working with children. Be sure to include welcome, transitional, and closing songs or activities to signify what is coming next. Don't be afraid to use the same ones; children take comfort in knowing what is coming next.

Opening Poem

"Today's My Favorite Holiday" from Nesbitt, Kenn and Ethan Long, illus. My Hippo Has the Hiccups: And Other Poems I Totally Made Up. Naperville, IL: Sourcebooks Jabberwocky, 2009.

Every day can be a holiday if you just have the right attitude. In this case, any day that ends in "Y" is a reason to celebrate. Full of positive language and celebratory vocabulary, this poem sets the mood for a holiday storytime.

Action Rhyme

Five Little Pumpkins

Five little pumpkins (show five fingers)
Sitting on a gate
The first one said (hold up one finger)
Oh my, it's getting late
The second one said (hold up two fingers)
There's mischief in the air
The third one said (hold up three fingers)
But we don't care
The fourth one said (hold up four fingers)
Let's run and run and run
The fifth one said (hold up five fingers)
We're ready for some fun
Then woosh went the wind (cross hands in front of you making whoosh noise)
And out went the light (clap)
And the five little pumpkins
Rolled out of sight. (roll hands)

Nonfiction for Storytime

Shea, Pegi Deitz, Cynthia Weill, and Tô Ngọc Trang and Phạm Viết Đinh, illus. Ten Mice for Tet. San Francisco, CA: Chronicle Books, 2003.
Mice from one to ten prepare to celebrate the Vietnamese new year. One sentence per page and embroidered illustrations give a quick introduction to the holiday. More information including approximate phonetic spellings for Vietnamese words is included in the back.

Early Literacy Tip:
Many holidays across cultures share celebratory activities. Even if no one in your storytime celebrates the Vietnamese new year, they can still be engaged by the festivities and start to see how we are all connected.

Transitional Song

See Welcome Song earlier.

Flannel Board Activity

Happy Birthday

Use the pattern attached to create a birthday cake and candles. You can start with five and count down, or see if anyone in storytime has a birthday soon, and place that number of candles on the cake.

Happy Birthday
By M. Follis
(Tune: Pop Goes the Weasel)

Today's a special day for me
And you have one too
It is the day when everyone says
Happy Birthday to You

And on my cake I have five candles
How many are on for you?
I take a breath, make a wish and then
Out all they blew!

Picture Books for Storytime

Mora, Pat and Rafael López, illus. Book Fiesta: Celebrate Children's Day/Book Day—Celebremos El día de los niños/El día de los libros. New York: HarperCollins Publishers, 2009.
Children's Day/Book Day is held every year on April 30, but every day can be a celebration of book in storytime. Told in both English and Spanish this book brings the adventure and imagination of books to life.

Silvano, Wendi and Lee Harper, illus. Turkey Trouble. Tarrytown, NY: Marshall Cavendish Children, 2009.
As Thanksgiving approaches, Turkey decides to disguise himself like other farm animals to avoid being eaten. While very creative, his costumes do not conceal his identity. Luckily he has one last costume up his sleeve (or up his feathers)—a pizza delivery man.

Closing Song

See Welcome Song earlier.

Follow-Up Activities

Arbor Day Seedlings

Depending on the time of year you are using this unit, you may want to check with your local nursery. Many of them will offer tree seedlings for free for you to distribute during storytime.

Plant a tree, and grow a new tradition for your storytime families.

Fireworks Craft

Materials:

- White paper
- Food coloring
- Straws

Directions:

- Put a couple drops of food coloring on the sheet of paper.
- Have the kids blow on the food coloring through the straw so that it splatters in a fireworks pattern.

Other Songs, Rhymes, and Fingerplays

Pledge of Allegiance

I pledge allegiance
To the flag
Of the United States of America
And to the Republic
For which it stands
One nation
Under god
Indivisible
With liberty and justice for all.

America the Beautiful

Oh beautiful for spacious skies
For amber waves of grain
For purple mountains majesties
Above the fruited plain

America, America! God shed his grace on thee
And crown thy good with brotherhood
From sea to shining sea

Over the River and through the Woods

Over the river, and through the wood,
To Grandmother's house we go;
The horse knows the way to carry the sleigh
Through the white and drifted snow.
Over the river, and through the wood,
To Grandmother's house away!
We would not stop for doll or top,
For 'tis Thanksgiving Day.

Jingle Bells

Dashing through the snow
In a one-horse open sleigh
O'er the fields we go
Laughing all the way

Bells on bobtail ring
Making spirits bright
What fun it is to ride and sing
A sleighing song tonight!

Jingle bells, jingle bells,
Jingle all the way.
Oh! what fun it is to ride
In a one-horse open sleigh.

Additional Poetry

Andrews, Julie and Emma Walton Hamilton, sel. and Marjorie Priceman, illus. Treasury for All Seasons: Poems and Songs to Celebrate the Year. New York: Little, Brown and Company, 2012.

From specific holidays to seasons, this collection of poems has it all. The table of contents is handily broken down by month so you can find a poem close to your current date or far away. Be sure to share selections about holidays that don't always get their own poem such as "Ground Hog Day" (p. 32) "Hang Out the Flag" (p. 87) for Flag Day.

Lewis, J. Patrick and Anna Raff, illus. World Rat Day: Poems about Real Holidays You've Never Heard Of. Somerville, MA: Candlewick Press, 2013.

Is today a crazy holiday? That depends. Is today January 16? Great, it's Dragon Appreciation Day. How about April 24? It's Bulldogs Are Beautiful Day. Quirky poems and clever illustrations cover the bases for 22 unique holidays.

Martin Jr., Bill, Michael Sampson, and various illustrators. The Bill Martin Jr. Big Book of Poetry. New York: Simon & Schuster, 2008.

Fun, short poems covering "New Year's Day" (Rachel Field, p. 53) Valentine's Day ("To My Valentine," Annon, p. 54), and the familiar Thanksgiving Day (L. Maria Child, p. 62) give you bite-sized bits to share with your young listeners. Also included are "Happy Hanukkah!" (Eva Grant, p. 64) and "Christmas Song" (Margaret Wise Brown, p. 65).

Vardell, Sylvia and Janet Wong, ed. The Poetry Friday Anthology for Celebrations. Princeton, NJ: Pomelo Books, 2015.

"New Year Is Here" by Kenn Nesbitt celebrates all the new challenges and opportunities a new year can bring. So "Let's shout! Let's cheer!" we can't wait for the New Year!

And if you need further reasons to celebrate in March, don't forget to remember Dr. Seuss, as Carole Gerber did in "Happy Birthday, Dr. Seuss" (p. 81). Fans of the good Dr. will love the cadence and the references to their favorite stories. We too are happy that he "served up Green Eggs and Ham!"

Is there another time of year when you can honestly say you are "friends with ghosts and witches?" I think not. Celebrate the fun of this candy filled night with Amy Ludwig VanDerwater's "Tonight" (p. 281).

And let's end with a bang and celebrate our freedom to eat picnics while watching fireworks bloom overhead in Linda Dryhout's "Independence Day" (p. 187).

Whitehead, Jenny. Holiday Stew: A Kid's Portion of Holiday and Seasonal Poems. New York: Henry Holt and Company, 2007.
The year is full of holidays: the first day of Spring, Flag Day, Grandparents Day, Valentine's Day. There's always a reason to celebrate, and this book covers them all. Read the poem for the holiday closest in date to your storytime or just pick your favorite holiday.

Worth, Valerie and Steve Jenkins, illus. Animal Poems. New York: Farrar Straus Giroux, 2007.
The "Groundhog" clambers back into bed because the sun is too weak in the sky. This logical poem is a fun Groundhogs Day addition.

Early Literacy Tip:
Remember that books, poems, songs, and rhymes don't always have to directly link to your topic. The "Groundhog" poem isn't specifically about Groundhogs Day, but the connection is strong enough to make it fun in a holiday storytime.

Additional Nonfiction

Barner, Bob and Teresa Mlawer, trans. The Day of the Dead/El Día de los Muertos. New York: Holiday House, 2010.
Told in English and Spanish, this simple story explains some of the practices and traditions of this special family holiday like paths of petal flowers to mark the way for the spirits. While this is designated as a nonfiction title, this can easily be read from start to finish and has the feel of a picture book.

Flanagan, Alice K. and Patrick Girouard, illus. Cinco De Mayo. Minneapolis, MN: Compass Point Books, 2004.
Each book in this series covers several aspects of holidays including the history and traditions. The books are detail oriented, and can be text heavy, but are easily scaled down for a younger audience, or read in completion for a slightly older audience. Detailed back matter including glossary, index, and additional sources for further information make this a useful resource for storytime planners. Other books in the series include *Carnival, Passover, Chinese New Year,* and more.

Gibbons, Gail. Thanksgiving Is . . . New York: Holiday House, 2004.
Clear and simple text accompanies big bold illustrations telling the story of Thanksgiving, and how we celebrate it today. Complete with parades! Gail Gibbons has written several other books on a variety of holidays which should be explored for any unit on holidays.

Merrick, Patrick. Fourth of July Fireworks. The Child's World, Inc., 2000.
Books in the Holiday Symbols series cover some of the trappings of many traditional holidays in the United States. Big bold photos, and explanatory text cover the reasons behind the symbols and how they came to be. This book is text heavy, but select passages can be used when working with a younger audience. Other books in the series include *Halloween Jack-O'-Lanterns, St. Patrick's Day Shamrocks,* and *Thanksgiving Turkeys.*

Rissman, Rebecca. Labor Day. Chicago, IL: Heinemann Library, 2011.
Part of the Holidays and Festival series of book, each title includes photographs and a simple sentence or two that is perfect for a young audience. Other books in the series include, but are not limited to: *Hanukkah, Earth Day, Diwali, Kwanzaa, Ramadan*, and *Id-ul-Fitr.*

Robert, Na'ima and Shirin Adl. Ramadan Moon. London: Frances Lincoln Children's Books, 2009.
A quiet homage to Ramadan, the holiday that begins with a "whisper and a prayer and a wish." A welcome addition for a holiday that is often overlooked, and most likely not understood. Beautiful collage overlays in the illustrations liven the pages.

Additional Fiction Picture Books

Katz, Karen. My First Chinese New Year. New York: Henry Holt and Company, 2004.
Brightly colored illustrations demonstrate the simple story about the festivities surrounding this special time of year. Although fictional, this title contains a wealth of information about Chinese New Year.

Katz, Karen. My First Ramadan. New York: Henry Holt and Company, 2007.
A simple introduction to the traditions and observations of the Muslim holiday. Check out other books by Karen Katz covering a multitude of holidays, offering information and treated with affection and respect.

Kimmelman, Leslie and Nancy Cote, illus. Happy 4th of July, Jenny Sweeney! Morton Grove, IL: Albert Whitman & Company, 2003.
Lots of preparation is needed before the grand parade and spectacular fireworks display in this small town. Rhyming text accompanies multicultural illustrations for the celebratory day.

Lin, Grace. Bringing in the New Year. New York: Alfred A. Knopf, 2008.
A young girl walks us through her family's preparation for Chinese New Year. She discusses the dragon dance, new clothes, and traditions like sweeping the old from your house. Back matter includes additional information for adults to share with their children. Readers get to enjoy the bright bold illustrations, many on pages with lucky red backgrounds.

Wong, Janet and Yangsook Choi, illus. This Next New Year. New York: Farrar, Straus and Giroux, 2000.
Janet Wong takes us through a young boy's preparations for "This Next New Year." He flosses his teeth "so I will have something smart to say," and clips his toenails so "luck can squeeze itself in there." Cheerful illustrations and fun explanations make this a holiday all children will want to celebrate.

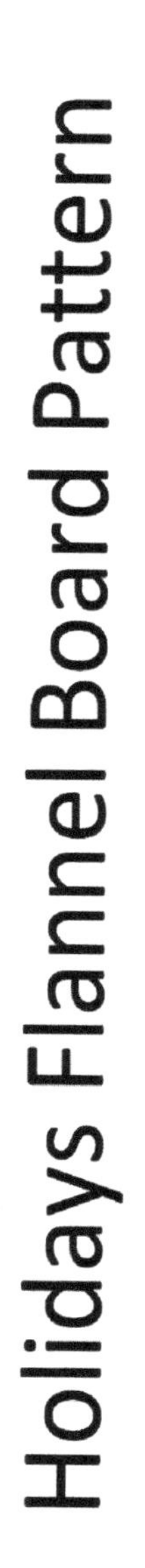
Holidays Flannel Board Pattern

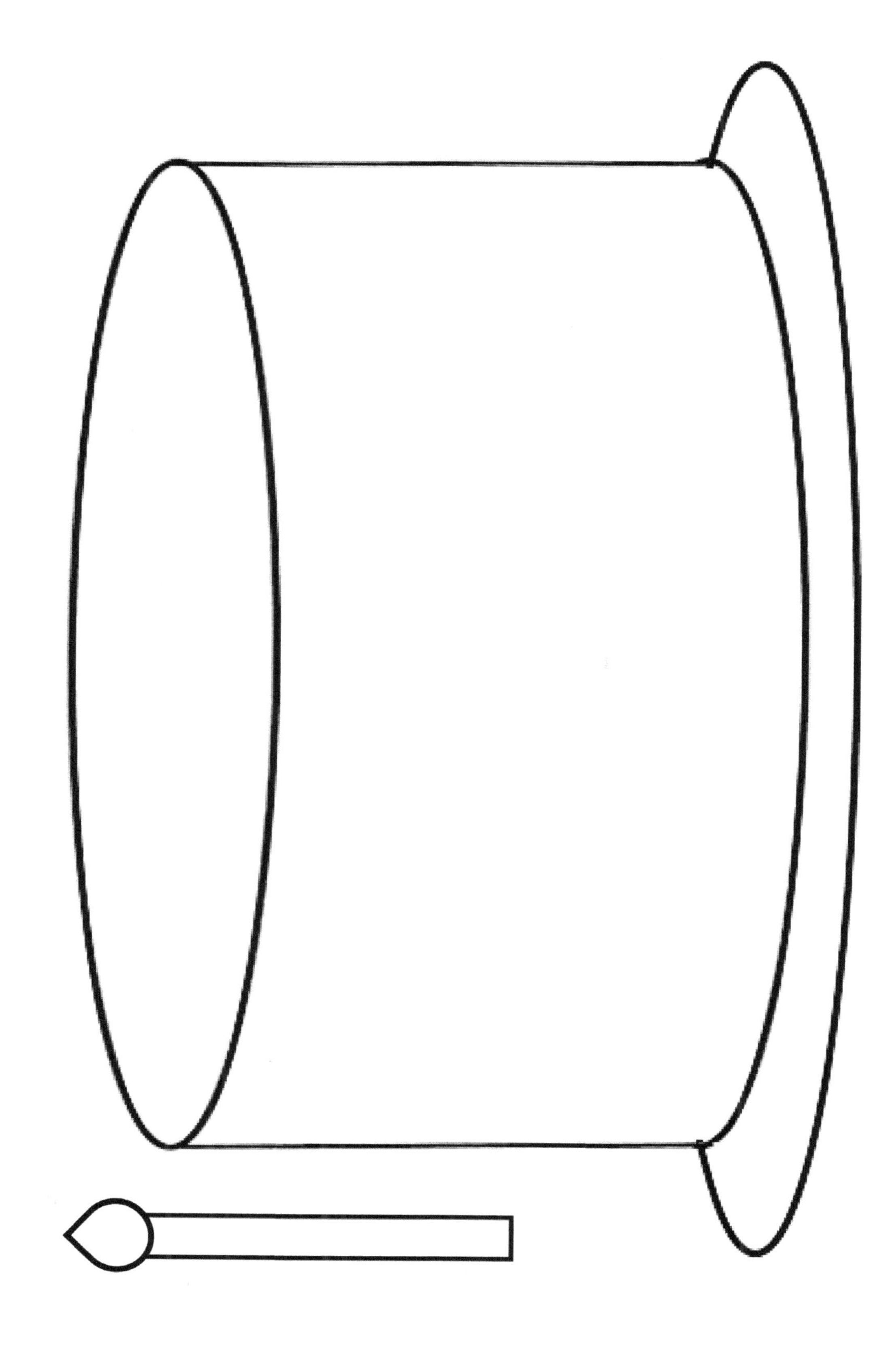

Humor

Ha ha ha! He he he! Everyone loves to laugh, even if it's different things that tickle our funny bone like a noodlehead story, a great knock-knock joke, or a fun play on words. Get ready for a good abs workout as you laugh through storytime.

Sample Storytime

Welcome Song

Routine is important when working with children. Be sure to include welcome, transitional, and closing songs or activities to signify what is coming next. Don't be afraid to use the same ones; children take comfort in knowing what is coming next.

Opening Poem

"Vacuum Cleaner's Revenge" by Patricia Hubbell from Janeczko, Paul B., ed. and Melissa Sweet, Illus. Dirty Laundry Pile: Poems in Different Voices. New York: HarperCollins Publishers, 2001.
A vacuum's life is a tough one. "I munch, I crunch, I zoom, I roar." With all of that work, and no play, you should probably keep a watchful eye on it. I think it is getting cranky.

Action Rhyme

If You're Silly and You Know It
Adapted by J. Dietzel-Glair
(Tune: If You're Happy and You Know It)

If you're silly and you know it laugh out loud (ha ha)
If you're silly and you know it laugh out loud (ha ha)
If you're silly and you know it
Then your laugh will surely show it
If you're silly and you know it laugh out loud (ha ha)

Additional verses:
If you're silly and you know it do a funny dance. . .
If you're silly and you know it stick out your tongue. . .
If you're silly and you know it wiggle your ears. . .

Nonfiction for Storytime

Hills, Tad. Knock, Knock! Who's There?: My First Book of Knock-Knock Jokes. New York: Little Simon, 2000.
Lift the flaps to reveal the answers to 10 simple knock-knock jokes appropriate for the preschool crowd.

Early Literacy Tip:
Jokes are an interesting way for children to acquire language, and find the humor in word play. But don't be surprised if they don't laugh at all of your jokes.

Transitional Song

See Welcome Song earlier.

Flannel Board Activity

Silly Faces

Materials:

- One big round felt circle—any color. (In order to avoid the issue of race, use a color that never matches skin tone.)
- Using the patterns at the end of the chapter, make multiple sets of eyes, noses, and mouths in random colors.

Directions:

- Tell everyone that you are going to make a picture of your mother.
- Put the big round circle on the flannel board.
- Then add two different colored eyes, a nose, and a funny colored mouth (e.g., one purple eye, one pink eye, one green nose, one orange mouth, and blue teeth)
- Ask everyone if they like the picture of your mother.
- "No? Well, let me try again." And make another crazy combination.
- After a few "failed" attempts you can give up and show them a real photograph of your mother.

Picture Books for Storytime

Czekaj, Jef. Oink-a-Doodle-Moo. New York: Balzar + Bray, 2012.
Pig shares his secret and asks rooster to pass it along. As each farm animal passes it, on they add their own animal sound to the message. Poor puppy, he just can't remember the whole thing. Animal sounds are fun to make and this crazy mix-up will leave everyone tongue tied.

Thomas, Jan. Can You Make a Scary Face? New York: Beach Lane Books, 2009.
When this silly ladybug invites the reader to play, pretend you can't help but play along. Everyone will be standing up, wiggling, and making faces while laughing uncontrollably. Everyone feels like part of the book since the ladybug speaks to and looks directly at the reader.

Closing Song

See Welcome Song earlier.

Follow-Up Activities

More Silly Faces

Children like to laugh at silly faces, but they don't always know how to make silly faces themselves. Give every child and caregiver pair a mirror and let them practice making silly faces together. Be sure to model a few ideas such as sticking your tongue out or scrunching up your nose.

Other Songs, Rhymes, and Fingerplays

Play around with familiar rhymes to bring giggles to your storytime crowd.

This Little Piggy
English Nursery Rhyme

This little piggy went to market
This little piggy stayed home
This little piggy had **watermelon** *(Substitute any food you wish.*
You can also do the rhyme multiple times asking the kids for suggestions.)
And this little piggy had none
And this little piggy went wee wee wee all the way home.

There Was an Old Lady
Adapted by J. Dietzel-Glair

There was an old lady
Who lived in a canoe
She had so many fish
She didn't know what to do
They swam round and round
In the bottom of her boat
I think I even saw one
Wearing a coat.

Apples and Bananas

This fun song plays with vowel sounds. A karaoke version can be found here: https://www.youtube.com/watch?v=OKEUAzzn-lg. If you have projection ability, show the video so everyone can sing along.

Additional Poetry

Agee, Jon. Orangutan Tongs: Poems to Tangle Your Tongue. New York: Disney* Hyperion Books, 2009.
Older preschoolers are learning to play around with words and language, and this poetry fits right in. A few of them are screaming for props to make them even funnier: a purple piece of paper for "Purple-Paper People," a pitcher filled with blue paper scraps (water) that can be poured over your head for "Walter and the Waiter," and a pair of underwear for "Undies." Warning, you'll probably want to practice these poems a few times before reading them to a group.

McNaughton, Colin. Wish You Were Here (And I Wasn't): A Book of Poems and Pictures for Globe Trotters. Cambridge, MA: Candlewick Press, 2000.
Tickle your funny bone with poems from this collection. Especially funny are "Miss Melanie Mish" and the illustration of a "beauty queen" from the "planet of Flong," "A I Went Walking" and all of its made-up words, and "Going Nowhere, Fast" which is perfect for acting out.

Vardell, Sylvia and Janet Wong, ed. The Poetry Friday Anthology for Celebrations. Princeton, NJ: Pomelo Books, 2015.
Did you know that there is a day set aside for celebrating jokes? There Is! No joke! "No Kidding!" by Michelle Schaub tickles your funny bone and reminds you share your favorite silly story and riddles on National Tell A Joke Day, August 16!

Additional Nonfiction

Freymann, Saxton, et al. Knock Knock!: Jokes by Fourteen Wacky & Talented Artists Inside! New York: Dial Books for Young Readers, 2007.
Tomie DePaola, Dan Yaccarino, Chris Raschka, and more have contributed a knock-knock joke to this hilarious collection. Each one is illustrated in their classic style. With so much variety, the entire book can be shared in one sitting.

Rosenberg, Pam, compiler, and Patrick Girouard, illus. Bug Jokes. Chanhassen, MN: The Child's World, 2007.
Everyone loves bugs so this collection of jokes is sure to be a treat.

Additional Fiction Picture Books

Barnett, Mac and Jen Corace, illus. Telephone. San Francisco, CA: Chronicle Books, 2014.
Have you ever played the game telephone? The message never comes out the same on the other end, even when a bunch of birds are playing. Laugh along as each bird shares his convoluted version of Peter's mom's message for her son.

Harrington, Tim. This Little Piggy. New York: Balzer + Bray, 2013.
We all know about the original five piggies, but what about the ones on the other foot? Those crazy piggies are dancing, selling hot dogs, and exploring outer space. Everyone will laugh at this silly extension of the popular rhyme.

Thomas, Jan. Rhyming Dust Bunnies. New York: Beach Lane Books, 2009.
Poor Bob the dust bunny. While his friends are playing rhyming games, he is trying to warn them about being swept up by a broom. The escape in the nick of time but can't avoid the vacuum cleaner. Soon to be a storytime favorite, the illustrations feature bold colors outlined by thick black lines that will show well across a room.

Early Literacy Tip:
Children start to pick up on rhyming words at an early age. Share books with rhymes then ask them to come up with rhymes to simple words like cat and bug.

Silly Faces Pattern

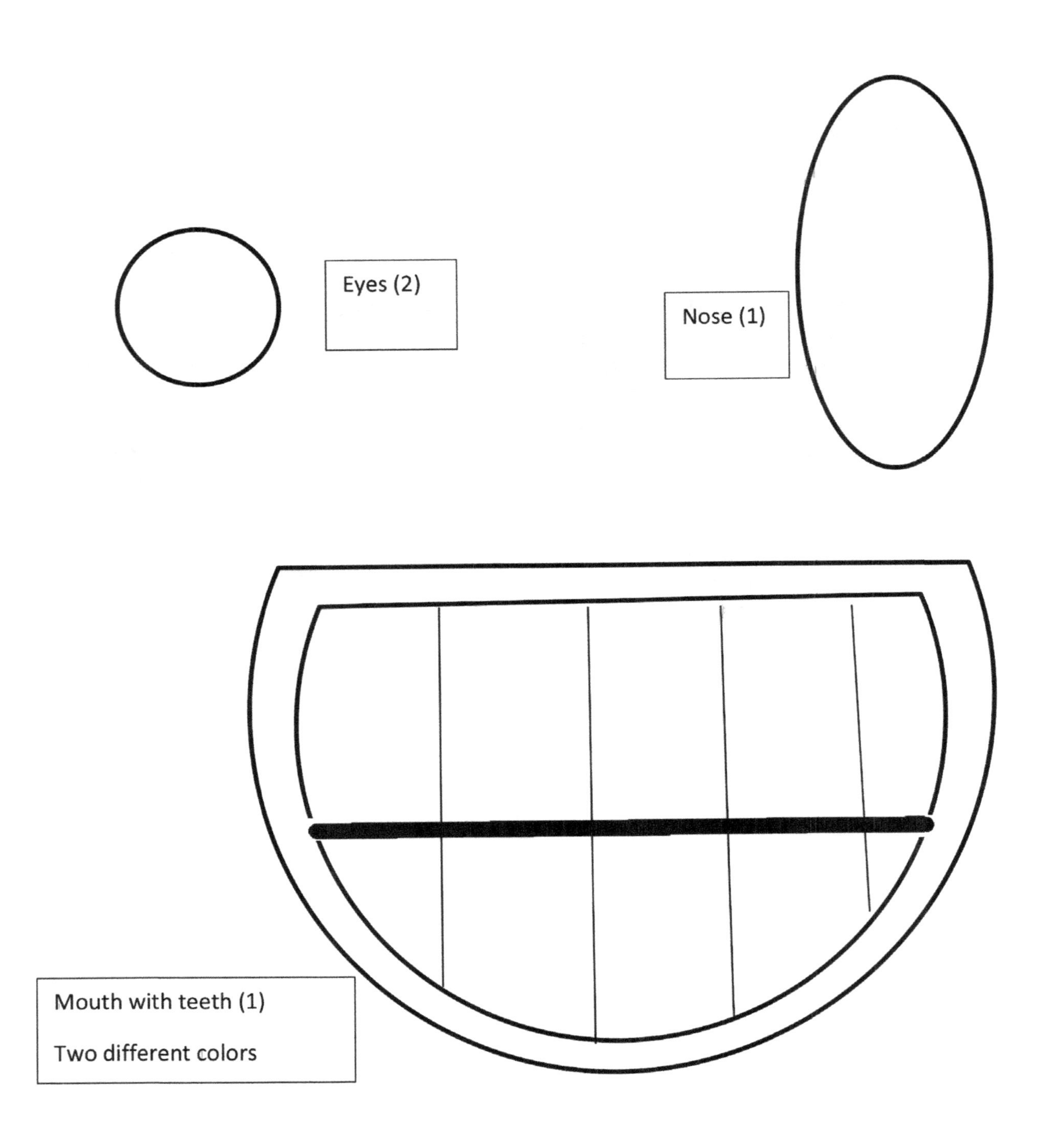

Insects

There is something innately and uniquely fun about insects. They both fascinate and frighten as they creep and crawl. They make you laugh while running in the other direction. All of this makes insects a fun topic for storytime.

Bug storytime also presents you with the perfect vehicle for using some great verbs: creep, crawl, scuttle, fly, soar, and slink, to name a few.

Sample Storytime

Welcome Song

Routine is important when working with children. Be sure to include welcome, transitional, and closing songs or activities to signify what is coming next. Don't be afraid to use the same ones; children take comfort in knowing what is coming next.

Opening Poem

"Ants" from Sidman, Joyce and Beckie Prange, illus. Ubiquitous: Celebrating Nature's Survivors. Boston, MA: Houghton Mifflin Harcourt, 2010.
"Ants" (p. 15) uses neat little lines and a quick short cadence to match the habits of these mighty moving machines. If you have access to a visual aid, such as an ELMO, show the poem in its original form. The poetic form of this poem is well suited for its subject.

Action Rhyme

This lively song is based on the popular Civil War era song, "When Johnny Comes Marching Home," and has no known author. Have your little ones march around the room with exaggerated arm movements. If you have instruments, you may want to designate a few line leaders to keep the beat. And don't forget when the lyrics state "go marching down into the ground" to make sure you bend your legs and march low to the ground.

If you aren't comfortable leading this song/chant, there are many recorded versions of this song. One recommended example can be found on YouTube at https://www.youtube.com/watch?v=Pjw2A3QU8Qg.

Early Literacy Tip:
Children learn phonological awareness through the cadence and rhythm of songs.

The Ants Go Marching

The ants go marching one by one.
Hoorah! Hoorah!
The ants go marching one by one
Hoorah! Hoorah!
The ants go marching one by one;
The little one stops to suck his thumb,
And they all go marching down into the ground

To get out of the rain.
Boom, boom, boom, boom!
Boom, boom, boom, boom!

The ants go marching two by two . . . The little one stops to tie his shoe
The ants go marching three by three . . . The little one stops to climb a tree
The ants go marching four by four . . . The little one stops to shut the door
The ants go marching five by five . . . The little one stops to take a dive
The ants go marching six by six . . . The little one stops to pick up sticks
The ants go marching seven by seven . . . The little one stops and looks to heaven
The ants go marching eight by eight . . . The little one stops to shut the gate
The ants go marching nine by nine . . . The little one stops to check the time
The ants go marching ten by ten . . . The little one stops to yell THE END!

Nonfiction for Storytime

Markle, Sandra. Insects: Biggest! Littlest! Columbus, OH: Boyds Mills Press, 2004.
This quick nonfiction book provides short simple sentences describing the perks of being small (and large) in the insect world. Small fact boxes are scattered throughout. Skip the fact boxes if you wish to read the text straight through in storytime.

Early Literacy Tip:
Before reading the book, hold up the cover and point out the title and author.

Transitional Song

See Welcome Song earlier.

Flannel Board Activity

While we are suggesting a flannel board activity, feel free to use a digital device if available.

Bug in a Rug

Materials:

- Clip art of six different insects such as a ladybug, beetle, bee, fly, ant, rolly polly
- Clip art of a colorful "rug"
- Glue a piece of felt to all of the clip art pieces so they will "stick" to the flannel board

Early Literacy Tip:
This highly interactive flannel board relies on the visual memory of your participants. This will help them build skills for recalling parts of a story.

Directions:

- Introduce each of the bugs used in the flannel board. You can also have the kids try to guess the types of bugs.
- As you introduce the bugs, place them near the rug on the flannel board.
- Turn the flannel board around so the children cannot see as you hide one of the bugs behind the rug.

- Turn the board back toward the children and chant

  Bug in a rug, bug in a rug, can you guess which bug is snug in the rug?
- Have children guess which bug is missing.
- Repeat, hiding each of the bugs.

Picture Books for Storytime

Diterlizzi, Angela. Some Bugs. Riverside, NJ: Beach Lane Books, 2014.
Big bold illustrations and a rollicking text make this a great book to share in storytime: "Some bugs FLUTTER. Some bugs CRAWL. Some bugs curl up in a BALL."

Early Literacy Tip: Books like *Some Bugs* are a great way to expand vocabulary.

Dodd, Emma. I Love Bugs. New York: Holiday House, 2010.
What wild life hides in your own backyard? Colorful illustrations show "jumpy leapy bugs, spiky spiny bugs, and brightly-colored-wing bugs."

Closing Song

See Welcome Song earlier.

Follow-Up Activities

Lady Bug Spots

This is a fun counting activity that helps build fine motor skills.

Materials:

- Two black circles. A smaller one for the head and larger one for the base of the body
- One large red circle cut in half for the segmented red wings
- Black dots (you can find these at an office supply store)
- Googly eyes (Warning: choking hazard. Use with adult supervision)
- Glue or glue sticks

Directions:

- Glue the head (small black circle) to one end of the body (large black circle).
- Glue the red wings to the body. Place them so they are slightly separated.
- Attach the black dots to the lady bug wings.
- Glue googly eyes for the finishing touch.
- Count the number of spots on the lady bug.

Other Songs, Rhymes, and Fingerplays

Bringing Home a Baby Bumblebee
Lyrics can be found on Kididdles: http://www.kididdles.com/lyrics/b002.html.

I Know an Old Woman Who Swallowed a Fly
Stories and Songs for Little Children by Pete Seeger. High Windy Audio, 2000 (B000008RZN).

Additional Poetry

Florian, Douglas. UnBEElievables: Honeybee Poems and Paintings. New York: Beach Lane Books, 2012.

Bright double-page spreads feature a poem on one side and an illustration on the other. Hold this book open for everyone in storytime to see as you read a poem of your choosing. The book also contains facts about honeybees on each page that can be shared.

Sidman, Joyce. Ubiquitous: Celebrating Nature's Survivors. Boston, MA: Houghton Mifflin Harcourt, 2010.

This collection contains many poems of creatures that others may not find worthy of praise. "The Beetle" poem (p. 10) presents a circular shape to chart the path of life, while the poem on "Ants" (p. 15) uses neat little lines and a quick short cadence to match the habits of these mighty moving machines.

Singer, Marilyn. Fireflies at Midnight. New York: Atheneum, 2003.

This collection includes poems for creatures according to time of day, including nighttime featuring spiders, ants, Monarch butterflies, and fireflies.

Yolen, Jane and Jason Stemple, photography. Bug Off: Creepy Crawly Poems. Honesdale, PA: Wordsong, 2012.

A swarm of poems highlighting the insect world that are short and provide a jaunty start to storytime. "Ants" (p. 12) uses a strong, peppy cadence to simulate the steady stream of marching ants that are so busy working they "don't stop for movies . . . (or to) dance."

Additional Nonfiction

Bugs (Look Closer) New York: DK Publishing, 2005.

Learn about less common bugs like the postman caterpillar, cardinal beetle, and parent bug. Each double-page spread features one bug displayed in a large photograph. Read just the largest font on each page to entertain the storytime crowd. Interested children can then look at the book with a caregiver to delve into more facts about each bug.

Evans, Lynette. Bug Life. San Rafael, CA: Insight Editions, 2013.

Evans provides a recounting of the life of a ladybug, without anthropomorphizing the insect. The incredibly realistic illustrations are big, bold, and lifelike, and would share well with a crowd of toddlers.

Rockwell, Anne. Bugs Are Insects. New York: HarperCollins, 2001.

Loads of facts presented in bite size morsels are accompanied by beautiful collage illustrations.

Additional Fiction Picture Books

Cyrus, Kurt. Big Rig Bugs. Gordonsville, VA: Walker & Co., 2010.

The author/illustrator uses a juxtaposition of size, placing these big bugs in the position of construction equipment. Great opportunities for experiments with word families as rhymes abound.

Morrow, Barbara Olenyik. Mr. Mosquito Put on His Tuxedo. New York: Holiday House, 2009.

Rhyming text proclaims the adventure of a mosquito that saves the insect ball from a bear that would surely ruin the evening. Insect lovers will be pleased to find bugs of all shapes and sizes from gnats to lice to bedbugs to crickets.

Stein, Peter. Bugs Galore. Boston: Candlewick, 2012.

Peter Stein presents all sorts of bright and colorful bugs illustrated by Bob Staake. While their definition of bugs is a rather loose one, the abundance of adjectives will make this a great book to share with young audiences.

Lady Bug Pattern

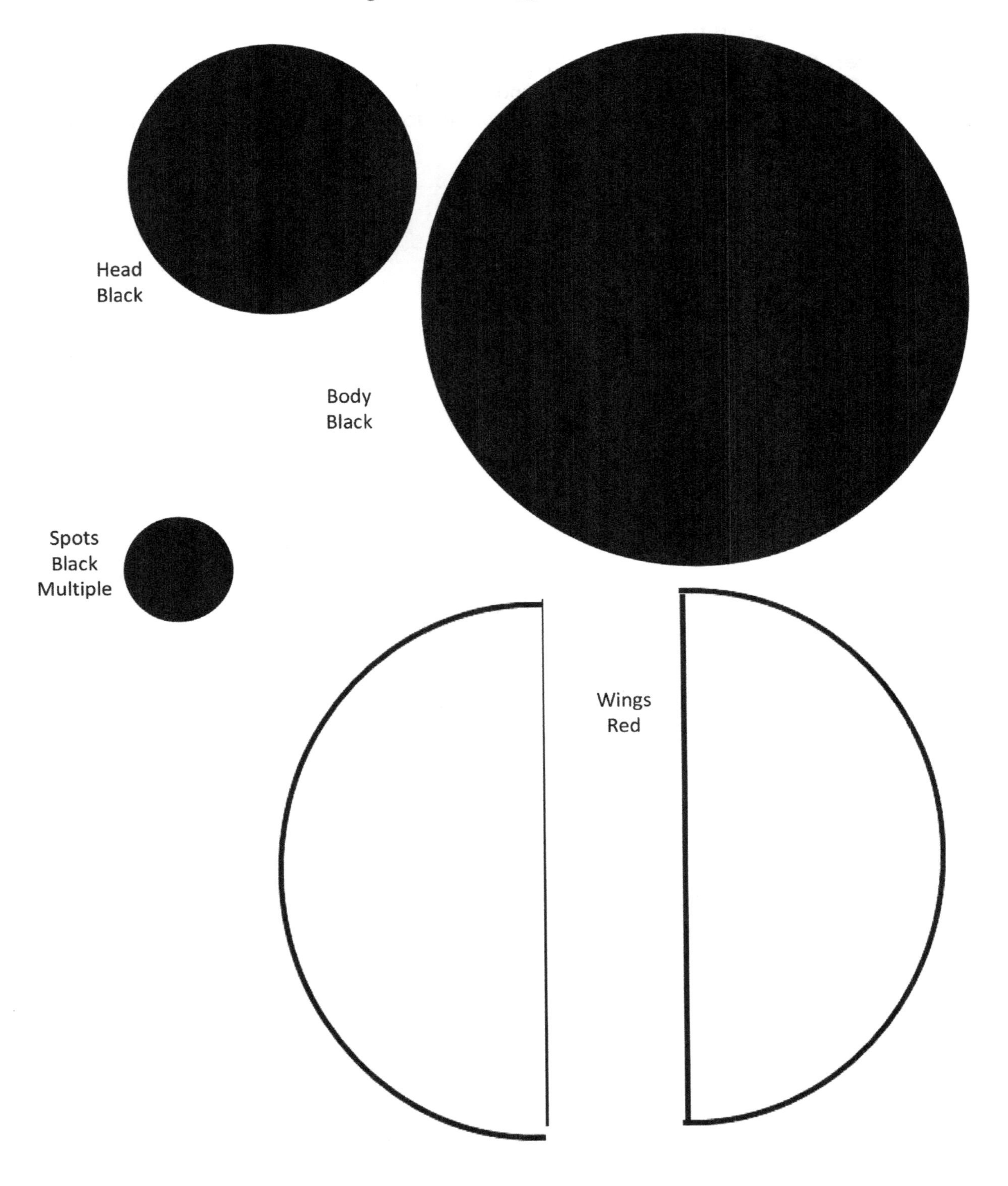

Math

One plus one equals two. Multiply that with books and songs and you have an exponentially greater percentage of fun for sharing

Sample Storytime

Welcome Song

Routine is important when working with children. Be sure to include welcome, transitional, and closing songs or activities to signify what is coming next. Don't be afraid to use the same ones; children take comfort in knowing what is coming next.

Opening Poem

"Time" from Hoberman, Mary Ann, ed. and Michael Emberley, illus. Forget-Me-Nots: Poems to Learn By Heart. New York: Megan Tingley Books, 2012.
As you listen to the clock chime you can actually hear the passing of time; one . . . two . . . three.

Action Rhyme

Hickory Dickory Dock
English Nursery Rhyme

Hickory dickory dock. Tick-tock (clap twice for tick-tock)
The mouse ran up the clock. Tick-tock.
The clock struck one.
The mouse ran down.
Hickory dickory dock. Tick-tock.

Nonfiction for Storytime

Brocket, Jane. 1 Cookie, 2 Chairs, 3 Pears: Numbers Everywhere. Minneapolis, MN: Millbrook Press, 2014.
Numbers really are everywhere! From 3 donuts on a napkin to 7 egg yolks in a bowl to 15 leaves on the ground. Photographs illustrate the numbers from one all the way up to twenty and then back down to zero.

Early Literacy Tip:
When reading a counting book, count up to the featured number on each page. While it may seem repetitive, you are actually reiterating the number sequence for blossoming minds.

Transitional Song

See Welcome Song earlier.

Flannel Board Activity

Sorting

Mariconda, Barbara and Sherry Rogers, illus. Sort It Out! Mt. Pleasant, SC: Sylvan Dell Publishing, 2008.

Packy the Packrat comes home with another load of stuff. When his mother tells him to sort everything and put it away he comes up with multiple ways to sort his objects. All sixteen items are illustrated on sorting cards in the back of the book. Make color copies of the cards, glue a piece of felt to the back of each, and sort along with Packy.

Picture Books for Storytime

Barnett, Mac and Kevin Cornell, illus. Count the Monkeys. New York: Disney*Hyperion Books, 2013.

Count the king cobra, the mongooses, the crocodiles are we ever going to get to the monkeys? With loads of audience participation right in the text, this is quite possibly the most fun counting book you'll ever share in storytime.

Wolff, Ashley. Baby Bear Counts One. New York: Beach Lane Books, 2013.

As the forest prepares for winter, baby bear counts animals (and eventually snowflakes) from one to ten. Be sure to point to each animal on the page as you count along with baby bear.

Closing Song

See Welcome Song earlier.

Follow-Up Activities

Numbers in Other Languages

Children are just learning to count, but this is still a great time to expose them to hearing other languages. Count from one to five (or up to ten) together in English then do the same thing in another language (or two). If you happen to have a native speaker on staff, ask them to come in for this portion of the storytime. Here are a couple examples to get you started.

Spanish

1—Uno	6—Seis
2—Dos	7—Siete
3—Tres	8—Ocho
4—Cuatro	9—Nueve
5—Cinco	10—Diez

French

1—Un	6—Six
2—Deux	7—Sept
3—Trois	8—Huit
4—Quatre	9—Neuf
5—Cinq	10—Dix

Other Songs, Rhymes, and Fingerplays

One, Two Buckle My Shoe
English Nursery Rhyme

One, two,
Buckle my shoe
Three, four,
Open the door
Five, six,
Pick up sticks
Seven, eight,
Lay them straight
Nine, ten,
A big, fat hen

This Old Man
English Children's Song

This old man, he played one,
He played knick-knack on my thumb;
With a knick-knack paddywhack,
Give the dog a bone,
This old man came rolling home.

This old man, he played two,
He played knick-knack on my shoe;
With a knick-knack paddywhack,
Give the dog a bone,
This old man came rolling home.

This old man, he played three,
He played knick-knack on my knee;
With a knick-knack paddywhack,
Give the dog a bone,
This old man came rolling home.

This old man, he played four,
He played knick-knack on my door;
With a knick-knack paddywhack,
Give the dog a bone,
This old man came rolling home.

This old man, he played five,
He played knick-knack on my hive;
With a knick-knack paddywhack,
Give the dog a bone,
This old man came rolling home.

This old man, he played six,
He played knick-knack on my sticks;
With a knick-knack paddywhack,
Give the dog a bone,
This old man came rolling home.

This old man, he played seven,
He played knick-knack up in heaven;
With a knick-knack paddywhack,
Give the dog a bone,
This old man came rolling home.

This old man, he played eight,
He played knick-knack on my gate;
With a knick-knack paddywhack,
Give the dog a bone,
This old man came rolling home.

This old man, he played nine,
He played knick-knack on my spine;
With a knick-knack paddywhack,
Give the dog a bone,
This old man came rolling home.

This old man, he played ten,
He played knick-knack home again;
With a knick-knack paddywhack,
Give the dog a bone,
This old man came rolling home.

Barefoot Books and Jill McDonald, illus. Over in the Meadow. Cambridge, MA: Barefoot Books, 2011.
Count from 1 to 10 with this adaptation of the well-known song. A CD with the song and a video animation is included with the book.

Murray, Alison. One Two That's My Shoe! New York: Disney*Hyperion Books, 2011.
This new version of "One, Two, Buckle My Shoe" has clear numbers and a playful puppy. Count teddy bears, flowers, and trees before the young girl is able to retrieve her shoe from the puppy.

Early Literacy Tip:
Help kids start to recognize numbers by putting a felt number on the flannel board for each verse of the song.

Additional Poetry

Brown, Calef. Soup for Breakfast. Boston: Houghton Mifflin Company, 2008.
"One to Ten (and Back Again)" is a counting rhyme akin to "One, Two, Buckle My Shoe" only this one adds humor through crazy ideas like underwater butterflies or babies with beards.

Franco, Betsy and Steven Salerno, illus. Mathematickles! New York: Margaret K. McElderry Books, 2003.
Words+math+seasons=Mathematicles. Poems covering the seasons are displayed as mathematical formulas.

Mannis, Celeste Davidson and Susan Hartung, illus. One Leaf Rides the Wind. New York: Viking, 2002.
Count the numbers 1 through 10in haiku fashion. Whether it be two carved temple dogs or six wooden sandals, each number is represented in a tranquil Japanese garden. There are 11 poems so the entire book can be shared in one sitting.

Martin Jr., Bill, Michael Sampson, and various illustrators. The Bill Martin Jr. Big Book of Poetry. New York: Simon & Schuster, 2008.
"Take a Number" by Mary O'Neill asks the reader to imagine life without numbers and lists all the things that wouldn't be, like birthdays, shoe sizes, and dates. An interesting approach to how we use math, measurements, and numbers every day.

Additional Nonfiction

Murphy, Stuart J. and Valeria Petrone, illus. Double the Ducks. New York: HarperCollins Publishers, 2003.
When a farmer's five ducks each bring home a friend, his work doubles. The numbers are prominent on the page, and you can count along from one farmer to ten ducks while reading this simple story about multiplication. Obviously, preschoolers are not going to understand multiplication but an understanding, or even knowledge, of the concept is not necessary to enjoy the story.

Stills, Caroline and Judith Rossell, illus. Mice Mischief: Math Facts in Action. New York: Holiday House, 2013.
Ten mice wake up and start to do their chores. One by one they get distracted into playtime. This introduction to addition can be used at a counting book in storytime. Count the number of mice doing each activity on each page. This gets especially fun when playtime starts taking over work time.

Additional Fiction Picture Books

Blechman, Nicholas. Night Light. New York: Orchard Books, 2013.
Can you guess the vehicle based on the lights you see through the cutout pages? Count from 1 to 10 with a helicopter, tugboat, street sweeper, and more.

Gregoire, Caroline. Counting with Apollo. La Jolla, CA: Kane/Miller Book Publishers, 2001.
Adorable, amusing Apollo is quite a handful even when trying to be helpful. He teaches the reader how to count from 1 to 10 by highlighting some of his strengths (he is very fast on four legs) and his weaknesses (sometimes he eats too many bones). Colors and numeral representations are also included. Apollo is a very talented (if sometimes naughty) dog!

MacDonald, Suse. Fish, Swish! Splash, Dash! Counting Round and Round. New York: Little Simon, 2007.
Cutouts in the pages add an extra layer of fun to this counting book from 1 to 10. When the book is done, flip it over to count backward with new fish.

Monkeys and Apes

What's more fun than a barrel of monkeys? Monkey storytime! These little creatures with their expressive faces and humanlike behavior are favorites of our own little monkeys. Since they have a reputation of naughty behavior, a storytime featuring these furry little ones is sure to be wild.

Sample Storytime

Welcome Song

Routine is important when working with children. Be sure to include welcome, transitional, and closing songs or activities to signify what is coming next. Don't be afraid to use the same ones; children take comfort in knowing what is coming next.

Opening Poem

"Howler Monkey" from Gibson, Amy and Daniel Salmeri, illus. Around the World on Eighty Legs. New York: Scholastic Press, 2011.
The very first poem in this collection speaks to the loud shrill of the howler monkey in the Amazon. Wake everyone up by reading this poem then making loud noises together.

Action Rhyme

Lead your little monkeys in this physical rhyme, which can be adapted to include other actions.

Monkey See, Monkey Do!
By M. Follis
(Tune: "This Old Man")

Monkey see, monkey do
Little monkey copies you
Let me see what you can do
*I can **turn around!** Can you? (turn around)*

Other verses: "Touch my toes"; "Touch my head"; "Jump up and down."
Be sure to act out each of the movements.

Nonfiction for Storytime

Sayre, April Pulley and Woody Miller, illus. Meet the Howlers! Watertown, MA: Charlesbridge, 2010.
A playful poem about papa, mama, brother, sister, and baby introduces readers to howler monkeys. While it reads like a story, the book provides information about these loud creatures. Additional information is provided in a smaller font for those who want to learn more.

Transitional Song

See Welcome Song earlier.

Flannel Board Activity

Five Little Monkeys

Materials:

- Clip art of a little monkey which you will use for all five of the monkeys
- Clip art of a bed. You may need to elongate the image to fit all of the monkeys
- NOTE: Laminating the clip art images helps increase their durability
- Glue and felt pieces or velcro to attach to the back of the clip art images

Early Literacy Tip:
We spend a lot of time counting forward, but backward is a bit harder. Using removable pieces in flannel board activities allows for concrete representation of subtraction.

Directions:

- Place the bed on the flannel board.
- Ask the children to count with you as you add the monkeys to the bed.
- Sing the following tune.

Five Little Monkeys
English Folk Song

Five little monkeys (show five fingers on your right hand)
Jumping on the bed ("bounce" right hand on flat left hand)
One fell off (indicate one [1] with index finger)
And bumped his head (touch head)
Mamma called the doctor (make pretend phone using thumb and pinkie and holding it up to your ear)
And the doctor said
"No more monkeys jumping on the bed!" (wag/shake index finger in "no" gesture)

- Ask children how many are left and count the remaining monkeys to reinforce their answer.
- Continue singing the song, changing the number until there are "No more monkeys jumping on the bed" gesturing to indicate "none."

Picture Books for Storytime

Browne, Anthony. One Gorilla: A Counting Book. Somerville, MA: Candlewick Press, 2012.
Count primates together from 1 gorilla to 10 lemurs. Browne's life-like illustrations add depth to this simple counting book. The inclusion of less common primates (colobus monkeys, macaques) provides a learning opportunity beyond math.

Early Literacy Tip:
We often think of picture books as just fun stories but most offer learning opportunities beyond the love of stories, books, and literacy.

McDermott, Gerald. Monkey: A Trickster Tale from India. Boston: Houghton, Mifflin, Harcourt, 2011.
Monkey needs help getting to the mango tree, but when a sneaky crocodile offers to help, monkey needs to use his

head to stay out of danger. With bold illustrations created using textured paper and paint, the monkey leaps off the page, while crocodile's scales sink stonily into the water.

Closing Song

See Welcome Song earlier.

Follow-Up Activities

Monkey Paper Plate Face

While many little ones are often called "little monkeys," this craft gives them a face to go with the name.

Materials:

- One brown paper plate (dinner size)
- One large pink oval for monkey nose
- Two medium brown circles for monkey's ears
- Two smaller pink circles for monkey's inner ears
- Two small white ovals for monkey's eyes
- Black dots (you can find these at an office supply store) to be used for nostrils and pupils
- Optional: Large googly eyes can be used in place of white ovals with black circles (Warning: choking hazard. Use with adult supervision)
- Glue or glue sticks

Directions:

- Glue the inner pink ear to the brown outer ear, then attach on the outer edges of plate
- Glue pink oval to the center of the plate. Pattern includes smile line, so be sure to make our little monkey "happy."
- Glue white ovals (or googly eyes) above the pink oval.
- Adhere black dots on pink oval to represent nostrils for monkey nose.
- Adhere black dots onto white ovals to represent the pupils of the eye.
- Popsicle stick can be added to make this a mask, or children can simply hold it up to their faces, which may be simpler and safer.
- Monkey around with your new masks!

Other Songs, Rhymes, and Fingerplays

The Silly Little Monkey
(Tune: Itsy Bitsy Spider)

There are many variation of this song. One is here: https://youtu.be/YMfj1xELL9c.

Five Little Monkeys Swinging on a Tree
English Folk Song

Five little monkeys (show five fingers)
Swinging on a tree (swing arms)
Teasing Mr. Crocodile: "You can't catch me!" (make teasing motion with thumbs in ears, waving fingers)

<sung softly>
Then along comes Mr. Crocodile, quiet as can be (put hands together and make a snaking motion)
<sing loudly>
Then SNAP! He grabbed that monkey off the tree! (make loud clapping noise at the word SNAP!)
Count backwards until all monkeys are gone.

Note: For those concerned about the implied violence of the song, a bonus last line can be added such as "And now it was the monkeys turn to be IT!"

Additional Poetry

Gibson, Amy and Daniel Salmeri, illus. Around the World on Eighty Legs. New York: Scholastic Press, 2011.
In addition to the Opening Poem mentioned earlier, this collection features poems on the acrobatic "Gibbon," large-nosed "Proboscis Monkey," thoughtful "Orangutan," and hot spring-loving "Macaque." The illustrations have an eclectic cartoon feel and should be shared as you read the poems.

Lewis, J. Patrick, ed. National Geographic Book of Animal Poetry: 200 Poems with Photographs That Squeak, Soar, and Roar! Washington, DC: National Geographic, 2012.
"Dear Orangutan" by David Elliott (p. 23) speaks to the special bond between humans and primates. "Proboscis Monkey Ponders Man" by Alice Schertle (p. 123) pokes a little fun at this odd-looking creature. Lastly, "Mountain Gorilla" by Janet S. Wong (p. 37) has an accompanying photograph that is like poetry without words.

Additional Nonfiction

Jenkins, Martin and Vicky White, illus. Ape. Cambridge, MA: Candlewick Press, 2007.
Share the lifelike illustrations of the five types of ape: orangutan, chimpanzee, bonobo, gorilla, and humans. The text is minimal and can also be shared with a group; however, the illustrations are so lovely that it is nice to simply talk about them in a program.

Simon, Seymour. Gorillas. New York: HarperCollins Publishers, 2000.
As is typical in Simon's books, the photography in this book is exquisite. Choose a few favorite pictures to share in storytime. You may also choose to do a photography tour of the book, pausing on each page to ask a question such as "What do you think this gorilla is thinking?" or "What do you think this gorilla is doing?" The book is a bit text heavy for storytime, but a family may wish to explore the book further one-on-one.

Additional Fiction Picture Books

Browne, Anthony. Little Beauty. Somerville, MA: Candlewick Press, 2008.
Inspired by the true story of a gorilla that learned sign language, this tale of friendship between a kitten and a gorilla will warm everyone's heart. Browne's gorilla illustrations are almost life-like, and the kitten is a whimsical ball of cuddly fur. The surprise ending may make everyone sigh in relief.

Gravett, Emily. Monkey and Me. New York: Simon & Schuster, 2007.
With its repetitive lines, "Monkey and me, Monkey and me, Monkey and me, we went to see, we went to see some . . ." children have a great way to interact with the text. Couple

this with the actions performed by the little girl and her stuffed monkey and this offers plenty of opportunity to engage in prediction and encourage movement. You can waddle, hop, lope, and jump as the young pair explore the zoo.

Monroe, Chris. Monkey with a Tool Belt. Minneapolis, MN: Carolrhoda Books, 2008.
Chico Bon Bon is no ordinary monkey. He is a monkey with a tool belt. He is great at problem solving and fixing things. But when Chico Bon Bon is captured by a monkey-less organ grinder and shipped off to the circus, he needs to use his tools to help him get back home.

Slack, Michael. Monkey Truck. New York: Henry Holt, 2011.
Are you in the jungle and in a jam? No worries. MONKEY TRUCK to the rescue! He is always ready to help, fueled by banana gas. With thicker, glossy pages, lively illustrations, and rolicking rhymes, this is sure to be a child-pleaser.

Townsend, Michael. Monkey & Elephant's Worst Fight Ever. New York: Alfred A. Knopf, 2011.
When Monkey's best friend Elephant throws a costume party and doesn't invite Monkey, a large and destructive fight that wreaks havoc for the entire animal community ensues. It's not until their mutual friends take drastic measures that the issues are resolved. Bright cartoon-like illustrations, complete with speech bubbles, make this a fun read-aloud.

Pattern for Monkey Face

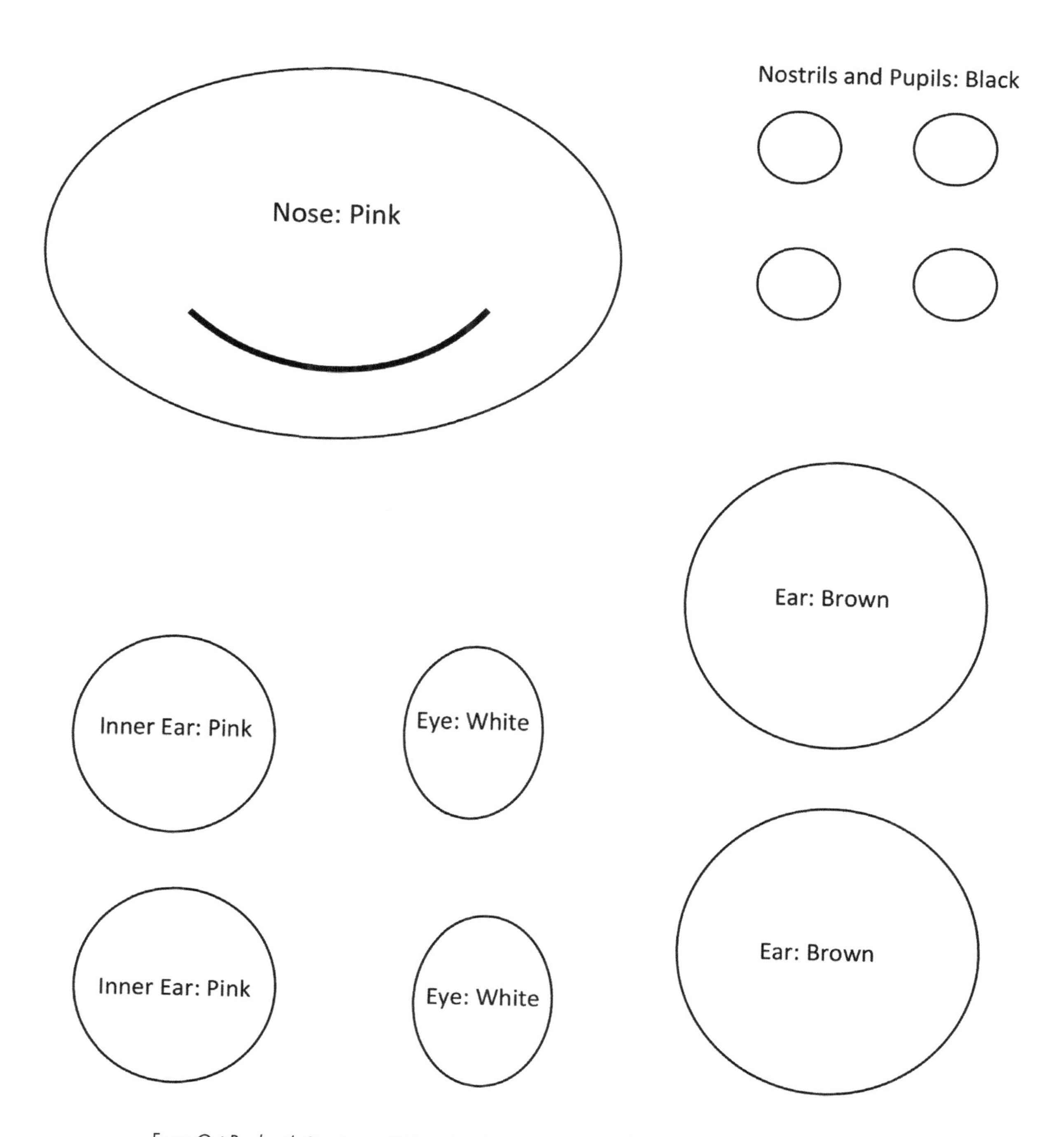

From *Get Real with Storytime: 52 Weeks of Early Literacy Programming with Nonfiction and Poetry* by Julie Dietzel-Glair and Marianne Crandall Follis. Santa Barbara, CA: Libraries Unlimited.

Music and Dance

Music, rhythm, beats, and movement are a part of every child's life, from the language they hear at home to the sounds of their environment. In addition to being everywhere, it's good for you. Studies have shown that the auditory system, rhythm, and language are linked in the brain. In addition, it provides a way to express yourself and burn off excess energy! So get on your feet, move to the beat, and sing!

Sample Storytime

Welcome Song

Routine is important when working with children. Be sure to include welcome, transitional, and closing songs or activities to signify what is coming next. Don't be afraid to use the same ones; children take comfort in knowing what is coming next.

Opening Poem

"We're Shaking Maracas" from Prelutsky, Jack and Doug Cushman, illus. *What a Day It Was at School!* New York: Greenwillow Books, 2006.

Judging by the illustration the teacher is not enjoying the raucous sounds of the class but they sure are having a great time with maracas and drums and tambourines. This poem mentions many instruments and encourages a free-spirited interpretation of music. (It may also be a subtle reminder to all adults in the room to let the kids have fun no matter how horrible the "music" sounds.)

Action Rhyme

My Grandfather Clock

Listen to Bob McGrath's version of this rhyme on the album "Songs and Games for Toddlers" or find it on YouTube at: https://www.youtube.com/watch?v=lnHmY-lZids.

Give everyone rhythm sticks to hit to the beat to make this rhyme interactive.

Nonfiction for Storytime

Ajmera, Maya, Elise Hofer Derstine, and Cynthia Pon. *Music Everywhere!* Watertown, MA: Charlesbridge, 2014.

Joyous photographs of children celebrate music throughout the world. Read just the large text or include some of your favorite captions in a storytime read.

Transitional Song

See Welcome Song earlier.

Flannel Board Activity

Musical Instruments

Using photographs or flannel pieces of a bass drum, tambourine, castanets, and triangle share this rhyme. You can make this activity more interactive by pretending to play each instrument together.

Oh, We Can Play
Traditional Rhyme

Oh, we can play on the big bass drum,
And this is the music to it;
Boom, boom, boom
Goes the big bass drum.
And that's the way we do it.

Oh, we can play on the tambourine,
And this is the music to it;
Chink, chink, chink
Goes the tambourine.
Boom, boom, boom
Goes the big bass drum
And that's the way we do it.

Oh, we can play on the castanets,
And this is the music to it;
Click, clickety-click
Go the castanets.
Chink, chink, chink
Goes the tambourine.
Boom, boom, boom
Goes the big bass drum
And that's the way we do it.

Oh, we can play on the triangle,
And this is the music to it;
Ping, ping, ping
Goes the triangle.
Click, clickety-click
Go the castanets.
Chink, chink, chink
Goes the tambourine.
Boom, boom, boom
Goes the big bass drum
And that's the way we do it.

Picture Books for Storytime

Gorbachev, Valeri. Catty Jane Who Loved to Dance. Honesdale, PA: Boyds Mills Press, 2013.
Catty Jane has always dreamed of being a ballerina. When she is finally enrolls in ballet school, she floats home and tells her friends. Of course, they want to dance as well, but

Catty Jane informs them that they are not really dancing. She eventually decides that there is plenty of room for anyone who loves to dance. A sweet story about friendship and dancing!

Singer, Marilyn. Tallulah's Tutu. New York: Clarion Books, 2011.

When Tallulah starts taking ballet lessons, she anxiously awaits the day when she finally gets her tutu. As days pass, she finally demands to know when the day will come. Dismayed to find that she has to practice a long time before earning her tutu, Tallulah quits dance. Or at least dancing lessons. When she finds herself dancing everywhere she goes, she realizes that some things are worth the wait. Lots of dancing vocabulary here and a great way to introduce young children to the language of ballet.

Early Literacy Tip:
When kids find a book or topic that they really like, they will ask for the same book over and over again. While parents may find this tiresome, it is an important step in reading development.

Closing Song

See Welcome Song earlier.

Follow-Up Activities

Dance Party

Create a kid-friendly play list and channel your inner DJ.

Here are some helpful hints:

- Plan a couple of guided songs and dances, like the Bunny Hop, Chicken Dance, Congo Line, and the Hokey Pokey.
- Don't be afraid to leave the rest unstructured.
- Use props if you have them:
  - Scarves, bells, shakers
- Party Rocker Wireless Speaker System with Light Show.
  - If funds permit and your needs warrant this additional purchase, personal experience finds that this product provides a fun disco style light show that is powerful enough to fill a nice-sized program room with lights and sound. Note: Check with parents first that their children are not epileptic.
- Enlist the help of the adults in the room to act silly along with you or to blow bubbles.

Staff Concert

Find out who on your staff plays an instrument. Ask them to bring in their instrument and have a short concert at the end of storytime. If everyone can learn to play the same song ("Mary Had a Little Lamb" or something else simple), they can take turns playing it. This will give the children the opportunity to hear the instruments individually so they can recognize the unique sound.

Musical Parade

Give every child an instrument (shakers, maracas, rhythm sticks, etc.) and play a festive song for them to march in their own parade. Look in your collection for John Philip Sousa's "Stars and Stripes Forever." It is hard to sit still during this familiar march.

Early Literacy Tip:
Leave instruments out for families to play with after storytime. Rhythm and language are linked in the brain.

Other Songs, Rhymes, and Fingerplays

Dance, Thumbkin, Dance
Traditional Nursery Rhyme

Dance, Thumbkin, dance, (wiggle your thumb)
Dance, Thumbkin, dance.
Thumbkin cannot dance alone,
So dance you merry men every one. (wiggle all your fingers)
Dance, Thumbkin, dance.

Dance, Pointer, dance, (wiggle your pointer finger)
Dance, Pointer, dance.
Pointer cannot dance alone,
So dance you merry men every one. (wiggle all your fingers)
Dance, Pointer, dance.

Dance, Longman, dance, (wiggle your middle finger)
Dance, Longman, dance.
Longman cannot dance alone,
So dance you merry men every one. (wiggle all your fingers)
Dance, Longman, dance.

Dance, Ringman, dance, (wiggle your ring finger)
Dance, Ringman, dance.
Ringman cannot dance alone,
So dance you merry men every one. (wiggle all your fingers)
Dance, Ringman, dance.

Dance, Baby, dance, (wiggle your pinkie)
Dance, Baby, dance.
Baby cannot dance alone,
So dance you merry men every one. (wiggle all your fingers)
Dance, Baby, dance.

Raposo, Joe and Tom Lichtenheld, illus. Sing. New York: Henry Holt and Company, 2013.
The song made popular on *Sesame Street* is handsomely illustrated to show a bird gaining confidence and the ability to fly through song. Sing the song as you flip the pages or play the CD included with the book.

Wright, Danielle, collected by, and Mique Moriuchi, illus. My Village: Rhymes from around the World. London: Frances Lincoln Children's Books, 2010.
Move to the beat as you read "Dance, Little One, Dance" a traditional German rhyme. "Let your shoes fly!"

Additional Poetry

Grimes, Nikki and Terry Widener, illus. Shoe Magic. New York: Orchard Books, 2000.
"Tap Shoes" has a toe-tapping beat and "Talisha's Toe Shoes" speaks of the toughness of a ballerina. Each poem is matched with an illustration of a person dancing.

Katz, Bobbi, sel., and Deborah Zemke, illus. More Pocket Poems. New York: Dutton Children's Books, 2009.
"Rain Dance" (p. 4) speaks to the rhythm of the rain and the tap, tap, tap you create in your rain-soaked ballroom.

Vardell, Sylvia and Janet Wong, ed. The Poetry Friday Anthology for Celebrations. Princeton, NJ: Pomelo Books, 2015.
Celebrate the rhythm, movement, and joy of dance in Jorge Argueta's "The Dancer" (p. 123). Who needs a single reason to dance, when *everything* is a reason to dance; and when you do, "the earth tickles (your) feet."

And don't forget to blow your own horn, and "Make a Joyful Noise" (p. 263). B.J. Lee's poem celebrates making music any way you can and "the whole day long."

Additional Nonfiction

Goodman, Joan Elizabeth. Ballet Bunnies. Tarrytown, NY: Marshall Cavendish Children, 2008.
Follow along in a ballet class from warmup to the ending bow with helpful bunnies. The illustrated bunnies demonstrate ballet positions and exercises. Read the book straight through like a story or stop and try some of the ballet as a group.

Nelson, Marilyn and Susan Kuklin, photography. Beautiful Ballerina. New York: Scholastic Press, 2009.
Photographs of African American students at the Dance Theater of Harlem complement this poem that begs to be read aloud. Each page is artfully designed with minimal text and a focus on the dancers.

Troupe, Thomas Kingsley and Heather Heyworth, illus. If I Were a Ballerina. Minneapolis, MN: Picture Window Books, 2010.
Information about being a ballerina, from practice to performance, is told in picture book story format. A glossary in the back can be shared with children who want to know more. Librarians looking for more diversity in storytime will note that the star character is African American.

Weatherford, Carole Boston and Sean Qualls, illus. Before John Was a Jazz Giant: A Song of John Coltrane. New York: Henry Holt and Company, 2008.
This accessible biography tells a picture book story about John Coltrane hearing music all around his childhood. Kids do not need to know who Coltrane is to enjoy the story that can be shared in storytime.

Additional Fiction Picture Books

Bradley, Kimberly Brubaker and R.W. Alley, illus. Ballerino Nate. New York: Dial Books for Young Readers, 2006.
When a young pup falls in love with the ballet, he is sad to hear his brother say that only girls can be ballerinas. Nate soon learns that there is room for boys at the ballet too!

Braun, Sebastien. Meeow and the Pots and Pans. New York: Boxer Books, 2010.
When Meeow and friends head to the kitchen in search of pots, pans and lids, the group's imaginative play leads them to music. With simplistic vocabulary and bright colors, this is a great choice for a younger crowd.

Cummings, Phil and Nina Rycroft, illus. Boom Bah! Tulsa, OK: Kane Miller, 2008.
What starts as a mouse playing on the teacups turns into a full-fledged band of animals. This rhythmic romp is full of fun sounds.

Feiffer, Jules. Rupert Can Dance. New York: Farrar Straus Giroux, 2014.
Rupert the cat loves watching his human Mandy dance, but when she sleeps, Rupert takes over. He doesn't want Mandy to know his secret because he is a free spirit and dances just for himself. Then one day, Mandy wakes up and discovers his secret. What will she do now that she knows that Rupert can dance?

Rabbits

We may not have a sound associated with rabbits (What do they say?) but that doesn't affect our fascination with these hopping, furry, cotton-tailed animals. So wiggle your nose and jump into this storytime.

Sample Storytime

Welcome Song

Routine is important when working with children. Be sure to include welcome, transitional, and closing songs or activities to signify what is coming next. Don't be afraid to use the same ones; children take comfort in knowing what is coming next.

Opening Poem

"Rabbit" from Lewis, J. Patrick, ed. National Geographic Book of Animal Poetry: 200 Poems with Photographs That Squeak, Soar, and Roar! Washington, DC: National Geographic, 2012.
Mary Ann Hoberman plays with the letters "bit" in this clever poem (p. 148) about a rabbit eating "an itty-bitty little bit of beet." Share the rabbit photograph on the page while reading the poem.

Action Rhyme

Little Bunny Foo Foo

Little bunny Foo Foo (hold up two fingers as if they are rabbit ears)
Hopping through the forest ("hop" the two fingers on the palm of your other hand)
Scooping up the field mice (make scooping motion with cupped hand)
And bopping them on the head (flatten palm onto fisted hand previously used to scoop)
Down came the Good Fairy, and she said (flutter fingers gently down)
"Little bunny Foo Foo (point index finger in a jutting motion, indicating talking to person before you)
I don't want to see you (wag index finger left and right)
Scooping up the field mice (repeat scooping motion)
And bopping them on the head." (repeat palm on closed fist)
"I'll give you three chances, (hold up three fingers)
And if you don't behave, I will turn you into a goon!"
(waggle fingers in a horizontal motion, indicating magic spell)

And the next day . . .

Little bunny Foo Foo (hold up two fingers as if they are rabbit ears)
Hopping through the forest ("hop" the two fingers on the palm of your other hand)
Scooping up the field mice (make scooping motion with cupped hand)
And bopping them on the head (flatten palm onto fisted hand previously used to scoop)

Down came the Good Fairy, and she said (flutter fingers gently down)
"Little bunny Foo Foo (point index finger in a jutting motion,
indicating talking to person before you)
I don't want to see you (wag index finger left and right)
Scooping up the field mice (repeat scooping motion)
And bopping them on the head." (repeat palm on closed fist)
"I'll give you two chances, (hold up two fingers)
And if you don't behave, I will turn you into a goon!"
(waggle fingers in a horizontal motion, indicating magic spell)

And the next day . . .

Little bunny Foo Foo (hold up two fingers as if they are rabbit ears)
Hopping through the forest ("hop" the two fingers on the palm of your other hand)
Scooping up the field mice (make scooping motion with cupped hand)
And bopping them on the head (flatten palm onto
fisted hand previously used to scoop)
Down came the Good Fairy, and she said (flutter fingers gently down)
"Little bunny Foo Foo (point index finger in a jutting motion,
indicating talking to person before you)
I don't want to see you (wag index finger left and right)
Scooping up the field mice (repeat scooping motion)
And bopping them on the head." (repeat palm on closed fist)
"I'll give you one more chance, (hold up one finger)
And if you don't behave, I will turn you into a goon!" (waggle fingers
in a horizontal motion, indicating magic spell)

And the next day . . .

Little bunny Foo Foo (hold up two fingers as if they are rabbit ears)
Hopping through the forest ("hop" the two fingers on the palm of your other hand)
Scooping up the field mice (make scooping motion with cupped hand)
And bopping them on the head (flatten palm onto
fisted hand previously used to scoop)
Down came the Good Fairy, and she said (flutter fingers gently down)
"Little bunny Foo Foo (point index finger in a jutting motion,
indicating talking to person before you)
I don't want to see you (wag index finger left and right)
Scooping up the field mice (repeat scooping motion)
And bopping them on the head." (repeat palm on closed fist)
"I gave you three chances and you didn't behave so . . . POOF."
She turned him into a Goon.
And the moral of the today is Hare today, Goon tomorrow!

Nonfiction for Storytime

Meister, Cari. Rabbits. Minneapolis, MN: Bullfrog Books, 2015.
Pet rabbits are adorable, but they also require work. Written for the youngest child, this book is a short introduction to rabbits and the care they require. The text is spare enough to read the entire book in a storytime while everyone oohs and ahhs over the rabbit photographs.

Transitional Song

See Welcome Song earlier.

Flannel Board Activity

Five Bunnies

Use the pattern at the end of the chapter to create five felt bunnies. Place all five bunnies on the flannel board before starting the rhyme.

Five Bunnies Hopping
By M. Follis

Five bunnies hopping
Across the woodland floor
One hopped away
Now there are four

Four bunnies hopping
Stopped under a tree
One hopped away
Now there are three

Three bunnies hopping
By flowers blue
One hopped away
Now there are two

Two bunnies hopping
In the sun
One hopped away
Now there is one

One bunny hopping
Finally made it home
How many are left
Now there are none.

Early Literacy Tip:
Rabbit and bunny are interesting words since they are used interchangeably to describe an adult rabbit. Using them as synonyms is second nature to most adults, and this storytime gives children lots of opportunities to hear both words.

Picture Books for Storytime

Battersby, Katherine. Squish Rabbit. New York: Viking, 2011.
Squish is a little rabbit and no one seems to notice him which makes it difficult to find a friend. Squish finally becomes friends with an equally small squirrel when he finds a big voice. Squish is a simple white rabbit with a bold black outline, but his emotions shine through on every page.

Surplice, Holly. Peek-a-Boo Bunny. New York: Harper, 2013.
Bunny and his friends love playing hide-and-seek, but Bunny is in such a hurry to find everyone that he misses their hiding spots. Take time to linger on the illustrations so storytime friends can find the animals on each page.

Early Literacy Tip:
The illustrations in picture books are equally as important as the words. Slow down and allow time for kids to really look at the pictures, especially when they can find things that the book characters cannot (like Bunny's friends in *Peek-a-Boo Bunny*).

Closing Song

See Welcome Song earlier.

Follow-Up Activities

The Bunny Hop

This classic party dance can be a fun addition to storytime. First you will need to find a recording of the song. Here is a clip from a Disney album that has instructions superimposed: https://youtu.be/4UwOa3agg2w.

The basic steps are as follows:

- Children form a line.
- Place hands on shoulders of the person in front of them.
- Kick twice to the left.
- Kick twice to the right.
- Hop forward.
- Hop back.
- Hop three time.
- Repeat as you circle around the room.

Other Songs, Rhymes, and Fingerplays

This Is the Way the Bunny. . . .
By M. Follis
(Tune: Here We Go Round the Mulberry Bush)

This is the way the bunny hops (hop through this verse)
The bunny hops, the bunny hops
This is the way the bunny hops
Through the wooded forest.

Additional verses:
This is the way bunny ears flop
(put open hands on head and flop forward and back)
This is the way a bunny nose wrinkles (scrunch your nose)

Little Cabin in the Woods
Traditional Rhyme

Little cabin in the woods
(outline a house shape with two index fingers)
Little man by the window stood (shade eyes with flat hand)
Saw a rabbit hopping by (use index and
middle finger to make rabbit and hop fingers left to right)
Knocking at his door (make knocking motion)

Help me, help me, help he cried (Hold two hands, open,
palms facing outwards, and then lower and
raise 90 degrees <like a bow down motion>)
Or the hunter will pop my head (flat hand on closed fist, make noise)
Little rabbit come inside (welcoming wave inward)
Safely to abide. (hug arms to self)

Additional Poetry

Brown, Margaret Wise and Wendell Minor, illus. Nibble Nibble. New York: HarperCollins Publishers, 2007.
Brown published these five poems in 1959. They are now accompanied by illustrations that appear as soft as bunnies at play. Choose a favorite from the bunch or share all five in storytime.

Worth, Valerie and Steve Jenkins, illus. Pug and Other Animal Poems. New York: Farrar Straus Giroux, 2013.
"Rabbits" are daring and peaceful and smart to stay "far enough away for safety." The two rabbits on the illustration seem to be looking at the poem and assessing its validity.

Additional Nonfiction

Endres, Hollie. J. Rabbits. Minneapolis, MN: Bellwether Media, 2008.
Zobel, Derek. Rabbits. Minneapolis, MN: Bellwether Media, 2011.
Part of emergent reader series about farm animals and backyard wildlife, these books feature sparse text on a clear white background, basic facts, and large photographs of a variety of types of rabbits. Beginning reader series like these can be made available after storytime for older preschoolers who may be trying to learn to read.

Additional Fiction Picture Books

Billingsley, Franny and G. Brian Karas, illus. Big Bad Bunny. New York: Atheneum Books for Young Readers, 2008.
Told in conflicting two-page spreads, we see BIG BAD BUNNY on one side, scratching, crashing, splashing, and chomping; on the other the quiet inside of the mouse house. But when BIG BAD BUNNY loses his or her way, Momma comes to the rescue. For anyone who has ever been tired of being the baby of the family.

Fleming, Candace and G. Brian Karas, illus. Muncha! Muncha! Muncha! New York: An Anne Schwartz Book, 2002.
Mr. McGreely is angry when he finds out that rabbits are sneaking into his garden at night and snacking on his plants. Each day he creates another obstacle and each night, the rabbits manage to get through. This cumulative tale is full of onomatopoeia and actions, sure to get your little listeners involved. And the twist at the end will be sure to have everyone reaching for a fresh crunchy carrot.

Galbraith, Kathryn O. and Joe Cepeda, illus. Two Bunny Buddies. New York: Houghton Mifflin Harcourt, 2014.
When two bunny buddies get tired and hungry, they argue and call names. But when they find themselves alone, they remember why they are friends. Sparse text and clean images make this a good choice for large crowds and knowing that you can argue with someone and still be friends.

Leathers, Philippa. The Black Rabbit. Somerville, MA: Candlewick Press, 2013.
Clever children will recognize right away that the black rabbit is simply a shadow but Rabbit is scared and tries to run away from this new creature. His attempts to outwit the black rabbit brings him face to face with a Wolf. Luckily, the Wolf is also foolish enough to think the black rabbit is a big scary creature.

Shea, Bob. Don't Play with your Food. New York: Disney Hyperion Books, 2014.
When Buddy, a fierce and grumpy monster, comes across some small peaceful bunnies, he wants to eat them. But these bunnies are as smart as they are cute and manage to put Buddy off day after day by offering up other ideas of fun things to do: eat cupcakes, go swimming, go to a carnival. When Buddy still wants to eat them, the very clever rabbits remind him about what you should not do with your food. The logic is flawless. This is a great book for readers' theater or animated tellings. Be sure to keep your eye on the ever-increasing number of bunnies.

Bunny Pattern

Rain

Drip! Drop! Umbrellas up! Rain can be experienced through all the senses: hear it fall, watch it stream down a window, smell the damp leaves, taste the crisp water, and feel the wetness on your skin. Appeal to all the sense with or without real puddles.

Sample Storytime

Welcome Song

Routine is important when working with children. Be sure to include welcome, transitional, and closing songs or activities to signify what is coming next. Don't be afraid to use the same ones; children take comfort in knowing what is coming next.

Opening Poem

"Let's Count the Raindrops" from Katz, Bobbi and Deborah Zemke, illus. More Pocket Poems. New York: Dutton Children's Books, 2009.
In this four-line chant-like verse by Alan Benjamin, raindrops are counted . . . "one million, two million, three million . . ." Because of the poems size and predictive nature this is one that you can teach young storytime goers quickly and one that they will enjoy repeating, especially during rainy seasons.

Action Rhyme

Itsy Bitsy Spider
Popular Rhyme

The itsy-bitsy spider
Climbed up the waterspout (match pointer fingers to thumbs on opposite hands and "climb" up)
Down came the rain (flutter your fingers down like rain)
And washed the spider out
Out came the sun (hold arms in a circle above your head)
And dried up all the rain (slowly lower arms)
And the itsy-bitsy spider
Climbed up the spout again ("climb" again)

Nonfiction for Storytime

Sayre, April Pulley. Raindrops Roll. New York: Beach Lane Books, 2015.
Simple sentences accompany high-definition photographs covering the impact of rain. Bugs seek shelter, spider webs glisten, mud is made, and beauty is uncovered. Simple enough to read aloud to a storytime crowd, with back matter to expand upon as needed by audience.

Transitional Song

See Welcome Song earlier.

Flannel Board Activity

Rainbow

Use the pattern at the end of this book to create a rainbow. As the colors are mentioned, place them on the flannel board. After initial reading, and placement, repeat the poem and point to the colors.

Rainbow
Adapted by M. Follis
(Tune: Did You Ever See a Lassie?)

Have you ever seen a rainbow,
A rainbow, a rainbow
Have you ever seen a rainbow
After a stormy sky?
With Red, Orange, Yellow,
And Green, Blue and Purple,
Have your ever seen a rainbow
After a stormy sky?

Picture Books for Storytime

Lichtenheld, Tom. Cloudette. New York: Henry Holt and Company, 2011.
Cloudette likes being a tiny cloud; it's just perfect for her personality and the games she likes to play with her friends. But sometimes she gets the desire to do something *big*. After a storm blows her to a faraway place, she finds her calling and makes a pond out of a sad, little puddle. This fun story introduces the concept of rain coming from clouds and includes some cloud/weather vocabulary like cold front and cumulus.

Root, Phyllis and Helen Craig, illus. Thirsty Thursday. Somerville, MA: Candlewick Press, 2009.
Everyone on Bonnie Bumble's farm is hot and thirsty. Will it ever rain? When a cloud finally blows by, Bonnie and the animals have to work together to tickle the cloud with a feather and make it rain.

Closing Song

See Welcome Song earlier.

Follow-Up Activities

Indoor Rain Storm

Materials:

- A spray bottle filled with water

Directions:

- As children leave the storytime space, lightly spray them with water.
- You are sure to get squeals of delight and kids asking for more.

Sprinkler Time

While the library most likely cannot hook up a sprinkler outside for kids to play in, you can encourage parents to do so when they get home. Remind them that this will further the child's exploration of water and rain. Of course, encourage this only if it's a warm day.

If it happens to be a rainy day when you do this storytime, encourage parents to put away the umbrellas and dance in the rain with their children.

Early Literacy Tip: Play is an important factor in a child's development. Play related to literature links the good feelings of play and stories together.

Other Songs, Rhymes, and Fingerplays

Rain, Rain, Go Away
English Nursery Rhyme

Rain, rain, go away,
Come again some other day
We want to go outside and play
Come again some other day

It's Raining, It's Pouring
English Nursery Rhyme

It's raining, it's pouring
The old man is snoring
He went to bed and he
Bumped his head
And couldn't get up
In the morning.

Wright, Danielle, collected by, and Mique Moriuchi, illus. My Village: Rhymes from around the World. London: Frances Lincoln Children's Books, 2010.
"Rain" is a traditional Norwegian rhyme that may quickly become a storytime favorite. It has an easy rhythm and fun little phrases like "zick, zack" and "tick, tack."

Additional Poetry

Gray, Rita, compiler, and Ryan O'Rourke, illus. One Big Rain: Poems for a Rainy Day. Watertown, MA: Charlesbridge, 2010.
While we often think of rain as an April occurrence, it falls year-round and each season's rain has a different mood. Explore the rain through haiku and other poetic forms by Robert Frost, Carl Sandburg, and Kyoshi. The colors of the illustrations match the temperature and look of the seasons as they change.

Kosaka, Fumi, illus. Let's Count the Raindrops! New York: Viking, 2001.
In this collection of poems about the weather, be sure to check out "Clouds" by Christina G. Rossetti and the title poem, "Let's Count the Raindrops" by Alan Benjamin. Short, simple, and sweet these are beautiful and child-friendly.

Martin Jr., Bill, Michael Sampson, and various illustrators. The Bill Martin Jr. Big Book of Poetry. New York: Simon & Schuster, 2008.
"Spring Rain" (p. 34) by Marchette Chute, with its chant-like rhythm, cheerfully recounts the sudden eruption of a spring shower. The cheerful meter and illustrations further the upbeat

attitude of a possibly uncomfortable situation. "I couldn't be much wetter . . ." yet no one is complaining.

Vardell, Sylvia and Janet Wong, ed. The Poetry Friday Anthology for Science: Poems for the School Year Integrating Science, Reading and Language Arts, K-5 Teacher Edition. Princeton, NJ: Pomelo Books, 2014.
The pattern of the rain cycle is told in a long thin stream of words that fall gently down the page in "Water Round" by Leslie Bulion (p. 124). Filled with action and sound, play with the pacing of your reading to reflect the action. Start fast as drops "splink" and "splash" and slow the pace as water drops "drip" and "seep" into the earth only to resurface as a bubbling brook, and finally back where it starts in dark heavy clouds.

Additional Nonfiction

Kaner, Etta and Marie Lafrance, illus. Who Likes the Rain? Tonawanda, NY: Kids Can Press, 2007.
A child likes the rain because it forms puddles, because it waters the plants, and because the air smells differently after a storm. Read about the delights of the rain then open the flaps to learn more about the science behind them. Share the basic storyline with a group and leave the information behind the flaps for one-on-one sharing.

Schaefer, Lola M. A Rainy Day. Mankato, MN: Pebble Books, 2000.
Part of a young nonfiction series, "What Kind of Day Is It?" this series explores daily weather in a manner suitable for the very young. Each double-paged spread contains a photo and a single sentence telling about the things you see, and that happen on a rainy day. The only drawback to this series is the small trim, but the content matter and child friendliness makes this worth using. Other books in the series: *A Cold Day, A Hot Day, A Snowy Day, A Sunny Day, and A Windy Day.*

Stewart, Melissa and Constance R. Bergum, illus. When Rain Falls. Atlanta, GA: Peachtree, 2008.
This softly illustrated picture book is perfect when you want to discuss rain, but not rely heavily on the water cycle. The narrator takes us to different locations so we can see what happens when rain falls in your neighborhood, in the forest, in the field, in the wetlands, and in the desert. The actions of inhabitants of these biomes are shared in multi-paneled frames. A great share across topics of wildlife, weather, and habitats.

Williams, Judith. Why Is It Raining? Berkeley Heights, NJ: Enslow Publishers, Inc., 2004.
Short, two-page chapters cover a wide variety of topics from how raindrops are formed, how rain is measured, and how clouds bring rain. This book can be used for older readers to explore the topic in a more complete manner, or chapters can be singled out for a younger audience. This title is part of the "I Like Weather" series. Other books include: *Why Is It Windy?, Why Is It Snowy? and How Does the Sun Make Weather?*

Additional Fiction Picture Books

Bluemle, Elizabeth and G. Brian Karas, illus. Tap Tap Boom Boom. Somerville, MA: Candlewick Press, 2014.
When a thunderstorm strikes in the city, everyone takes shelter in the subway station. With lots of rhymes, taps, and booms, this book is a lot of fun to read. Like any feel good story, it ends with a rainbow.

Early Literacy Tip:
Books can put a positive spin on things (like thunderstorms) that scare many children.

Mack, Jeff. Good News Bad News. San Francisco, CA: Chronicle Books, 2012.
With just two words of text and some expressive characters, a series of good and bad events tell the tale of an unfortunate picnic.

Weeks, Sarah and Jane Manning, illus. Drip, Drop. New York: HarperCollins Publishers, 2000.
A leaky roof keeps Pip Squeak up all night finding pots, pans, and cups to fill up with rainwater. Rhyming text with a peppy beat makes this a fun read-aloud.

Willems, Mo. Are You Ready to Play Outside? New York: Hyperion Books for Children, 2008.
When best friends Gerald and Piggie get ready to play outside, they are dismayed at the rain. Good thing they have some friends to show them how much fun puddles can be.

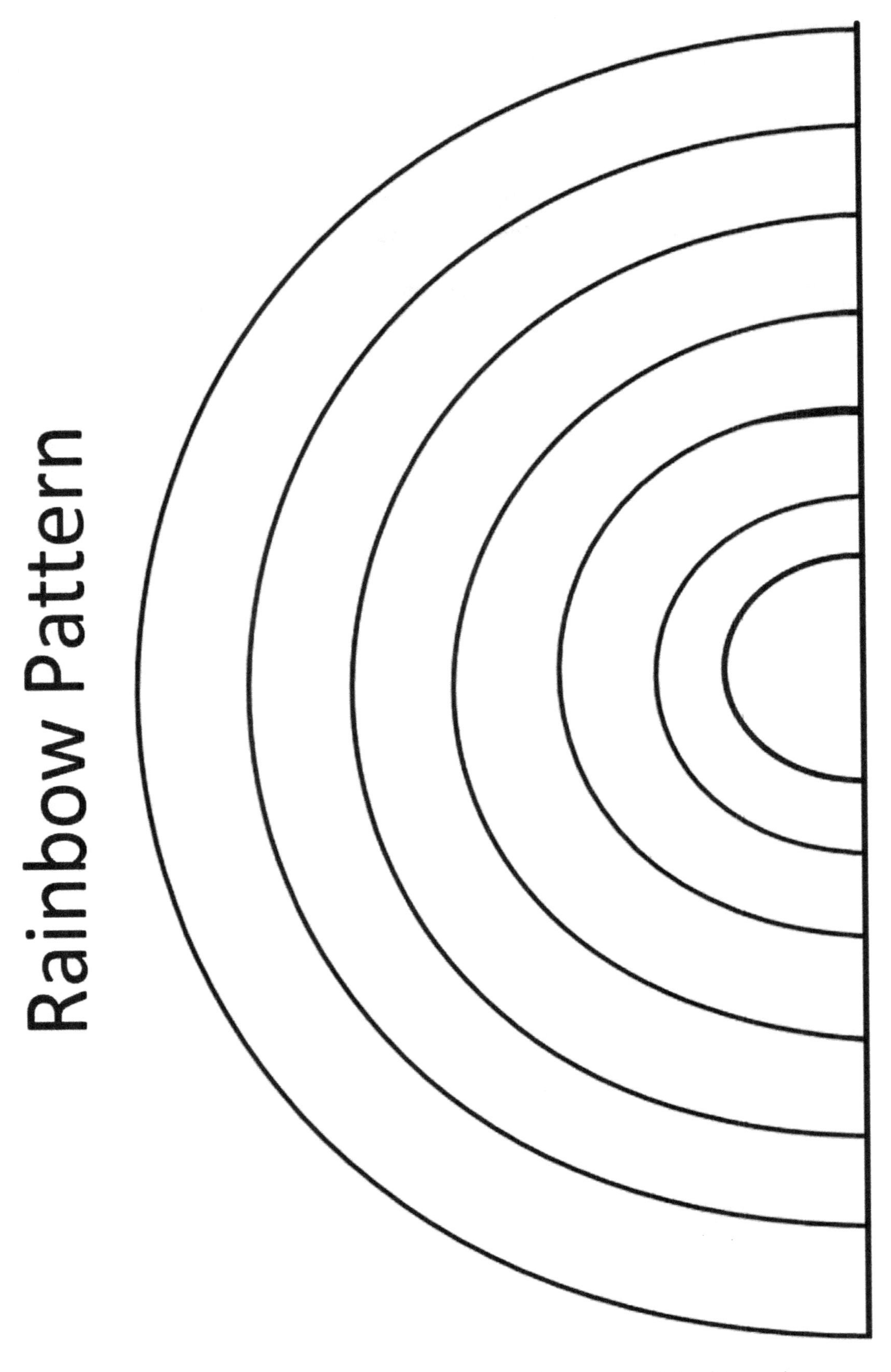
Rainbow Pattern

Reptiles

Things that slither, things that crawl, things with scales that scale the walls! It seems that people either love or fear the creatures of the reptile world. Slither your way into a fun storytime.

Sample Storytime

Welcome Song

Routine is important when working with children. Be sure to include welcome, transitional, and closing songs or activities to signify what is coming next. Don't be afraid to use the same ones; children take comfort in knowing what is coming next.

Opening Poem

"Turtles" from Lewis, J. Patrick, ed. National Geographic Book of Animal Poetry: 200 Poems with Photographs That Squeak, Soar, and Roar! Washington, DC: National Geographic, 2012.

Turtles (p. 95) are slow, shy creatures, and Charles Ghigna has captured their essence in this quick poem.

Action Rhyme

Alligator Alligator

Alligator alligator (open your arms wide, one up one down,
and close them like an alligator mouth)
Sitting on a log
Down in the water (hold your hand up to your forehead
like you are looking at something)
He sees a frog
Down goes the alligator (shoot one hand quickly down)
Around goes the log (roll your hands like the wheels on the bus)
Away swims the frog (pretend to swim)

Nonfiction for Storytime

Cowley, Joy and Nic Bishop, photography. Chameleon, Chameleon. New York: Scholastic Press, 2005.

Information about chameleons is presented through a story about a chameleon searching for food. Kids will especially like the photograph of the chameleon catching a caterpillar with his tongue. With minimal text and large photographs, share this whole book with a storytime crowd.

Transitional Song

See Welcome Song earlier.

Flannel Board Activity

Chameleon Chameleon

Find a simple chameleon clip art image, one that you can either print on colored paper, or can color. Be sure to scale the chameleon and leaf and petals so that the chameleon can "hide" behind the leaf. Create pairs of leaves and petals, and their coordinating chameleons. Patterns for the leaves and petals are at the end of the chapter.

You will want to start with a typical green chameleon, and prepare additional flannel pieces in pairs with the newly colored chameleon behind the leaf.

So, when you place the red leaf down, you will place the red leaf and chameleon together. When you remove the leaf, the chameleon will seem to have changed color.

Explain to children that chameleons can change colors in order to hide themselves in their environment. Have children fill in the blanks for the color to encourage participation.

Chameleon, Chameleon
By M. Follis

Chameleon, chameleon
Sitting on a wall
Chameleon, chameleon
Watching leaves fall

One just landed on his head.
Now our chameleon is turning _____ (red)

Oh look, another just fell down
Now our chameleon is turning _____ (brown)

One landed on his nose, lucky fellow
Now our chameleon is turning _____ (yellow)

A blossom fell down and landed with a "plink"
Now our chameleon is turning _____ (pink)

Floating through the air, are these flower petals, two
Now our chameleon is turning _____ (blue)

Picture Books for Storytime

MacDonald, Margaret Read and Deborah Melmon, illus. Give Up, Gecko!: A Folktale from Uganda. Las Vegas: Amazon Children's Publishing, 2013.
The animals are thirsty and decide to stomp on the ground to dig for water. The first one to find water will be their new chief. The big animals STOMP! The medium animals STOMP! The little animals STOMP! Everyone gives up. Except for Gecko, he keeps trying and trying and trying until he finds water. Everyone can join along "Heavy! Heavy! Heavy! Stomp! Stomp! Stomp!"

Early Literacy Tip:
Many folktales are a bit long for storytime. Look for ones that provide opportunities for audience participation to successfully share these stories with a group.

Sherry, Kevin. Turtle Island. New York: Dial Books for Young Readers, 2014.
Turtle is huge. Yet even a giant animal can feel lonely in the great big sea. When four animals are shipwrecked, they take refuge on his shell and Turtle is thrilled to have friends. When they return to their families, he is distraught. But all is well when they return to set up a permanent settlement with their families. Turtle takes up most of the space on the pages showing the vastness of his size and his heart.

Closing Song

See Welcome Song earlier.

Follow-Up Activities

Turtle Craft

Materials:

- Paper plates
- Green tissue paper (multiple shades of green)
- Glue or glue sticks
- Green construction paper
- Googly eyes or crayons (optional)

Directions:

- Cut the tissue paper into approximately one inch squares.
- Use the pattern at the end of the chapter to make a turtle head, legs, and tail out of green construction paper.
- The kids glue the tissue paper squares onto the back of the paper plate creating their own turtle back design.
- Glue the head, legs, and tail from the underside of the shell.
- Add googly eyes or draw eyes with crayons if you wish.

Other Songs, Rhymes, and Fingerplays

Slow Pokey Turtle
By M. Follis

Slow pokey turtle
Looks for some fun
Slow pokey turtle
Finds some sun
She climbs upon a rock
And goes into her shell
And the slow pokey turtle
Into sleep fell.

Crocodile
By J. Dietzel-Glair
(Tune: I Wish I Were an Oscar Mayer Weiner)

I wish there wasn't a crocodile beside me
That is what I really want today

'Cause if there wasn't a crocodile beside me
It wouldn't have to quickly run away

There Once Was a Turtle
Traditional Rhyme

There was a little turtle (make a fist)
He lived in a box (outline box in air)
He swam in a puddle (pretend to swim)
He climbed on the rocks (pretend to climb)
He snapped at a mosquito (snap fingers and thumb together in a mouth chomping motion)
He snapped at a flea (snap fingers and thumb together in a mouth chomping motion)
He snapped at a minnow (snap fingers and thumb together in a mouth chomping motion)
He snapped at me (snap fingers and thumb together in a mouth chomping motion)
He caught the mosquito (clap)
He caught the flea (clap)
He caught the minnow (clap)
But he didn't catch me! (shake finger no)

For this poem, see if you can find a piece of clip art that has a snake in an S shape. Enlarge and make into a flannel piece. As you read the poem, trace your finger along the S shape. If you would rather not use the flannel board, trace the S shape in the air in front of you, and invite adults to assist youngsters in doing the same.

S Is for Snake
By M. Follis

S is for "slither"
S is for "scales"
S is the sound of a hiss (ssssssss)
Be careful of their tails!

Early Literacy Tip:
Tracing letters (on a page or in the air) helps with letter recognition.

Additional Poetry

Florian, Douglas. Lizards, Frogs, and Polliwogs. San Diego: Harcourt, Inc., 2001.
Slither in for a scaly poem about a skink, tortoise, crocodile and alligator, iguana, cobra, komodo dragon, gila monster, box turtle, chameleon, and diamondback rattlesnake. Especially fun are the poems that take a shape like "The Gecko" and "The Python."

Janeczko, Paul B., ed. and Melissa Sweet, illus. Dirty Laundry Pile: Poems in Different Voices. New York: HarperCollins Publishers, 2001.
In "Old Tortoise" by Madeleine Comora, our reptile comments that while you, passing by far too quickly, might think he is a rock, he is not. And if you slow down to his pace, you will not only "hear the old rocks breathe" but will be privy to all of the wonder around us. If. You. Just. Slow. Down. Another poem, "Turtle in July" by Marilyn Singer tells of the wisdom of a turtle, happily submerged in a pond, with only his nose above water in the "heavy hot thick sticky icky" July heat.

Lewis, J. Patrick, ed. National Geographic Book of Animal Poetry: 200 Poems with Photographs That Squeak, Soar, and Roar! Washington, DC: National Geographic, 2012.
Open up a quick conversation about snakes shedding their skin after reading "Dressing Like a Snake" by Georgia Heard. Or, perhaps, speak to the quiet ease of having a snake as a pet in Rebecca Kai Dotlich's "Pet Snake." Both poems can be found on p. 156. Then slowly travel to page 164 for a photograph of a yellow-spotted Amazon river turtle accompanied by three poems.

Additional Nonfiction

Arnosky, Jim. Slither and Crawl: Eye to Eye with Reptiles. New York: Sterling, 2009.
This attractive book includes fold-out pages with life-size paintings of reptiles. Use this book to introduce a reptile storytime by looking at and commenting on the illustrations. Would you want to meet these reptiles in the wild?

Maylan, Sue. Reptiles. New York: DK Publishing, Inc., 2005.
Look eye to eye with geckos, snakes, and turtles. Children will love looking at the photographs while you read the large font text on each page. Further information is shared on each page for families who wish to learn more.

Rathmell, Donna and Barbara J. Bergwerf, photography. Carolina's Story: Sea Turtles Get Sick Too! Mt. Pleasant, SC: Sylvan Dell Publishing, 2005.
Follow Carolina from her rescue on a beach, through her treatment at a turtle hospital, to her eventual release back into the wild. The author infers Carolina's feelings throughout the process helping children empathize with her plight. Large photographs make this a viable storytime choice.

Additional Fiction Picture Books

Bergman, Mara and Nick Maland, illus. Snip Snap! What's That? New York: Greenwillow Books, 2005.
Would you be scared if an alligator came into your home? The suspense builds until three scared children have had enough, "Alligator, you get out!" The slightly scary story ends on a funny note as the tables turn and the alligator gets scared.

Gorbachev, Valeri. Red Red Red. New York: Philomel Books, 2007.
Turtle is in a rush. He is off to see something red and he doesn't have time to tell the other animals what it is. Curious, they all follow him to the top of the hill where they all see a magnificent red sunset.

Gorbachev, Valeri. Turtle's Penguin Day. New York: Alfred A. Knopf, 2008.
After a bedtime story featuring penguins, Turtle decides he wants to go to school dressed as a penguin. His teacher decides to expand on the concept and Turtle and his friends spend the day learning about and acting like penguins. But what will Turtle decide he wants to be next?

Gravett, Emily. Blue Chameleon. New York: Simon & Schuster Books for Young Readers, 2010.
Poor little chameleon is sad and lonely. In effect, he is blue. He tries to make friends, and fit in with all sorts of things; a yellow banana, a brown boot, a striped sock, but nothing works. It isn't until he meets a kindred colorful spirit that he can truly be himself.

Na, Il Sung. Hide & Seek. New York: Alfred A. Knopf, 2011.
When elephant and his friends play hide and seek, Chameleon always wins!

Watt, Mélanie. Leon the Chameleon. Tonawanda, NY: Kids Can Press, 2001.
Leon the Chameleon doesn't fit in with the rest of the other chameleons. When everyone else is green against the grass, Leon turned red. Being different brings out a slew of emotion for Leon; frightened, embarrassed, and lonely. But one day Leon is given the chance to see how the thing that makes him different also makes him Leon.

Willems, Mo. Can I Play Too? New York: Hyperion Books for Children, 2010.
Snakes cannot play catch but this Snake is willing to try. As it turns out, it is impossible for Snake to play catch because he doesn't have arms. That doesn't matter to Gerald and Piggie, they can find another way to include Snake in their game of catch.

Reptile Pattern

Turtle Pattern

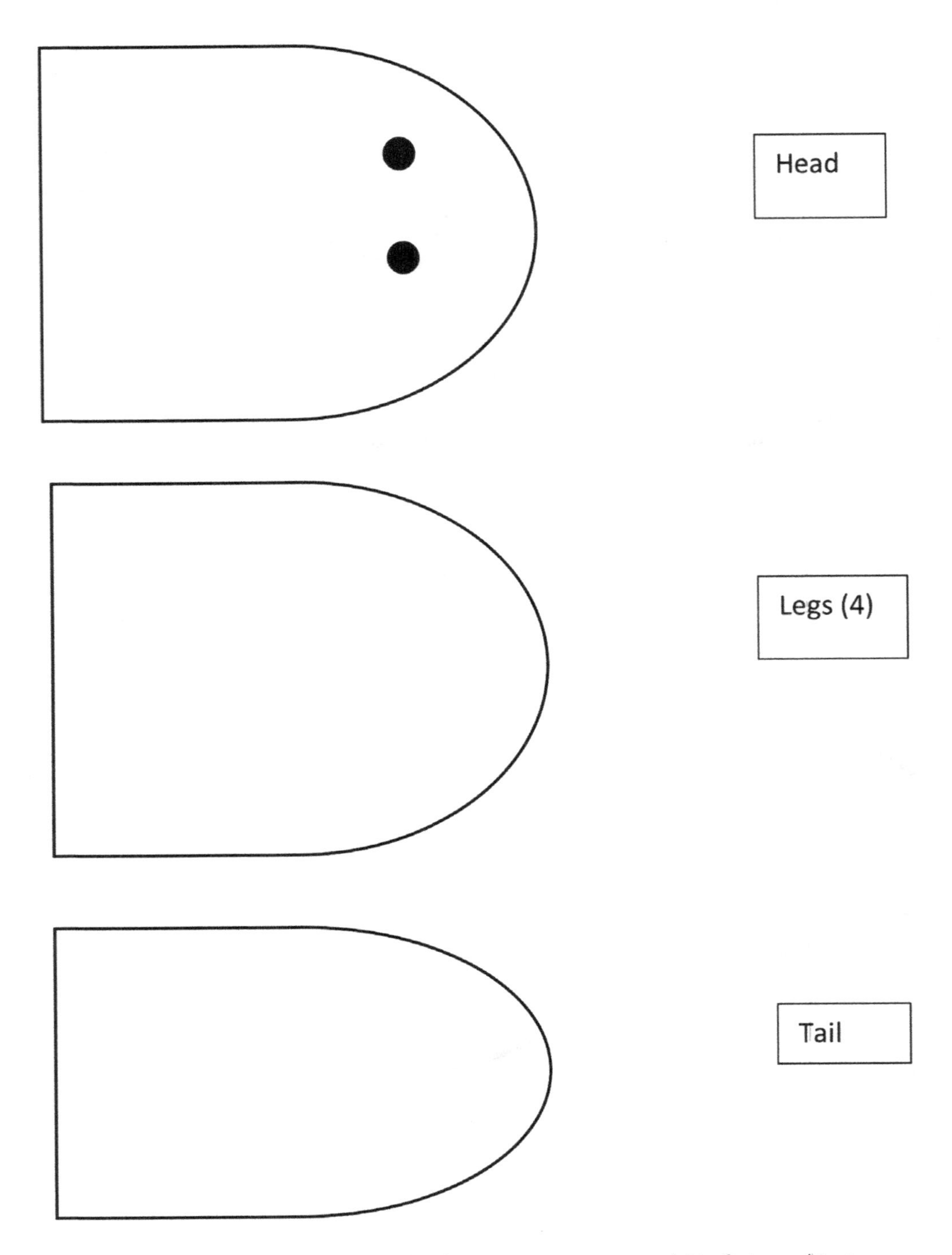

Rocks, Dirt, and Mud

Whether smoothed perfectly by the sea, or roughly protruding from the ground, rocks are little bits of treasure. Whether dry and crumbly, or wet after the rain, dirt makes for grubby fun.

Sample Storytime

Welcome Song

Routine is important when working with children. Be sure to include welcome, transitional, and closing songs or activities to signify what is coming next. Don't be afraid to use the same ones; children take comfort in knowing what is coming next.

Opening Poem

"Making Soup" from Singer, Marilyn and LeUyen Pham, illus. A Stick Is an Excellent Thing: Poems Celebrating Outdoor Play. New York: Clarion Books, 2012.
The only thing better that mud pies is mud soup and this chant-like poem deserves to be shouted while you combine the magic ingredients: "grass and stones and mud (one scoop)."

Early Literacy Tip:
Playing is a great way for little ones to practice life skills. Making mud pies is practice for young ones.

Action Rhyme

I Like to Dig
Adapted by M. Follis
(Tune: Three Blind Mice)

I like to dig (mime digging)
I like to dig
In the dirt (mime digging)
In the dirt
I like to dig in the cold wet ground
Dirt on my fingers and rocks all around
The slimy wet mud makes a squishy sound
I like to dig

Nonfiction for Storytime

Aston, Dianna Hutts and Sylvia Long, illus. A Rock Is Lively. San Francisco, CA: Chronicle Books, 2012.
We tend to think of rocks as stagnant objects. In reality, they are ever-changing, useful, and beautiful objects. Read just the cursive text to share this lovely title with a storytime crowd.

Transitional Song

See Welcome Song earlier.

Flannel Board Activity

Here Is a Rock

This flannel board allows for an expanding vocabulary and entry points for discussing the various types of rocks and why they are smooth, like a pebble from erosion done by water, disintegrated like sand, from the pounding of the ocean and how rock has another meaning, as a type of music.

Create your own pebble, boulder flannel pieces, or use the pattern included at the end of this chapter.

Here Is a Rock
By M. Follis

Here is a pebble, found in a stream
Here is some sand, rocks that used to be
Here is a boulder, blocking a path
And here is some music, oh what a blast!

Put the flannel board pieces up as you mention them in the poem. Have an iPod or CD player on hand and hit play when you mention the last kind of rock!

After you put up the flannel pieces, discuss how they are the same and different and what makes them so.

Early Literacy Tip:
This flannel board activity is one example of how you can expand the vocabulary of young storytime goers by including words and discussing their meanings. How are they alike and different? Be sure to point out when words have more than one meaning, like rock.

Picture Books for Storytime

Barnett, Mac and Jon Klassen, illus. Sam & Dave Dig a Hole. Somerville, MA: Candlewick Press, 2014.
Two friends and a dog, armed with shovels, chocolate milk, and animal crackers, set out on a mission: to dig a hole. How will they know when they are done digging? "We won't stop digging until we find something spectacular." Readers are privy to the buried gems all around Sam and Dave, but each time they get close, they change directions. Please have your storytime goers pay close attention to the dog in the story as Jon Klassen tells a story all his own!

Hillenbrand, Jane and Will. What a Treasure! New York: Holiday House, 2006.
When little mole gets a new shovel, he sets off to look for treasure. While the twig, shell, and other items found are not quite what the mole seeks, they are treasures to others! Eventually mole makes a great find, a new friend. Bright egg tempera and oils combined with friendly faces make this a book young storytime goers will really dig.

Closing Song

See Welcome Song earlier.

Follow-Up Activities

Rock Walk

Families often go on nature walks. They look for flowers, trees, and animals along their path. Why not expand that activity into a rock walk. Much like searching for seashells on a beach, you can look for colorful, unusual, or eye-catching rocks. Take your storytime group outside your library on your quest for rocks.

If there is time, have everyone bring their chosen rock back to the storytime room. Ask questions to help them describe their rock: Is your rock smooth? Is your rock bumpy? What color is your rock? Is it big? Is it heavy?

An added benefit to this activity is the fact that families can easily replicate it on their own at a later date.

Pet Rock

Materials:

- Medium-sized rocks (about the size of a fist)
- Paint brushes
- Brightly colored paint
- Paper plates

Directions:

- Put dabs of paint on the paper plates.
- Let everyone paint their rock with a design of their own creation.
- Share the rhyme "Pet Rock" found later in this chapter.

Other Songs, Rhymes, and Fingerplays

I'm A Rock
By M. Follis
(Tune: I'm a Nut)

Way below the cold hard ground,
That is where I can be found
If you dig in dirt you'll see
Loads of others just like me
I'm a rock
I'm a rock
I'm a rock I'm a rock, I'm a rock

Some are rough and some are smooth
Some and small and some are huge
I build walls and surround seas
Rocks are all around you see.
I'm a rock, I'm a rock, I'm a rock, I'm a rock, I'm a rock

Pet Rock
By J. Dietzel-Glair

This is my pet rock
I take him everywhere I go

I used paint to decorate him
Now he's a bright sunny yellow

This is my pet rock
Isn't he cool?
I just wish he would do more
Than sit quietly on a stool.

Additional Poetry

Foxworthy, Jeff and Steve Björkman, illus. Dirt on My Shirt. New York: HarperCollins, 2008.
There is something so freeing about getting dirty. This child is a mess and he loves it. Even the page looks like it's been splattered in mud. Share this book's title poem and relish the thought of getting messy.

Heard, Georgia, ed. Falling Down the Page. New York: Roaring Brook Press, 2009.
In "Show-and-Tell Rocks" by Terry Webb Harshman a young collector lists all of the many kinds of rocks they collect and excitedly exclaims that "if rocks could talk, the secrets we'd hear!" Rich in vocabulary-expanding words like geodes, mica, and so much more.

Martin Jr., Bill, Michael Sampson, and various illustrators. The Bill Martin Jr. Big Book of Poetry. New York: Simon & Schuster, 2008.
"The Muddy Puddle" by Dennis Lee (p. 32) waxes poetic about the "muddiness of mud." You will need a bath after sharing this one! You can also read "Kick a Little Stone" by Dorothy Aldis (p. 112) and spend some time walking while kicking a little stone ahead of you.

Vardell, Sylvia and Janet Wong, ed. The Poetry Friday Anthology for Science: Poems for the School Year Integrating Science, Reading and Language Arts, K-5 Teacher Edition. Princeton, NJ: Pomelo Books, 2014.
What can you make with this delicious mud recipe from Rebecca Kai Dotlich? Follow the directions in "Water = Dirt =" (p. 37) to find out. The toe squishiness is a bonus!
Then turn to where Ken Slesarik asks "Are rocks living?" in "My Rock" (p. 47). This is a great way to engage in descriptive language and explore what is "alive."

Additional Nonfiction

Christian, Peggy. If You Find a Rock. San Diego: Harcourt, 2000.
There are so many kinds of rocks. Rocks perfect for skipping, perfect for writing with and some that have no practical uses except to remind you of a time and place when you found the perfect rock. Words stand like a solid pillar running down the page, surrounded by plenty of whitespace and sepia-toned photographs. A calm, quiet, and beautiful book for sharing.

Rosinsky, Natalie. M. and Matthew John, illus. Rocks: Hard, Soft, Smooth, and Rough. Minneapolis, MN: Picture Window Books, 2003.
The different types of rocks (igneous, sedimentary, and metamorphic) are explained in easy-to-understand text. The illustrations give visual clues on the rocks but, if possible, bring in samples for everyone to see and feel (granite, limestone, etc.—maybe not the rubies and diamonds).

Additional Fiction Picture Books

Fleming, Denise. Underground. New York: Beach Lane Books, 2012.
It's not just children who love to dig. Each rhyming double-page spread takes you "way down, underground" to see the creatures that dig and live beneath your feet. Appropriate

for a wide range of young readers, especially with the additional information included in the back matter. Fleming's pulp painting takes on earthy hues with plenty of details for individuals to pour over.

Lopez, Mario, Marissa Lopez Wong, and Maryn Roos, illus. Mud Tacos! New York: Celebra Children's Books, 2009.
Brother and sister Mario and Marissa play pretend restaurant, where MUD TACOS are on the menu! Using mud, twigs, flowers, and worms the fun lasts for hours. A great take on mud pies, and the power of imaginative play.

McGuirk, Leslie. If Rocks Could Sing: A Discovered Alphabet. Berkeley, CA: Tricycle Press, 2011.
Just like seeing shapes in the clouds, rocks can look like lots of fun things. In this case, rocks can look like something from each letter of the alphabet. Show the entire book or choose a few favorite pages, perhaps E is for elephant, K is for kick, or T is for toast.

Salas, Laura Purdie. A Rock Can Be. Minneapolis, MN: Millbrook Press, 2015.
Poetic lines about all of the things a rock can be aside from its mineral elements. It can be a "volcano flower . . . lake skimmer . . . hopscotch maker . . . fire sparker." Interesting back matter continues the discussion on how different rocks work to be all of these things.

Flannel Board Patterns

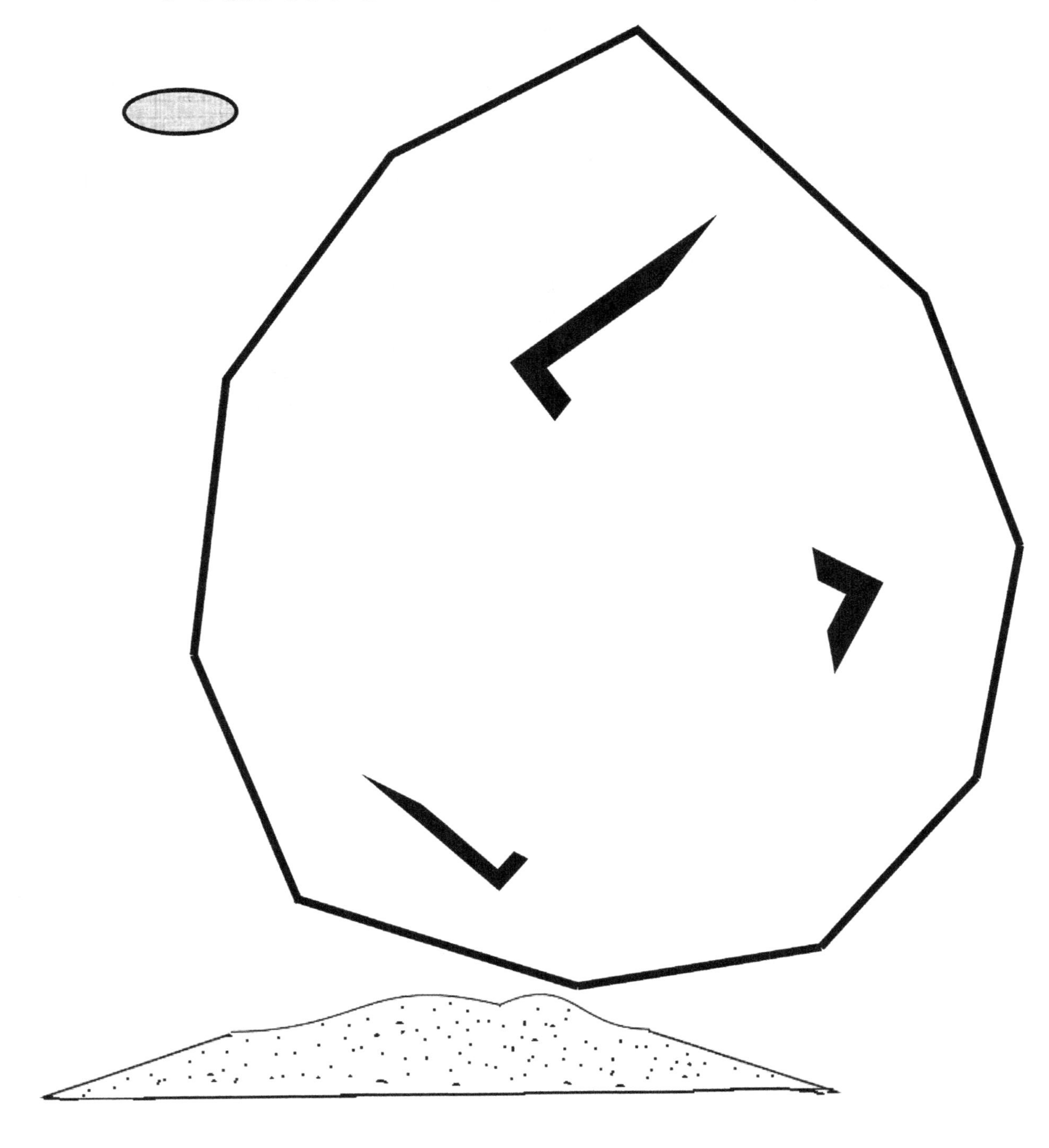

School

More and more of our little ones are attending preschool before heading off to kindergarten. Even if they are not in a formal classroom setting, they understand that school is where the big kids go and learn things like counting and the alphabet. Having storytimes on the topic can help make the leap to big kid school a bit easier.

Sample Storytime

Welcome Song

Routine is important when working with children. Be sure to include welcome, transitional, and closing songs or activities to signify what is coming next. Don't be afraid to use the same ones; children take comfort in knowing what is coming next.

Opening Poem

"Good Morning! How Are You Today" from Calmenson, Stephanie and Melissa Sweet, illus. Kindergarten Kids: Riddles, Rebuses, Wiggles, Giggles, and More! New York: HarperCollins Publishers, 2005.

This poem leads right into the day's storytime by ending with the line "Who's ready to start our Kindergarten day?" Make the poem interactive by having everyone raise their hands when the questions about the moods pertain to them.

Action Rhyme

Go to School
By M. Follis

1 + 1 = 2 (put up one finger on each hand and bring them together indicating addition)
2 + 2 = 4 (put up two fingers on each hand and bring them together indicating addition)
Go to school
You'll learn much more

3 + 3 = 6 (put up three fingers on each hand and bring them together indicating addition)
4 + 4 = 8 (put up four fingers on each hand and bring them together indicating addition)
Go to school
Don't be late

5 + 5 = 10 (put up five fingers on each hand and bring them together indicating addition)
I'm out of fingers
Let's start again! (REPEAT)

Nonfiction for Storytime

Carr, Aaron. The School. New York: AV2 by Weigl, 2014.

Kids can be anxious about starting school, but this short introduction shows them the types of things they will find there: teachers, desks, a gym, and activities. The best part? Everyone in the two-page photographs looks like they are having so much fun!

Transitional Song

See Welcome Song earlier.

Flannel Board Activity

School Bus

Use the pattern found at the end of this chapter to create this flannel board. As each child is mentioned, add their face to the school bus window.

The School Bus
By M. Follis

Mrs. Shriver, the school bus driver
Pick up all of us kids
She makes her stops
Around our blocks
And greets each one of us at the bus door

First she picks up Joe, who everyone knows
Lives on Honeysuckle Road.

Second is Sue whose house is blue
And shows off her new shoes.

Third is Stan, who has a plan
To be the smartest man.

Fourth is Beth whose hair is wet
In a hurry to get out of the door.

Last is me and as you can see
I keep some funny company.

Mrs. Shriver, the school bus driver
Lets us off at school
And tells us to have a good day.
I wonder where they go
Does anyone know
How does she spend the rest of her day?

Early Literacy Tip:
Children can learn things that may be difficult through singing and rhymes. In this rhyme activity, we are discussing first, second, third, fourth, and last.

Picture Books for Storytime

Calmenson, Stephanie and Abby Carter, illus. Ollie's School Day: A Yes-and-No Book. New York: Holiday House, 2012.
Covering the activities of a school day from getting dressed to returning home, readers are asked which of Ollie's actions are appropriate for school. When asked a question, will he do a back flip, will he sing? NO! He will raise his hand. A humorous and interactive take on school behavior.

Early Literacy Tip:
Children are not born with innate knowledge about how to behave in storytime and in school. Experience and books like *Ollie's School Day* can help them learn what is appropriate.

Cuyler, Margery and Bob Kolar, illus. The Little School Bus. New York: Henry Holt and Company, 2014.
This personified school bus tells his story of how he picks up children for school with his driver, Bob. Riding the bus can be scary for some kids, but this book makes it look fun and easy.

Closing Song

See Welcome Song earlier.

Follow-Up Activities

School Bus Practice

Many kids are very excited about going to school, but their first trip on a school bus can still cause some jitters; the steps are steep and the seats look huge. Help to quell some of this apprehension by arranging for a school bus to visit after storytime. Let everyone practice getting on and off the bus.

Other Songs, Rhymes, and Fingerplays

Alphabet Song

Letters are one of the first things children learn in school. Sing the ABC song together.

I Like to Go to School
By M. Follis
(Tune: The Farmer in the Dell)

I like to go to school
I like to go to school
It's where I go
To learn all I know
I like to go to school

I like to go to school
I like to go to school
Books and friends
The fun never ends
I like to go to school

Every Day at School
By M. Follis
(Tune: Here We Go Round the Mulberry Bush)

This is the way we learn our letters
Learn our letters, learn our letters
This is the way we learn our letters
Every day at school

Other verses:
Count our numbers
Read our stories
Play with our friends

Additional Poetry

Martin Jr., Bill, Michael Sampson, and various illustrators. The Bill Martin Jr. Big Book of Poetry. New York: Simon & Schuster, 2008.
"First Day of School" by Aileen Fisher (p. 84) covers all of the wonders of the first day of school.

Trapani, Iza. Rufus and Friends School Day. Watertown, MA: Charlesbridge, 2010.
Fourteen traditional poems, placed in a school setting for a fresh approach. The end of the book offers young readers a chance to return to the pages to complete a scavenger hunt style quest.

Additional Nonfiction

Adamson, Heather and Gail Saunders-Smith, Phd, consultant. School in Many Cultures. Mankato, MN: Capstone Press, 2008.
"Students go to school in many different cultures. How is your school like other schools?" The following pages follow a double-page format with some activities that all schools share, but the setting is diverse; from students studying science in a park in Vietnam to children enjoying recess in Africa.

Layne, Steven L. and Deborah Dover Layne, and Doris Ettlinger, illus. T Is for Teacher: A School Alphabet. Chelsea, MI: Sleeping Bear Press, 2005.
For those entering school, this is an alphabet that takes you through some of the people, places, and activities of school. Each page covers a letter of the alphabet and a related school-themed blurb. Additional information is provided on side panels.

Additional Fiction Picture Books

Brown, Peter. My Teacher Is a Monster (No I Am Not). New York: Little, Brown and Company, 2014.
When a little boy encounters his monster of a teacher outside of the classroom, he slowly begins to see her in a new light.

Dodd, Emma. Foxy. New York: Harper, 2012.
Emily is nervous about the first day of school. Fortunately she has her friend, Foxy and his magic tail, to help. Unfortunately, Foxy's magic isn't always perfect. Eventually, they make sure she has everything she needs for a successful first day.

Portis, Antoinette. Kindergarten Diary. New York: HarperCollins, 2010.
The diary of a young girl during her first month of Kindergarten displays her fears about going to school and the pleasant surprises she faces in the classroom. A fun way to ease the fears of little ones as they go off to school.

Yolen, Jane and Mark Teague, illus. How Do Dinosaurs Go to School? New York: Blue Sky Press, 2007.
Recess, show and tell, and riding the bus, these dinosaurs know how to do it all with class. While it may be crazy to have a silvisaurus sitting in the next desk, this book reminds us all how to be friendly and courteous. Look closely in the illustrations for the name of each dinosaur.

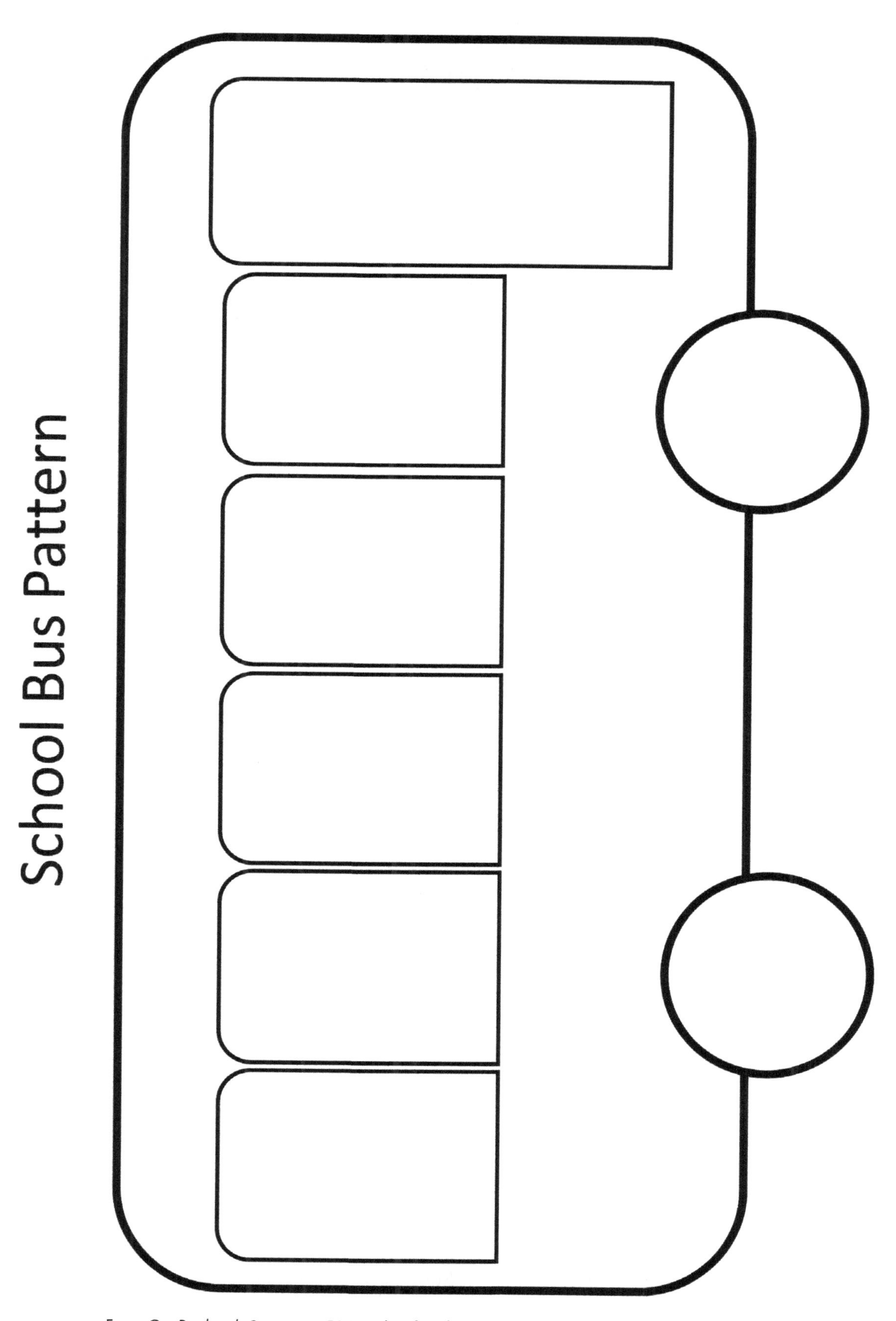
School Bus Pattern

School Bus Pattern

Faces are scaled to fit School Bus Windows

Sea Animals

There is something magical about sea animals. To be able to live under the surface of the water where they breath and swim seems impossible. Add to that the variety of life that can be found in the deep sea, and you have an endless supply of surprises for this storytime.

Sample Storytime

Welcome Song

Routine is important when working with children. Be sure to include welcome, transitional, and closing songs or activities to signify what is coming next. Don't be afraid to use the same ones; children take comfort in knowing what is coming next.

Opening Poem

"The Jellyfish" from Ode, Eric and Erik Brooks, illus. Sea Star Wishes: Poems from the Coast. Seattle, WA: Sasquatch Books, 2013.
Jellyfish sometimes seem to be nothing at all as reflected in this astute poem. The page in the book has illustrations of jellyfish, or you can show photographs of the real thing while reading the poem.

Action Rhyme

Fishey Hokey Pokey

Use the regular tune for Hokey Pokey but substitute, fins, and tails for arms and legs and instead of the line "turn yourself about" you may want to swim!

Nonfiction for Storytime

Rose, Deborah Lee and Hiroe Nakata, illus. Ocean Babies. Washington, DC: National Geographic, 2005.
From huge whales to tiny fish, new babies are born every day in the ocean. Illustrated like a storybook, this title can be shared with a large group. A paragraph of further information is provided in the back for each featured animal.

Transitional Song

See Welcome Song earlier.

Flannel Board Activity

Early Literacy Tip:
Flannel board activities offer a very visual element to knowledge acquisition for children.

Sea Animals Song

Using the Internet to find free clip art, collect images of the following: whale (with a waterspout), crab, octopus, shark, clam, and fish. Try to find images that are similar in type. You don't want to mix a very realistic photo of a shark, with a cute cartoonish oyster, although either/or is fine. Size appropriately, print, laminate, and adhere with flannel or velcro, to work with your display.

When introducing the activity, tell the children that you are going to share some creatures that live under the sea and ask them if they know their names. Once they have guessed correctly, be sure to offer a tidbit about each, which you will sing about.

Example: Do you know what this is? That's right! It's a whale! Now you know that whales live in the sea, but do you know why they blow water out of their blowhole? The blowhole is their nose, and when they blow air out it is just like when you exhale. Can you all blow air out of your nose? Good job! Now let's sing.

The Animals in the Sea
Adapted by M. Follis
(Tune: The Farmer in the Dell)

The whale lives in the sea
The whale lives in in sea
Heigh-ho, watch him blow
The whale lives in the sea

Repeat this process, using the following facts and verses.

Crabs walk sideways because of the way their legs are bent and attached.
The crab lives in the sea (Heigh-ho they scurry so)

The octopus lives in a den, a hole they find under rocks. If they can't find one, they dig one!
The octopus lives in the sea (Heigh-ho they live in holes)

Do you know that some sharks swim in their sleep? They are constantly on the go!
The shark lives in the sea (Heigh-ho watch them go)

Clams don't have arms or legs, but they use inside muscle to dig, or burrow themselves below the sand. This makes them harder to catch! Now wonder they look like they are smiling!
The clam lives in the sea (Heigh-ho the burrow below)

Fish follow the buddy system. They know they are safe when they are with their friends and families. They swim in large groups called "schools."
The fish lives in the sea (Heigh-ho in schools they go)

Early Literacy Tip:
Stop and repeat all the (possibly) new words contained in this flannel board: blowhole, waterspout, exhale, scurry, den, burrow, and school.

Picture Books for Storytime

Krosoczka, Jarrett J. Peanut Butter and Jellyfish. New York: Random House, 2014.
Best friends Peanut Butter (a seahorse) and Jellyfish explore the ocean, ignoring the taunts of the perpetually grumpy Crabby, but when Crabby gets trapped, they work together to set him free. A touch of the Lion and the Mouse and good opportunities to discuss bullying set against the bold and vibrant undersea illustrations make this an ideal share with storytime crowds.

Peck, Jan. Way Down Deep in the Deep Blue Sea. New York: Simon & Schuster, 2004.
When a small boy goes "way down deep in the deep blue sea," he discovers a plethora of sea creatures. The vibrant colors and hidden features in the illustrations offer plenty of discussion for prediction and discussion. The repetition of story pattern "Hello ____, (action)_____, see you later ____, swim away" is great perfect for participation of audiences of all ages. The surprise at the end is good for a sure laugh!

Closing Song

See Welcome Song earlier.

Follow-Up Activities

Draw Sea Creatures

Court, Rob. How to Draw Underwater Animals. Chanhassen, MN: The Child's World, 2007.
Using only four simple steps each, this title gives instructions on how to draw a fish, turtle, jellyfish, crab, shark, clam, sardines, puffer fish, starfish, lobster, eel, sea horse, dolphin, and octopus. Draw one of the animals together in the program or put the book on display for families to try at home.

Floating Jellyfish Craft

Example of completed craft included at the end of this chapter.

Materials:

- White paper plates
- Pastel watercolors
- Paintbrushes
- Pastel crepe paper
- Glue or glue sticks
- Hole punch
- Yarn
- Googley Eyes

Directions:

- Take a paper plate and cut it in half.
- Have children use watercolors to paint the white plate.
- Have children glue strips of pastel crepe paper as tentacles.
- Adhere eyes to jellyfish.
- Use hole punch for the top of the jellyfish and string a piece of yarn through it.

Other Songs, Rhymes, and Fingerplays

Fish Are Swimming
By M. Follis
(Tune: Are You Sleeping?)

Fish are swimming, fish are swimming
In the sea, in the sea

A-splishing and a-splashing, a-splishing and a-splashing
Look and see, look and see

Whale are blowing, whales are blowing
In the sea, in the sea
Water spouts everywhere, water spouts everywhere
Look and see, look and see

Dolphins jumping, dolphins jumping
In the sea, in the sea
Flipping and diving, flipping and diving
Look and see, look and see.

I'm a Fishey
Adapted by M. Follis
(Tune: I'm a Little Teapot)

I'm a little fishey, I can swim
Here is my tail and here is my fin
When I want to have fun, with my friends
I wiggle my tail and dive right in

Wright, Danielle, collected by, and Mique Moriuchi, illus. My Village: Rhymes from around the World. London: Frances Lincoln Children's Books, 2010.
"Big Whale" is a traditional rhyme from New Zealand that has been translated into English to be shared with your storytime.

Additional Poetry

Elliott, David and Holly Meade, illus. In the Sea. Somerville, MA: Candlewick Press, 2012.
Vibrant woodcuts accompany poems about a variety of sea creatures. With short poems and interesting illustrations, you can share a few selections in each storytime.

Janeczko, Paul, ed. and Robert Rayevsky, illus. Hey You! Poems to Skyscrapers, Mosquitoes and Other Fun Things. New York: HarperCollins, 2007.
Included among the pages of this collection are "Dear Shell" by Karla Kuskin, "Conch Shell" by Beverly McLoughland, "The Octopus" by Ogden Nash, and "The Sea Horse" by Douglas Florian. Enough to keep your storytime afloat in sea animal poetry.

Ode, Eric and Erik Brooks, illus. Sea Star Wishes: Poems from the Coast. Seattle, WA: Sasquatch Books, 2013.
Find poems dedicated to curious animals of the sea including the sea urchin, barnacle, octopus, and sea cucumber. Many of the poems and illustrations have a hint of humor.

Additional Nonfiction

Gibbs, Edward. I Spy Under the Sea. Somerville, MA: Templar Books, 2011.
Can you identify the sea animal peeking through the circular hole? Read the short fact before turning the page to see if you are right. Everyone in storytime will get involved with this guessing game.

Malyan, Sue. Sea Creatures. New York: DK Publishing, Inc., 2005.
Get up close and personal with a hermit crab, octopus, strawberry shrimp, crab, sea cucumber, queen scallop, seahorse, sea star, and giant blue cram. In typical DK fashion,

there is fascinating information all over the page. Read just the largest text on each page to share it with a storytime crowd.

O'Connell, Jennifer. The Eye of the Whale: A Rescue Story. Gardiner, ME: Tilbury House, Publishers, 2013.
This picture book recounts the 2005 story of a humpback whale tangled in crab-trap lines and her rescue by divers. Children will be entranced by the tale of a huge whale needing the assistance of humans.

Additional Fiction Picture Books

Magoon, Scott. Breathe. New York: Simon & Schuster Books for Young Readers, 2014.
Follow a little beluga whale on his adventure. Many of the pages have only one word but take the time to linger over the illustrations. Great for a storytime, this book is also wonderful as a bedtime book.

Marino, Gianna. Following Papa's Song. New York: Viking, 2014.
Little Blue is uncertain about the migration he is about to undertake. He gets curious along the way and loses the rest of the pod. Luckily he remembers his father's advice to listen for the other whales and he finds his way back. Illustrated in blue and green tones, readers will be immersed in this under the sea adventure.

Shea, Bob. I'm a Shark. New York: Balzer + Bray, 2011.
This awesome shark isn't scared of anything. In fact, everything else is scared of him. Just don't mention spiders because he'll swim away really fast. Everyone will be giggling at shark's boastful interactions.

Jellyfish Craft Example

Seasons

For the very young, the idea of seasons might be difficult to grasp. When you have only had three winters, the pattern of the changing seasons may not yet be apparent. But the changing seasons has a very real impact on their lives like what you wear and what is happening in the weather.

Sample Storytime

Welcome Song

Routine is important when working with children. Be sure to include welcome, transitional, and closing songs or activities to signify what is coming next. Don't be afraid to use the same ones; children take comfort in knowing what is coming next.

Opening Poem

"Spring" from Zolotow, Charlotte and Eric Blegvad, illus. Seasons: A Book of Poems. New York: HarperCollins Publishers, 2002.
Five short lines describe the sweet transition of winter into spring asking readers "What does this gentle wind sing?" Yes, the excited answer is spring.

Action Rhyme

The Leaves Are Falling Down
Adapted by M. Follis
(Tune: The Farmer in the Dell)

The leaves are falling down (wiggle fingers in a downward motion)
The leaves are falling down (wiggle fingers in a downward motion)
Flutter slowly to the ground (wiggle fingers in downward motion)
The leaves are falling down

My father rakes the leaves (act out raking)
My mother rakes the leaves (act out raking)
Gathering slowly from the ground (act out raking)
My family rakes the leaves

We jump into the pile (jump)
We jump into the pile (jump)
All the leaves are in the air
We jump into the pile (jump)

But guess what?

The leaves are falling down (wiggle fingers in a downward motion)
The leaves are falling down (wiggle fingers in a downward motion)
Flutter slowly to the ground
The leaves are falling down (wiggle fingers in a downward motion)

Early Literacy Tip:
Singing songs with exaggerated words and meter helps little ones recognize that language is broken down into smaller sounds.

Nonfiction for Storytime

McKneally, Ranida T. and Grace Lin, illus. Our Seasons. Watertown, MA: Charlesbridge, 2006.
Starting with autumn, find questions to answers relating to each season: Why do leaves change color? Why is there frost on the window? What makes a thunderstorm? Why do fireflies glow? Each page is illuminated with child-friendly haikus. Share the poetry with a group and make the book available for one-on-one sharing afterward.

Transitional Song

See Welcome Song earlier.

Flannel Board Activity

Map to Spring

"Map to Spring" by Rebecca Kai Dotlich reads like street directions. Create a map on your flannel board that you can follow with a toy car as you read the poem. Use the image found at the end of this chapter or create your own.

"Map to Spring" can be found in:

Hopkins, Lee Bennett, selector, and David Diaz, illus. Sharing the Seasons: A Book of Poems. New York: Margaret K. McElderry Books, 2010.

Picture Books for Storytime

Lyon, George Ella and August Hall, illus. What Forest Knows. New York: Atheneum Books for Young Readers, 2014.
Textured illustrations accompany lyrical text as the seasons come and go in the forest. Search for the dog on each page, sometimes just a tail, to add extra fun to this read-aloud.

Schertle, Alice and Matt Phelan, illus. Very Hairy Bear. Orlando, FL: Harcourt, Inc., 2007.
Bear doesn't mind his "no-hair nose" when he catches fish in the spring, when searching for honey in the summer, or when the leaves fall in autumn. But when the snow falls, he has to find a way to keep his nose warm so he can sleep.

Closing Song

See Welcome Song earlier.

Follow-Up Activities

Fall Leaves

Materials:

- Tree pattern (you can find a pattern at the end of the Trees chapter)
- Fall colored tissue paper
- Glue

- Crayons
- Paper plate
- Paint brushes

Directions:

- Photocopy tree pattern.
- Cut tissue paper into small squares, approximately 1 inch square.
- Pour glue onto a paper plate.
- Allow children to color the tree if desired.
- Using paint brush, dab dots of glue onto the tree branches and at the bottom of the trunk.
- Crumple bits of tissue paper and stick onto the dabs of glue to imitate fall leaves.

Other Songs, Rhymes, and Fingerplays

Buttercups and Daisies
Mary Howitt
Public Domain

Buttercups and daisies,
Oh what pretty flowers,
Coming in the springtime,
To tell of sunny hours!
While the trees are leafless,
While the fields are bare,
Buttercups and daisies,
Spring up everywhere.

A Tree's Year
By M. Follis

In the winter time, trees are bare
No leaves on branches, and a chill in the air

In spring time, trees are full of blooms
Pale new colors and sweet perfume

In summer time, trees are full of green
Giving you a nice shady place to read

But autumn in best of all
When fireworks of color around you fall

Down by the Bay
Traditional song

Down by the bay, (have audience echo)
Where the watermelons grow (echo)
Back to my home (echo)
I dare not go (echo)
For if I do (echo)
My mother will say (echo)

Did you ever see a pig, dancing a jig? (storyteller sing)
Down by the bay (together)

Additional verses:
Did you ever see a whale with a polka dot tail?
Did you ever see a bear combing its hair?
Did you ever see a moose kissing a goose?
Did you ever see a bee with a sunburned knee?

Early Literacy Tip:
The repetition in this song helps children learn the words. Since each verse is the same except for one line, children will catch on quickly.

Additional Poetry

Farrar, Sid and Ilse Plume, illus. The Year Comes Round: Haiku through the Seasons. Chicago: Albert Whitman & Company, 2012.
Although brief, haiku adds so much lyrical vocabulary to a child's life. Travel through the year one month at a time according to the Gregorian calendar.

Franco, Betsy and Steven Salerno, illus. Mathematickles! New York: Margaret K. McElderry Books, 2003.
Words+math+seasons=Mathematickles. Poems covering the seasons are displayed as mathematical formulas.

Janeczko, Paul B, sel., and Melissa Sweet, illus. Firefly July: A Year of Very Short Poems. Somerville, MA: Candlewick Press, 2014.
What season are you celebrating? This book includes selections by poets such as the great William Carlos Williams, Langston Hughes, and Robert Frost. Engaging illustrations will keep the attention of preschoolers while you read a few selections.

Katz, Bobbi, sel. and Deborah Zemke. More Pocket Poems. New York: Dutton Children's Books, 2009.
This collection of short sweet poems that you can put in your pocket (or tuck away in the corner of your mind and heart to bring out later to sit on your tongue) contains several perfect for sharing through the many seasons of the year including: "Spring" by Prince Redcloud (p. 8); sometimes it only take six words to express happiness over being warm. "August Ice Cream Cone Poem" by Paul B. Janeczko, you have to be quick and two words will do it! "Summer" by Myra Cohn Livingston (p. 12) compares the bright colors of summer found in the sky's fireworks and earth's flower beds. "A Winter Thought" by Bobbi Katz (p. 24), a good thought: "kids and hills . . . snowy weather" are things that should always go together. "Read This with Gestures" by John Ciardi (p. 25), both title and direction, read this poem as you mime the action of forming and throwing a snowball.

Muth, Jon J. Hi, Koo!: A Year of Seasons. New York: Scholastic Press, 2014.
Experience a full year with Koo the panda. Twenty-six poems start with the leaves falling in autumn and end quietly thinking about the year. For a storytime group, choose one season and read all of the poems like a story.

Vardell, Sylvia and Janet Wong, ed. The Poetry Friday Anthology for Celebrations. Princeton, NJ: Pomelo Books, 2015.
"Spring" by Jane Lichtenberger Patton (p. 91) celebrates that spring is here and that winter has "at last. . . . it's passed" along with frigid air. Celebrate the new season and all it brings.

Zolotow, Charlotte and Eric Blegvad, illus. Seasons: A Book of Poems. New York: HarperCollins Publishers, 2002.

Divided into four season poetic chapters like "Spring Things" and "The Feel of Fall" this book provides storytime-friendly short poems for each of the seasons. Not all poems are about the weather or seasons per se, but encompass things felt, seen, and thought throughout the year.

Additional Nonfiction

Rotner, Shelley, photography, and Anne Love Woodhull. Every Season. New Milford, CT: Roaring Brook Press, 2007.

There are so many reasons to love every season. From green grass to straw hats and pumpkin picking to snow angels. Photographs and lyrical text show the joys of each season starting in spring and then coming back full circle.

Additional Fiction Picture Books

Crausaz, Anne. Seasons. Tulsa, OK: Kane Miller, 2010.

Every season has unique tastes, smells, and sounds. Use all your seasons to experience spring, summer, fall, and winter. Read this on a hot summer day and feel the chill of winter.

Fogliano, Julie, and Erin E. Stead, illus. And Then It's Spring. New York: Roaring Book Press, 2012.

A young gardener worries and waits while the world turns from brown to green and his seeds into young plants.

Na, Il Sung. Snow Rabbit, Spring Rabbit: A Book of Changing Seasons. New York: Alfred A. Knopf, 2010.

No season change is more exciting and refreshing than the transformation from winter to spring. Rabbit observes how various animals adjust to the cold temperatures and then smiles on the last page when spring finally arrives.

Seven, John and Jan Christy, illus. A Year with Friends. New York: Abrams Appleseed, 2012.

Many season books start in a particular season then go through the year. This one starts in January and provides a tiny tidbit of celebration for that month. Bright yet gentle illustrations accompany the short text.

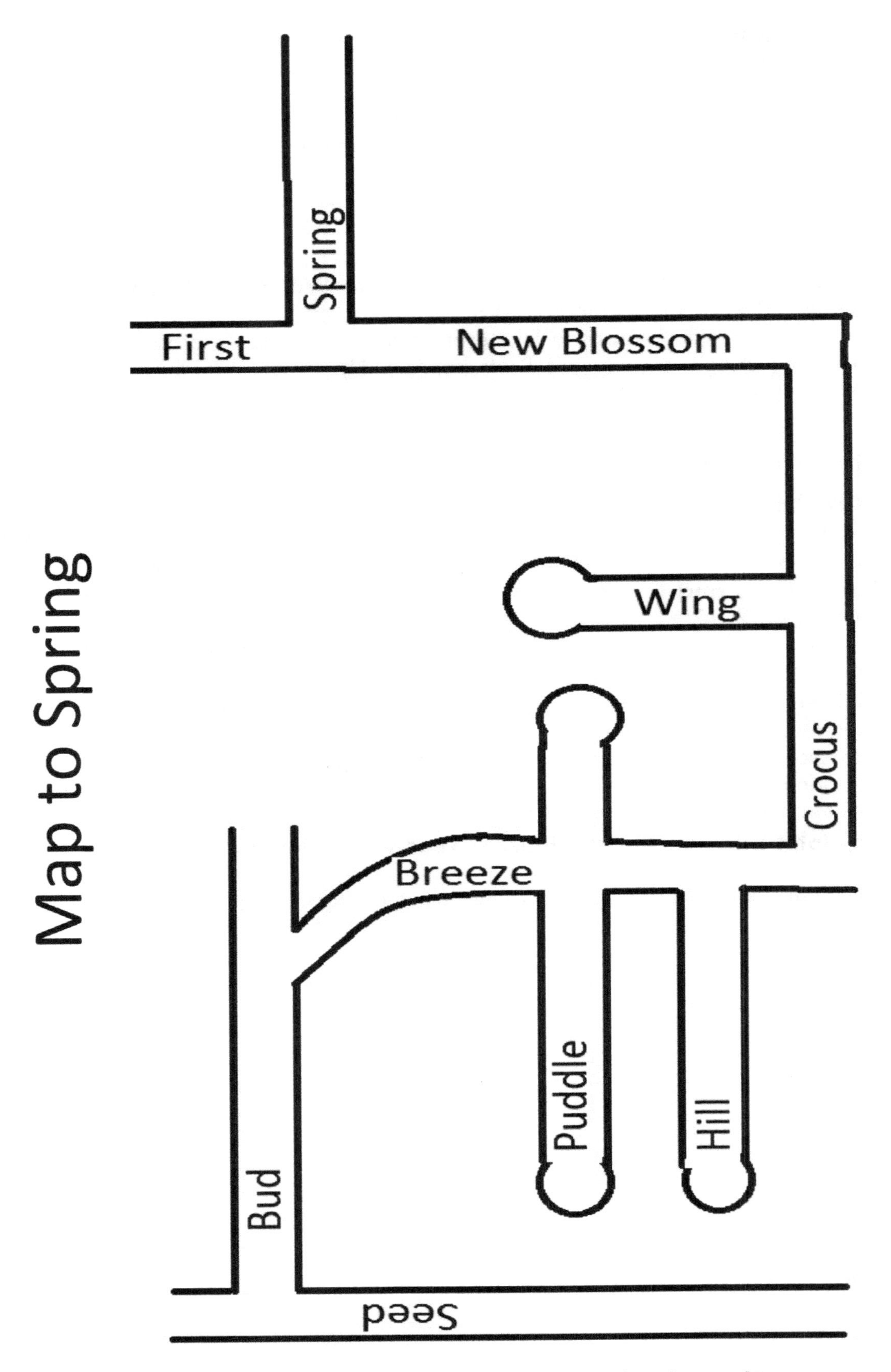
Map to Spring
Spring
First
New Blossom
Wing
Crocus
Breeze
Puddle
Hill
Bud
Seed

Shapes

Shapes, along with colors and letters, are one of the first things we teach children. Reinforce their education with a shapes storytime. Shapes are all around us!

Sample Storytime

Welcome Song

Routine is important when working with children. Be sure to include welcome, transitional, and closing songs or activities to signify what is coming next. Don't be afraid to use the same ones; children take comfort in knowing what is coming next.

Opening Poem

"A Circle of Sun" from Yolen, Jane and Andrew Fusek Peters, collector, and Polly Dunbar, illus. Here's a Little Poem: A Very First Book of Poetry. Cambridge, MA: Candlewick Press, 2007.
This lively and colorful ray of sunshine dances across the page in a "Circle of Sun" by Rebecca Kai Dotlich.

Action Rhyme

Depending on the size of your group, you can do this all together, or if you have a larger crowd, have adult and their child form a smaller "ring."

Ring around the Rosie
Traditional Rhyme

Ring around the Rosie
A pocket full of posies
Ashes, ashes
We all fall down

Early Literacy Tip:
Singing, movement, and early literacy go hand in hand. Reach out!

Nonfiction for Storytime

Gunzi, Christiane. My Very First Look at Shapes. Princeton, NJ: Two-Can Publishing, 2001.
Colorful pages feature multiple real-life examples of each shape. On the circles page you'll find a cake, buttons, marbles, and more. Each page also has a quick question that focuses on one object, for example "What color is the yo-yo?" See if you can find examples of each shape in your storytime space after each page.

Transitional Song

See Welcome Song earlier.

Flannel Board Activity

Perfect Square

Hall, Michael. Perfect Square. New York: Greenwillow Books, 2011.

With a little preparation, this book can easily be transformed into a flannel board story. Start with red, orange, green, teal, blue, and purple felt squares. Cut each square ahead of time to match the concept in the book and create mountains, fountains, and bridges like magic in storytime. Rather than quickly trying to create a perfect square out of multiple pieces you can place the pieces in their "square" form on another piece of felt before storytime. Simply put the "perfect" square on the flannel board then dissect it to create the shapes.

Early Literacy Tip: Shape recognition is vital in learning letters. Be sure to point out different shapes as you see them during your day. The ability to differentiate between them is the same skill we use in reading.

Picture Books for Storytime

Bertier, Anne. Wednesday. New York: Enchanted Lion Books, 2014.

Each Wednesday two friends get together and play a game. Big Square and Little Round dissect their shape into pieces and create and re-create themselves into a wide assortment of objects. Pages are filled with plenty of whitespace and simple text, which allows for the shapes to take front and center.

Bingham, Kelly L. and Paul O. Zelinsky, illus. Circle, Square, Moose. New York: Greenwillow Books, 2014.

Moose is up to his old tricks. While the narrator is trying to tell the reader about shapes, Moose, well. . . . Moose gets in the middle of things. A true friend until the end, Moose helps Zebra get to his favorite shape: the star.

Closing Song

See Welcome Song earlier.

Follow-Up Activities

Shape Puzzles

There are many toys that teach shapes. There are chunky wooden puzzles. There are plastic shape sorters with holes that fit certain shaped pieces. These tactile activities are a great way for kids to put their hands (literally) on shapes. Put out as many toys as you can and let everyone explore on their own.

Other Songs, Rhymes, and Fingerplays

The Queen of Hearts
Traditional Rhyme

The Queen of Hearts
She made some tarts,
All on a summer's day;

The Knave of Hearts
He stole those tarts,
And took them clean away.
The King of Hearts
Called for the tarts,
And beat the knave full sore;
The Knave of Hearts
Brought back the tarts,
And vowed he'd steal no more.

Round the Maypole
Traditional Rhyme

Round and round the maypole
Merrily we go
Singing hip-a-cherry,
Dancing as we go
All the happy children
On the village green
Sitting in the sunshine
Hurrah for the queen

Round and Round the Garden
Traditional Rhyme

Round and round the garden (swirl index finger in child's palm)
Went the little bear
One step, two steps (walk index and middle finger up child's arm)
Tickle under there! (gently tickle child under the arm)

Round and round the garden (swirl index finger in child's palm)
Went the little mouse
One step, two steps (walk index and middle finger up child's arm)
In his little house (gently tickle child under the arm)

Note: There are many, many versions of this rhyme. Use this one, or make up your own!

Stevesongs and David Dim, illus. The Shape Song Swingalong. Cambridge, MA: Barefoot Books, 2011.
Sing along with Stevesongs as you learn about lines, circles, squares, and triangles. Movements for the song are included in the colorful artwork. Read the book as a story or play the accompanying CD to "read" the book as a song.

Additional Poetry

Sidman, Joyce and Beth Krommes, illus. Swirl by Swirl: Spirals in Nature. Boston: Houghton Mifflin Books for Children, 2011.
Shapes are more than circles, triangles, and squares. They are the coil of a snake or a seahorse tail. They are strong and they are clever. Sidman's poetic words are an ode to many types of spirals found in nature.

Yolen, Jane and Stemple, photography. Shape Me a Rhyme: Nature's Forms in Poetry. Honesdale: PA: Wordsong, 2007.
Shapes can be found all throughout nature as is readily evident by Stemple's stunning photographs. Yolen then adds elegant poems relating the shape to the image. Common shapes like circle and triangle are complemented by spirals, waves, and fans.

Additional Nonfiction

Dotlich, Rebecca Kai and Maria Ferrari, photography. What Is a Triangle? New York: HarperFestival, 2000.
Rhyming text and real-life examples show triangles from a candy corn to a birthday hat. The final page features many shapes and a challenge to pick out the triangles.

Micklethwait, Lucy. I Spy Shapes in Art. New York: Greenwillow Books, 2004.
On each page, readers are directed to find a particular shape in a famous work of art. This book is great for a detail-oriented child who loves to sit and study illustrations.

Pistoia, Sara, and David M. Budd, photography. Shapes. Chanhassen, MN: The Child's World, 2007.
Shapes are one of the earliest math concepts that children can learn. Help them identify circles, triangles, squares, cylinder, and spheres in their everyday world. After reading the book see if you can spot any shapes in your storytime space.

Additional Fiction Picture Books

Fleming, Denise. Go, Shapes, Go! New York: Beach Lane Books, 2014.
Shapes slither, roll, slide, and bounce to create something new. A fall knocks the shapes out of place, and its creator isn't happy with the new configuration. Good thing shapes can go in many patterns!

Hall, Michael. My Heart Is Like a Zoo. New York: Greenwillow Books, 2010.
My Heart Is Like a Zoo presents the heart as similes using zoo animals. It's "as eager as a beaver, steady as a yak . . ." and so on. The zoo animals are created using the whole and pieces of the traditional heart shape.

MacDonald, Suse. Shape by Shape. New York: Little Simon, 2009.
Page cutouts of circles, triangles, crescents, semicircles, oval, and diamonds slowly create a large fold-out brachiosaurus. The inclusion of less common shapes makes this a unique addition to a shape storytime.

Schoonmaker, Elizabeth. Square Cat. New York: Aladdin, 2011.
It's not easy being a square cat but with the help of her friends Eula discovers some simple and humorous benefits to her shape. The white background makes it easy for everyone to distinguish her shape. Celebrate individuality, friendship, and squares all in one book.

Walsh, Ellen Stoll. Mouse Shapes. New York: Harcourt, Inc. 2007.
Once again our three creative mice are hiding from the cat, this time among a pile of shapes. Once safe, they build a variety of objects with the shapes, and eventually find a way to turn the tables on the cat.

Snow

When you think about it, the idea of white fluffy, moldable, edible playstuff falling from the sky seems magical. This storytime allows you to explore the science behind the magic, while keeping company of the lyrical wonder that can be found in poetry and prose.

Sample Storytime

Welcome Song

Routine is important when working with children. Be sure to include welcome, transitional, and closing songs or activities to signify what is coming next. Don't be afraid to use the same ones; children take comfort in knowing what is coming next.

Opening Poem

"Snowflake Wakes" from Sidman, Joyce and Rick Allen, illus. Winter Bees and Other Poems of the Cold. Boston: Houghton Mifflin Harcourt, 2014.
Snow can seem silent and lifeless but this poem proves that all wrong. Snowflakes laugh and tickle, whirl and drift, before settling down to earth.

Action Rhyme

Snowball Fight
By M. Follis

Slowly, slowly falling down (flutter fingers down)
Little snowflakes all around (flutter fingers down)
When they gather on the ground (mime gathering snow from ground and form a ball)
Chilly fun is sure to be found! (throw imaginary snowball)

Nonfiction for Storytime

Fisher, Carolyn. The Snow Show. Orlando: Harcourt, Inc., 2008.
Quiet on the set! Join Chef Kelvin as he mixes up a fresh batch of snow while introducing vocabulary like evaporation and precipitation. The book is full of humor and includes a recipe for polar pops in the back.

Transitional Song

See Welcome Song earlier.

Flannel Board Activity

Fleming, Denise. The First Day of Winter. New York: Henry Holt and Company, 2005.
A snowman is built slowly over the course of 12 days, each day adding a countable item. Example: "On the fifth day of winter my best friend gave to me . . . Five bird seed pockets"

(and then you recite all of the previously added items). The story can be sung to the tune of "Twelve Days of Christmas."

Create a white felt snowman shape and use the pattern found at the end of this chapter to create the snowman accessories.

Early Literacy Tip:
Cumulative tales and songs are great ways to increase memory in little ones.

Picture Books for Storytime

Messner, Kate and Christopher Silas Neal, illus. Over and Under the Snow. San Francisco, CA: Chronicle Books, 2011.
Things may look quiet and peaceful above the snow, but down below is a whole secret world of animals living, eating, and sleeping. As a child and father ski through the woods, readers see the animals beneath them. The back pages have information about the featured animals for readers who want more.

Norman, Kim and Liza Woodruff, illus. If It's Snowy and You Know It, Clap Your Paws! New York: Sterling Children's Books, 2013.
Set to the tune of the familiar song, this book features a variety of animals enjoying a winter wonderland. They go skiing, build a fort, and make a snowman. But like all children, they eventually get cold and curl up together in a nice toasty heap inside.

Closing Song

See Welcome Song earlier.

Follow-Up Activities

Pine Cone Feeders

Materials:

- Pine cones (one per child)
- Peanut butter
- Bird seeds
- String
- Plastic spoons or knives
- Wax paper

Directions:

- Tie a string around one end of the pine cone so it can be hung from a tree.
- Slather a thin coat of peanut butter using a spoon or knife.
- Spread seeds on wax paper.
- Roll the peanut butter coated pine cone in the seeds so that the seed stick.
- Hang the pine cone from a tree branch for the animals.
- Read *In the Snow* by Sharon Phillips Denslow.

Denslow, Sharon Phillips and Nancy Tafuri, illus. In the Snow. New York: Greenwillow Books, 2005.
A child sets out seeds in the snow and the reader gets to see the birds, squirrels, and rabbits that get a winter meal.

Early Literacy Tip:
Activity extensions on books make the book and the activity more memorable to young children.

Other Songs, Rhymes, and Fingerplays

Getting Dressed
Adapted by M. Follis
(Tune: Farmer in the Dell)

I'm putting on my coat . . .
I'm putting on my coat . . .
Hi-Ho, it's cold outside
I'm putting on my coat!

Additional verses: hat, scarf, and mittens

Mittens on My Hands
(Tune: Wheels on the Bus)

The classic version of this song can be found here: https://youtube/UjQXMRZc1dM.

Additional verses
Scarf around my neck . . .
Hat on my head . . .
Boots on my feet . . .

Winter Warm Up
Adapted by M. Follis
(Tune: Head, Shoulders, Knees and Toes)

Boots, mittens, scarf and hat, scarf and hat
Boots, mittens, scarf and hat, scarf and hat
I'll never get cold when I'm wearing all of that
Boots, mittens, scarf and hat, scarf and hat!

Snowballs
By M. Follis
(Tune: Daisy, Daisy)

Snowballs, snowballs
What's a kid to do? (shrug shoulders)
I can't wait to throw a ball or two
Pack the snow tightly into a ball so round (mime making snowball)
Let it fly, high, over the frozen ground! (throw ball)
DUCK! (duck!)

I'm a Little Snowman
Traditional Rhyme
(Tune: I'm a Little Teapot)

I'm a little snowman, short and fat.
Here is my scarf and here is my hat. (gesture to a pretend scarf and hat)
Pebbles for my buttons (point to three spots on your shirt)
Carrot for my nose (hold a pretend carrot near your nose)
Made of snow from head to toes (touch your head then your toes)

Additional Poetry

Cleary, Brian P. and Andy Rowland, illus. Ode to a Commode: Concrete Poems. Minneapolis, MN: Millbrook Press, 2015.
Why are snowmen only given a scarf and a hat to keep warm? This snowman would sure like to know. Shaped like a snowman, show this poem as you read it.

Heard, Georgia, ed. Falling Down the Page. New York: Roaring Brook Press, 2009.
"Winter's Presents" by Patricia Hubbell tells all of the gifts that snow brings, without ever stating the word snow as seen here: "Stars for all mittens." A gift of a poem.

Janeczko, Paul, ed. and Robert Rayevsky, illus. Hey You! Poems to Skyscrapers, Mosquitoes and Other Fun Things. New York: HarperCollins, 2007.
"To a Snowflake" by X.J. Kennedy. A small child wonders as a snowflake falls slowly to the ground, how they decide where to land and "wish to spend tonight." This sweet dreamy poem assigns intention and whimsy to each delicate flake.

Schnur, Steven and Leslie Evans, illus. Winter: An Alphabet Acrostic. New York: Clarion Books, 2002.
Winter is frozen apples in the orchard, sitting by the fireplace, and maple syrup. An acrostic poem for every letter of the alphabet traces the winter season until a warm breeze starts to blow. Bright linoleum-cut illustrations capture the essence of each poem.

Sidman, Joyce and Rick Allen, illus. Winter Bees and Other Poems of the Cold. Boston: Houghton Mifflin Harcourt, 2014.
As winter approaches the animals prepare for the long, cold season. Some, like the moose, trudge along through the harsh environment. Others, like bees, huddle together for warmth. Allen's illustrations capture the crisp and frosty environment.

Additional Nonfiction

Cassino, Mark, Jon Nelson, Ph.D., and Nora Aoyagi, illus. The Story of Snow: The Science of Winter's Wonder. San Francisco, CA: Chronicle Books, 2009.
Photographs of real snow crystals are the stars of this book. A wealth of information is provided but you can decide how much to share. Each page has three different font sizes; read just the largest text to give a storytime crowd a hint of information about snow.

Flanagan, Alice K. Snow. Mankato, MN: The Child's World, 2010.
Very simple text explains how snow is formed. Corresponding photographs give children something to look at while you read.

Kaner, Etta and Marie Lafrance, illus. Who Likes the Snow? Tonawanda, NY: Kids Can Press, 2006.
Why are some days better for making snowballs? Why doesn't my sled work on hill without snow? Why does snow make a crunching sound? Find the answers to these questions and more. This title is perfect for that inquisitive child and the parent who just wants some quick answers.

Stewart, Melissa and Constance R. Bergum, illus. Under the Snow. Atlanta, GA: Peachtree Publishers, 2009.
The world seems still and silent when there is snow on the ground, but much is happening under the snow in fields, forest, ponds, and wetlands. See illustrations of the animals in their winter habitats as they wait for spring. Kids will be excited to see how their favorite animals spend the winter months.

Additional Fiction Picture Books

Gill, Deidre. Outside. New York: Houghton Mifflin Harcourt, 2014.
When his brother doesn't want to go outside to play in the snow, a little boy creates his own fun and playmates. This book heralds the beauty of outside play and imagination.

Hubbell, Patricia and Hiroe Nakata, illus. Snow Happy! Berkeley, CA: Tricycle Press, 2010.
Frolicking rhyming words dance across the page as youngsters play in the snow making snow angels, igloos, have snowball fights and more. Such fun to be had, and everyone is "snow happy!" Bright colors pop off of a pale background adding to the action.

Judge, Lita. Red Sled. New York: Atheneum Books for Young Readers, 2011.
When a young child leaves a red sled outside, it sparks the curiosity of nearby creatures, who take it out for a joyride. This story is nearly wordless except for the onomatopoetic expressions of snowy joy.

Kuskin, Karla and Fumi Kosaka, illus. Under My Hood I Have a Hat. New York: HarperCollins, 2004.
"Under my hood I have a hat. Under that . . . my hair is flat." A little girl undressing and dressing for the cold reveals layer after layer of winter clothing. While all of the layers keep her warm, she warns against falling down. Simple sweet illustrations and rhyming text make this a fun share that will warm up any storytime.

Neubecker, Robert. Winter Is for Snow. New York: Disney Hyperion Books, 2013.
Brother and sister have very different opinions on snow. While brother loves it, sister just thinks winter is for staying warm inside. After sharing all the joys of snow, he finally wins her over. Young readers will discover all the fun contained in those little white flakes.

Sakai, Komako. The Snow Day. New York: Arthur A. Levine Books, 2005.
A little rabbit wakes up to discover a snow day. He explores the still, quiet world with his mother. Illustrations are done in a muted palette reflecting the hush of this still and quiet tale.

Young, Ned. Zoomer's Summer Snowstorm. New York: Harper, 2011.
Nothing cools off a hot summer day like a gigantic snowstorm. When Zoomer inadvertently causes a storm by overrunning his snow-cone machine, he makes amazing snow sculptures in his yard. Read this in winter to make everyone think warm thoughts.

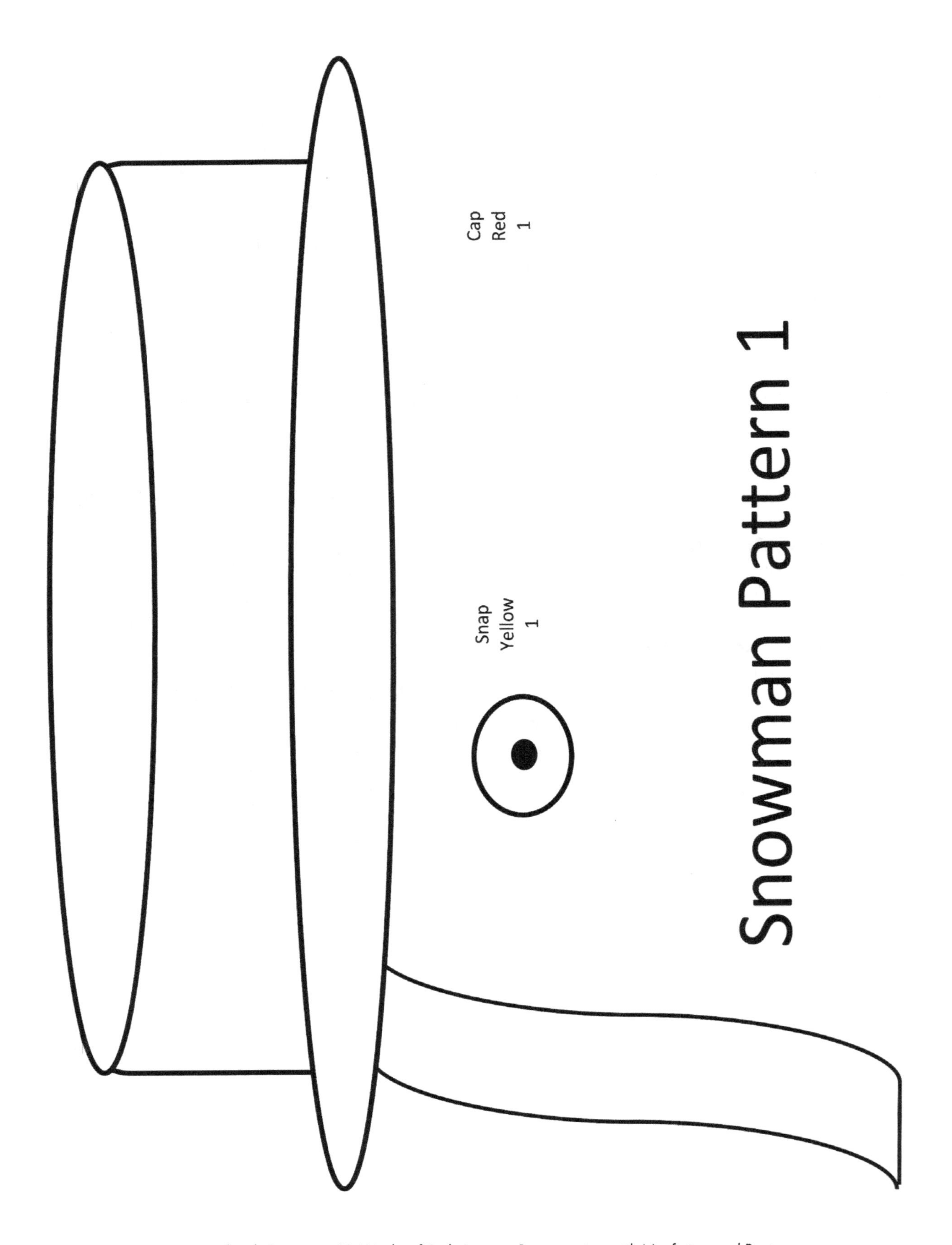
Snowman Pattern 1
Cap
Red
1
Snap
Yellow
1

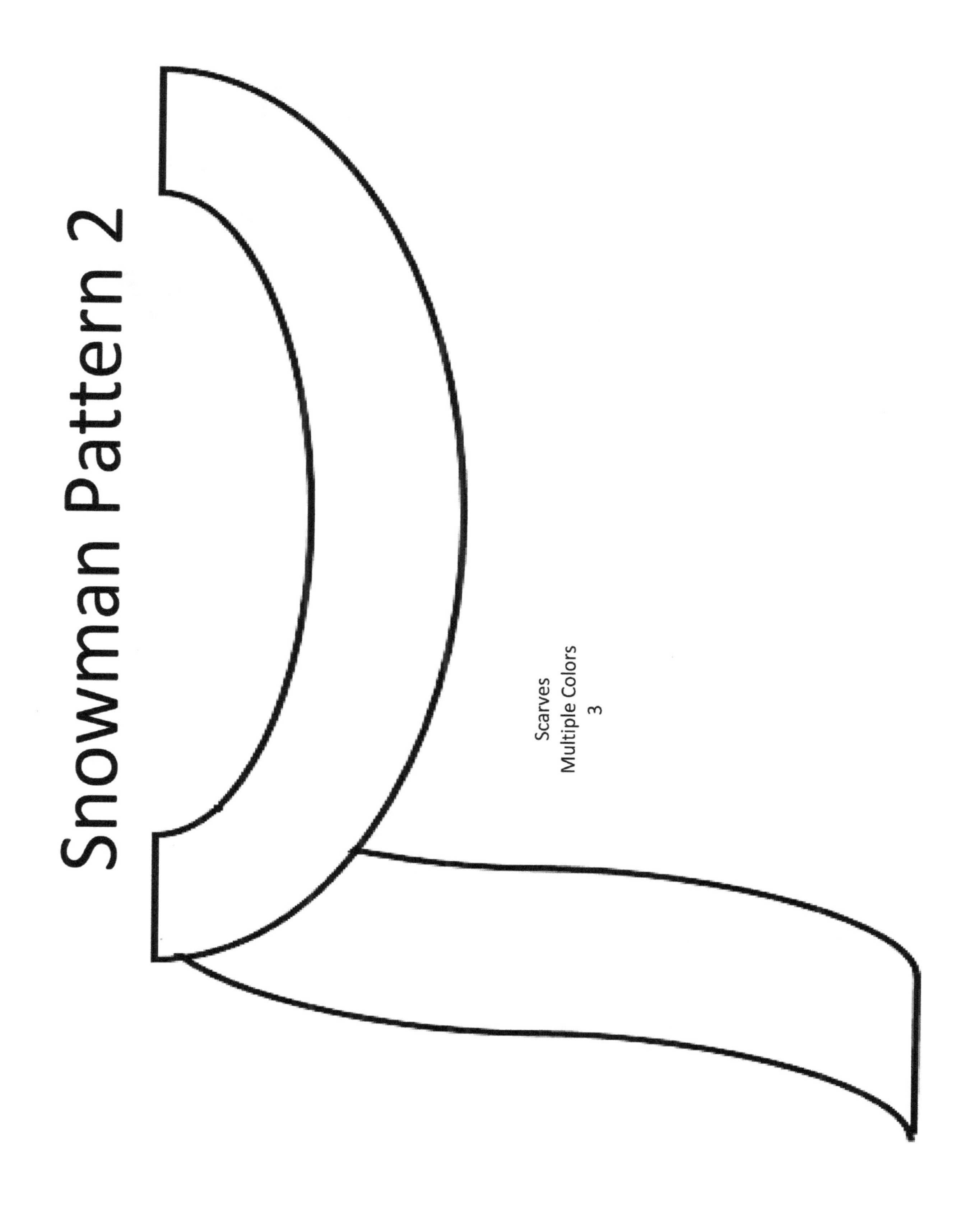
Snowman Pattern 2
Scarves
Multiple Colors
3

Snowman Pattern 3

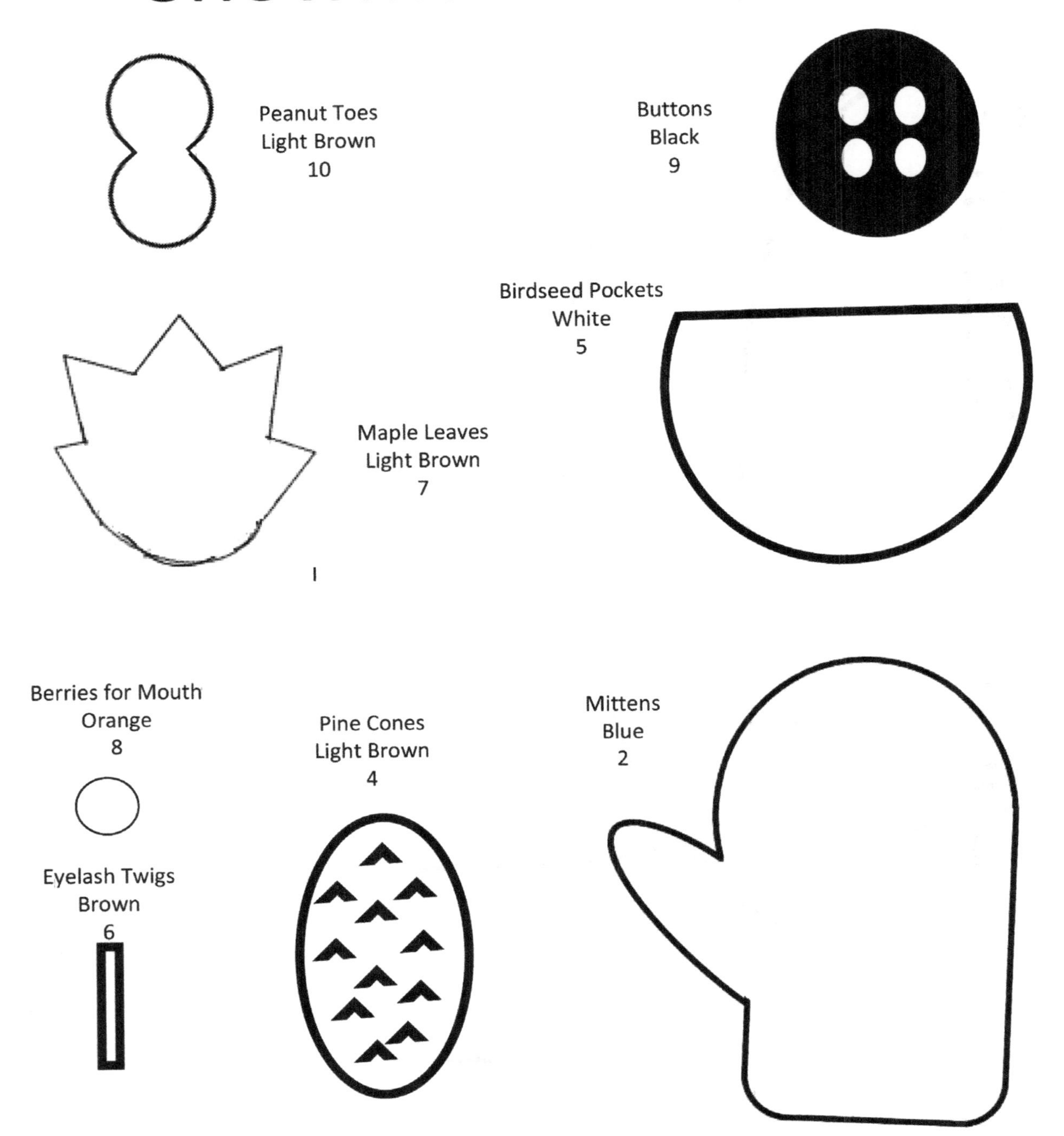

Space

Outer space is all over the place! And now in storytime, too. The sky above offers a great deal to look at, but especially at night. The moon, the stars, and their formations can be part of a little one's bedtime routine. Plan this storytime around a full moon and ask participants to make it a point to look upward before bed that evening.

Sample Storytime

Welcome Song

Routine is important when working with children. Be sure to include welcome, transitional, and closing songs or activities to signify what is coming next. Don't be afraid to use the same ones; children take comfort in knowing what is coming next.

Opening Poem

"The Comet" by Florian, Douglas. Comets, Stars, the Moon, and Mars. New York: Harcourt, 2007.
Made of gas, metal, ice dust, and other space debris, a comet is the "biggest snowball that you'll ever see." Relating the makeup of a hard-to-imagine object to something most children can understand really brings this far out concept down to earth.

Action Rhyme

Twinkle, Twinkle Little Star
English Lullaby

Twinkle twinkle little star (open and close hands like a twinkling star)
How I wonder what you are
Up above the world so high (raise hands above your head)
Like a diamond in the sky (create a diamond shape between hands)
Twinkle twinkle little star (open and close hands like a twinkling star)
How I wonder what you are

Nonfiction for Storytime

Houran, Lori Haskin and Francisca Marquez, illus. A Trip into Space: An Adventure to the International Space Station. Chicago: Albert Whitman & Company, 2014.
Follow along as two astronauts blast off to the International Space Station and join the crew for work. This accessible title has rhyming text and double-spread illustrations. More information is found in the back for families wishing to know more.

Transitional Song

See Welcome Song earlier.

Flannel Board Activity

E-A-R-T-H

Have die-cut letters that spell Earth, and place each one as mentioned.

(Tune: Bingo)

We live on a big blue planet
And Earth is its name-o
E-A-R-T-H
E-A-R-T-H
E-A-R-T-H
And Earth is its name-o

Picture Books for Storytime

Jeffers, Oliver. How to Catch a Star. New York: Philomel Books, 2004.
Everyone wishes upon a star, but this little boy wishes *for* a star. After numerous unsuccessful attempts to catch one, he is just about to give up when a star falls from the sky onto the beach just for him.

Mayo, Margaret and Alex Ayliffe, illus. Zoom, Rocket, Zoom! New York: Walker & Company, 2011.
Words like "pow!" "bam!" and "oops!" add another level to an already high-interest topic. Travel in a rocket to the moon and space station to see the astronauts hard at work.

Closing Song

See Welcome Song earlier.

Follow-Up Activities

Spacescape

Materials:

- White paint
- Paint brushes
- Safety scissors
- Construction paper in:
    - black
    - orange
    - pink
    - red
    - yellow
- Glue or glue sticks
- Crayons
- Star stickers in silver and gold

Directions:

- Give each child a piece of black construction paper.
- Allow them to drop small drips of white paint on the paper and put it aside to dry.
- Give children the opportunity to practice their cutting skills by offering them circles (planets) to cut. Simply trace a variety of circle sizes in many colors for them to choose from for their spacescape.
- Decorate the planets with crayons (if desired).
- Glue the circle planets onto the painted black construction paper.
- Adhere silver and gold stars if desired.

Early Literacy Tip: Shape recognition is vital in learning letters. Be sure to point out different shapes that you see around you, like in this craft. The ability to differentiate between them is the same skill we use in reading.

Other Songs, Rhymes, and Fingerplays

Bend and Stretch
By M. Follis

Bend and stretch
Up to the stars
Stretch left to Jupiter
Stretch right to Mars

Bend and stretch
Up to the sky
Lean back and marvel
At the starry sky

I'm a Little Astronaut
Adapted by M. Follis
(Tune: I'm a Little Teapot)

I'm a little astronaut (point to self)
In my suit
Here is my helmet (point to head)
Here are my boots (touch toes)
When I board my spaceship (pretend to climb)
You will see (hold hands up to eyes)
Outer space is all around me (stretch hands out wide)

Little Astronauts
Adapted by M. Follis
(Tune: Ten Little Indians)

One little, two little, three little astronauts
Four little five little, six little astronauts
Seven little, eight little, nine little astronauts
10 astronauts floating in space

Watch them as they launch into the sky
See them float as shooting stars fly
Faster as the planets pass by
10 astronauts in space

Star Light, Star Bright
English Nursery Rhyme

Star light, star bright,
First start I see tonight,
I wish I may, I wish I might
Have the wish I wish tonight,

Oh, Mr. Sun

Try sharing this YouTube version of the song complete with hand movements: https://www.youtube.com/watch?v=0j3PPukoErE. Show the video in storytime and follow along or use the video to learn the song yourself.

Additional Poetry

Florian, Douglas. Comets, Stars, the Moon, and Mars. New York: Harcourt, 2007.
With poems that span the universe, Florian address out of this world topics such as stargazing, galaxies, each planet in our solar system, even poor demoted Pluto. Cutouts on each page provide dimension and a sneak peek (or look back) at a topic's surroundings. Thought provoking, interesting, and always in awe of the space we inhabit, these poems will find an audience in a wide range of ages and interests.

Heard, Georgia, ed. Falling Down the Page. New York: Roaring Brook Press, 2009.
Bobbi Katz lists some of the many roles the sun plays in "Things to Do If You Are the Sun." A great conversation starter that is both factual and lyrical. "Shooting Star" by Avis Harley shoots down the page in fleeting lines ending with "a wishing time, before I sleep."

Hopkins, Lee Bennett, compiler, and Mariusz Stawarski, illus. Sky Magic. New York: Dutton Children's Books, 2009.
Celebrate the sun, moon, and stars with poems by Tennessee Williams, Carl Sandburg, and Ashley Bryan. "Moon's Poem" is a soothing entrance into dreamworld. "Last Song" speaks of the sun, moon, and stars, and would close a space storytime on a quiet note.

Janeczko, Paul, ed., and Robert Rayevsky, illus. Hey You! Poems to Skyscrapers, Mosquitoes and Other Fun Things. New York: HarperCollins, 2007.
"To an Astronaut" by Beverly McLoughland. A young reader ponders what life is like for an astronaut so far from home and wonders if when they see the small green and blue planet "Do you love it even more?"

Martin, Jr., Bill, Michael Sampson, and various illustrators. The Bill Martin Jr. Big Book of Poetry. New York: Simon & Schuster, 2008.
"The Star" by Jane Taylor (p. 44) takes the well-known rhyme "Twinkle, Twinkle, Little Star" and expands upon it. Children will take comfort and enjoyment in hearing the familiar. Myra Cohn Livingston's "My Star" (p. 118) shares the joy of star gazing from the comfort of your bed.

Sklansky, Amy E. and Stacey Schuett, illus. Out of This World: Poems and Facts about Space. New York: Alfred A. Knopf, 2012.
More than just wordplay, the poems in this title teach the reader about space and exploration. Additional facts are included in paragraph form on each page. Mirroring the vast darkness of space, most of the poems are accompanied by dark hued illustrations; yet the glossy pages make it possible to share the book with a crowd. Share favorite poems and a couple of interesting facts with a storytime group.

Additional Nonfiction

Dahl, Michael, Derrick Alderman and Denise Shea, illus. On the Launch Pad. Minneapolis, MN: Picture Window Books, 2004.
A fun, space rocket-themed countdown book to lift-off highlights equipment and other equipment found on the launch pad. In addition to the spelled-out numbers, there are objects to count, and a numeric representation of the number, with dots for additional counting and visual representation.

McCarthy, Meghan. Astronaut Handbook. New York: Alfred A. Knopf, 2008.
Study hard and be a team player and you might be able to go to astronaut school. Cartoon illustrations accompany child-friendly information about what it takes to be an astronaut. Set aside extra time to look closely at the page with the space toilet.

McReynolds, Linda and Ryan O'Rourke, illus. Eight Days Gone. Watertown, MA: Charlesbridge, 2012.
The story of the eight-day mission of *Apollo 11* is told in one four-line verse per page. Appealing illustrations will make you want to linger on the page even after the text is read. The Author's Note in the back provides more information for a storytime attendee who loves the book.

Early Literacy Tip: It's okay to break up the rhythm of a book in order to focus on high-interest pages. Nonfiction books offer many opportunities for slowing down and savoring the information.

Additional Fiction Picture Books

Arnold, Tedd. Green Wilma, Frog in Space. New York: Dial Books for Young Readers, 2009.
Poor Green Wilma is minding her own business trying to catch a fly when she gets mistakenly taken on board an alien space ship. In her typically mischievous manner, she ends up back where she belongs, on her log!

Kelly, Mark and C.F. Payne, illus. Mousetronaut. New York: Simon & Schuster Books for Young Readers, 2012.
Meteor is smaller than the rest of the mice but he has a real desire to go to space. It's a good thing he is chosen because his small size comes in handy when a key is lost in a tiny crack. While the mice on Kelly's space mission stayed in their cages, this story is inspired by one mouse that seemed to enjoy the trip.

Loomis, Christine and Ora Eitan, illus. Astro Bunnies. New York: G.P. Putman's Sons, 2001.
Some imaginative bunnies take a trip on a rocket ship and explore the great big milky way, always returning home.

Mayo, Margaret and Alex Ayliffe, illus. Zoom, Rocket, Zoom! New York: Walker & Company, 2011.
Perfect for storytime, Zoom, Rocket, Zoom! has big bold illustrations and load of action words describing many space travel topics and their actions. "Moon buggies are good at roll, roll, rolling, round wheels turning, soft dust gripping . . . across the humpy, lumpy moon . . . bumpety-bumping. Exploring up in space." Out of this world fun.

Scribens, Sunny and David Sim, illus. Space Song Rocket Ride. Cambridge, MA: Barefoot Books, 2014.
With a catchy refrain built on the tune "The Green Grass Grows All Around" this song takes you for a ride through space in a rocket. Bright cheerful colors and roughhewn illustrations make this a fun visual treat, too!

Shaw, Nancy and Margot Apple, illus. Sheep Blast Off! Boston: Houghton Mifflin Company, 2008.
Deciding to upgrade from their Jeep, the sheep take off in an alien spacecraft for some extraterrestrial fun.

Spiders

Creepy and crawly, friend and foe; spiders are all around us in the real world and in the books and songs for children. This combination makes for a great crossover storytime that can be used to bridge fact and fiction, making this unit shine. Some might even say that it is "radiant."

Sample Storytime

Welcome Song

Routine is important when working with children. Be sure to include welcome, transitional, and closing songs or activities to signify what is coming next. Don't be afraid to use the same ones; children take comfort in knowing what is coming next.

Opening Poem

"Night Spider's Advice" by Sidman, Joyce and Rick Allen, illus. Dark Emperor & Other Poems of the Night. New York: Houghton Mifflin Books for Children, 2010.
At night the world of the spider comes alive. This spider offers advice on building "the world" each and every night by creating a frame and going around and around until the perfect web is spun.

Action Rhyme

Itsy Bitsy Spider
Popular Rhyme

The Itsy Bitsy Spider (make a spider by aligning thumb and index finger with backwards configuration on the opposite hand)
Went up the waterspout (walk index and thumb upwards)
Down came the rain (use fingers to represent sprinkling of rain)
And washed the spider out (cross both arms indicating out)
Up came the sun (use index and thumb to form circle above your head)
And dried up all the rain (wave fingers as if to indicate steam)
So the itsy bitsy spider
Went up the spout again (again walk index and thumb upwards)

Nonfiction for Storytime

Bishop, Nic. Nic Bishop Spiders. New York: Scholastic, 2007.
The stunning photographs taken by the author make this book stand out. While there is a great deal of information here, the book is created in such a way that you can simply read the bolded line on each double-paged spread for the perfect read-aloud in a crowd, but you may want to skip a page or two when using with a very young audience.

Transitional Song

See Welcome Song earlier.

Flannel Board Activity

Little Miss Muffet

Find or create flannel pieces for the following rhyme:

Early Literacy Tip:
While this is a simple rhyme, it offers plenty of opportunities for vocabulary: tuffet, curds and whey, and frightened.

Little Miss Muffet
Traditional Rhyme

Little Miss Muffet (gesture to flannel piece)
Sat on her tuffet (put her on tuffet)
Eating her curds and whey (give her a bowl)
Along came a spider (if possible, put the spider
on a piece of thread or yarn and
dangle it in front of Miss Muffet)
Who sat down beside her
And frightened Miss Muffet away
(you may want to make Miss Muffet cry out,
and run off the flannel board)

Go over some of the words in the rhyme. Repeat the rhyme again, replacing the original words so with more current words. Ask the children how it sounds and which version they like better.

Rhyme with more current words:

Little Miss Muffet sat on her "footstool"
Eating her "cottage cheese"
Along came a spider
Who sat down beside her
And scared her so she ran away

Picture Books for Storytime

Harper, Charise Mericle. Itsy Bitsy the Smart Spider. New York: Dial Books for Young Readers, 2004.
Tired of the same old version of Itsy Bitsy? This spider uses her brain and problem solves the whole "washed the spider out" issue. Sweet, funny, and a fresh take on a classic story.

Monks, Lydia. Aaaarrgghh! Spider! Boston: Houghton Mifflin Company, 2004.
A sad and lonely spider wants to be a family's pet, so he sets out to impress them by how well he can feed and clean himself, as well as how entertaining he can be when dancing on the ceiling. Alas, his efforts are met with screams of "Aaaarrgghh! Spider! Out you go!" Storytime goers will happily join you in the chorus, but what will this poor spider have to do in order to impress his would-be family? Brightly colored pages and big eyes set the tone, as do the silvery gleams of magical web.

Closing Song

See Welcome Song earlier.

Follow-Up Activities

Spider Legs

Materials:

- Black construction paper for legs—cut into strips that are 1 inch long and ¼ inch wide
- Die cuts of number 8 in black construction paper
- Googly eyes
- Glue

Directions:

- Give each child a number 8 (spider body) and discuss that spiders are arachnids and have eight legs.
- Give each child eight black strips of paper to glue onto the body of the spider.
- Give each child two googly eyes to glue onto the "face" of the spider.

Other Songs, Rhymes, and Fingerplays

There's a Spider on the Floor!

Words by Bill Russell and notably recorded by Raffi.

You can find the words online and listen to Raffi's rendition here: https://www.youtube.com/watch?v=9ShsC8srN0E&feature=youtu.be.

It is always fun to have a clip art spider printed and laminated. Give these to the kids and they can move the spider along with the pattern of the song.

I Know an Old Lady Who Swallowed a Fly

Words by Rose Bonne, tune by Alan Mills.

This cumulative tale is a favorite in storytime. There are many versions of the song, but here is a link to the Simms Taback version produced by Weston Woods. https://youtu.be/WzGLUINCT-g.

Early Literacy Tip:
Cumulative tales and songs are great ways to increase memory in little ones.

Additional Poetry

Andreae, Giles and David Wajtowycz, illus. Bustle in the Bushes. Wilton, CT: Tiger Tales. 2011.
"Spider" (p. 11) describes the pride a spider feels waking up to its web glittering with the morning dew.

Lewis, J. Patrick, ed. National Geographic Book of Animal Poetry: 200 Poems with Photographs That Squeak, Soar, and Roar! Washington, DC: National Geographic, 2012.
"The Spider Is a Lovely Lady" (p. 55) by Frank Asch gives a lofty, beautiful aura to an eight-legged creature. The delicate petals on which she rests in the photo are the perfect backdrop for the dainty mother of tiny babies.

Additional Nonfiction

René, Ellen. Investigating Spiders and Their Webs. New York: PowerKiDS Press, 2009.
Each two-page spread has an up close photograph of a spider. Share the pictures and read just the captions for a creepy storytime.

Wadsworth, Ginger and Patricia, J. Wynne, illus. Up, Up, and Away. Watertown, MA: Charlesbridge, 2009.
Facts about the life cycle of a spider are woven like a web throughout this tale of a spider from birth to death. Readers and listeners will feel a connection to the female spider as she struggles to survive.

Additional Fiction Picture Books

Chapman, Keith and Jack Tickle, illus. Itsy Bitsy Spider. Wilton, CT: Tiger Tales, 2006.
The traditional tale of the Itsy Bitsy Spider takes on a new twist when he visits the farm. He bounces from animal to animal with some great barnyard sounds. Glitter streams across the page mimicking the silvery web until Itsy is back at home with mom.

Cronin, Doreen and Harry Bliss, illus. Diary of a Spider. New York: Joanna Cotler Books, 2005.
A young spider shares his thoughts and daily activities through a diary. Fun facts and sweet stories are woven together in a clever story form.

Cummings, Troy. The Eensy Weensy Spider Freaks Out! (Big Time!) New York: Random House, 2010.
What starts as a traditional song becomes an entire story about getting back up and trying again. When Eensy is embarrassed by her fall down the waterspout, she is encouraged by her ladybug friend to climb something else. Before you know it, Eensy has climbed higher than any bug has ever been.

Shea, Bob. I'm a Shark. New York: Balzer + Bray, 2011.
Shark thinks he is pretty amazing. He doesn't cry when he gets a shot. He isn't afraid of the dark, or a giant squid. His friends are pretty impressed too until someone mentions spiders. Everyone is afraid of something! Big, bold, toothy illustrations will have children chuckling, and the sly asides will make adults giggle too. As long as they aren't afraid of spiders.

Finished Spider

Spider Pattern

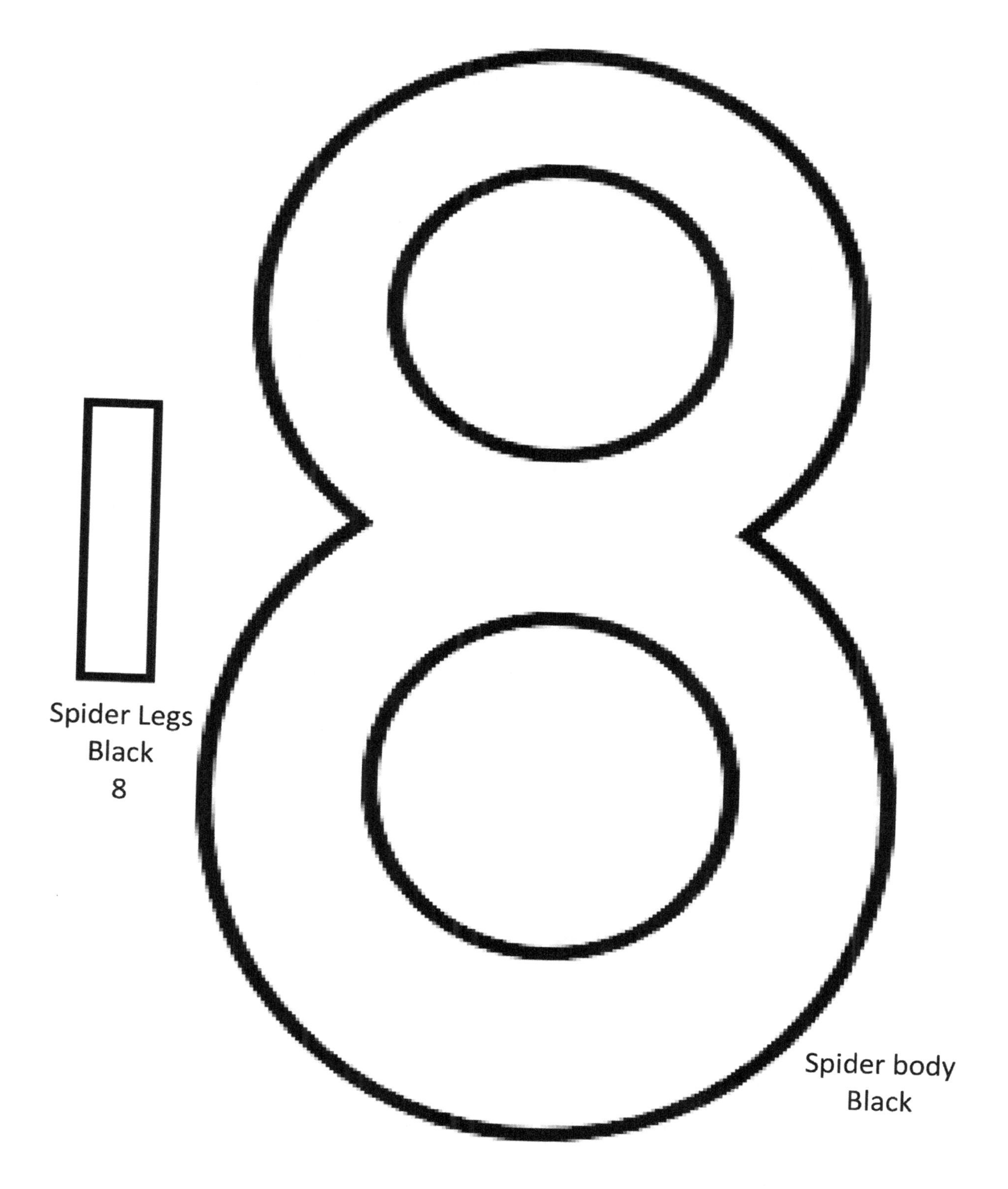

Sports and Games

Balls are one of the first toys we give little ones. They are great for developing motor skills and eye-hand coordination. As children grow, they are often surrounded by a variety of balls that accompany many sports. Then we have our body; designed to run, jump, and throw, sports are often a natural extension of how we work. Rouse up some team spirit with this active storytime.

Sample Storytime

Welcome Song

Routine is important when working with children. Be sure to include welcome, transitional, and closing songs or activities to signify what is coming next. Don't be afraid to use the same ones; children take comfort in knowing what is coming next.

Opening Poem

Prelutsky, Jack and Chris Raschka, illus. Good Sports. New York: Knopf, 2007.
Half way through the book, two sets of four lines describe the freedom and perceived speed of being on wheels, "I'm faster than an asteroid" and the reader, knowing that even if it isn't true, that's how it feels. This easy-going rhyme is embellished by terrific words, the epitome of poetry.

Action Rhyme

Playground!
By M. Follis

Bounce, hop, skip and pass (pretend to bounce a ball, hop, skip, and pass a football)
Jog real slow (jog in place—slow)
Run real fast (run in place—fast)
Jump up high (jump)
Feet off the ground
Spin yourself (spin in place)
Round and round
The things you can do with your body!
Your all time favorite . . . playground!

Nonfiction for Storytime

Nevius, Carol and Bill Thomson, illus. Baseball Hour. Tarrytown, NY: Marshall Cavendish Children, 2008.
Teamwork is key when a baseball team practices together. Illustrations made to look like sepia-toned photographs give unique perspective to the baseball drills. Rhyming text

provides an easy read that will make everyone feel like they are part of the team. Also look for ***Karate Hour*** (2004) and ***Soccer Hour*** (2011) by the same author and illustrator.

Transitional Song

See Welcome Song earlier.

Flannel Board Activity

Seek and Find

While hide-and-seek may be a bit rambunctious for inside a library, you can still get everyone involved in a searching game. Grab a collection of easy-to-identify flannel board shapes (letters, animals, shapes). Remember that you don't need to make new pieces for every storytime, use flannel pieces you have from previous programs. Place them in a haphazard fashion on the flannel board. Invite children to come up one by one to find a specific shape.

If your group is too large to invite children up to the flannel board, you can make this a group activity. Move your hand slowly around the flannel board and ask the children to yell loudly when your hand is near the requested shape.

Picture Books for Storytime

Chase, Kit. Oliver's Tree. New York: G.P. Putnam's Sons, 2014.
Oliver is upset when he can't get to his friends hiding in the trees during a game of hide-and-seek. Luckily, Charlie and Lulu are such good friends that they find a way for everyone to enjoy the trees.

Thompson, Lauren and Jarrett J. Krosoczka, illus. Hop, Hop, Jump! New York: Simon & Schuster, 2012.
What do you need to have endless fun? Nothing but yourself! Your body is capable of many fun things: wiggle, hop, jump, and wag and see what you can get up to!

Closing Song

See Welcome Song earlier.

Follow-Up Activities

Indoor Games

There are many indoor games that you can play after storytime is over. Consider the following:

Freeze

Turn on some music and invite the children to dance and be silly.

Without them seeing you, turn off the music and say "freeze!"

For older children you can have people who continue moving to be considered "out" of the game, but with younger children this may not be appropriate or very fun.

Repeat!

Simon Says

Let your children know that this is a listening game and that they need to pay close attention to what you are saying.

Lead children through a series of directions for activities such as "Simon Says touch your nose. Simon Says touch your toes."

Then give directions without the phrase "Simon Says." Those who do the activity are "out."

Again, with younger children you can skip the "out" portion of the game.

Tic Tac Toe

Cut four long pieces of felt and either position together or hot glue together to create a board. Use the patterns attached, or make your own Xs and Os, and invite families to play this simple, yet strategic game on the flannel board.

Early Literacy Tip:
Play helps make some abstract concepts more concrete. For example, when playing Tic Tac Toe, you are using words like above, below, across. A lot of learning goes into even a simple game.

Other Songs, Rhymes, and Fingerplays

Cheer for Reading!
Adapted by M. Follis

Give me a R
Give me an E
Give me an A
Give me a D
What's that spell?
READ!
(jump and cheer!)

Early Literacy Tip:
Simple chants like this one help improve letter knowledge. As you go through your day, be sure to point out letters or spell familiar words out.

Take Me Out to the Ball Game

Take me out to the ball game,
Take me out with the crowd;
Just buy me some peanuts and Cracker Jacks,
I don't care if I never get back.
Let me root, root, root for the home team,
If they don't win, it's a shame.
For it's one, two, three strikes, you're out,
At the old ball game.

Wright, Danielle, collected by, and Mique Moriuchi, illus. My Village: Rhymes from around the World. London: Frances Lincoln Children's Books, 2010.
"Song of Kites" is a traditional Japanese rhyme translated into English. "Don't forget to hold on tight!" "Let's Play" is a traditional Iranian rhyme about balls, slides, swings, and toys.

Let's Go Fly a Kite

This is a fun song to sing with juggling scarves. Let everyone play with their "kite" as you play the song from the Mary Poppins soundtrack. Or you may choose to show that portion of the movie from YouTube: https://www.youtube.com/watch?v=BA-g8YYPKVo.

Additional Poetry

Cleary, Brian P. and Andy Rowland, illus. Ode to a Commode: Concrete Poems. Minneapolis, MN: Millbrook Press, 2015.
"What about Me?" is told from the point of view of a poor football that never gets any of the glory when the game is won. Shaped like a football, show this concrete poem while reading if possible.

Lewis, J. Patrick, ed. National Geographic Book of Animal Poetry: 200 Poems with Photographs That Squeak, Soar, and Roar! Washington, DC: National Geographic, 2012.
Can you imagine watching the slowest animals possible trying to play soccer together? Kenn Nesbitt can in "I Saw a Sloth Play Soccer" (p. 160). Well, actually, he has to try to real hard just to see them move. Read this poem with the passion and determination you can muster if you were a sloth, tortoise, or snail.

Lillegard, Dee and Valeri Gorbachev, illus. GO!: Poetry in Motion. New York: Alfred A. Knopf, 2006.
This title contains short poems about a variety of things that go, from roller skates to tugboats. Look for the ones that relate to sports and exercise to share with this storytime: "Bike and Trike," "Scooter," "Roller Skates," Skateboard," "Skis," "Sled," and "Ice Skates." All of the lively illustrations feature animals on the go!

Prelutsky, Jack and Chris Raschka, illus. Good Sports. New York: Knopf, 2007.
Run, jump, kick, and score and sometimes even fumble in this collection of short, jaunty poems featuring sports and play of all forms. Poems are accompanied by Chris Raschka's fluid and animated watercolor and ink illustrations, which leap off the page.

Singer, Marilyn and LeUyen Pham, illus. A Stick Is an Excellent Thing: Poems Celebrating Outdoor Play. New York: Clarion Books, 2012.
Fun poems celebrating all sorts of sports and play from jacks to jump rope.

Vardell, Sylvia and Janet Wong, ed. The Poetry Friday Anthology for Celebrations. Princeton, NJ: Pomelo Books, 2015.
What can you do with a body like ours? "Let's Go" (p. 135) by Merry Bradshaw has a few ideas! With this action-filled poem, you can get your young audience off their feet and ready to go! On your mark.

Additional Nonfiction

Gordon, Sharon. We Are a Team = Somos un equipo. New York: Marshall Cavendish, 2007.
This bilingual book reads almost like a chant or cheer that a team does together before a game. Each page ends with the words "We are a team." The accompanying photographs show little league kids playing baseball.

Kuklin, Susan. Hoops with Swoopes. New York: Hyperion Books for Children, 2001.
Celebrate basketball from dribbling to defence to shooting hoops. Photographs of retired WNBA player Sheryl Swoopes stand out against a white background. Read the minimal text with a sports announcer's voice for extra fun.

Additional Fiction Picture Books

Cronin, Doreen and Scott Menchin, illus. Stretch. New York: Atheneum Books for Young Readers, 2009.
We all need to be reminded to stretch more (adults included) and this book makes it look less like exercise and more like fun. Try acting out some of the stretches as you read.

Pizzoli, Greg. Number One Sam. New York: Disney*Hyperion Books, 2014.
Sam always wins, except when he doesn't. After the next race, Sam's friends show him that winning comes in many different forms. Bright during high moments, blue during Sam's sad times, the colors used in this book reflect Sam's changing mood.

Rodriguez, Edel. Sergio Makes a Splash! New York: Little, Brown and Company, 2008.
Sergio the penguin loves water, as long as it's not the deep kind he is scared to swim in. His very supportive friends help him see how much fun he can have if he just takes the plunge. Splashes of orange add to the cool black, white, and blue tones of the illustrations. Also look for ***Sergio Saves the Game!*** (2009) to see the Penguins beat the Seagulls in soccer.

Wheeler, Lisa and Barry Gott, illus. Dino-Basketball. Minneapolis: Carolrhoda Books, 2011.
It's epic battle on the court between the meat-eating and the plant-eating dinosaurs. Follow the play-by-play, through the half-time show, until the meat-eaters win the game. Red and green text helps readers can keep the players on each team straight. Also look for ***Dino-Baseball*** (2010) and ***Dino-Hockey*** (2007) by the same author and illustrator.

Willems, Mo. Can I Play Too? New York: Hyperion Books for Children, 2010.
What do you do when a snake wants to play catch? If you are Gerald and Piggie you keep trying until you find a way that everyone can play. This is a hysterical story of friendship and sportsmanship.

Trains

With steam coming from their stacks, the bright flashing lights as the safety arm blocks crossing, and the loud noise as they pass, trains provide stimulation for almost all of the senses. This storytime engages most of them while keeping kids on track for becoming fans of trains.

Sample Storytime

Welcome Song

Routine is important when working with children. Be sure to include welcome, transitional, and closing songs or activities to signify what is coming next. Don't be afraid to use the same ones; children take comfort in knowing what is coming next.

Opening Poem

"Freight Train" from Lillegard, Dee and Valeri Gorbachev, illus. Go! Poetry in Motion. New York: Alfred Knopf, 2006.
With an onomatopoetic refrain of "clickety click click . . ." children will be in a hurry to "come quick" to this poem of a favorite vehicle.

Action Rhyme

This song is best done sitting on the floor with your legs extended. Parents of small children may want to sit their little ones on their laps and help them with the chugging motion.

Before the song starts, demonstrate the chugging motion by holding your arms bent at the elbows, imitating pistons. Make a train sound: "chugga, chugga, chugga, chugga."

Choo-Choo Train
Traditional Rhyme

Here is the Choo-Choo Train, chugga, chugga,
chugga, chugga
Chugging down the track, chugga, chugga, chugga, chugga
Now it's going forward (bend your torso toward your knees)
Chugga, chugga, chugga, chugga
Now it's going back (lean backward)
Chugga, chugga, chugga, chugga
Now the bell is ringing (mimic pulling bell string)
Ding, ding, ding!
Now the whistle blows
Toot, toot, toot! (make toot noise through almost closed fist)
What a lot of noise it makes (cover hands over ears)
Chugga, chugga, chugga, chugga
Everywhere it goes
Chugga, chugga, chugga, chugga.

Early Literacy Tip:
If you choose to do this rhyme with the child on your lap, you are adding a level of closeness between parent and child. This positive touch adds to the child's (and parent's) enjoyment and makes them associate words and language with happy feelings.

Nonfiction for Storytime

Simon, Seymour. Seymour Simon's Book of Trains. New York: HarperCollins Publishers, 2002.

From steam locomotives to electric trains to mountain trains, there are so many different types of locomotives. Kids will love the large photographs on one side of each double-page spread. Read just the page headings (types of trains and train cars) when sharing with a large group. Be sure to leave the book out after a program for families who want to learn more.

Transitional Song

See Welcome Song earlier.

Flannel Board Activity

The Little Steam Engine

Create flannel pieces using the patterns at the end of the chapter.

The Little Steam Engine
Adapted by M. Follis
(Tune: This Old Man)

The little steam engine, painted black
It goes racing down the track
With a chug chug, choo choo
And a whistle blow
The little steam engine is on his way home

The passenger car, painted yellow
Is such a mighty fine fellow
With a chug chug, choo choo
And a whistle blow
The little yellow car is on its way home

The caboose is last, bright shining red
Takes its passengers home to bed
With a chug chug, choo choo
And a whistle blow
The little train is on its way home

Picture Books for Storytime

Rockwell, Anne and Vanessa van der Baan, illus. Whoo! Whoo! Goes the Train. New York: HarperCollins, 2009.

A young kitten obsessed with trains is excited by all the things he sees and does on his first ever train trip. Perfect for those young readers who share this obsession.

Steggall, Susan. Rattle and Rap. London: Frances Lincoln Children's Books, 2008.

More than a train ride, this is a journey for the senses. Rumble and sway as the whistle blows and the train crosses sky-high tresses. Use different voices to add intensity and excitement to the ride.

Closing Song

See Welcome Song earlier.

Follow-Up Activities

Train Game

This train storytime is full of sound and movement. Continue this after storytime by playing "TRAIN."

Materials:

- Train music or sound effects
- Speakers or sound system to play music or sound effects

Directions:

- Have children line up, with someone designated as the Engine and someone as the Caboose.
- Form a line and circle around the room while playing train music.

You can find fun train sound effects through an APP like TRAIN SOUNDS where you can choose the train and loop the sound effect while sounding a horn in a layered effect (Android App—free).

There are also a variety of sound recordings you can use for this activity. Your library's collection may have a few, but you can also purchase select tracks on iTunes or Amazon. You may want to check out the Thunder on the Steel CD.

Early Literacy Tip:
There is a lot of talk and research about the downfalls of using technology with children. Technology, such as the train sounds app, can be a positive influence when used to enhance communication and playtime between parent and child.

Other Songs, Rhymes, and Fingerplays

I've Been Working on the Railroad
American Folk Song

I've been working on the railroad
All the live long day
I've been working on the railroad
Just to pass the time away
Can't you hear the whistle blowing,
Rise up so early in the morn;
Can't you hear the captain shouting,
"Dinah, blow your horn!"
Dinah, won't you blow,
Dinah, won't you blow,
Dinah, won't you blow your horn?
Dinah, won't you blow,
Dinah, won't you blow,
Dinah, won't you blow your horn?
Someone's in the kitchen with Dinah

Someone's in the kitchen I know
Someone's in the kitchen with Dinah
Strummin' on the old banjo.
Singin' fee, fie, fiddly-i-o
Fee, fie, fiddly-i-o-o-o-o
Fee, fie, fiddly-i-o
Strummin' on the old banjo.

Down by the station
Folk song

Down by the station
Early in the morning
See the little pufferbellies
All in a row

See the station master
Turn the little handle
Puff, puff, toot, toot
Off we go!

The Last Train by Gordon Titcomb: https://www.youtube.com/watch?v=q1h-1iCme3k.
The YouTube video is the trailer for the audiobook of:

Titcomb, Gordon and Wendell Minor, illus. The Last Train. New York: Roaring Brook Press, 2010.
The trailer includes over half of the book, illustrations from the book, and live-action additions. Watch the YouTube video or play the song without video while turning the pages of the book.

Additional Poetry

Martin Jr., Bill, Michael Sampson, and various illustrators. The Bill Martin Jr. Big Book of Poetry. New York: Simon & Schuster, 2008.
For many young storytime goers, the subway is part of their daily lives. If you are in a more rural area, this may need a bit of an explanation. "Subways Are People" by Lee Bennett Hopkins (p. 71) focuses less on the actual train than the people who ride it; some "people I will never know." If you have ridden on the subway, you know the rocking and rhythm of the train cars. Channel that as you read.

Additional Nonfiction

Coppendale, Jean. Trains. Laguna Hills, CA, 2007.
Full-color, double-page photo spreads give this book a visual punch. Each double page explores a topic such as What Is a Train. Simple sentences make this an easy share, although you may want to skip some lines for easier storytime sharing.

O'Brien, Patrick. Steam, Smoke, and Steel: Back in Time with Trains. Watertown, MA: Charlesbridge, 2000.
Train designs have changed tremendously over the years. One young boy provides a tour of trains through generations of his family's history. Every other turn of the page has a double-page illustration of a train going back through history; show and read just these pages in a storytime group to garner interest in the book. For extra fun, look for the cat in each illustration.

Ryan, Phillip. Steam-Powered Trains. New York: PowerKiDS Press, 2011.
Full color illustrations with simple sentences make this an easily readable and accessible story for sharing in storytime. Train specific vocabulary words are bolded, with a glossary in the back of the book, making this also appropriate for newly independent readers.

Additional Fiction Picture Books

Barton, Chris, and Tom Lichtenheld, illus. Shark vs. Train. New York: Little Brown and Company, 2010.
Join this epic battle as two powerhouses, one of the land and one of the sea, duke it out to see who is the "best." In the water? SHARK! On the land? TRAIN! Young readers will enjoy chiming in with their guesses on who end up on top of the (toy) heap!

Cooper, Elijah. Trains. New York: Orchard Books, 2013.
Readers are invited "all aboard" several different types of trains and they journey through cities and towns, following tracks, and learning more about what each type of train carries and does.

McMullan, Kate and Jim McMullan, illus. I'm Fast! New York: Balzer + Bray, 2012.
Who's going to get to Chicago first? The speedy car or the freight train? With lots of "Vruummmm" and "Chooka chooka" everyone can get into the action of this story.

Piper, Watty and Loren Long, illus. The Little Engine That Could. New York: Philomel Books, 2005.
New steam has been added to this classic tale with art by Loren Long. Add this revised classic to your train storytimes. Will it garner new fans? I think it can!

Sturges, Philemon and Shari Halpern, illus. I Love Trains! New York: Harper-Collins. 2001.
A rocking rhyme takes young readers along the train tracks, starting with the engine and ending with the caboose. A fun celebration of the love of trains!

Engine Pattern

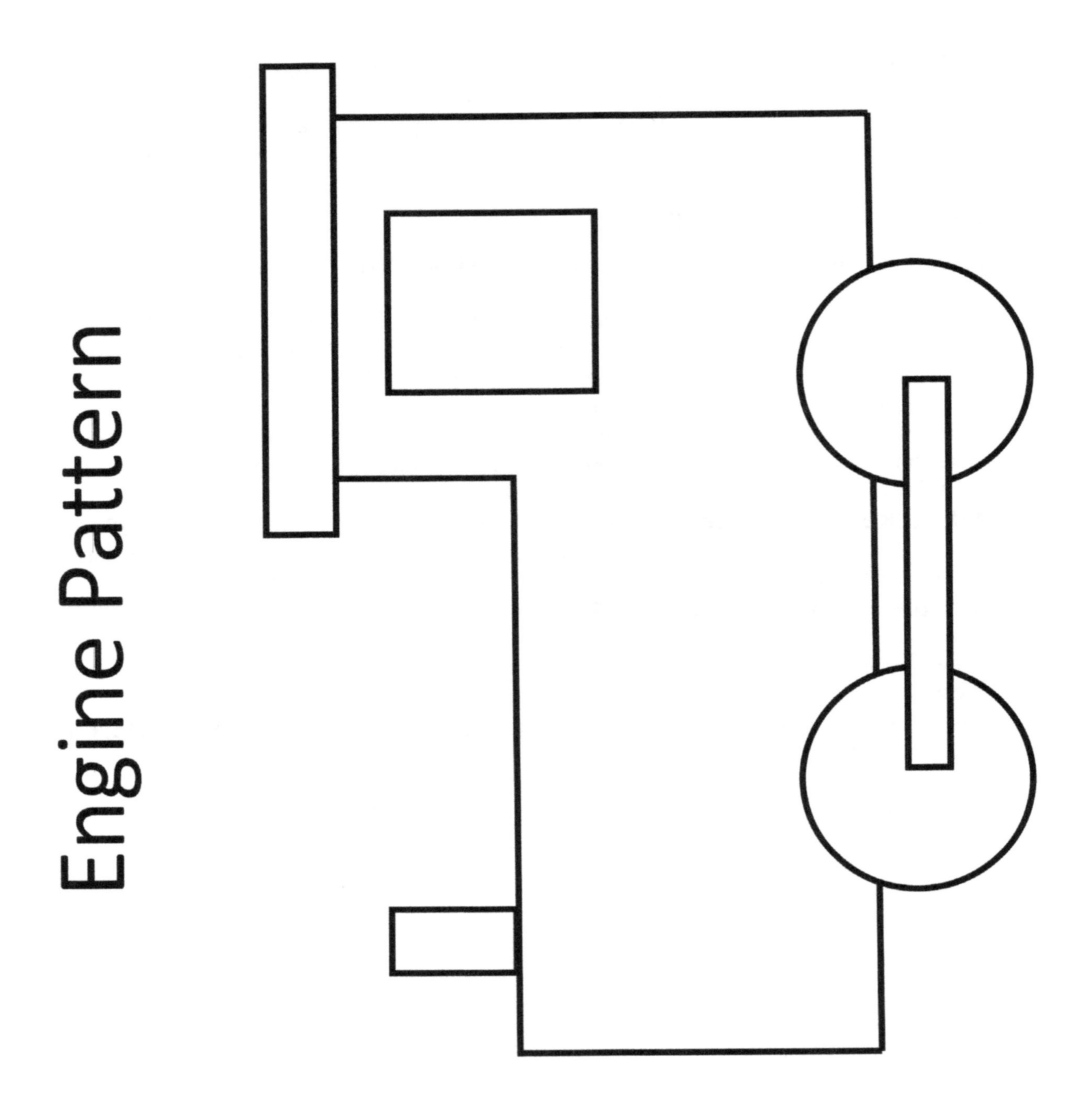

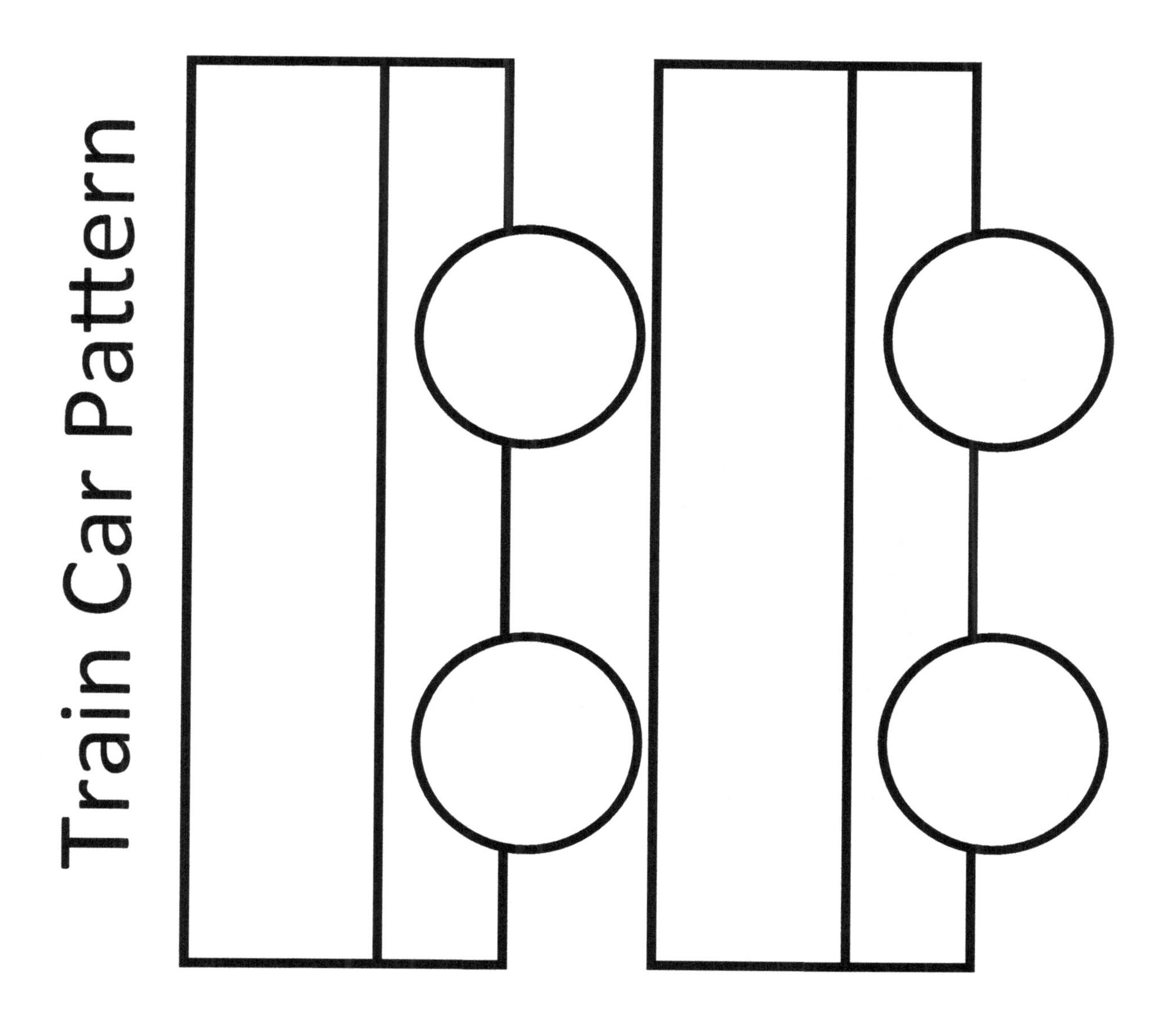
Train Car Pattern

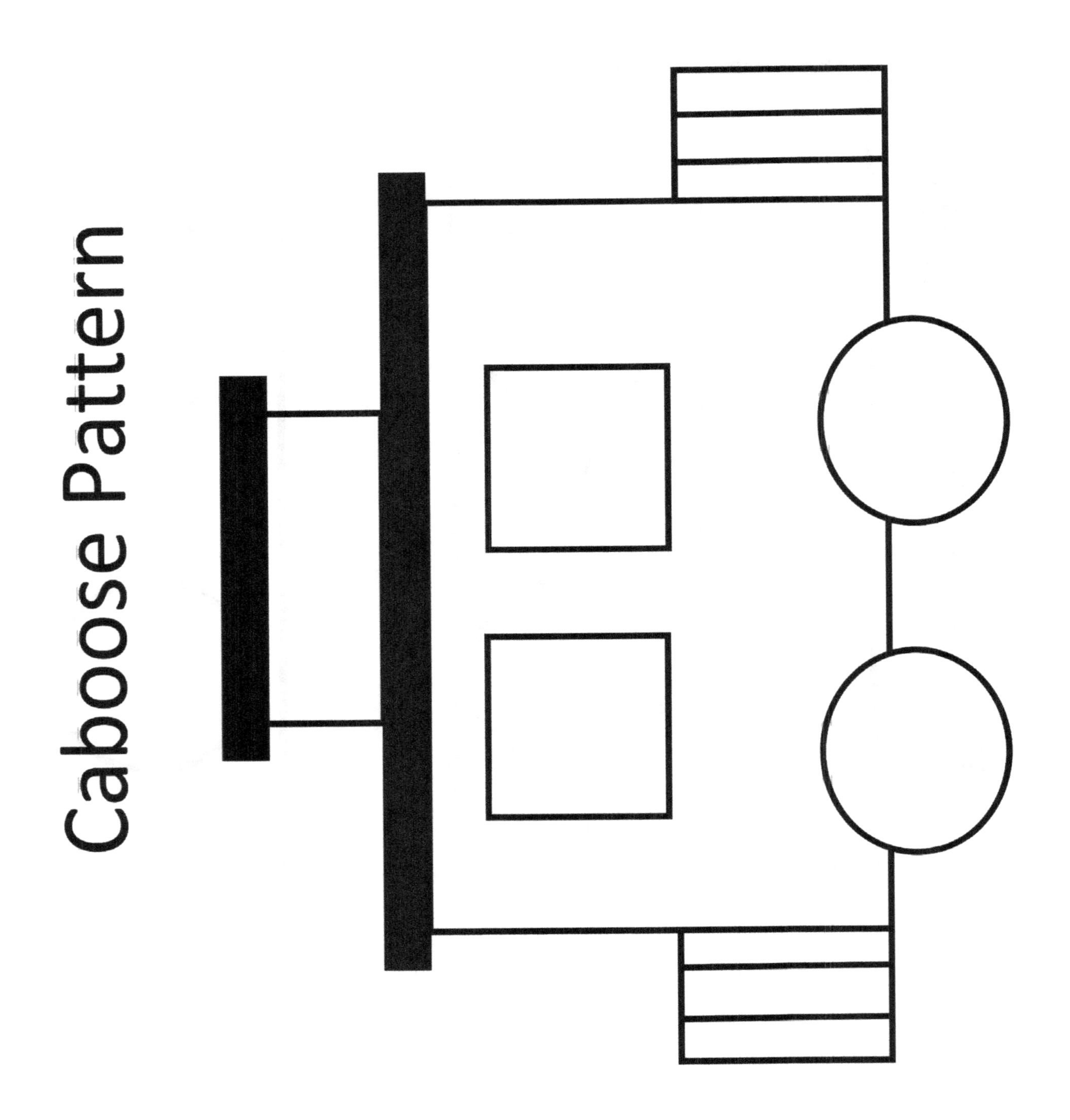
Caboose Pattern

Trees

There are so many different types of trees. Some have leaves that stay green and on the tree all year long. Other have leaves that change color and fall to the ground. Hopefully your little ones have trees in their lives, even if they live in an urban environment. Be sure to call their attention to them and expand on vocabulary like deciduous, rough, smooth, autumn.

Sample Storytime

Welcome Song

Routine is important when working with children. Be sure to include welcome, transitional, and closing songs or activities to signify what is coming next. Don't be afraid to use the same ones; children take comfort in knowing what is coming next.

Opening Poem

Heard, Georgia, ed. Falling Down the Page. New York: Roaring Brook Press, 2009.
"Tree Song" by George Ella Lyon is a tall, slender poem that falls down the page as gently as leaves in the fall. Have your little ones stand and unfold as the poem does, from the roots up.

Action Rhyme

What Does a Tree Do?
By M. Follis

A tree has roots that plant themselves into the ground.
(Ask your young people to stand with legs hip distance apart and "plant" themselves into the ground.)

A tree grows taller and taller reaching up and all around
(Reach up overhead and rise up on your tippy toes)

A tree has branches that reach up to the sky
(Plant feet shoulder width apart and spread arms wide and pretend that your arms are branches swaying in the wind)

A tree stands still while the world goes quickly by
(Lead children into the yoga "Tree" pose. Have them stand on one foot, and either place the other foot by their ankle, or on their calf. Have them try to maintain this balanced pose)

Early Literacy Tip: Storytime is the perfect time to expand vocabulary. Be sure to ask children about words that may be new to them. What are roots and branches? In the preceding poem you might ask if children where their roots would be if they were a tree. How about branches?

Nonfiction for Storytime

Gerber, Carole and Leslie Evans, illus. Leaf Jumpers. Watertown, MA: Charlesbridge, 2004.
Learn about the shapes and colors of the autumn leaves of eight different trees. The illustrations clearly show each leaf so the book can be used as a small field guide. The text evokes the smell, feel, and fun of the falling leaves.

Transitional Song

See Welcome Song earlier.

Flannel Board Activity

Use the patterns included at the end of this chapter, or create your own. You will need one bare tree, and two to three canopies, depending on your preference.

For the spring canopy, use a light green, maybe adding a few pink dots indicating blooms; for summer, a dark green. If you don't want to use felt, you can photocopy the pattern onto colored copy paper. If you are artistically inclined, you can pen in leaf shapes to color.

For the autumn canopy, you can use the small leaf pattern included to make a colorful confetti of leaves. A scrapbooking hole punch would also work. Feel free to use the canopy as well, but just be sure to adjust it to reflect the colors of the poem.

Place the bare tree on the flannel board to start, and then read the following poem, switching out leafy tree canopies as indicated.

A Tree's Year
By M. Follis

In the winter time, trees are bare
No leaves on branches, and a chill in the air

In spring time, trees are full of blooms
Pale new colors and sweet perfume

In summer time, trees are full of green
Giving you a nice shady place to read

But autumn in best of all
When fireworks of color around you fall

Picture Books for Storytime

Jeffers, Oliver. Stuck. New York: Philomel Books, 2011.
When young Floyd's kite gets stuck in a tree, he has a great idea. He will throw other objects up into the tree to knock his kite loose. First his shoe, then his cat, followed by a ladder . . . and after that . . . everything gets stuck. A fun, cumulative, tall tree tale.

Reid, Barbara. Picture a Tree. Chicago: Albert Whitman & Company, 2011.
Reid's unique Plasticine illustrations add so much texture and life to the magic of trees. They provide shade and oceans of green and imaginary places. After reading this book you may never think of a tree as just a plant ever again.

Closing Song

See Welcome Song earlier.

Follow-Up Activities

Leaf Pile

Materials:

- Fake leaves from a craft store or leaves cut out of construction paper (You can use real leaves that you collect outside but fake ones are just as fun and half the mess.)

Directions:

There are a variety of ways to interact with the leaves:

- Create small piles for kids to jump and play in.
- Sort the leaves by shape, color, or size.
- Hold leaves in your hands and pretend that your arms are branches.
- Throw the leaves up in the air and let them fall around you like a fall day.

Early Literacy Tip:
Play is an important skill in early literacy and helps children experience the world in new and safe ways. While engaging in play, little ones can practice all sorts of skills without even knowing it. For example, when little ones are in the leaf pile activity above, ask them to collect all the yellow leaves.

Make a Leaf Mask

Materials:

- Green construction paper (or you can include red, orange, yellow, and brown for fall leaves)
- Leaf pattern at the end of the chapter
- Popsicle sticks
- Tape or glue
- Crayons and/or stickers
  - Suggestion: Use stickers of animals that can be found around trees—insects, birds, and so on.

Directions:

- Use the leaf pattern to pre-cut enough masks for everyone.
- Let everyone decorate their leaf as they wish.
- With the help of an adult, tape or glue the popsicle stick to the bottom of the leaf so the mask can be held in front of the child's face.

Other Songs, Rhymes, and Fingerplays

Plant a Tree
By J. Dietzel-Glair and M. Follis
(Tune: Are You Sleeping?)

Plant a tree, plant a tree (wave hands above your head like tree branches)
Dig a hole, dig a hole (pretend to dig a hole with a shovel)
Make sure it gets water, make sure it gets water (pretend to use a watering can)
It will grow, it will grow. (squat down, slowly stand up like you are growing, and raise your hands in the air)

All the Leaves
By M. Follis
(Tune: London Bridge)

All the leaves are turning green,
Turning green, turning green.
All the leaves are turning green,
It is spring time!

All the leaves are giving shade,
Giving shade, giving shade.
All the leaves are giving shade,
It is summer!

All the leaves are falling down,
Falling down, falling down.
All the leaves are falling down,
It is autumn!

All the leaves have gone away,
Gone away, gone away.
All the leaves have gone away,
It is winter!

Five Little Birds, Five Little Trees
Traditional Rhyme

Five little birds without any home,
Five little trees in a row.
Come build your nests
In our branches tall.
We'll rock you to and fro.

Additional Poetry

Florian, Douglas. Poetrees. New York: Beach Lane Books, 2010.
Turn this book on its end to read the poems about trees that stretch to new heights. Learn about different types of trees from Japanese Cedar to the mighty Oak or read a poem about tree rings or leaves.

Heard, Georgia, ed. Falling Down the Page. New York: Roaring Brook Press, 2009.
"Oak Tree" by Georgia Heard is to be read backward from the bottom up as a small acorn takes root and "reaching up, up . . . touching sky." Another poem that would be perfect to add movement to, with young listeners starting in a crouch, and then ending on tippy toes.

Lewis, J. Patrick and Ethan Long, illus. Countdown to Summer: A Poem for Every Day of the School Year. New York: Little, Brown and Company, 2009.
"American Autumn." This concrete poem is an ode to the oak tree that has left the gift of leaves on the doorstep of the narrator who has "piles to go . . . I must sweep." This poem is best shared visually so that your young audience can see the shape of the poem and guess why it is so.

Additional Nonfiction

DePalma, Mary Newell. A Grand Old Tree. New York: Arthur A. Levine Books, 2005.
Told as the life story of one fictional tree, readers see the tree bloom, lose her leaves, and eventually fall. The story doesn't end with the tree "dying," instead the trunk becomes a home for other animals. The story-like feel of this book makes it especially appealing to a storytime crowd.

Gerber, Carole and Leslie Evans, illus. Winter Trees. Watertown, MA: Charlesbridge, 2008.
Trees look very different in the winter covered in snow. A boy and his dog take a walk through a forest identifying the trees as they go.

Smith, Danna and Laurie Allen Klein, illus. Balloon Trees. Mt. Pleasant, SC: Sylvan Dell Publishing, 2013.
See trees in a different light after rhyming text explains the balloon-making process. Look for the inquisitive bird included in each double-page illustration.

Additional Fiction Picture Books

Chase, Kit. Oliver's Tree. New York: G.P. Putman's Sons, 2014.
Oliver the elephant loves playing with his friends, a bird and a bunny. Their favorite game is hide-and-seek and his friends favorite hiding spots are trees. Too big for trees, Oliver says "That's not fair." So the friends set off to find the perfect tree for Oliver and after some comical mishaps, they do!

Lurie, Susan and Murray Head, photo. Frisky Brisky Hippity Hop. New York: Holiday House, 2012.
Based on a poem written 140 years ago by Alexina B. White, this story follows the lively life a squirrel living in a tree.

MacKay, Elly. If You Hold a Seed. Philadelphia, PA: Running Press Kids, 2013.
Follow the story of a young child who watches and waits for his seed to grow. The sweet slow story covers seasons and years until finally the "tree will grow SO LARGE it will hold you." Mixed media collage in warm tones gives the book the dream like quality of memories.

Nichols, Lori. Maple. New York: Nancy Paulsen Books, 2014.
When Maple was a baby, her parents planted a tree in her honor. As they both grew, Maple learned to take care of the tree. When her parents plant another tree, Maple soon learns to take care of her baby sister too, Willow.

Reid, Barbara. Picture a Tree. Chicago, IL: Albert Whitman & Company, 2011.
A sweet story of all the things a tree can be; a tunnel, an ocean, and so much more. It's all in how you picture a tree. Big bold textured illustrations are easily shared with a storytime crowd, but filled with details found after further inspection.

Stein, David Ezra. Leaves. New York: G.P. Putnam's Sons, 2007.
Bear is confused when the leaves fall off the trees during his first autumn. He wonders if the trees are okay but becomes too sleepy to do much about it. After a long hibernation he is excited to welcome the leaves back to the trees.

Stein, David Ezra. Ol' Mother Squirrel. New York: Nancy Paulsen Books, 2013.
Ol' Mother Squirrel is protective of the tree she and her babies call home. If you try to get near it, she will run out and yell at you! "Chook chook chook! Get away from my tree! Get away from my babies!" But even Ol' Mother Squirrel is no match for a bear. Good thing she has friends!

Stoop, Naoko. Red Knit Cap Girl and the Reading Tree. New York: Megan Tingley Books, 2014.
On a hot sunny day, Red Knit Cap Girl and friends work together to build a special place to read and share books: a library!

Verburg, Bonnie and Mark Teague, illus. The Tree House That Jack Built. New York: Orchard Books, 2014.
This classic cumulative tale has been given a new spin, when young Jack builds a tropical tree house. When the wild animals have pestered each other enough, Jack rings a bell and they all settle in for storytime. Guess what book they read?

Zweibel, Alan and David Catrow, illus. Our Tree Named Steve. New York: G.P. Putnam's Sons, 2005.
One tree has stood tall besides this family's home through a generation becoming a part of the family. Catrow adds many visual jokes to this sentimental story told as a letter from a father to his children after Steve the tree has fallen in a storm.

Tree Pattern

Tree Canopy Pattern

Leaf Patterns

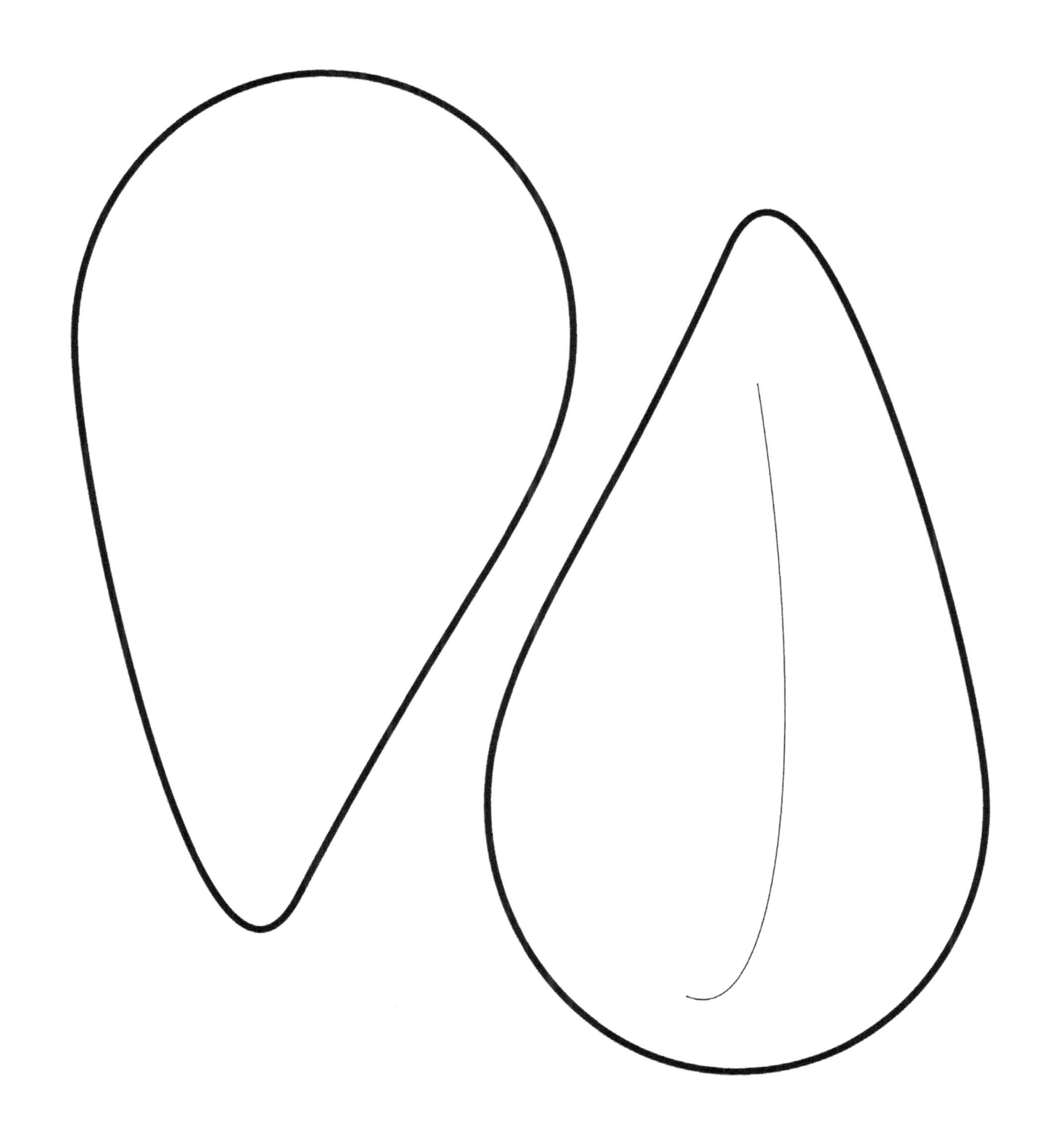

Wild Animals

Roar, soar, crawl, and paw. What's not to love about getting wild once in a while? Wild things are fun, colorful and well, wild. They run and make noise and behave in ways that may be considered naughty by adults. Maybe that is one of the main reasons children love them so! From a librarian's point of view this topic presents opportunities to showcase many areas of their collection while expanding vocabulary. Oh the verbs!

Sample Storytime

Welcome Song

Routine is important when working with children. Be sure to include welcome, transitional, and closing songs or activities to signify what is coming next. Don't be afraid to use the same ones; children take comfort in knowing what is coming next.

Opening Poem

"The Wolf" from Elliott, David and Holly Meade, illus. In the Wild. Somerville, MA: Candlewick Press, 2010.
Gather everyone's attention as you howl "Ahooooo!" at the end of both stanzas of this ode to the nighttime canine.

Action Rhyme

Five Little Monkeys Swinging on a Tree
English Folk Song

Five little monkeys (show five fingers)
Swinging on a tree (swing arms)
Teasing Mr. Crocodile: "You can't catch me!"
(make teasing motion with thumbs in ears, waving fingers)
<sung softly>
Then along comes Mr. Crocodile, quiet as can be
(put hands together and make a snaking motion)
<sing loudly>
Then SNAP! He grabbed that monkey off the tree!
(make loud clapping noise at the word SNAP!)

Count backwards until all monkeys are gone.

Note: For those concerned about the implied violence of the song, a bonus last line can be added such as "And now it was the monkeys turn to be IT!"

Nonfiction for Storytime

Jenkins, Steve, illus. and Robin Page. Creature Features: 25 Animals Explain Why They Look the Way They Do. Boston: Houghton Mifflin Harcourt, 2014.
Why is a giraffe's tongue purple? Does a bighorn sheep's horns get in the way? Kids (and adults) will love learning some quick facts about funny-looking creatures. Read the whole book or choose a couple favorite pages to share.

Transitional Song

See Welcome Song earlier.

Flannel Board Activity

Animals and Their Sounds

If you already own animal flannel pieces, repurpose them for this song. If not, you may want to go online and find some free wild zoo animal clip art. You will also need die-cut letters to spell "Z-O-O."

NOTE: Since this song requires animal sounds, be sure your animals have sounds that can be easily replicated.

Sing:

Mrs. Gnu Has a Zoo
Adapted by M. Follis
(Tune: Old MacDonald)

Mrs Gnu has a zoo, Z-O-O (place letters on flannel board)
And on that zoo she has a ____________ Z-O-O (place wild zoo animal clip art on board)
With a ________, ______, here and a ______, ______ there
(fill in the blanks with the appropriate wild sound)
Here a ____ there a _____
Everywhere a ________, _________
Mrs. Gnu has a Zoo, Z-O-O

Picture Books for Storytime

Craig, Lindsey and Marc Brown, illus. Dancing Feet! New York: Alfred Knopf, 2010.
One by one, wild animals are introduced along with their dancing feet. With a rolicking rhyme and sing song beat, you too will soon have many dancing feet! Young readers will have fun guessing whose feet are dancing and will be out of their seats in excitement.

Fleming, Candace and Eric Rohman, illus. Oh No! New York: Schwartz & Wade, 2012.
When a small mouse falls into a large hole, his friends come to the rescue. This story escalates when one wild

Early Literacy Tip:
Involving children as active participants in storytime, like joining in during a repeated chorus, encourages active engagement and increases print motivation; otherwise known as "the love of reading and books!"

creature after another tries to help their friends with some interesting results. With a chorus of "Oh No!," young listeners can sympathize and then cheer them on.

Closing Song

See Welcome Song earlier.

Follow-Up Activities

Lion Mask

Materials:

- Paper plates
- Construction paper in:
    - brown
    - orange
    - pink
    - white
    - black
- Glue or glue sticks
- Craft sticks

Directions:

- Cut out the pattern pieces ahead of time from the appropriate color construction paper.
- Glue the inner pink ear to the outer orange ear, then attach on the outer edges of plate.
- Adhere black dots onto white ovals to represent the pupils of the eye and place them in the appropriate place as shown in pattern.
- Glue brown oval "muzzle" to the center of the plate.
- Glue the black triangle nose to the top of the brown oval muzzle in an inverted manner, to serve as nose (see pattern).
- Adhere pink triangle mouth to the bottom of the brown oval muzzle.
- Adhere long skinny black "whiskers" to the brown oval muzzle to represent whiskers.*
- A craft stick can be added to make this a mask, or children can simply hold it up to their faces, which may be simpler and safer.
- Now give a ROAR!

*Did you know that the whisker placement on a lion's muzzle is as unique as a fingerprint?

Other Songs, Rhymes, and Fingerplays

In the wild
Adapted by M. Follis
(Tune: If Your're Happy and You Know It)

What does a lion say in the wild? ROAR! ROAR!
What does a lion say in the wild? ROAR, ROAR
If you're a wild lion and you want the world to know it
If you're really wild give a roar! ROAR ROAR

What does a monkey say in the wild? Eeek Eeek!
What does a monkey say in the wild? Eeek Eeek!
If you're a wild monkey and you want the world to know it
If you're really wild give an Eeek! Eeek, Eeek!

What does an crocodile do in the wild? Snap, Snap!
What does a crocodile do in the wild? Snap, Snap!
If you're a wild crocodile and you want the world to know it
If you're really wild give a snap! SNAP, SNAP

What does a kangaroo do in the wild? HOP, HOP
What does a kangaroo do in the wild? HOP, HOP
If you're a wild kangaroo and you want the world to know it
If you're really wild give a Hop. HOP HOP!

The Elephant
Traditional Rhyme

The elephant goes like this, like that,
He's terribly big, and he's terribly fat. (hold out your arms and legs to make yourself big)
He has no fingers, he has no toes, (hold up your fingers then point to your toes)
But goodness gracious, what a nose! (hold up your arm to your nose like an elephant trunk)

We're Going on a Bear Hunt
Traditional Folk Song

We're going on a bear hunt, (slap hands on thighs to mimic sound of walking)
We're gonna catch a big one,
What a beautiful day,
We're not scared.
Oh oh!
Grass,
Long, wavy, grass.
We can't go over it,
We can't go under it,
We've gotta go through it!
Swishy swashy, swishy swashy. (rub hands together in a back and forth motion)

We're going on a bear hunt,
We're gonna catch a big one,
What a beautiful day,
We're not scared.
Oh oh!
Mud,
Thick, oozy mud.
We can't go over it,
We can't go under it,
We've gotta go through it!
Squelch squelch, squelch squelch (lift feet slowly as if feet are stuck in mud)

We're going on a bear hunt,
We're gonna catch a big one,

What a beautiful day,
We're not scared.
Oh oh!
A river,
A deep, cold river.
We can't go over it,
We can't go under it,
We've gotta go through it!
Splish splosh, splish splosh. (pretend to swim through the water)

We're going on a bear hunt,
We're gonna catch a big one,
What a beautiful day,
We're not scared.
Oh oh!
A cave,
A scary, dark cave.
We can't go over it,
We can't go under it,
We've gotta go through it!
Tiptoe, tiptoe. (crouch low and tiptoe)
(Say the following verse all together and quickly.)
OH NO IT'S A BEAR!!!

Quick! (do all actions quickly in reverse)
Through the cave, tiptoe, tiptoe,
Through the river, splish splosh, splish splosh,
Through the mud, squelch squelch, squelch squelch,
Through the grass, swishy swashy, swishy swashy.
Run to the house, run up the stairs, (pretend to run with arms racing at sides)
Oh oh forgot to shut the door!
Run back downstairs, shut the door, (run and mime shutting door)
Run back up, to the bedroom, (run)
Jump into bed, pull up the covers, (mime pulling covers overhead)
WE ARE NEVER GOING ON A BEAR HUNT AGAIN!!

Early Literacy Tip:
Singing songs helps develop listening and memory skills, especially songs with repeated choruses.

Additional Poetry

Elliott, David and Holly Meade, illus. In the Wild. Somerville, MA: Candlewick Press, 2010.
These poems and woodcuts just beg to be shared. The large trim size, colorful illustrations, and tight poetry allow for the entire book to be read aloud in one sitting. Who's your favorite wild animal? The sloth? The kangaroo? The lion?

Florian, Douglas. Bow Wow Meow Meow: It's Rhyming Cats and Dogs. San Diego, CA: Harcourt, Inc., 2003.
This title has easy-to-understand poems about a cheetah, lion, leopard, jaguarundi, and black panther. Each double-page spread features one poem and an illustration. Hold up the book as you read the poem.

Lewis, J. Patrick, ed. National Geographic Book of Animal Poetry: 200 Poems with Photographs That Squeak, Soar, and Roar! Washington, DC: National Geographic, 2012.

This title has so many child-friendly poems that it's difficult to pick just a few to highlight. Take your chances and flip to a random page, you are certain to find a wild animal, an amazing photograph, and poem to share with storytime.

Schwartz, David M., Yael Schy, and Dwight Kuhn, illus. Where Else in the Wild? More Camouflaged Creatures Concealed . . . and Revealed. Berkeley, CA: Tricycle Press, 2009.

Part poetry, part nature photograph, part puzzle, all fun. Each poem describes an animal that blends in with its environment. Search for the animal in the photograph then lift the flap for more information and a reveal of the animal's hiding spot. Choose one or two pages to share with the group. Be sure to have more copies on hand as this title is certain to be popular with a variety of ages. You can also share the first book in this series: ***Where in the Wild? Camouflaged Creatures Concealed . . . and Revealed*** (2007).

Vardell, Sylvia and Janet Wong, ed. The Poetry Friday Anthology for Celebrations. Princeton, NJ: Pomelo Books, 2015.

The narrator of "Tiger" by Bruce Balan (p. 317) admires to colors and ferocity of the tiger, but doubts they would feel the same "with no fence in between." And who would?!

Vardell, Sylvia and Janet Wong, ed. The Poetry Friday Anthology for Science: Poems for the School Year Integrating Science, Reading and Language Arts, K-5 Teacher Edition. Princeton, NJ: Pomelo Books, 2014.

"The Leopard Cannot Change His Spots" by Lesléa Newman is a funny poem about being happy with our lot (or spots) in life. An assortment of animals present some of the things they would like to change, including the leopard not being able to alter his "spots into stars or polka-dots." The great cadence is sure to be a hit at storytime.

Wheeler, Lisa and Zachariah Ohora, illus. The Pet Project: Cute and Cuddly Vicious Verses. New York: Atheneum Books for Young Readers, 2013.

When a little girl asks her parents for a pet, they ask her to do some research and "formulate a query . . . plan your bestiary." And she does in poetic forms while exploring the pros and cons of a variety of pets, some quite wild! With great words like observation, notes, and query in context this book can be used when discussing scientific method as well as animals.

Additional Nonfiction

Jenkins, Steve and Robin Page. What Do You Do with a Tail Like This? Boston: Houghton Mifflin Company, 2003.

The concept of the book is to explain that animals have special body parts that have developed to aid the animal in its daily life. "What do you do with a nose like this?" one double page asks, displaying an assortment of noses. The follow pages answer, by identifying the creature to whom the nose belongs, and explaining how its special features aid the creature. For example, did you know that a mole's nose helps the mole find its way when it is burrowing in the ground? Beautiful collage art allows for terrific up close detail, and back matter offers additional material for closer reading.

Neuman, Susan. Go, Cub! Washington, DC: National Geographic. 2014.
This beginning to read title includes engaging photographs that National Geographic is known for. With minimal text, the entire book can be read in storytime.

Schaefer, Lola and Geoff Waring, illus. Just One Bite: 11 Animals and Their Bites at Life Size! San Francisco, CA: Chronicle Books, 2010.
How much can a worm eat? How about a rabbit? Or a sperm whale? Life-size illustrations add energy to this seemingly larger-than-life book, even the trim size is big. Kids will be clambering to read the further facts about each animal after a storytime read.

Early Literacy Tip:
The older children in a preschool storytime may be starting to read. Display extra copies of this title as well as other National Geographic beginning reader books about animals for families to check out after the program.

Additional Fiction Picture Books

Brown, Peter. Mr. Tiger Goes Wild. New York: Little Brown and Company, 2013.
Mr. Tiger's life is quite calm and civilized, but he feels like something is missing. That's when he decides to return to his roots and GO WILD! But even then Mr. Tiger realizes that finding balance in life is key. Perfect for readers learning that there is a time to behave and time to let loose!

Buzzeo, Toni and Mike Wohnoutka, illus. Just Like My Papa. New York: Disney-Hyperion Books, 2013.
Join a lion and his cub through their day on the savanna. Rhythmic text and vibrant illustrations will draw the attention of big cat lovers.

Cuyler, Margery and Joe Mathieu, illus. We're Going on a Lion Hunt. Tarrytown, NY: Marshall Cavendish, 2008.
The familiar song "We're Going on a Bear Hunt" is adapted to a search for a fierce lion. Rather than being scary, the lion looks more confused and perhaps friendly. The adventurous movements add opportunity for an active read-aloud.

Hall, Michael. My Heart Is Like a Zoo. New York: Greenwillow Books, 2010.
Filled with hearts and similes, *My Heart Is Like a Zoo* introduces heart-shaped animals and compares the reader's heart to some of their attributes. "My heart is as jumpy as a frog . . . eager as a beaver, etc." A great way to expand the vocabulary of the little ones you love.

Ohora, Zachariah. Stop Snoring Bernard! New York: Henry Holt, 2011.
Bernard the otter loves his life in the zoo. Sadly, not everyone loves his snoring. When he is asked to find somewhere else to sleep, Bernard the snoring otter encounters the same complaint! "STOP SNORING BERNARD!" With a cool retro palette and hand-lettered speech bubbles, the book has a fun and funky feel. Ask your little ones to join you in the chorus, or better yet . . . SNORE!

Reynolds, Aaron and Dan Santat, illus. Carnivores. San Francisco, CA: Chronicle Books, 2013.
A lion, a great white shark, and a timber wolf want to know why no one likes them, so they form a support group. After trying to modify their behavior and blend in, they finally come to the realization that they are carnivores and eating meat is just what they do. Sly humor and detailed expressions on the illustrations make this a great choice for a slightly older crowd and the adults reading to them.

Shea, Bob. Cheetah Can't Lose. New York: Balzar & Bray, 2013.
Cheetah thinks he can win every possible race. Readers will enjoy being in on the joke as the little cats trick him into losing the last race. This humorous tale is told entirely through the voices of Cheetah and the cats so it is best done with multiple voices or readers.

Sierra, Judy and Marc Brown, illus. Wild about Books. New York: Knopf, 2004.
When the bookmobile accidentally ends up at the zoo, the librarian introduces the wonderful world of books to the zoo animals. They go wild for them!

Stein, David Ezra. Pouch! New York: G. P. Putman's Sons, 2009.
A shy and timid baby kangaroo explores the big new world, but quickly returns to the safety of his mother when he meets new and startling creatures. "Pouch" he shouts and jumps back home to his mother. Eventually he grows more confident, especially when making a new friend.

Sample Lion Mask

Lion Mask Pattern

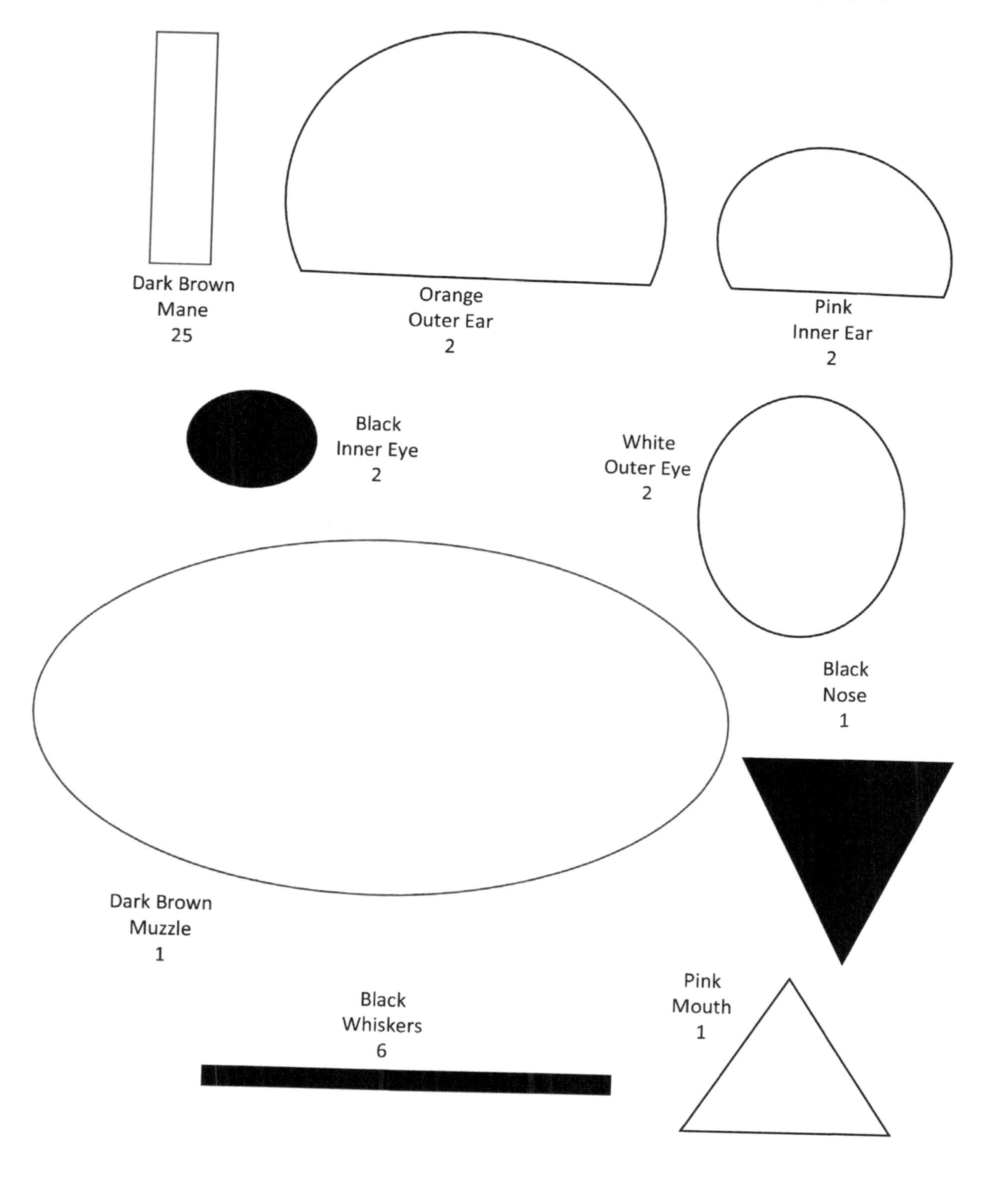

Lion Mask Pattern

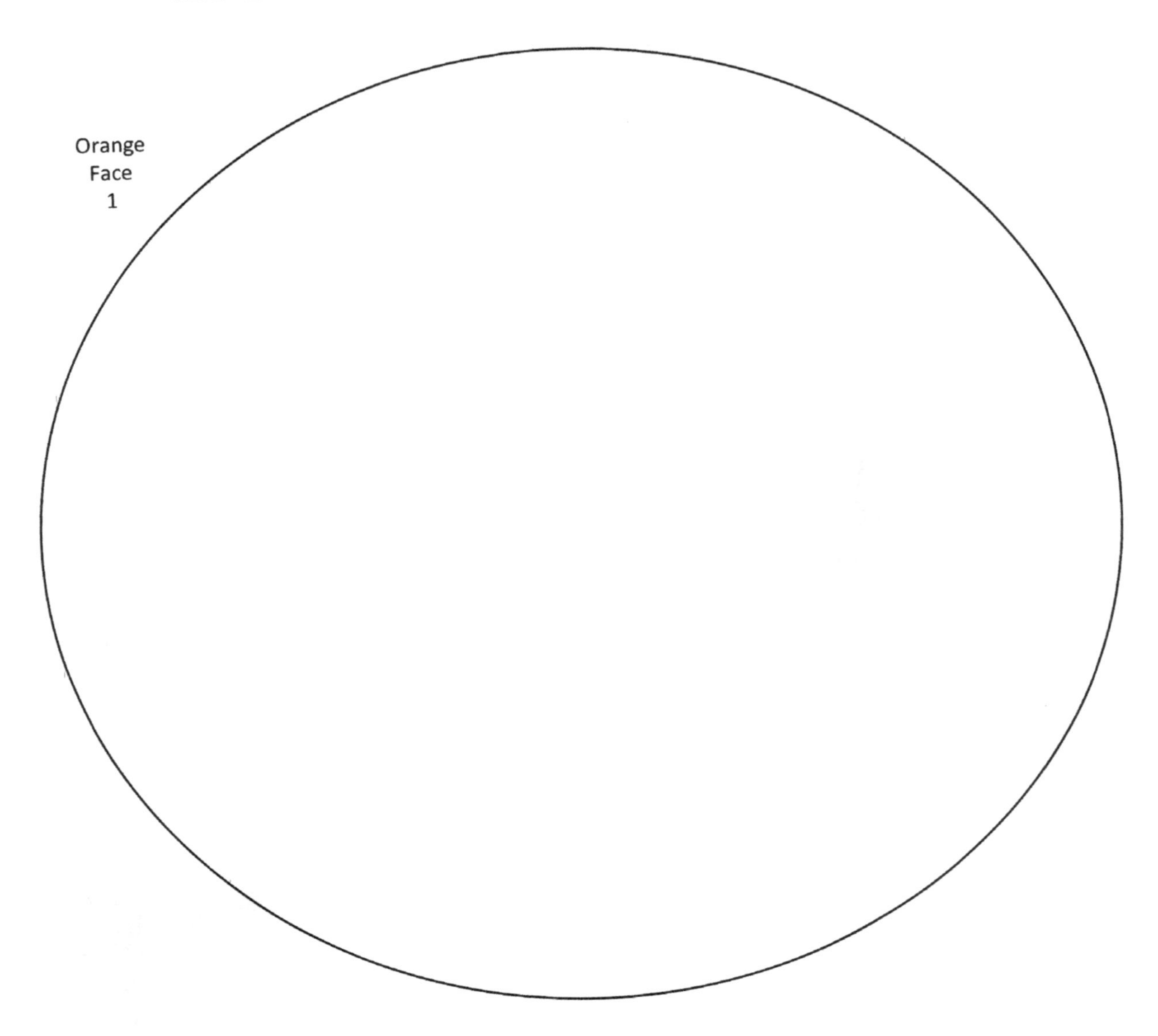

Note: If you have orange paper plates on hand, you can use them instead of this circle.

Author Index

Title Index

Poem Index

About the Authors

JULIE DIETZEL-GLAIR is a freelance writer and library consultant. Previously, she was a children's librarian and then an assistant children's services coordinator in Maryland public libraries for 11 years. She is the author of *Books in Motion: Connecting Preschoolers with Books through Art, Games, Movement, Music, Playacting, and Props* and the *2015 Collaborative Summer Learning Program Early Literacy Manual*. Dietzel-Glair provides training sessions for library staff and others interested in early literacy, presents special programming for children, and works on other special library projects. She is active in the Association for Library Service to Children, the Children's Services Division of the Maryland Library Association, and Capitol Choices. Her website is www.juliedietzelglair.com and her Twitter username is @JulieDGWrites.

MARIANNE CRANDALL FOLLIS, PhD, is senior librarian specializing in youth services at the Valley Ranch (Irving) Public Library. She has spent the past 11 years working in Texas public libraries, serving young people and the adults who care for them. She has taught undergraduate and graduate classes in children's literature at Texas Woman's University, where she recently earned her doctorate in library science. Follis is active in the American Library Association, the Association for Library Service to Children, and the Texas Library Association as well as its Children's Round Table.